# The Economic History of India, 1857–1947

# The Economic History of India, 1857–1947

*Tirthankar Roy*

**OXFORD**
UNIVERSITY PRESS

# OXFORD
UNIVERSITY PRESS

YMCA Library Building, Jai Singh Road, New Delhi 110001

Oxford University Press is a department of the University of Oxford. It furthers the
University's objective of excellence in research, scholarship, and education
by publishing worldwide in

Oxford   New York

Athens   Auckland   Bangkok   Bogota   Buenos Aires   Calcutta
Cape Town   Chennai   Dar es Salaam   Delhi   Florence   Hong Kong   Istanbul
Karachi   Kuala Lumpur   Madrid   Melbourne   Mexico City   Mumbai
Nairobi   Paris   Sao Paolo   Shanghai   Singapore   Taipei   Tokyo   Toronto   Warsaw
with associated companies in Berlin   Ibadan
Oxford is a registered trade mark of Oxford University Press
in the UK and in certain other countries

Published in India
By Oxford University Press, New Delhi

ISBN   019   565154 5

Typeset in Palatino 10.5 on 12 by Jojy Philip, New Delhi 110 042
Printed at. Tushar Printers, Delhi 110 032
Published by Manzar Khan, Oxford University Press
YMCA Library Building, Jai Singh Road, New Delhi 110 001

*for Dharma Kumar*

# Preface

This is a textbook on the economic history of colonial India. A compulsory course in most Indian universities, there is at present no detailed and updated text on the economic history of India. This book is targeted to help students at both undergraduate and postgraduate levels. Further, it is hoped that the book will serve as a handy reference on the subject for teachers and researchers in economics and history. The standard reference now available is the *Cambridge Economic History of India*, Vol II (*CEHI*, 1983). This is much too detailed to be either a convenient teaching aid or a quick guide. It also predates a vast quantity of new research on old themes and the emergence of new themes such as common property, labour, and small-scale industry. Yet, the *CEHI* is indispensable. In a way, this book aims to be no more than an updated and shorter version of the *CEHI*. With this mixed readership in mind, the book tries to be comprehensive in content, but as simply and easily written as possible.

One of the overall aims of the book is to show how history can explain the roots of economic growth and stagnation in South Asia. The belief that the past does explain the present is not a new one. It has been a key element in scholarly and popular views about colonialism in the region. There are old undying controversies about how past matters continue to stimulate researchers in this field. At the same time, new research enhances the level and complexity of these debates. The book tries to capture the changes that the subject has undergone both in terms of description and interpretation.

A word is needed on the citation style. Where the scholarship is of manageable scale, it has been more or less completely covered by the reading list at the end of the chapter. In such cases, footnotes in the text have been avoided. In the case of some other chapters, notably Chapter 3 on agriculture, the scholarship is very large and it is not realistic to expect students to read all of it. The chapter cites many works as footnotes purely for reference purposes. The reading list covers only a small set of these works, sufficient for a guided tour.

The idea of the book was initiated in 1995-6 in an informal proposal. After lying dormant for two years, the project was completed over 1998 and 1999, and behind this Nitasha Devasar of the Oxford University Press has significant contribution. Those who read some of the draft chapters and gave detailed comments include G. Balachandran, Kunal Sen, Haruka Yanagisawa, a referee of the Oxford University Press, and especially, Marcia Frost and Douglas Haynes. I am indebted to them all. Morris D. Morris's library of books and articles, part of which is now stored in the Indira Gandhi Institute of Development Research library, was an invaluable resource for me. Sudakshina Roy provided many-sided support at home and work.

The book is dedicated to Dharma Kumar who, through her own work, her inspiration, and encouragement to a large number of scholars, and by building up a leading journal in the field, has had a pervasive influence on the teaching and research of economic history in India.

October 2000                                   TIRTHANKAR ROY
Mumbai

# Contents

# Tables

# Maps

# Abbreviations

| | |
|---|---|
| CEHI 1 | Tapan Raychaudhuri and Irfan Habib (eds) (1983), *The Cambridge Economic History of India* Vol 1, c. 1200–c. 1750, Cambridge. |
| CEHI 2 | Dharma Kumar (ed.) (1983), *The Cambridge Economic History of India* Vol 2, c. 1757–c. 1970, Cambridge. |
| EPW | *Economic and Political Weekly* |
| IESHR | *Indian Economic and Social History Review* |
| MAS | *Modern Asian Studies* |
| UP | United Provinces or Uttar Pradesh according to context |

❦

1

# Introduction

## INDIA, 1857–1947

From the end of the eighteenth century, India began to experience three overlapping waves of change that fundamentally transformed patterns of production and consumption in the region. These were, the rise of colonial rule, extension of market economy, and the rise of a modern economy based on machinery and wage labour. In 1947, India was one of the poorest countries in the world, having seen rather low rates of economic growth in the late nineteenth and the early twentieth centuries. The book describes the changes in the structure of the economy and their effects on the population by summarizing a large and growing literature. It also examines the questions, why India grew slowly in the colonial period, and what role the colonial rule played in growth and stagnation in the long run.

The first of these processes, that is, the rise of colonial rule, was under way almost exactly over a century, 1757 to 1856. During this period the English East India Company annexed the Indian territories that came to constitute British India. In 1856, after Awadh was annexed, a little over 60 per cent of land area in the present India, Pakistan and Bangladesh belonged to British India (see Table 1.1). After this date, and after the Indian mutiny of 1857 that occurred partly as a response to the annexations, no further conquests took place. But the British maintained close control over the affairs of the princely states. This relationship has been called 'indirect rule'.

The second process of extension of the market economy was active from the beginning of the nineteenth century, but it gathered force only after 1850. About this time, the whole world was turning into a supplier of food and raw material to industrializing Europe. Peasants and merchants in India also responded to these immense opportunities. Production for export increased. A rough measure of 'commercialization' is the annual growth of foreign trade. This growth was consistently large from 1835 until the First World War. Along with trade, international capital movements grew rapidly further integrating India into the world economy. Within India, institutions and infrastructure necessary for a market economy to function smoothly were set up. These included uniform weights and measures, contract law, uniform currency system, the railways, the telegraph, and a powerful state committed to defending private property rights. The third process, employment of machinery, more or less began after the 1850s.

TABLE 1.1
Major Annexations by Year, 1757–1857

|  | Territories annexed | Area ('000 square miles) | |
| --- | --- | --- | --- |
| 1757 | Bengal and Bihar | 15 | |
| 1765 | Carnatic | 4 | |
| 1766 | Northern Sarkars | 2 | |
| 1775 | Benares | 1 | |
| 1792–9 | Dindigul, Malabar, Canara, etc. | 4 | |
| 1801 | 'Ceded Districts' | 7 | |
| 1803–18 | Maratha territories | 19 | |
| 1825–42 | Northeast and Burma | 15 | |
| 1843 | Sind | 5 | |
| 1848 | Satara | 1 | |
| 1849 | Punjab | 10 | |
| 1853 | Jhansi, Nagpur, Hyderabad assigned | 13 | |
| 1856 | Awadh | 2 | |
| Total | Annexation | 98 | (62%) |
|  | Indian states remaining | 59 | (38%) |
|  | India | 157 | |

Note: Not all were immediate annexation.
Source: Michael H. Fisher, *The Politics of British Annexation of India 1757–1857*, Oxford University Press, Delhi, 1993, p. xvi.

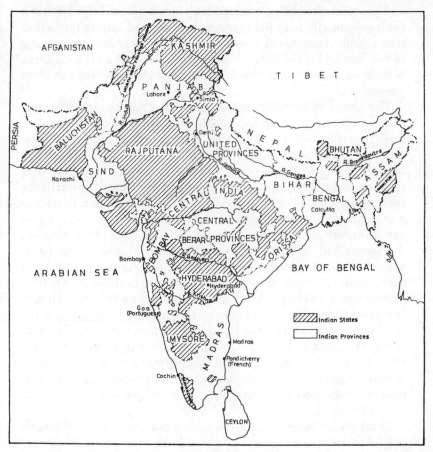

MAP 1.1: INDIA, 1939

The above chronology suggests why we start from 1857. The book deals only briefly with the changes that occurred during the period when British rule was still settling down. Chapter 2 introduces the broad facts and major debates on this period. But the main concerns of the book are with 'commercialization' and the growth of a modern economy.

The rise of British rule was not just a political change. The new rulers did not arise from the established ruling classes. They were foreigners. The British were a mercantile population turning industrial by the end of the eighteenth century, whereas India was overwhelmingly agricultural. Being foreigners and merchants, the new regime could initiate economic policies and principles of governance that upset the established (agrarian) order as never before. In science and technology, political organization, and economic activity, eighteenth century Europe was modernizing at unprecedented speed. Europeans had the military and the ideological means, the 'hardware' and the 'software' necessary to create a far more centralized and bureaucratic state in India than what the region had seen before. Politics aided the integration of India into world trade and an unfolding international division of labour. The British had access to superior knowledge about industry and trade, which the empire brought within the reach of Indians. Thus, major forms of transformation—class structure, commercialization, formation of a modern state, technology—had roots in the colonial encounter. Independent India took over from the political–economic–administrative structure created by the British rule.

Dramatic as these changes were, they did not result in dramatic improvement in average incomes or standards of living. Except for sometime in the late nineteenth century, total and average real incomes in India grew at rates that were poor by contemporary world standards. Several countries in South America, for example, grew far more rapidly. Japan is the country with which nineteenth century India tends to be frequently compared since Japan and India had similar levels of living about 1850. Given its rate of growth, colonial India would have needed several centuries to double its standard of living, a feat Japan achieved within a few decades. The paradox here is best expressed in the words of Raymond Goldsmith

If a percipient and knowledgeable economist, for example, John Stuart Mill or Karl Marx, had been asked in 1870 whether a century later India or Japan would be more advanced economically and financially and thus closer to the levels of Western Europe and North America, it is possible, and indeed likely, that he would have named India. To justify his choice, he might have pointed to the facts that India, as a result of its connection with Great Britain, possessed a unified currency and the rudiments of Western-type banking system, as well as easy access to the British capital market and British industrial and financial technology, then the most advanced available. Japan, on the other hand, was just emerging from a decaying feudal system; its modern sector was negligible; its currency was in chaos; and it lacked modern financial institutions. Neither Mill nor Marx would ever have envisaged the abysmal difference that marks the observed economic and financial development of the two countries.[1]

Stimulated by this puzzle, historians of India have debated the effects of the colonial encounter. Why did India grow slowly? Were British policies responsible for the stagnation? Or was stagnation a result of adverse initial conditions that British rule was too weak to change?

The present work is an interpretive summary of scholarship on economic change during the British rule. This whole story can be told in two ways. Seen as local history, a story about India primarily, the facts speak for themselves. Seen as global history, facts are more than just facts. They are the means to test theories about why economic growth happens or does not happen. It is useful, therefore, to digress briefly into theories of economic history, and see how they can be used to formulate questions about colonial India or to answering them.

## ECONOMIC HISTORY

The basic question that concerns economic history is, why have some countries grown rich, and some others remained poor? In other words, what causes economic growth and what prevents growth? Economics and economic history both try to answer these questions, but their methods differ. These differences give us a clearer idea about economic history as a separate discipline. There are three main differences.

The causes of economic growth are not one, but several. Some of them, say a new policy on taxation or money supply, act relatively quickly. Some other processes work more slowly. Economists usually study the former type of forces, historians the latter. An analogy is the human body. The health of the human body depends on temporary

[1] Raymond Goldsmith, *The Financial Development of India, Japan and the United States*, Yale University Press, New Haven and London, 1983, pp. 4–5.

infections and medicines available to cure them, as well as on such long term factors as immunity, genetic traits or lifestyle. In the context of economics, examples of variables of the latter kind are, quality of the environment, population, law, cultural change or changes in mentalities, scientific and technological change, and industrial organization. Perhaps the most familiar example of all is 'commercialization' or creation of markets. Economic theory and a large part of development studies take the existence of 'markets' more or less for granted. Economic history usually deals with the process by which markets get created. Therefore, economic history also deals with the question, why transactions happen and what effects such transactions have when markets in the modern sense are still evolving.

Secondly, economic history recognizes, more than economic theory, the importance of specific events and individuals. Great events such as the Depression of 1929 or the World Wars have had such long-term and global impact that we still have not finished understanding them. Economic theory finds it difficult to handle 'path dependence', the condition when a single event changes behaviour and institutions. Historians routinely deal with it.

Thirdly, economic history tends to be inter-disciplinary in nature. Economic actions depend on economic stimuli (such as calculations of profit and loss) as well as on cultural and social norms. In the short run, these two aspects can be easily separated out, for it is possible to assume that socio-cultural norms change rather slowly. The longer the time span over which human activity is explained, the harder it becomes to separate out the economic from the non-economic factors. For example, in explaining changes in population growth, it may be necessary not only to look into the economic costs and benefits of having large families, but also how a woman's role in society has evolved over time. In this book, noneconomic variables play an important and explicit role in the context of demography (see Chapter 9), the role of social structure in agricultural production (see Chapter 3), consumption of industrial goods (see Chapter 4), etc.

In practical terms, historians' research consists of two types of work. The first type builds up plausible stories from a body of data, and the second illustrates models or theories by means of data. Usually, both progress simultaneously and complement one another. But the second stream of research is rather special in that it has seen attempts to theorize, build models, and compare countries—consequently, it has been prone to debates and controversies. A few typical models are described in the next section.

## THEORIES OF ECONOMIC HISTORY

Attempts to answer the question, what causes economic growth, with the help of general models has a long history. It began with Adam Smith's *Wealth of Nations* (1776). The appeal of Adam Smith, despite constant attempts to revise and qualify his theory, has endured for a very long time.

### Market-led Growth

In Smith's view, the key to economic growth is the productivity of labour. Only by increasing the quantity that each individual is able to produce can the average consumption or income increase. What causes productivity to grow? By the premise that each individual concentrates on performing one task rather than dividing up energy and resources to doing too many (division of labour), and that each individual concentrates on that task which he or she is best able to do (specialization). Smith attributed the invention of machinery to the fact that 'men are much more likely to discover easier and readier methods' when they direct all their attention to doing one task. It is the process of continuous increase in division of labour and specialization that results in economic growth.

What drives such a process is the market or the possibility of exchange. Individuals begin to produce more than their own needs only when there is a prospect of selling off the surplus. Markets create incentives. When in isolation, individuals cannot know which decisions benefit them. Markets create examples of success that can be replicated. The more markets expand, the more surplus they produce, the more specialized they get. And the more specialized they get, the more dependent the individuals become on the market. Further on in his book, Smith also added that markets, to perform this role to the fullest, must not be restrained. That is, markets must be competitive. Otherwise they tend to push up costs of production.

In a classic work published in 1969, John Hicks developed a view of European history as expansion and maturation of markets. Smith had not distinguished between markets for products and markets for factors of production. By contrast, Hicks argued that markets for factors such as land or labour develop more gradually and hesitantly because they tend to be rooted in social custom and political power. Hicks also showed how a mercantile economy could force changes in laws that enabled markets to function properly. Smith could not quite foresee the extent of technological change that the west was to experience in the nineteenth century. Hicks emphasized that competition drove innovation and technological development.

This is a simple tale, but one with a powerful moral. The moral is that commerce, competition, and competence are interdependent. History of economic growth upholds this powerful and creative role of markets, in so far as the world knows of no instance of sustained economic growth that does not utilize this role. 'Commercialization' is of fundamental importance in economic history. Still, if commercialization is necessary for growth, it cannot be seen as a condition sufficient to ensure economic growth. The history of the developing countries seems to suggest that slow economic growth can arise despite vigorous trade.

Search for explanations of why markets are not sufficient has followed broadly two roads. One emphasizes the role of institutions; the other emphasizes unequal power.

## Institutions

Economic theory recognizes that if markets are imperfect, transactions that benefit an individual may result in the society being a loser, or transactions that benefit the society may not be undertaken at all. Two common sources of market imperfection are uncertainty and inadequate information.

An example of how uncertainty matters is poor enforcement of property rights. Trade can give rise to gains. But few will trade if the traders are not sure of being able to enjoy the gains. Such a situation can occur if a mafia can easily plunder these gains because property rights are not well defined or are not enforced by a strong police system. If routine disputes between transacting parties cannot be easily settled because the courts are too slow, few will trade. If an inventor cannot enjoy the returns from an innovation because patent rights are not well defined, few will be encouraged to innovate.

An example of information problems is 'asymmetric information', or a situation when transacting parties are unequally informed about the quality of the product they are dealing in. In that case, the party better informed can gain by cheating the other. If the sellers are better informed about the product, they may be tempted to cheat the buyers and sell them poor quality. But cheating leads to loss for society because if it continues, the buyer may simply refuse to buy, thereby destroying the market. This problem, where asymmetric information leads to wrongful behaviour is called 'moral hazard'.

Yet another contradiction between private and social gains arises in the case of 'public goods', that is, goods whose usage cannot be restricted. Major forms of productive capital such as roads, water supply or irrigation canals, if left up to individuals to build, will not be built at all because an individual cannot restrict the use of the facility only to those who pay for it.

The message is, in an unsafe and amoral economic world, growth will not take place, and markets will lead to as much loss as gain. The society needs mechanisms to ensure that actions compatible with economic growth are taken. These mechanisms are called 'institutions'. Examples are, systems of police and justice, a government that provides public goods, regulation of monopolies and unfair practices, associations of businessmen that enable free flow of information, etc. If the path to economic growth is so evident, why do some societies find it earlier than others? Why do some societies never find it at all? The answer to these questions is neither simple, nor clear in every case. But one immediate reason is that those who gain from market imperfections have too much political power, including the power to persuade the citizens that they are in fact serving social interests whereas in reality they pursue private interests.

## Class and Power

If transacting parties have unequal power, one party can influence the terms of trade and appropriate the gains from transaction. Further, gains from market–exchange can be appropriated by the rulers and their cronies. Examples of both situations can be found in plenty in the real world. In the Marxist tradition of economic history and development scholarship, the idea has played a central and systematic role. Barring some extreme positions, the Marxist tradition does not really dispute Adam Smith's model. But it suggests that politics influences markets much too often.

Classical Marxist writings generalized on the basis of the study of nineteenth century Europe. In this tradition, 'bourgeois–democratic' revolution was seen as a precondition for economic growth. This meant that the entrepreneurs who invested in production, and the workers of these enterprises, should become free of the dominance of old political and legal systems. These old powers were based on landed wealth. They did not contribute to new enterprises such as industry but exploited them and extracted rent from them. Later Marxist writings began by asking why such a revolution did not take place in the developing countries.

In this tradition, the answer focused not only on class–structure within these countries, but also on the nature of their relationship with the rich countries. The essential message was that trade between countries of unequal political power resulted in greater gains for the strong than for the weak. This was because, power ensured that wages remained low and labour remained unfree in the weaker country. In its most famous application, the idea has been used to explain rise in inequality between Western Europe on the one hand, and Asia and Africa on the other, from the fifteenth century onward.

The central idea in the 'world systems' school, for example, is that the origins of growth and origins of underdevelopment are connected through politics and long term trends in the world economy. Between approximately the fifteenth century and the mid-nineteenth century, trade between Europe and the modern developing world expanded, and the Europeans turned the terms and conditions of trade in their favour. Using superior military power and advanced business organization, the Europeans forced the persistence of exploitative forms of labour control in the 'periphery'. Open play of power declined thereafter. But implicitly the same process continued. During colonial rule, the colonist countries were vitally dependent on the markets and resources of their colonies. They created a system of trade that mainly benefited traders from their countries. Peasants of the colonized countries were forced by various means to specialize in the production of raw material for the industries located in the colonist countries. The artisans in the colonies were rendered unemployed in the face of competition from manufactured goods imported from the colonist countries. Commerce was forced. It destroyed livelihood, and it destroyed food security, as peasants shifted out of production of food for their own subsistence to production of industrial raw materials.

What happened after colonialism ended? Most authors in this tradition answer that the rule of the strong over the weak continued. But precisely how it adapted to the changed political conditions is a matter of debate. Based on these theories, major writers within this tradition have contended that economic growth for the poor countries is impossible unless they stop trading with the rich, which in turn calls for a political revolution. But these strands in the literature need not concern us.

## Applications

Economic historians' answer to the question 'how the West grew rich' has followed mainly the Smithian and institutionalist lines of explanation, with an important qualification from economic demography.[2] The standard view is that, economic growth in the West arose from 'the development of private property rights, the possibility of pursuing business relatively free of political or religious interference ... all stimulated by expansion of trade and commercial activity'.[3] These conditions encouraged innovations, technological progress, increasing employment of capital, and productivity growth. An important factor in speeding up these changes was the decline in population growth rates. It led to increasing shortage of labour relative to capital and resources, and therefore, encouraged more efficient use of labour. The timing of the 'demographic transition' and its relationship with other economic changes are matters of debate.

At different periods in the twentieth century, parts of East Asia have 'grown rich' rather rapidly. The standard story for East Asia too has the same major ingredients—property rights, free markets, more markets, and demographic transition. However, there were differences between Asia and the West in minor aspects, such as the nature of innovative activity, sources of investment capital, and most importantly, the role of the government in stimulating consumption, innovation, and capital formation.

By and large, the scholarly tradition that dealt with the question 'why the West grew rich' ignored the counterpart question 'why the South stayed poor'. This oversight has been so profound that even today no coherent non-Marxist theory on the origins of underdevelopment is available. The theory of the history of underdevelopment became a preoccupation of those scholars who believed that political inequality played a central role in rising international economic disparity. The most famous school to have expounded such a view is the 'world systems school'. Within India, the idea that colonialism meant economic exploitation via trade, investment, and political domination became very popular.

The Marxist and the 'world systems' approach have been criticized on several grounds. First, their tendency to ignore local and regional particularities has been repeatedly criticized in historical scholarship. Secondly, the inference that the West grew rich by exploiting the non-western world is strongly contradicted by empirical evidence (See Appendix A). This evidence suggests that the non-western colonies

---

[2] The term appears in N. Rosenberg and L.E. Birdzell, *How the West Grew Rich*, Tauris, London, 1986.

[3] N.F.R. Crafts, 'Economic History', in *The New Palgraves Dictionary of Economics*, Macmillan, London and Basingstoke, 1986, 2, p. 40.

were a rather small source of accumulation for the West during the period of rising inequality. Third, these approaches paint an unrealistically grim view of trade. They over-emphasize the role of coercion and underplay freedom of choice and gains from trade. Open play of power, in terms of military action, is least visible in periods of most vigorous trade in the late nineteenth century. More recently, rapid economic growth in some developing countries of Asia and Latin America has reinforced faith in Adam Smith's engine of growth. Lastly, the Marxist approach suffers from what econometricians call an 'identification problem'. Low wages can mean either abundance of labour or political weakness of labour. What Marxists often mistake for unequal power could simply mean relative scarcity or abundance of different factors of production. These criticisms of the Marxist theories of underdevelopment do not deny that power can influence the outcome of exchange. It can do so not only internationally, but also locally. India's home-grown caste system is no less impressive an example of coercion.

Some of these arguments and positions have deeply influenced theories about colonial India. This chapter ends with a general idea of the range of existing positions. Specific debates will be introduced in the other chapters.

## ECONOMIC HISTORY AND INDIA

The colonial period in India was one of accelerated commercialization. Therefore, commercialization has been the central theme in Indian economic history of this period. A large number of historians, especially among those working in India, believe that Adam Smith's theory failed in the Indian case. According to this informal consensus, growth of markets under the colonial situation retarded India and enriched Britain. Such a view originated from several distinct intellectual traditions. These include, an Indian nationalist critique of British rule articulated chiefly by R.C. Dutt and Dadabhai Naoroji at the end of the nineteenth century, a revival of the nationalist critique in the 1950s and the 1960s articulated, for example, in books by Surendra Patel and B.M. Bhatia, classical theories of imperialism, and Marxian interpretations of nineteenth century Indian history.[4] We shall call the common core of these views the 'left–nationalist' paradigm.

[4] S.J. Patel, *Agricultural Labourers in Modern India and Pakistan*, Current Book House, Bombay, 1952; B.M. Bhatia, *Famines in India*, Asia Publishing House, Bombay, 1951. See also the readings list for this chapter ('Economic History and India: The Left–nationalist Paradigm'), and the discussion in Chapter 3.

## The Left–nationalist Paradigm

Economic and political changes from the eighteenth century led to decline in some activities and growth in some others. Fundamentally, the left–nationalist interpretation is built around two beliefs about the aggregate effects of this change. First, decline outweighed growth, and second, both decline and growth were derived from colonial policies.

Broadly, the mechanism was as follows. During colonial rule, high revenue demand in cash forced peasants to produce commercial crops in place of subsistence food crops. Such a shift exposed the rural population to increased risks of famine. Further, commercial production was not always profitable enough and therefore, peasants fell into debts. Many were forced to sell their land to moneylenders and become labourers or tenants. Moneylenders represented a class of people distinct from peasants. In particular, they were not interested in investing profits in improving the productivity of land. So, the more powerful the moneylender, the greater was the agricultural stagnation, rural poverty and inequality. At the same time, import of British manufactures destroyed India's traditional industry or handicrafts, which added to the number of agricultural labourers. Not only was there an absolute decline in industry, there was also a relative decline in India's position as a manufacturer. Around 1750, India supplied nearly a quarter of the world's manufacturing output. By 1900, it supplied as little as 1.7 per cent.

The growth of large-scale industry, government, and infrastructure partly compensated for this retardation in the villages and traditional industry. But even in these spheres, colonial policies affected Indian interests adversely. Thus, in large-scale industry, colonial rule sustained unfair competition where British and Indian capitalists were rivals. The government supervised a transfer of wealth from India to Britain in the form of profits of foreign business and government charges, which the nationalists called 'drain'. Foreign business in India created limited income or wealth within India. At best it created a modern 'enclave' that had little contact with the traditional economy. As for modern infrastructure, it was built by the British with the purpose of transporting Indian wealth abroad and facilitating the modern enclave. Therefore, it had little impact on the traditional economy and society.

In the 1950s, early statements of the left–nationalist paradigm projected precolonial rural India as a cluster of self-sustaining village communities oriented to subsistence production. These consisted of peasants and artisans, and did not have a large class of agricultural labourers. Over the last twenty years or so, the idea of early–modern India has undergone a great change. The notion of self-sufficient rural communities has been more or less discarded in favour of a view that admits of a great deal of trade and commerce in rural India. In trade, industry, and urbanization, the immediate pre-colonial period is seen to be more dynamic than was earlier believed. For example, there was an expansion in cotton textile exports to Europe. This trade encouraged long-distance domestic trade in foodgrains and raw cotton. In a way, the change in perspective makes the left–nationalist case even stronger, for it can now be argued that the Indian economy was already on the verge of a commercial and industrial revolution, when it was impeded by colonialism.

## Critique of the Left–nationalist Paradigm

That the eighteenth century saw commercialization in some regions in a few select sectors cannot be questioned. But the inference that this momentum could have been a more powerful stimulus for growth if colonialism had not intervened is difficult to accept. Firstly, what might have happened is a speculative question that cannot be tested. Secondly, there is no quantitative data to measure how large the commercialized segments were in the eighteenth century relative to the traditional sector of economy still oriented to subsistence production.

As for the nineteenth century, the left–nationalist picture of a net decline does not stand up to empirical evidence. Research shows that colonial India experienced positive economic growth. The claim that growth in colonial India was not just faster but also spread over a wider area *vis-à-vis* pre-colonial India is fairly credible. Three key factors encouraging economic growth in the nineteenth century were growth of world trade, a strong state, and modern transport and communication. All were of recent origin.

Nearly every major research studying rural inequality in different regions has found the extent of inequality more or less unchanged in a quantitative sense. The British rule did not create labourers. Pre-colonial rural India already had a large number of agricultural labourers bonded to land by custom. Colonialism in fact weakened this customary bondage. The notion that commercialization was forced upon the peasants by taxes or debts, and not driven by profit motive, is seriously disputable. Statistical data on agriculture show a strong association between rates of profit, growth in productivity, and com-mercialization across crops and across regions. The Smithian logic did work—rise of markets did lead to productivity gains. There was an increase in rural indebtedness but there was no large-scale dispos-session of land by moneylenders. 'Moneylenders' cannot even be defined as a distinct class.

There was certainly a relative decline in India's position in the world as an industrial country. This was a result of the Industrial Revolution in Europe. India was among the countries that saw their comparative advantage in industry partially eroded by technological change. But was there an absolute decline in industry? The answer is, almost certainly, no. As late as 1931, more than 90 per cent of the Indian industrial work-force was engaged in handicrafts, and their average earning capacity was certainly not declining. The reason why handicrafts as an industry was so stable was that India's com-parative advantage in labour-intensive industry did not disappear. Drain of resources from India to Britain can neither be precisely de-fined nor correctly measured.

A further criticism of the left–nationalist paradigm is that it ignores factors other than colonial strategies with a possible role in promoting growth or stagnation. Neither growth nor stagnation were India-wide features, but characterized specific sectors in specific periods. Real income in industry and services grew rapidly throughout the colonial rule. Real income in agriculture also grew in the nineteenth century, but remained nearly stagnant in the inter-war period. The stagnation was however confined to certain regions. Hence, any ex-planation of slow growth rates must focus on the role of local char-acteristics and peculiarities that made the regions different from the rest of the country.

## Limits to Economic Growth in Colonial India: Alternative Views

### Market-failure or Government Failure?

In 1968, Morris D. Morris questioned the left–nationalist paradigm and suggested an alternative explanation for limited economic growth in colonial India.[5] Morris's grounds for questioning the paradigm were based on several assumptions about the nineteenth century growth pattern. Some of them later research validated, and some

[5] Morris D. Morris, 'Towards a Reinterpretation of Nineteenth-Century Indian Eco-nomic History', *IESHR*, 5(1), 1968. See also the other contributions in the same issue of the journal.

turned out to have been rather simplified. His basic premise was that the period 1860–1920 saw economic growth, and probably on an unprecedented scale. Later research on national income showed that Morris was right. He further speculated that growth slowed down after 1920. There is evidence to establish this too. In the 1920s, international trade, one of the engines driving the world economy during the preceding 50 years, slowed down. Morris concluded that in colonial India, the market did work as expected—further growth might have occurred if the government had invested to create more assets and markets.

Surely, any regime that rules over a region for as long as a century, and fails to generate a big momentum for growth, must be seen as a failure in one key aspect of governance. However, the argument that the government failed in British India has two drawbacks. First, it is rather general, and does not explain regional differences very well. Second, it ignores conditions within India that needed to change for more rapid growth to occur.

Resource Endowments

Resource endowments form the basis of a hypothesis on stagnation that is more sensitive to regional differences. For growth to occur, a sustained expansion in markets is not enough. Resources are needed to enable sustained increase in supply. Peasants in nineteenth century India could access plenty of land, but faced a severe scarcity of water. Agricultural growth almost always occurred in the presence of investment in irrigation mainly in the form of government canals. Wherever land was plentiful and water became available by new investments, growth occurred too. Examples are Punjab, coastal Madras, or western Uttar Pradesh (UP). Where population density on land was too high and/or investment in irrigation was not significant, growth was either weak or entirely absent. Examples are, most parts of eastern India and parts of the dry southwestern India. When arable land became scarce and investments in irrigation slowed down, growth slowed down too. This is what happened after 1920 in many regions. At the same time population growth rate accelerated, intensifying the shortage of land.

Industry in nineteenth century India could get plenty of labour, and use cheap natural resources, but could not get capital easily enough. Large-scale industry took birth when the capital constraint eased somewhat due to growth of foreign trade. Even so, scarcity of capital was always present and always acute. All forms of new enterprise within both large-scale and small-scale industry were necessarily intensive in natural resources and labour, and avoided capital-intensive or innovative but risky ventures. A process of labour-intensive industrialization can expand total incomes, but it cannot generate big gains in labour productivity because the existence of surplus labour discourages investment in the efficient use of labour.

The inadequate government investment in water can be seen as evidence of government failure. However, we need to remember that the investments that did occur in this period go to the credit of this regime. Conceivably, factor endowments could have changed if the government had pursued some of its basic duties more actively. Sustained investment in irrigation could have mitigated land-shortage. Investment in education could have enhanced the capability of human beings and make them less dependent on manual labour and investment in health care could have been a step towards decline in population growth rates. The British rule was not politically capable of making such investments to the extent needed. Nor, interestingly, were the post-colonial regimes.

Other Factors

Scarcity of critical resources was one of the factors that constrained economic growth. There are other important determinants of growth:

a) Some works cited in Chapter 3 suggest that caste influenced market transactions and introduced market imperfections. This condition was weakening in colonial India but only very slowly and with some reverses. The reverses occurred because the upper castes had better access to economic opportunities and could reinforce their social power.

b) Chapter 7 suggests that high risks might have inhibited investment. A risky environment induces more precautionary savings, such as savings in gold, and discourages productive investment. Agriculture, the mainstay of the economy, was subject to high climatic risk. Neither precolonial India nor colonial India could develop adequate alternative systems of reducing these risks or insuring against them.

c) Chapters 4 and 9 reveal the inferior position of female workers. Their position probably worsened in the colonial period in the course of commercialization of labour. These facts reflect the universal neglect of women as an economic asset. Though the British rule did not create this handicap, it did little to change it. It shows up in the low work-participation of women, and in the persistence of the traditional role of women as homemakers.

In all these three respects, independence from British rule made little difference.

## CONCLUSION

The experiences, on the one hand, of mass poverty and deprivation, and on the other, of colonialism and lack of political freedom, are overpowering ones. The former tends to make the study of economic history of India a diagnostic exercise—a relentless search for causes of underdevelopment. The latter induces the belief that colonialism must have been responsible, somehow, for the underdevelopment. This second belief in particular is not confined to history textbooks—it underlies the average Indian's sense of history. While the historical root of underdevelopment is an interesting issue, debates about it can have a deceptive appeal. They can lead to two forms of shortsightedness. One is to read history in a narrow way, solely to find out what went wrong. The more serious bias is to read history in a pre-ordered way, to find support for what the reader had already decided, went wrong.

It is necessary, therefore, to take leave of generalizations from time to time and step into history. In that spirit, the next chapter sets the scene with a survey of major economic trends during 1757–1857, the period of consolidation of British rule in India.

## ANNOTATED READINGS
### The Political Evolution of British India

Michael H. Fisher, *The Politics of the British Annexation of India 1757–1857*, Oxford University Press, Delhi, 1993. C.A. Bayly (ed.), *An Illustrated History of Modern India 1600–1947*, Oxford University Press, Oxford, 1990, Section II.

### Theories of Economic History

On the market model of growth, the best readings are the original statements by Adam Smith, *An Inquiry into the Nature and Causes of the Wealth of Nations*, in Edwin Cannan (ed.), Modern Library, New York, 1937, Chs I–III. Also strongly recommended are John Hicks, *A Theory of Economic History*, Clarendon Press, Oxford, 1969, and Hla Myint, 'The "Classical Theory" of International Trade and the

Underdeveloped Countries', *Economic Journal*, 1958. On institutions, Douglass North and R.P. Thomas, *The Rise of the Western World*, Cambridge, 1973, Ch. 1. The survey by J.L. Anderson, *Explaining Long-Term Economic Change*, Macmillan, Basingstoke, 1991 is useful. So are the initial chapters in any standard development economics textbook, for example, R. Grabowski and M.P. Shields, *Development Economics*, Blackwell, Cambridge Massachusetts, 1996, pp. 2-18.

## How the West Grew Rich, and the South Stayed Poor

On the mainstream explanation on how the west grew rich, N.F.R. Crafts, 'Economic history', in *The New Palgraves Dictionary of Economics*, Macmillan, London and Basingstoke, 1986, is adequate. On the Marxist theory of the origins of underdevelopment, see the three articles, 'Colonialism', 'Development' and 'Dependency' in *The New Palgraves*.

## Economic History and India: The Left–nationalist Paradigm

An early and influential restatement of this paradigm is S.J. Patel, *Agricultural Labourers in Modern India and Pakistan*, Current Book House, Bombay, 1952. For more recent statements, see Sumit Sarkar, 'The Colonial Economy', *Modern India: 1885–1947*, Macmillan, Delhi, 1983; Irfan Habib, 'Colonialization of the Indian Economy, 1757–1900', *Social Scientist*, 3(8), 1975; and Amiya Kumar Bagchi, *The Political Economy of Underdevelopment*, Cambridge, 1982, Sections 4.3–4.5, which place India in a general account of colonial exploitation.

## Imperialism

The readings listed here also relate to Appendix A at the end of the book. J. Gallagher, *The Decline, Revival and Fall of the British Empire*, Cambridge, 1982; D.K. Fieldhouse, *The Colonial Empires*, Weidenfield and Nicholson, London, 1965; P.J. Cain and A.G. Hopkins, 'Gentlemanly Capitalism and British Expansion Overseas II: New Imperialism, 1850–1945', *Economic History Review*, 40, 1987; P.K. O'Brien and L. Prados de la Escosura, 'The Cost and Benefits of European Imperialism from the Conquest of Ceuta, 1415, to the Treaty of Lusaka, 1974', in C-E Núñez (ed.), *Debates and Controversies in Economic History*, proceedings of the 12th International Economic History Congress, Madrid, 1998. The essay last mentioned is the best recent survey of research on the economic costs and benefits of empires. See also on the same theme, P. O'Brien, 'European Economic Development: The Contribution of the Periphery', *Economic History Review*,

35(1), 1981. For international comparisons of average incomes, see Paul Bairoch, *Economics and World History*, The University of Chicago Press, Chicago, 1993, Ch. 9, and Angus Maddison, 'A Comparison of Levels of GDP per capita in Developed and Developing Countries, 1700–1980', *Journal of Economic History*, 48(1), 1983.

## 2

# The Background: 1757–1857

### CONDITIONS ABOUT 1750

Early British administrators tended to believe that the eighteenth century was a period of political instability and insecurity of life and property. This period saw the decline of the Mughal Empire and the rise of new regimes in its place often through armed conflict. In some regions, the safety and security of the people deteriorated under threat from marauders who were often remnants of Mughal, and later Maratha armies. Conflicts did give rise to depopulation and decline in cultivation in some parts of India. But on the whole, evidence of general anarchy and economic dislocation is not strong.

### Conditions of Agriculture

Agriculture was the most important occupation both before the British rule, and during it. Any inquiry about long-term changes in economic conditions must begin from agriculture and the people dependent on it. There is no evidence that in the aggregate, agriculture was adversely affected by changes in the political map in the eighteenth century. One reason for this stability was the rise of strong states such as the Marathas in western and central India and Hyderabad in the south. Another reason was that the agricultural production went overwhelmingly to meet the subsistence needs of the peasants and residents of the village, and thus responded slowly to changes outside it.

That does not mean that the economic life of rural India was a tranquil one. Climate caused great uncertainty. A large part of India is located on latitudes that pass through some of the world's greatest deserts. That India escaped being a desert is due to the river system created by the Himalayas in conjunction with the monsoon rains. Rainfall is usually adequate to raise one or two food crops in the months following the monsoons. But rainfall is rarely adequate for winter crops, and marginally adequate in some of the drier regions even for the main food crop. In the eighteenth century, when investment in irrigation systems was insignificant, if the rains failed even slightly, the monsoon crops could fail and result in sudden and widespread starvation. The prospect of famine was intrinsic in monsoon agriculture.

In theory, high risk can discourage private investment in agriculture the returns on such investment being uncertain. One way to alleviate such risks is for the government and collective institutions to create systems that store and distribute water. Nearly every major regime has played a role in building irrigation systems. In some regions rural collectives played such a role. Yet, given the enormity of the need, such capital was rare in India. High risk and low investment characterized Indian agriculture both before and during the colonial period.

## Agrarian Relations

Landed classes can be classified by the type of land rights held. In general, land rights tended to be correlated with political power, the capacity to withstand famine, and quite often, caste. A useful way to understand rights in precolonial India is to make a distinction between rights of revenue collection and rights to property. The rights and obligations concerning the state were usually of the former kind. A massive and pyramidal system of leasing and sub-leasing of revenue collection functioned in the major regimes before the British, and for some years into the British rule in Bengal.

Sometimes, certain tiers could be leased out by auction to the highest bidder. This practice was known as 'revenue farming'. Revenue farming tended to become popular in a condition of weakening authority of the ruling power over their subjects. It was also popular when the area farmed out happened to be a new acquisition, such that there were questions about the local officers' loyalty to the new right-holder. On the other hand, certain other tiers could hold rights that were not usually transferred. While not hereditary in theory, from long practice or the weakness of the imperial State, such rights could become as good as hereditary rights.

Of these contractors and sub-contractors, especially well-known were the *zamindars* and *talukdars* of Bengal and Awadh. Some of them had held the revenue collection right for many generations, held hereditary positions in the courts, and supplied troops to the Nawabs. But several other families of prominent right-holders had risen during the eighteenth century when extensive revenue farming enabled some groups of magnates to rise above the cultivating population. In all regions of India, revenue farming appears to have increased in the eighteenth century. Thus, when the British began to restructure revenue systems, land control was vested not only in the hands of the old nobility, but also with great many tax farmers of this kind, who were moneyed people or former officials who had bid successfully in revenue auctions. The pre-British *zamindars* were in practice, more administrators of their territory than collectors. The *zamindari* charter was non-hereditary in theory but hereditary in practice. The *zamindars* were in charge of law and order, they settled local disputes, and were required to supply forces to the State army if necessary. In eighteenth century Bengal, the Maratha raids of the 1740s was the most important occasion when *zamindari* troops thus needed to be mobilized.

In other parts of the country, exact counterparts of the northern *zamindars* were rare. In southern Andhra there were the warrior chieftains the British called 'poligars'. In areas close to Ahmedabad in Gujarat, there were similar local chiefs whom the British called *talukdars*. All such people strengthened their rule over land as the regional ruling power weakened.

The actual cultivators of the soil included, broadly, 'two distinct classes ... a relatively small group of "owners" with hereditary transferable rights in land ... and the many who tilled the land without such rights.'[1] Below the cultivators were the agricultural labour castes some of whom were little better than slaves and not ordinarily entitled to superior rights. Such people were common in the regions of Tamil Nadu and Kerala, but less common elsewhere. Within this hierarchy were many types of tenants whose rights to cultivate, or 'occupancy rights', were hereditary and transferable in different degrees.

A hereditary right to sell, transfer (gift or bequest) and mortgage property is the modern sense of the term 'property rights'. However, even superior proprietary rights to land in the pre-British period were rarely rights in all of these senses. There were no well-defined

[1] T. Raychaudhuri, 'The Mid-Eighteenth Century Background' in *CEHI 2*.

proprietary rights. And yet rights could function as more or less proprietary according to local custom.[2] Among those who held superior rights it is possible to make a distinction between three general categories. These are, individual cultivators, individuals holding a share in jointly owned village land, and holders of offices who were granted revenue-free or lowly-assessed land, better known as *inam* land. Individual elite proprietors existed usually in fertile regions such as the eastern Gangetic plains, and were drawn from the upper castes. Their prosperity clearly depended on the level of rents the land could sustain, and the amount of land they had control over. Thus, their hold could weaken in areas with low land–man ratio and high population density. In the eighteenth century, revenue farming and the rise of the *zamindars* seriously jeopardized their position.

In regions around Delhi, by contrast, the usual proprietary body was represented not by an individual but a collective of kinsmen who managed the administrative and economic affairs of a village. Some of these 'village republics', as the British called them later, arose from pastoral groups acquiring land in the course of the eighteenth century. In western and southern India in general, the proprietary right was expressed as a share in total village land. The root of the northern, the southern, and the western systems was the notion of a 'coparcenary' community of landholders that seems to appear in muted forms in many regions of India. In southern and western India, such share-holders were called *mirasdars*. The term literally meant holder of a hereditary right. In practice they were substantial cultivators claiming descent from an original settler family or lineage. *Mirasi* rights were saleable. Such sales were rare in western India, but not uncommon in southern India. *Mirasdars* could lease their land to tenants, but tenants in *mirasi* areas were a minority.

In western and southern India, joint landlordship went with a distinct and important role of offices of the State located in or near the village. Two offices were critical and universal, headman and accountant. Here there was a contrast between western and southern India. Offices of a varied kind were performed by *mirasdars* in Tamil villages. The most important duties were revenue collection and investments in agriculture such as construction of irrigation systems. However, such offices were performed by State appointed officials in the Peshwa territory. By 1800, towards the end of Peshwa rule,

[2] In some regions that experienced growth of commerce in the eighteenth century, there was a trend towards old rights of usage turning into alienable property rights.

rampant revenue farming weakened their power. These officials were the main holders of *inam* land. *Inam* lands could also arise from gifts made to temples, village servants, artisans, and men of special merit. The area where *inam* was especially large was southern Andhra, where *inam* probably increased in the course of weakening central authority in the eighteenth century. On the other hand, *inam* was rarer in Tamil villages, but here the *mirasdars* appear to have enjoyed greater bargaining power over revenue rates.

## Land Revenue

In Mughal India, the official revenue rate was about half of average produce. Among the Marathas and in south India, rates like 50 per cent of gross produce off irrigated land, and one-third off dry land, seem to have been usual. Actual collection was almost invariably less than the stated rate, and the revenue system had a history of remissions and rescheduling in times of stress. In Maratha territories, a great deal of the revenue remained in the village itself. A regime of high revenue benefited those who had some role in State offices. Yet, the burden of taxation on the poorer cultivators was by modern standards a heavy one, and probably removed the bulk of the surplus over subsistence needs. Further, a uniform tax-rate for all tax-payers is, by modern judgement, a 'regressive' system. Such regressive and extortionate elements were pervasive in relations between the State and the producers such as peasants and artisans. What was left in the village after taxes were taken was mainly used for consumption. The likelihood that the State attempted to take away almost the entire surplus over subsistence from land leads to the conclusion that the market for mass consumption goods was 'severely restricted'.[3] Consequently, while rural industry was widely dispersed, its consumption, technology and organization were of the crudest sort. Rural industry, therefore, was owned and operated largely by family units using simple locally fabricated tools for the subsistence consumption of the villagers.

The tax collected from land was used to maintain a public administration and meet the consumption needs of those directly or indirectly connected with the state. Even here, inequality was extreme. By far the greater part of collection went to the emperor directly. Productive public investment consisted of roads and irrigation. These

---

[3] T. Raychaudhuri, 'The Non-agricultural Economy: The Mughal Empire', *CEHI 2*, p. 306.

were neither a sustained nor a large commitment, and fell far short of the level required to make a significant difference to rural producers. Those connected with the state were on average wealthy and their consumption basket provided a sustained demand for high-quality crafts and services. Numerically speaking, the consumers of high-quality crafts were a small minority compared to the cultivating population. However, if one believes that half or more of agrarian production was taken away by the state, one may safely conclude that their total income or purchasing power was not small. Trade between rural consumers and urban producers was virtually non-existent. Trade between rural producers and urban consumers was limited to a few goods such as raw silk, indigo, sugar, salt and saltpetre. The greatest sphere of trade was that within and between the towns, or between towns and specialized manufacturing villages in a relatively highly urbanized north India.

## Village Community

Early British views on the Indian village were dominated by the notion of the *jajmani* system. In this view, the bulk of the rural manufactures and services were exchanged within the village by various artisans and suppliers of services who received fixed shares of the total grain retained by the village. Such a system of barter could naturally arise in a situation were long-distance trade was difficult or costly.[4] That apart, fixed share of crop has been seen as a kind of insurance against famine extended by landed people to the non-landed ones.[5] There is, however, no direct evidence to support the existence of this motive. It seems unlikely that customary obligations would be more powerful than survival instincts when the village really starved during a famine.

No matter what the motivation, barter exchange of grain for labour or grain for manufactures, and to a small extent, production for sale, were universal features in pre-colonial rural India. However, the scale of such local and barter exchange varied between regions and over time. It may have been more articulate in western or northern India than in Bengal, and may have been weakened by 1750 compared to the earlier periods. Rarely were such transactions confined within one village. More usually, a cluster of villages or a small region

[4] The term 'long-distance trade' would mean export, or trade with Indian markets accessible mainly by mass transportation systems that existed then, such as pack bullocks and large boats.

[5] Raychaudhuri, 'Non-Agricultural Economy', p. 280.

transacted within itself, the bulk of what it needed. To that extent, small market-places and weekly or periodic markets had a function within this local barter exchange.

*Jajmani* has tended to be seen, partly by the British administrators and partly by Indian nationalists, in normative terms, as a system that made the village integrated, self-sufficient, non-commercial, unchanging, and egalitarian. This was not entirely true. Markets did exist in villages. Some products such as cloth were rarely a part of the product-sharing process. The egalitarianism is a myth—no matter how transactions happened, inequality between superior right holders or village officials and labourers was deep and ingrained. In 1813 in southern Andhra villages, a rich cultivator's average consumption was about twice that of the poorest.[6] In the nineteenth century, those who died during famines were predominantly small farmers and labourers. There is no reason to believe that the situation was any different in periods before.

Shorn of this image, a system of rural transaction called *jajmani*, the broad features of which were barter, customary dues, production of manufactures for local consumption, and a caste-based specialization, did exist in large parts of India, and not until the end of the nineteenth century did it finally crumble.

## Industry

Rural and urban artisans produced mainly for local consumers. Rural industries included textiles of the coarser kind, pottery, agricultural implements made of wood and iron, sugar, leather and oil. The main unit of production was the family, and sometimes, small collectives of artisan families. The organization of production was simple and rarely involved extensive division of labour or specialization by task. Some other rural products, such as raw silk, salt, saltpetre, and indigo, were produced in the villages by part-time peasants, but were traded more widely.

Urban industries included finer textiles, carpets and shawls, decorative metal-ware and pottery, wood and ivory carving, manufacture of arms and musical instruments, etc. The superior economic and political power of the consumers led to very high degrees of refinement in urban craft. Proximity to power was important for these crafts in two ways, consumption, and protection from piracy. By and

---

[6] Burton Stein (ed.), *The Making of Agrarian Policy in British India, 1770–1900*, Oxford University Press, Delhi, 1992, p. 9.

large, industry and trade in high-quality goods were 'dependent entirely on the "affluence of ruling aristocracies and land controlling elites"'.[7]

Proximity to power also led to economic subordination of producers to the consumers. Some of these crafts were performed in *karkhanas* (literally factories) or departments owned by the courts and other wealthy consumers. Unlike pre-modern European industry of the towns, the presence of guilds is extremely rare, almost unknown, in India. There are some examples in Gujarat. But even these were not institutions with well-defined economic functions and as powerful as the European guilds frequently could become. Broadly speaking in pre-colonial India, '[Virtually] every relevant feature of the economy, society and state was designed to hold the artisan firmly down to his lowly place ... '[8]

Political decentralization in the eighteenth century dispersed the urban skilled crafts that earlier had a strong bias for a few cities in the Mughal heartland, notably Lahore, Agra, Delhi and Multan. Now, skilled crafts flourished, or began to congregate, in such towns as Banaras, Farrukhabad, Lucknow, Moradabad, Jhansi and Gwalior in north India, Bijapur, Ahmadnagar, Aurangabad and Warangal in the Deccan, and Madurai in the south. Each one of these sites was similar to craft towns in Mughal north India, in that they flourished because of aristocratic consumption and protection. Nevertheless, the dispersal was significant for the pattern of regional industrialization in the long run.

Relative to the rural crafts, the refinement attained by the urban crafts was enormous. This was evident not so much in technology, but in the use of costly materials like gold thread or pashmina. Division of labour and specialization were more advanced in the urban industries. Consequently, craftsmanship reached great heights of proficiency. There was greater degree of mercantile activity in high-quality industrial goods. For, these goods occasionally used imported raw material and were sometimes exported. Money and credit were also more prevalent in these transactions. Ship-building was a highly developed semi-urban industry in certain towns located on western and eastern coasts. Unlike the rural industries, it served a wider market. Unlike the urban industries, it served trade rather than rich consumers.

[7] T. Kessinger, 'Regional Economy: North India', *CEHI 2*, p. 246.
[8] T. Raychaudhuri, 'Non-agricultural Production' *CEHI 1*, p. 284.

## Export of Textiles

An export market for industries expanded from the seventeenth century and was flourishing in the first half of the eighteenth. This market was mainly for Indian cotton textiles consumed in Europe. The most popular items in this trade were not the most refined varieties made in the capital cities. Europeans were primarily interested in cheap, mass consumable cloth. Among designed garments, prints suited them because printing is cheaper than woven designs. Because of this bias for cheapness and simplicity, the purchases tended to come from the rural areas, or rather, large villages that were somewhat more proficient than the smaller ones. The purchase of such textiles was active in three coastal regions, Gujarat, Coromandel, and increasingly Bengal. Initially the purchasers included a number of European countries, but the English and the Dutch increasingly dominated the trade. The English trade was under the monopoly of the East India Company. The Company, however, could not always protect its monopoly from many European private traders.

In all these regions, the production organization in textile trade was different from the usual ones in domestic markets. Here, rural production coordinated with merchants located in towns.[9] The rural production was not completely dispersed, but clustered around the European Companies' trading stations. Such a pattern of location and the ethnic composition of buyers and producers ensured a very important role for Indian merchants and intermediaries in this system. When eventually this trade dwindled from about 1820, (see section on foreign trade), it left behind a prosperous group of Indian merchants who had risen from the textile trade, and were often weavers by hereditary occupation. In Bengal, such people included the *Basaks*, who were among the prominent early Indian residents of Calcutta town. These Indian merchants contracted with the weavers by giving advances of money and raw material, a system known as *dadni*. As

---

[9] In the early stages of industrialization in some parts of Europe, external markets, rural production and urban capital had combined in this way to generate a process of rapid capital accumulation. In some views, this episode was preparatory to the more capital-intensive industrialization that followed. The process is known as 'proto-industrialization', and is significant for a number of changes that it is said to have introduced in the economy and society of the rural artisans in western Europe. For a collection of essays covering most of these aspects, see S.C. Ogilvie and M. Cerman (eds), *European Proto-industrialization*, Cambridge, 1996. Early-modern Europe and India are compared by Frank Perlin, 'Proto-industrialization and Pre-colonial South Asia', *Past and Present*, 98(1), 1983.

such, *dadni* does not stand for a special system of contract. For advances can be features of numerous types of contractual sale. But in this case, the *dadni* could sometimes be used as a tool of bargaining, or involve an element of coercion. *Dadni* could be forced onto a weaver, or threat applied towards fulfilment of contract once *dadni* was taken.

The Europeans paid for Indian goods not with their own goods, but with gold and silver. There was, thus, great inflow of bullion into the exporting regions. What effect these imports had, and where they eventually went, are questions historians of this trade are still debating. Import of gold and silver is an important and little understood peculiarity of Indian foreign trade. We shall have to deal with this aspect of saving behaviour at different points, most importantly Chapter 7. Indians heavily imported gold not just in this period, or not only due to European trade, but as a long-term enduring habit. Whether the gold imports in the eighteenth century functioned mainly as currency or mainly as savings is an open question.

It is not possible to know what proportion of contribution the three main types of market—rural, urban and export—made in the total manufacturing production and employment in the eighteenth century. The export market was evidently an important one for Bengal and Coromandel, and the trade contributed to the fact that Bengal was among the most prosperous regions of pre-colonial India. The trade also contributed to the rise of cities such as Madras and Calcutta. However, in relation to the possible scale of textile production in India or even Bengal, the export market was a rather small one. At 1790, export of cloth was an estimated 50 million yards,[10] which probably represents 1–2 per cent of total cloth production in India at that time.

## Internal Trade and Finance

Several authors have tried to visualize a hierarchy of markets in pre-British India highlighting the varying importance of commerce for different segments of the economy. In one such scheme for northern India, three types of markets or market-networks are distinguished. At the lowest level is exchange of rural produce with or without local markets. The markets, usually periodic, were located in large villages —commodities traded were mostly necessities of life. At the next level was limited regional trade again mainly in necessities based in

[10] M.J. Twomey, 'Employment in Nineteenth Century Indian Textiles', *Explorations in Economic History*, 20(1), 1983, Table 1.

small towns with permanent markets, or *qasba*. Besides necessities, the *qasba* trade also dealt in higher valued goods such as sugar, oil, ghee, better cloth, etc. The range of supplies has been roughly placed at 50–100 miles.[11] The range probably expanded where water transport was available. Above this was the entirely urban, long-distance trade in luxuries.

Conspicuously absent from this scheme is long-distance trade in rural produce for the home market. Examples would be trade in grain, or industrial raw material. Long-distance trade in such low-value high-bulk goods is certainly not unknown in India. They tended to use systems such as caravans of pack bullocks driven over badly maintained and highly insecure roads that were not travelworthy for rainy months of the years. Such systems implied astronomically high real cost of overland transport. Nevertheless, such trade may have actually expanded in the eighteenth century. There is some sign that grain trade began to expand, when political decentralization increased the scope for inter-regional trade.

Political decentralization seemingly also strengthened a financial sector dominated by firms that performed four functions: converting currencies, bill discounting, remittances, and lending to the local elite. Families that performed one or more of these functions were called *shroffs*. They were an important part of the urban economy and long-distance trade. Decentralization of power led to a dispersion of *shroff* activities, and possibly led to a considerable rise in their political power. An example of the latter would be the Jagatseth house in Bengal.

## The Rise of British Rule

By the end of the eighteenth century, the English East India Company was less a trading house and more a rentier. It had rights to the revenue of large states. The income from export trade declined after peaks attained in the 1790s. Already by then, the English Company had become the effective ruler of Bengal, partly in attempts to defend trade from political interference, and partly as a result of conflicts that the Company was sometimes accidentally drawn into. Land revenue in any case became a convenient means of payment for Indian textiles. It is possible that the decline in export incomes strengthened the Company's dependence on land revenue, and thus, on direct rule As the territory under their control expanded, the regions in their

---

[11] Kessinger, 'Regional Economy', p. 247.

possession began to feel the new regime in unprecedented ways. In trade, agrarian relations, industry, and infrastructure, the European connection had begun to produce significant impact. The most important changes are described in the three sections that follow.

## FOREIGN TRADE

The integration of Indian trade with world trade had begun before the eighteenth century, but speeded up from about 1800. The major impetus to this process was the Charter Act of 1813 that curtailed the official monopoly of the East India Company in trade. The long-term result of integration was fairly rapid growth in export and import between 1800 and 1850, and almost explosive growth from 1850 down to the beginning of the First World War. The composition of trade, however, had changed dramatically in the course of this long expansion. An examination of export and import data estimated by K.N. Chaudhuri suggests the following conclusions about this 'commercialization'.[12]

The first conclusion relates to the importance of trade for the economy as a whole. An approximate but acceptable measure of the importance of trade and markets for the economy is the contribution of foreign trade (or export) to national income. The rate at which national income at current prices was growing over the period 1868–1913 was well below 1.5 per cent per annum. Although we have no time-series for incomes for periods before the 1860s, from what we know about prices and economic structure of the time, for the rate of growth of nominal national income to exceed the above rate in the period 1800–1850, one would need to assume absurdly high growth rates in real income and prices. Growth rates of export and import were considerably higher, at 4–5 per cent during 1834–1913 ( see Table 2.1). It follows that the ratio of trade (or export) in income was rising rapidly all through the nineteenth century. In quantitative sense, the nineteenth century was a period of unprecedented commercialization. We also need to remember that growth rates in trade did not decline as the scale of trade expanded. In other words, compared to any two years in the early nineteenth century, the same annual growth rate of 4 per cent in the late nineteenth meant immensely larger volume of transactions.

The second conclusion relates to comparison between the eighteenth

---

[12] 'Foreign Trade and Balance of Payments', *CEHI 2*.

century, and the nineteenth or the colonial period. Nationalist as well as recent writings suggest that with the rise of the British rule in India, a commercialized economy retreated from trade. There is no question that in *textiles*, India's position in the world regressed from that of a net exporter in the eighteenth century to a net importer in the nineteenth, and that there was decline in a highly commercially-oriented sector of the economy. But can we generalize from textiles to trade as a whole?

We cannot be sure that foreign trade played a bigger role in the Indian economy at, say, 1750, compared to 1835 or later. From available trade figures (see Table 2.1) such a conclusion seems questionable. The levels of export and import almost steadily increased from the eighteenth century down to 1913. As far as one can see, there is no evidence that the scale of export from India at any time during the early modern period was higher than at any time in the nineteenth century. It is also not reasonable to say that the share of trade in national income in 1750 was any higher than it was in 1835. Before the nineteenth century, foreign trade was certainly important for some coastal regions. But it was a rather negligible activity for the economy as a whole. Quantitatively, its potential to generate economic growth was small. Foreign trade really grew in importance after British rule began.

The third conclusion is about composition, which changed quite dramatically. At its peak, the early modern trade was dominated by two items—textiles in export, and bullion in import. Between 1800 and 1850, both components began to lose importance. Bullion was not needed to pay for Indian goods as the Company could now use its land revenue for the purpose. That did not stop bullion imports, for the demand for precious metals was entrenched. But it did reduce the scale of imports. Export of cotton cloth dropped sharply after 1800, and import of machine-made cloth and yarn expanded. Textiles began to be replaced by new exportables such as indigo, opium, silk, tobacco and cotton, and to a limited extent salt, sugar, and saltpetre. The region that benefited most from this shift was the larger area served by the network of transportation and trade along the Ganges river. Elsewhere, commercialization was considerably less obvious, if not absent altogether.

In 1811, the most important export from India was cloth (33 per cent of export value). Next in importance were opium (23.8 per cent), indigo (18.5 per cent), raw silk (8.3 per cent), raw cotton (4.9 per cent), and sugar (1.5 per cent). Already by then, the share of cloth had been falling, and that of the other goods rising. Around 1850, this trend grew stronger. The five most important exports in that year were, opium (30.1 per cent of value), raw cotton (19.1 per cent), indigo (10.9 per cent), sugar (10 per cent) and foodgrains (4.1 per cent). After the 1850s, composition of exports changed further. Indigo and opium were replaced by cotton, jute, tea and leather. Composition of import was much simpler. Textiles and metals accounted for nearly 60 per cent of import value in 1850. This pattern changed from the 1870s in that the importance of textiles declined in favour of machinery and intermediate goods.

Finally, there is a point to be made about fluctuations in trade. Eighteenth century trade was notorious for fluctuations, a feature that derived from weaknesses in infrastructure and information. Partly in response to these problems, the bulk of the trade took place in 'consignments' rather than on order. That is, a certain quantity of goods was bought, kept in an inventory, and sold in the final market at whatever price it fetched from whichever buyer it could attract. Usually, goods in consignment trade were auctioned. Naturally, price fluctuations were very large, and the trade suffered from what economists call 'adverse selection', the problem that speculative profits tend to attract risk-takers, making matters worse. This feature continued in the 1800–50 period. The two crashes in Calcutta, in 1830–3 and 1847, led to violent declines in export prices each lasting several years. Such fluctuations were considerably reduced in the latter half of the century, as consignment trade slowly faded away.

TABLE 2.1
Scale of Foreign Trade (excluding treasure), 1813–1913

| | Value of trade (Rs mn) | | Per cent share of trade in National Income |
|---|---|---|---|
| | Import | Export | |
| Bengal | | | |
| 1813[a] | 16 | 46 | – |
| 1839[b] | 57 | 120 | – |
| India | | | |
| 1835 | 48 | 111 | 1.1 to 2.4[c] |
| 1857 | 153 | 275 | 3.6 to 4.8[c] |
| 1913 | 1913 | 2490 | >20[c] |

| | Average annual growth rate (per cent) | |
| --- | --- | --- |
| | Import | Export |
| Begal | | |
| 1813–27[a] | 6.5 | 2.4 |
| 1828–39[b] | 1.1 | 1.9 |
| India | | |
| 1835–57[d] | 6.3 | 4.9 |
| 1858–1913 | 5.0 | 4.5 |
| 1858–1913[e] (excluding 1866) | 5.0 | 5.3 |

[a] Figures available in Sicca, Madras and Bombay rupees.
[b] Figures converted into Company's rupees.
[c] These percentages are based on the premise that national income at current prices grew within a range 0.5 to 1.5 per cent per year (compound) between the pairs of dates. There are two assumptions behind this range. First, in the early nineteenth century real national income could not have grown at a rate very different from the 0.9 per cent or so observed for the early twentieth century. And second, there was no secular and large increase in prices in the early nineteenth century. Both assumptions are modest.
[d] Although the data series begins from 1834, the first year is excluded because it was a year of unusually low level of trade.
[e] 1866 was again an outlier, and the last row recalculates the growth rates excluding that year.
Source: K.N. Chaudhuri, 'Foreign Trade and Balance of Payments', *CEHI 2*, Tables 10.4–10.7c. S. Sivasubramonian, 'Revised Estimates of the National Income of India, 1900–1 to 1946–47', *IESHR*, 34(2), 1997.

1800–50 was the indigo–opium era. Cotton too was emerging in a small way as an export item in India's trade with Britain (see Chapter 3). Indigo was the main dye used in cotton textiles. The world trade in indigo began to rise after the establishment of a machine textile industry in England. At first supplies came from the West Indies, but this source became uncertain during the Napoleonic wars. As Bengal had conditions suitable for indigo cultivation, it seemed a better option. European capitalists engaged in textile trade found in indigo a new and profitable investment. European firms based in Calcutta who supplied capital and handled marketing and shipment of indigo were known as agency houses. Cultivation and trade in indigo expanded rapidly until the 1850s when synthetic substitutes began to replace natural indigo. The growth, however, was marked by sharp fluctuations. The cultivation of indigo in Bengal is a long-remembered example of the abuses of the *dadni* system. Opium, again, was produced in Bengal under government monopoly. It was a small item of export to China in the late eighteenth century. The scale of exports rose enormously as the East India Company found it a convenient means of payment for the Chinese tea, silk and porcelain it exported to Europe. Opium was contraband in China, and the Company and its authorities fought two wars with China to stave off threats to stop the trade. The trade finally stopped after agreements were signed between India and China in the early twentieth century. By then, the special significance of opium as a balancing item in Britain's trade between India, China and Europe had more or less disappeared. These two goods, indigo and opium, and to a smaller extent sugar and raw cotton, sustained the commercialization of the eastern Gangetic economy in the first half of the nineteenth century.

## AGRARIAN CHANGE
### General Tendencies

During the first three or four decades of British rule, maximization of land revenue was pursued with great determination. Revenue demand on land was fixed in cash rather than as proportion of output, and the assessments were universally exorbitant. They were especially severe in the *ryotwari* (see the following sub-section on agrarian relations) settlement areas between 1820 and 1850. The burden was probably increasing in real terms, as prices fell. A large variety and number of tax-free tenures were subject to taxation. Taxes were collected more efficiently than before. Cash transactions in the rural economy probably expanded, partly as a result of revenue demand in cash, and partly due to production of cash crops like sugar, cotton, indigo and opium. It is possible that the decision to raise these crops was influenced by the need to gather cash for the payment of revenue.

Sale and auction of land tended to increase with revenue defaults, and as proprietary rights became increasingly well-defined. Rural creditors including grain traders found their position relatively strengthened for they could acquire some of the land that was transferred. Also, the cash economy depended on financiers. Revenue demand in cash hurt poorer peasants in general and part-time peasants in particular. The latter group included communities that lived primarily on livestock rearing, cultivation being a subsidiary occupation.

After 1858, the impact of high revenue demand was eased to an extent. In revised settlements the revenue rates were brought down. In regions that grew the most successful commercial crops, the real revenue burden eased via expansion in irrigation, cultivation of arable wastes, and rising prices and profits.

## Agrarian Relations

Well before 1857, new or modified revenue collection and proprietary rights had come in place. They had been at work in regions such as Bengal for over 60 years. The result was substantial re-ordering of rural class structure. The major part of historical research on colonial India has been about these changes in relations between rural classes. The abundance of British records on the subject has aided such studies.

Three topics of analytical interest have driven much of this research. The British wanted to introduce property rights in land, and thus redefine the relationship between the cultivators and the State. There is first of all the question of the intellectual roots of this attempt. What did the British think they were doing in Indian agriculture? Such doctrinal roots of policy on rent and property have been traced to various sources. Eric Stokes, for example, traced it to the influence of the Ricardian idea that rent is the only income that can be taxed without discouraging production.[13] Others have traced it to ideologies that considered property rights to be the main stimulus behind enterprise, or to the way the new regime interpreted past Indian practice, especially customs and laws of the Mughal state. Secondly, were the British guided mainly by these theories or by local conditions? Third, how far did British rule actually change local conditions? The answers to the second and third questions depend largely on the quality of interaction between the new regime and the classes that were formerly powerful. The latter, the British sometimes suppressed and sometimes collaborated with. Collaboration, in turn, was one massive example of 'asymmetric information' between the rulers and the ruled. Therefore, it could produce outcomes very different from what the rulers intended.

The new regime defined itself as the supreme landlord, which it thought was a long established Indian custom. In the interest of better cultivation (and therefore larger revenue), it decided to define ownership or proprietary right in land, and began to search for suitable hands to give this gift to. The general ideology was to fuse revenue collection with proprietorship, that is, to contract with proprietors rather than middlemen for payment of revenue. Such contracts were

---

[13] Eric Stokes, *The English Utilitarians and India*, Oxford University Press, Oxford, 1959.

called 'settlements'. These ideas were not always practicable in the early years. So a great deal of continuity with the old power structure was forced upon the reformers. The State uniformly tried to demilitarize those of the old nobility who had revenue collection rights. The village offices were left in place, but much reduced both in importance and in share of revenue. *Inam*, interestingly, was left more or less untouched. But very heavy revenue demands were imposed almost uniformly across all regions until the 1830s and the 1840s, which happened to be a period of falling prices. Demands were fixed in money rather than in kind.

The new proprietary body varied according to local conditions. In Bengal and central Doab, proprietary rights were granted to *zamindars*. These included a mixed class of people who had been *zamindars* during the pre-British periods, as well as some who had acquired *zamindari* rights through revenue farming. The decision was partly a result of the fact that *zamindars* were far too powerful in this region. But partly, it was a case of 'mistaken identity'. The British wrongly thought that the *zamindar* was like the 'landlord' in Britain, that is, a superior cultivator. The most famous example of *zamindari* settlement is the Permanent Settlement of Bengal (1793), extended in the next decade to coastal Madras and North-Western Provinces (eastern UP). It is noteworthy that usually *zamindari* areas were highly fertile areas that created enough rent to support a landlord–tenant–labourer hierarchy. In some parts of *zamindari* this condition was weak, defaults excessive, and these were later changed to different forms of settlement.

By the *zamindari* settlement, the government granted *zamindars* ownership rights subject to the payment of fixed sum of money. After the British came to control the revenue of Bengal, in the 1760s, revenue farming continued out of necessity, with the change that auctions became more open and the terms of the lease shorter. As usual with revenue farming, such a course diluted the composition of *zamindars*. Moreover, the highest price at the auction was frequently too high relative to the area's ability to pay. The right holders in that case either defaulted, or tried to collect exorbitant rents from their tenants, who in turn fled from their land. Revenue farming, therefore, was both unpopular and inefficient. After this experience, the Company turned back to the old *zamindars* and tried to settle with them directly. The Permanent Settlement was the final result of this process. It gave the *zamindars* ownership and security provided they paid their tax. In effect, the *zamindars* were also allowed to continue as mini-monarchs in their own domain. The tax was initially set so high that extensive default and sale of *zamindari* followed, with the result that more non-landed people came to acquire *zamindari*. While there was such reshuffling at the top, at the village level, the imposition of new title holders on actual cultivators initiated a long process of adjustment. Exactly what the nature of this adjustment was like is a matter of debate. Positions in this debate depend on how the tenancy situation is interpreted. Ratnalekha Ray, for example, argued that taking advantage of the *zamindars'* own distance from land and unstable economic conditions, wealthy peasants with superior tenancy claims extended their land-holdings, so much so that they put limits on the *zamindars'* ability to take closer hold of actual cultivation. Rajat Datta, on the other hand, has argued that except in a few districts, the small peasant dominated Bengal agriculture in the eighteenth century.[14]

In other areas of India, change came more slowly. In western India where the British took over from the long established Maratha bureaucracy, the first impulse was continuity rather than reform, so as not to upset revenue collection. But in the long run, change did come. Outside *zamindari* settlement areas, the practice was to 'settle' with dominant cultivating groups. In the upper Doab and Rohilkhand, *talukdars* were suppressed and the 'village republics' were recognized as the proprietary body. The joint-landlords of village lands were collectively responsible for the revenue. Agriculture was too insecure and population too thin here to generate large rent. Therefore, joint rights cemented by clan or kinship were possible. The early years of overassessment, however, made these rights unattractive, and they were practically unmarketable. The 1830s saw the first assessments of the individual shares in village lands. As these shares were defined, they became marketable, and began to come into the market in large extent.

By and large in southern and western India, *mirasdars* were granted proprietary rights. The *mirasdars* being technically holders of shares in village land, this system and joint-landlord kind of assessment could become in many cases indistinct. The political prelude to this system in the south was the suppression of *poligars* in 1799–1800. They were somewhat like the northern *zamindars*. A few of them did

---

[14] Ratnalekha Ray, *Change in Bengal Agrarian Society, c. 1760–1850*, Manohar, Delhi, 1979, and Rajat Datta, 'Agricultural Production, Social Participation and Domination in Late Eighteenth Century Bengal: Towards an Alternative Explanation', *Journal of Peasant Studies*, 17(1), 1989.

become *zamindars* under British rule. But they were considerably fewer and more distant from the land than the *zamindars*. The type of settlement where cultivators individually received proprietorship was known as *ryotwari*.[15] By the time *ryotwari* was established (1800–20), the minds of the major reformers had turned against *zamindari* from a sense that the *zamindars* were really more middlemen than cultivators. Early British rule continued with an old practice of assessments over the entire village. The cultivators were expected to allocate the revenue among them. Gradually, individual shares and assessments on them came to be measured. The shares were called *pattas*. This process enabled easier sale of such rights. Tolerable rates of revenue generally came to be levied in the 1830s and 1840s, after new assessments. The 1835 Bombay Survey was an important model that was followed elsewhere.

*Ryotwari* was, in principle, a direct contract between the ryot, or the cultivator, and the State. Thus, theoretically, it should have eliminated the need for any intermediary between them. As we have seen, offices of the State were important in the villages in western and southern India before British rule. These offices were sometimes performed by *mirasis*, as in southern India, and sometimes by stipend or salary earning employees of the State, as in the west. Did these offices actually decline after *ryotwari*? This question has engaged a lot of attention. Scholars agree that initially there was an attempt to destroy or reduce the offices. The move in some cases impaired the cohesion and internal management of the village. It also seems that the British realized in some areas that it would be wise to go slow on this course. In the long run, there could be one of three outcomes—a permanent weakening of office holders in the rural economy, their evolution into substantial cultivators, and a more mixed situation where a few among the office holders could evolve as substantial cultivators. Western India is seen to be an example of the first situation. The *ryotwari* of the south-eastern coast, and partly the Tamil region, evolved more in the lines of the second possibility. In some cases of western India, the third outcome was observed. In all cases, where old officers benefited or survived, the main instrument or privilege that enabled them to do so was *inam* land. *Inam* was substantial in certain parts of the south, mainly in southern and coastal Andhra. It is a puzzle that such extensive revenue discounts were permitted while at the same time there was every attempt to wrest from the village as much as

---

[15] The Arabic word *raiyat*, by which peasants were called in pre-British sources, meant 'subjects'.

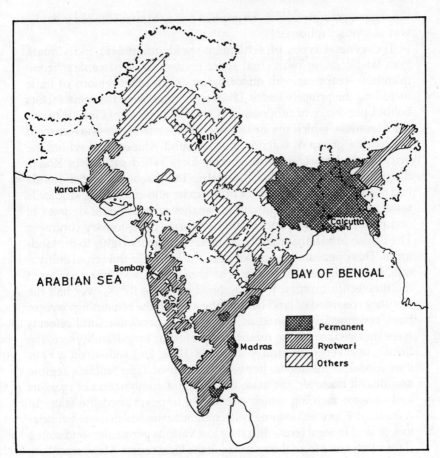

MAP 2.1: TYPES OF SETTLEMENT, C. 1858

the regime possibly could. An implicit policy to spare the old notables was obviously followed.

The general types of settlement—with prominent individuals, joint landlords, or individual share-holders in co-parcenary[16] communities—reappear with minor variations in other regions of India including the princely states. Local conditions were the main factors behind the choice of proprietary body. In the areas of Gujarat under the Marathas, which the British acquired, settlements were entered into with a group of warrior chiefs around Ahmedabad whom the British called *talukdars*; with shareholders called *patidars* in Kheda district; and with individual cultivators in Broach. Pre-British Kerala had a system of tenancy where upper caste non-cultivating landlords rented out land to a hierarchy of tenants with different degrees of occupancy rights and under different forms of customary contracts. The British in Malabar readily granted proprietary rights to the landlords. This opened a breach between the land and the actual cultivators, that is the tiers of tenants. The breach widened in the course of the nineteenth century. In Hyderabad until the 1850s, over half the territory consisted of land held by the king. In the remaining *ryotwari* land, revenue farming and its abuses were pervasive until reforms were initiated under the ministership of Salar Jang-I. In Mysore, the British intervened in land systems in 1831, and settled on a *ryotwari* model in the 1860s. Between the end of Tipu Sultan's regime and British takeover, the state was under a combination of *ryotwari* and revenue farming which eventually impoverished the state. In Awadh, the former revenue collectors or *zamindars* became proprietors of land in legal terms. But they lost various perquisites and status claims that arose from their service in the local courts. Many members of their extended families claimed rights to the land, a factor that led to subdivision of these estates. On the other hand, many forms of customary tenants found their claim to tenure bereft of proper legal protection. Both these problems defied easy solution.

## INDUSTRY AND FINANCE

In industry, there was no significant state intervention, quite clearly because it was not a source of revenue. The formation of a new regime did not mean a significant change for industry. But economic circumstances affected industry deeply. The manufacture of better quality

[16] The term used in revenue administration for members of a group of dominant families.

articles and long distance trade in Indian manufactures were under stress in the early nineteenth century from three sources. First, there was decline in European import of Indian textiles. Second, there was import into India of British textiles. And third, there was decline in demand due to the depleted and impoverished state of the Indian aristocracy. Foreign trade with a now rapidly industrializing Britain greatly reduced India's position as a supplier of cloth to the world. It also reduced the position of the textile industry in the domestic market. There is considerable quantitative data from south India, central India and eastern India confirming that employment declined in textiles. The timing of this decline varied somewhat. In central India it may have peaked after 1860s when the region was connected with the ports by rail. The price depression of the 1830s and 40s in western India was attributed by some contemporaries to the collapse of textile trade. The most significant drop in employment was seen in spinning. Women in many regions were engaged in hand spinning of cotton yarn as a part-time activity. This activity was more or less terminated by British yarn.

The left–nationalist school of historiography has suggested that foreign import of textiles led to 'de-industrialization' or shift of population from industry to agriculture. Such a trend does not necessarily mean increasing poverty. But in this case, the implication is that it did cause increasing poverty, that is, a fall in incomes. It is plausible that the proportion of working population engaged in industry was higher at 1800 (possibly 15–18 per cent) than at 1900 (about 10 per cent). In that strict sense de-industrialization did take place. However, some qualifications are needed here—first, many people who gave up industry in this period were working only part-time; second, the major reason behind the decline, import of machine-made goods, applied only to textiles; third, in parts of the Gangetic plains, agriculture was not doing too badly in the early nineteenth century. If there was a fall in textile employment, there was a rise in employment in indigo, opium and saltpetre. However, we do not know whether the latter compensated for the former. Finally, cheaper cloth would have benefited rural consumers, and cheaper yarn would have reduced the costs of production of handloom weavers. The changes introduced by foreign textiles did not necessarily have adverse effects on levels of income or consumption. Whether they were adverse in the net cannot be determined without better quantitative data on income and expenditure. 'De-industrialization' will be discussed further in Chapter 4.

Early British rule is believed to have been a period of decline in indigenous banking and finance. The *shroff* houses thrived in the presence of many currencies. They gradually lost the business of money-changing after unification of currency about 1835. In the eighteenth century, almost all the independent states were heavily dependent on financiers. This was so partly due to mismanagement and wars, and partly for the same reason that they became dependent on revenue farmers, that is, inadequate knowledge or control over relatively new territories. This dependence faded or disappeared with the rise of British rule. Finally, the general importance of tax farming declined and so did the fortunes of many mercantile-financial houses for whom this had been an important source of income.

But new opportunities were opening up. In the mid-eighteenth century, foreign trade of India was in the hands of three communities—the Europeans dominated trade with Europe; and Armenians and Arabs that with the Middle East; close behind were the Indian merchants such as the Parsis of the western coast. The Chettis in southern India, and Indian and European traders of Calcutta, were prominent in trade with East and South-east Asia, and domestic trade between the interior and the ports. Along with trade, the Indian merchants were involved in shipbuilding and shipping, revenue farming, banking and currency exchange. They were dominant in the relatively new foreign trades, such as opium and raw cotton in western India, and opium and indigo in the east. This profile fits the larger Parsi, Chetti and Bengali houses engaged in foreign trade in the early nineteenth century. By the middle of the century, their enterprise was in a state of flux—for Indians withdrew from large-scale shipping. Foreign trade became centred in Britain. A series of speculative bubbles destroyed many of the Indian firms. The Indian capitalists who survived this crisis did so by turning their attention to different commodities and to industry.

One major episode has drawn special attention from scholars. By the very end of the eighteenth century, European merchants and former employees of the East India Company were setting up firms in Calcutta in collaboration with Bengali capitalists. These firms were known as 'agency houses'. They traded in some of the goods then in great demand, such as opium, indigo, silk, foreign textiles, and sugar. They were also engaged in a limited way in banking and insurance. Until about 1834, they received deposits of Company officials attracted by speculative interest rates and the exchange rates offered on remittances. This was a major source of their capital and an impetus to their banking services.

The demand and price of indigo were notoriously unstable. A violent crash in the early 1830s drove many of these firms to the. wall. Thereafter, deposits of Company officials dried up. The agency houses began to rely more on Indian partners for capital and management. These firms entered banking, insurance, coal mining, silk filature, ship-building, along with indigo, opium and sugar. Some of them ambitiously diversified into manufacturing based on machinery. In the case of Jessop & Co., one of the oldest engineering firms in India, this diversification involved collaboration between agency houses and artisan-mechanics.

There were several Indian individuals and families that became millionaires during this brief period of Indian dominance in Calcutta's commerce and industry. Notable examples are, Dwarakanath Tagore, Rustomji Cowasji, Motilal Seal, the Law family, etc. The first three names commanded immense credit in the money market. The firm Carr Tagore is the best-known example for three reasons. It was the largest in scale and had the most diversified interests. Rabindranath Tagore was Dwarakanath's grandson. And Dwarakanath was a great philanthropist and *zamindar*. He had official connections with the government. He used his talents and resources productively, to develop a major financial and commercial house of the time. His interests included colliery, tea, salt, steamboats, indigo, and a major bank of the time. His own *zamindari* estate grew indigo. His own bank, the Union Bank, dominated the financing of indigo trade.

The end of these partnerships came with another crash in 1847–8, when the Union Bank collapsed. This date effectively marked the permanent end of Bengali involvement in large-scale business. Thereafter, Bengali moneyed people tended to invest in *zamindari*. Various authors have tried to explain this regression. The three main explanations are, attraction of *zamindari* as an investment and as a way of life, European dominance in large-scale trade and industry, and speculative mentality. The third factor is a reminder that the history of these partnerships was never a sound one. Fraud, disputes, cliquism, and distrust were widespread because both the local and the foreign partners were driven by a mentality that N.K. Sinha has called 'predatory capitalism'. The majority of the foreign partners were determined to get rich quickly and return home. In this prevailing mood, no stable rules, institutions, or a foundation of trust could take shape. Both the Indo-European collaborations and the financial capacity of the ventures they floated were thus basically unsound and fragile. They were too weak internally to survive the crash of 1847–8.

A further reason can be advanced as to why the Bengalis did rather poorly in industry and commerce. During the interwar period many Marwari firms replaced Bengalis engaged in mining and trade based in Calcutta. The former's relative strength was seen to be 'the good backing' they received from among the community 'which helps them to tide over difficulties when they occur'.[17] Bengalis, in the 1840s and in later periods, conspicuously lacked such systems and tradition of community support. Chapter 5 will discuss the importance of the 'community' as a business resource.

After 1848, commerce and industry in Calcutta were dominated by British capital, and by capitalists who were willing to make long-term investment commitments in India. The most prominent group among their Indian business associates was the Marwaris.

INFRASTRUCTURE

Along with agriculture, one field in which the rise of British power had direct effect was in the creation of physical and institutional infrastructure. In the last quarter of the eighteenth century, administrative districts in Bengal were more clearly defined than in the pre-British regimes. A system of district officers maintaining peace and collecting revenue came in place. Between 1800 and 1835, weights and measures were unified, many currencies were replaced by those issued from time to time by the East India Company, transit duties that had proliferated during the decentralization of power in the eighteenth century were abolished, and an old profession tax was abolished. The legal framework promoted private property rights and contract law more explicitly than most Indian regimes. A centralized system of police was coming into place. Justice acquired its separate institutional identity through a series of 'regulations' and a gradual process of separation from the Company's administration.

Government investment during the Company's rule consisted mainly of repair, enlargement, and unification of ancient irrigation systems. These works were located on the Jamuna (from 1817 to the 1840s), the deltas of the Cauvery (1830s and 1840s), Godavari and Krishna (1840s and 1850s). Most of the ancient systems of canals were in a state of disrepair decades before the Company's rule began. The

[17] 'Jute Industry', *Career Lectures*, Appointments and Information Board, Calcutta University, Calcutta, 1939, pp. 229–30. This is a collection of popular lectures by persons established in commerce and industry in Calcutta, designed to make students, especially Bengali students, familiar with business vocations.

returns to such investment were expected to come in two forms, indirectly as increased revenue charged on irrigated land or as prevention of famines, and directly as water rates. Although no precise accounting was possible on the contribution of irrigation to government's income, some calculations did show that these were remunerative investments. In north India, such investments had some strategic value and were thus in the hands of the Military Board. Public works remained with this department until the 1870s when public works departments were set up in various provinces.

Ships of iron powered by steam, in place of wooden ones run on sails, had begun to revolutionize both coastal and inland transport from the 1830s. They also effectively terminated the Indian shipbuilding tradition. Between 1835 and 1855, grounds were cleared for very rapid development of the postal system, the railways, and telegraph. Between 1809 and 1843, the government established three joint-stock banks, the 'Presidency Banks' of Bengal, Madras and Bombay. These banks were initially the government's banker. Over time, they expanded their business with the private sector. The three main businesses were, discounting of bills and securities, advance of short-term credit, and acceptance of deposits. They were not permitted to deal in foreign exchange. 'Exchange Banks' were established by first Indian, and later, European capitalists to finance foreign trade and remittances.

These changes cleared the road for a macroeconomic transformation that will occupy the rest of the book.

## Conclusion

The eighteenth century was a period of transition in both political and economic terms. The basic structure of the land revenue system had been established by 1857. The burden of taxation in the early British rule was generally high. Possibly, the taxed proportion of output was no higher than that in the previous regimes but taxes were collected more efficiently. This may have had a depressing effect on agriculture. The decline of textile exports to Europe and the import of British textiles were other factors that are likely to have had depressive effects in the early nineteenth century.

Do these signs of a depression in the early nineteenth century suggest that a commercialized economy of the eighteenth century regressed in the early nineteenth? The question cannot be satisfactorily answered for, data on incomes is not available. Plausible calculations suggest that export of Indian textiles was not quantitatively a very large force before the nineteenth century, even though it may have been significant in certain regions. Furthermore, markets were expanding in a number of commodities that were poorly traded earlier. Studies of the eighteenth and early nineteenth centuries have seen a surge in mercantile activity in northern India, a possible expansion in employment, but no significant improvement in the conditions of peasants and artisans. The benefits of this commercialization largely went to the merchants and landowners.

Thus, it is not clear yet whether the first half of the nineteenth century was a generally depressed period or not. It is clear, however, that after 1860, the economy was growing under the impetus of easier tax burden and significant expansion in market opportunities. Already, before 1860, commercialization, property rights, infrastructure and a crushing burden of revenue had created a market in land. After 1860, profitability of land was another factor behind the growth of a land market.

Did these tendencies favour the more efficient cultivators or the more extortionate and powerful rural bosses? How far was British intervention responsible for the changes that occurred? How large was the impact of commercialization? The next chapter considers answers to some of these questions.

## Annotated Readings

### Conditions at 1750

Read the surveys by Irfan Habib, 'The Systems of Agricultural Production: Mughal India', Tapan Raychaudhuri, 'Non-Agricultural Production: Mughal India' and a few other articles in CEHI 1. Also, Raychadhuri, 'The Mid-Eighteenth Century Background' in CEHI 2. B.R. Grover, 'An Integrated Pattern of Commercial Life in the Rural Society of North India during the Seventeenth and Eighteenth Centuries', in Sanjay Subrahmanyam (ed.), Money and the Market in India 1100–1700, Oxford University Press, Delhi, 1994.

### Agrarian Relations

It is neither necessary nor possible to make an exhaustive list of works on this very well-researched theme. Presented below is a list of some of the useful surveys, followed by a few widely cited works on each of the major topics. The student should begin with the surveys.

Surveys

The four articles by Eric Stokes on agrarian relations in northern India, B. Chaudhuri on eastern India, H. Fukuzawa on western India, and Dharma Kumar on south India, in *CEHI 2*. Neeladri Bhattacharya, 'Colonial State and Agrarian Policy', and Burton Stein, 'Introduction', in Burton Stein (ed.), *The Making of Agrarian Policy in British India 1770–1900*, Oxford University Press, Delhi, 1992.

Intellectual Roots of British Agrarian Policy

Eric Stokes, *The English Utilitarian and India*, Oxford University Press, 1959, especially Ch. 2; R. Gush, *A Rule of Property for Bengal: An Essay on the Idea of Permanent Settlement*, Mouton, Paris, 1963; A.T. Ember, 'Landholding in India and British Institutions', in R.E. Frykenberg (ed.), *Land Control and Social Structure in Indian History*, University of Wisconsin Press, Madison, 1969; and Burton Stein, *Thomas Munro: The Origins of the Colonial State and His Vision of Empire*, Oxford University Press, Delhi, 1989, Chs. 2 and 3.

Northern and Eastern India

Sugata Bose, *Peasant Labour and Colonial Capital: Rural Bengal since 1770*, Cambridge, 1993, pp. 45–52, 68–79, 114–22. Ratnalekha Ray, *Change in Bengal Agrarian Society c. 1760–1850*, Manohar, Delhi, 1979. Rajat and Ratna Ray, 'Zamindars and Jotedars: A Study of Rural Politics in Bengal', *MAS*, 9(1), 1975. Rajat Datta, 'Agricultural Production, Social Participation and Domination in Late Eighteenth Century Bengal: Towards an Alternative Explanation', *Journal of Peasant Studies*, 17(1), 1989. Asiya Siddiqui, *Agrarian Change in a North Indian State: Uttar Pradesh, 1819–33*, Oxford University Press, Delhi, 1978. Eric Stokes, *The Peasant and the Raj: Studies in Agrarian Society and Peasant Rebellion in Colonial India*, Cambridge, 1978.

South India

Dharma Kumar, *Land and Caste in South India*, Cambridge University Press, 1965. R.E. Frykenberg, *Guntur District: 1788–1848, A History of Local Influence and Central Authority in South India*, Oxford University Press, Oxford, 1965. N. Mukherjee and R.E. Frykenberg, 'The Ryotwari System and Social Organization in the Madras Presidency', in R.E. Fykenberg (ed.), *Land Control and Social Structure in Indian History*, University of Wisconsin Press, Madison, 1969. David Ludden, *Peasant History in South India*, Princeton University Press, Princeton, 1985, pp. 101–15.

Western India

Sumit Guha, *The Agrarian Economy of the Bombay–Deccan, 1818–1941*, Oxford University Press, Delhi, 1985, Ch. 2. R.D. Choksey, *Economic History of the Bombay–Deccan and Karnatak (1818–68)*, published by author, Poona, 1945.

Inams

An essay on the role of *inams* in different systems of assessment by Eric Stokes, 'Privileged Land Tenure in Village India in the Early Nineteenth Century', in R.E. Frykenberg (ed.), *Land Tenure and Peasant in South Asia*, Manohar, Delhi, 1984.

## Trade, Industry, Finance, Infrastructure

Essential Readings/Surveys

R.S. Rungta, *The Rise of Business Corporations in India, 1851–1900*, Cambridge, 1970. The five articles by Tom G. Kessinger on regional economy in north India, S. Bhattacharya and B. Chaudhuri both on eastern India, V.D. Divekar on western India, and Dharma Kumar on south India, in *CEHI 2*. Rajat K. Ray, 'Introduction', in Rajat Ray (ed.), *Entrepreneurship and Industry in India 1800–1947*, Oxford University Press, Delhi, 1992, pp. 18–30.

Other Readings

K.N. Chaudhuri, 'Foreign Trade and Balance of Payments', in *CEHI 2*, especially pp. 813–60. N.K. Sinha, 'Indian Business Enterprise: Its Failure in Calcutta 1800–48', in R.K. Ray (ed.), *Entrepreneurship and Industry in India 1800–1947*, Oxford University Press, Delhi, 1992. Blair B. Kling, *Partners in Empire*, Firma KLM, Calcutta, 1981. Lakshmi Subramanian, 'Banias and the British: Role of Indigenous Credit in the Process of Imperial Expansion in Western India in the Second Half of the Eighteenth Century', *MAS*, 21(3), 1987. Elizabeth Whitcombe, 'Irrigation', *CEHI 2*, pp. 678–92. Samuel Schmitthener, 'A Sketch of the Development of the Legal Profession in India', *Law and Society Review*, 3 (2–3), 1968–9. Ratnalekha Ray, *Change in Bengal Agrarian Society*, pp. 79–88 on changes in systems of governance in Bengal during early British rule.

# 3

# Agriculture and Common Property Resources

Two sets of general questions usually motivate studies on agriculture in colonial India. First, why was agriculture stagnant in the first half of the twentieth century? Throughout the colonial period the primary sector employed nearly 70 per cent of the economically active population. Agricultural growth or stagnation, therefore, largely explains rates of growth in national income. In the late nineteenth century, growth rates in agriculture and Net Domestic Product (NDP) were above 1 per cent per annum, and well above the population growth rate. After 1900 agriculture was not capable of generating rapid economic growth. Why this stagnation?

Secondly, whatever the factors behind the stagnation, they must be long-standing—for the regional pattern of agricultural growth and stagnation after independence has been very similar to the regional pattern of growth and stagnation in the colonial period. Pockets of rural poverty today were pockets of rural poverty in the past. Areas that experienced 'green revolution' in the 1970s and 1980s had started on the road to prosperity even during the British rule. This correlation has been getting weaker. But it has not disappeared yet. The past explains the present of Indian agriculture in an obvious and direct way. How is this continuity to be explained?

This chapter will describe agrarian change over the period, 1858–1947. Once the description is complete, the two questions posed above will be taken up for discussion. The chapter is divided into six sections—trends in agricultural production, expansion in markets, effects of market expansion, explaining stagnation, common property resources, and summary and conclusion.

TABLE 3.1

Growth Rates of Net Domestic Product (NDP),
Total and in Agriculture, 1868–9 to 1946–7

*(annual trend growth rates in per cent)*

|  | Agriculture | NDP | Population | Per capita NDP |
|---|---|---|---|---|
| 1868–98 | 1.01 | 0.99 | 0.40[a] | 0.59 |
| 1882–98 | 1.08 | 1.29 | 0.51[b] | 0.78 |
| 1900–46 | 0.31 | 0.86 | 0.87[c] | −0.01 |

[a] Growth rate between 1872 and 1901.
[b] Growth rate between 1881 and 1901.
[c] Growth rate between 1901 and estimated 1946.

*Notes:* '1898' stands for average of three years, 1896–7, 1897–8 and 1898–9. '1900' and '1946' are similarly averages of three years.

*Sources:* Alan Heston, 'National Income', in *CEHI 2*, Table 4.3A, for 1868–98; S. Sivasubramonian, 'Revised Estimates of the National Income of India, 1900–01 to 1946–47', *IESHR*, 34(2), 1997.

PRODUCTION, INVESTMENT, TECHNOLOGY

### Agricultural Production Data

How did agricultural income change over time? This question, though a critical one for economic historians of colonial India, cannot be answered simply, because the statistics on agricultural output has serious limitations. Scholars disagree on how serious these limitations are, and how one could get round them. These disagreements have generated alternative series of national income and led to different views on regional agricultural performance. For the period before 1890, the problem of inadequate data is so serious that all India estimates of agricultural output and income seem impossible. Some broad conclusions can be drawn about trends in major crops and major regions, which are stated below.

### Agricultural Production before 1890

Two general conclusions can be drawn from crop and region-specific data.

(i) In major regions, the second half of the nineteenth century saw a significant expansion in net sown area or land under cultivation. This was a universal phenomenon. But it was more pronounced in crops that were traded widely.

(ii) In specific commercial crops, such as cotton and wheat, there is evidence of rise in yield per acre during the nineteenth century. Based on these findings, it seems certain that the latter half of the nineteenth century saw expansion in output in almost all the major regions. National income data confirms this contention. The growth is mainly owed to increasing area under cultivation. Cultivable wastes and large areas of otherwise uncultivable wastes were made cultivable by canal irrigation in the late nineteenth century.

## Agricultural Production, 1890–1947

For the period 1890–1947, the All India database is considerably richer. The main published sources on area and output of major crops by districts are the following—*Season and Crop Report* issued by the Department of Agriculture or land records in each province, *Agricultural Statistics of India* and *Estimates of Area and Yield of Principal Crops in India*, both published by the Director General of Commercial Intelligence and Statistics. Across these publications, the coverage, content and presentation of data differ somewhat. But fundamentally, the sources of the raw data on which these reports are based did not differ much. The data was collected mainly by village officials such as the *patwaris* and *chowkidars*,[1] and district-level officials of revenue administration who also checked and compiled these figures. In the Permanent Settlement areas, the village administrative tradition had become weak. Consequently the quality of data suffered. In the other areas, the data collection system at the local level was more developed because the revenue rates were expected to adjust to prevailing agricultural conditions.

### Method of Estimating Production for Survey Purposes

Total agricultural output in a year for a crop was calculated as follows:

Production = area cultivated in that year × 'standard yield' per acre × 'condition factor' for that year

The standard yield meant an average or normal yield in a normal season. It was estimated by crop-cutting experiments in sample plots

---

[1] *Patwaris* were accountants or village registrars and *chowkidars*, village watchmen who held hereditary offices under the *zamindars* in north India.

in a normal season. It was meant to be periodically revised by means of similar experiments. The condition factor was actual yield as a ratio of the normal yield.[2] In a drought year, the condition factor should be less than one, in an exceptionally good year it should exceed one.

In each harvest season, the village officials gave figures for the area cultivated and the condition factor locally. The district officials sometimes revised these figures before sending them to the Department of Agriculture. The standard yield was estimated independently, and did not vary annually. There was considerable guess-work involved in both the acreage and the condition factor estimates. Both were essentially subjective figures until independence. Village officials often arrived at these figures based on very general impressions. Acreage may have been systematically underestimated as a result. But acreage in any case varied rather slowly and to a limited extent, so the problem is not considered a serious one.

The condition factor, on the other hand, was supposed to be a function of the season, and fluctuated to a much greater extent. In practice, the condition factor was almost always reported to be less than one. It rarely exceeded one, no matter how good the season. There are three explanations for this. First, the standard yield was set too high. Second, the officials misinterpreted standard yield to mean the best possible output rather than the normal or average output. And third, the officials suffered from a universal and persistent pessimism about agricultural conditions. Sometimes they might have deliberately reduced the condition factor to press for revenue remissions. These problems should make the estimated levels of crop output rather unreliable. However, it is unlikely that the village officials made an error in judging whether the harvest was going to be a good one or a bad one. That is, the variations in the condition factor should capture fluctuations in output correctly. A test of this is the apparently strong positive correlation between rainfall, the most important factor behind seasonal fluctuations, and the condition factor.

Was there a long-term trend in the condition factor? The presence of a long-term trend would provide adequate cause for doubting the statistics. For the condition factor is by definition only a measure of fluctuations. In his contributions on revised agricultural output and national income, Alan Heston argued that the condition factor for the Bombay Presidency showed a downward trend between the 1890s

---

[2] Accountants estimated the yield for a particular year in comparison with the yield they thought 'normal' in their villages. District figures for condition factor were based on the sum of village-level observations.

and the 1940s.[3] However, this conclusion, as well as its validity for the rest of India, has been questioned by a number of authors. The standard yield was possibly overestimated for British India. More serious, variations in standard yield for major regions and for all of India have been repeatedly questioned. The over- and under-estimation in yields came to light when the results of more accurate crop-cutting experiments in the 1940s and immediately after independence were compared with the yield estimates from fifty or sixty years ago. This difference was the basis for an alternative national income estimate that Heston developed.

How far do these problems bear on the utility of agricultural statistics in colonial India? Clive Dewey, in a well-known paper, offered a very pessimistic assessment of this dataset.[4] Other historians, while alive to the problems, are more hopeful about the inferences from analysis of the data. The village reporting system in areas outside Permanent Settlement was not as bad or as arbitrary as was sometimes made out in colonial reports. The overestimation of standard yield and underestimation of condition factor partially compensated each other in the aggregate. So, the colonial yield figures are usable. Having said that, the problems in the collection system did become serious in particular regions, as we shall see.

Major Features of Agricultural Production in the Period
The standard series of agricultural production owes to a monumental work by George Blyn.[5] Blyn's work is famous not only for the quality of statistical work, but also for its major conclusions. The most widely used national income series, by S. Sivasubramonian or Heston, build on Blyn's database. Tables 3.2–3.6 contain the essential results of Blyn's work.

Blyn's work suggests seven basic findings:
(i) Over 1891–1946, average growth rate of crop output was small at 0.37 per cent (see Table 3.2). Alternative estimates of agricultural output do not question the low level of growth.
(ii) The experience of foodgrains and non-foodgrains differed

[3] 'Official Yield per Acre in India, 1886–1947: Some Questions of Interpretation', first published in 1973, reprinted in Sumit Guha (ed.), *Growth, Stagnation or Decline? Agricultural Productivity in British India*, Oxford University Press, Delhi, 1992.

[4] 'Patwari and Chaukidar: Subordinate Official and the Reliability of India's Agricultural Statistics', in Dewey and A.G. Hopkins (eds), *The Imperial Impact: Studies in the Economic History of Africa and India*, London, 1978.

[5] George Blyn, *Agricultural Trends in India, 1891–1947: Output, Availability, and Productivity*, University of Pennsylvania Press, Philadelphia, 1966.

sharply. Foodgrain output was practically stagnant, whereas non-foodgrain output was growing quite rapidly (see Table 3.2).

(iii) Output growth rate was small because of two reasons. Firstly, acreage growth was small, because there was not much cultivable waste land left after 1891. Secondly, yield per acre grew slowly, and in fact, declined in food crops (see Table 3.2).

(iv) Until the First World War, yield per acre of both food and non-food crops were growing. But in the interwar period, food crops experienced a precipitous decline (see Table 3.3).

TABLE 3.2
Trend Growth Rates of Crop Output,
Acreage and Yield For British India 1891–1946

(per cent per annum)

| | Growth in output | Growth in acreage | Growth in yield per acre | Growth and stagnation in yield per acre in selected periods | | |
|---|---|---|---|---|---|---|
| | | | | 1891–1916 | 1916–21 | 1921–46 |
| All crops | 0.37 | 0.40 | 0.01 | 0.47 | −0.36 | −0.02 |
| Foodgrains | 0.11 | 0.31 | −0.18 | 0.29 | −0.63 | −0.44 |
| Non-foodgrains | 1.31 | 0.42 | 0.67 | 0.81 | 0.34 | 1.16 |

Note: The trend rates are average of ten rates, each relating to a 5-year period. Blyn divided the entire period into ten such parts.
Source: Blyn, *Agricultural Trends in India*, Appendix Table 5A.

TABLE 3.3.
Trend Growth Rates of Output of
Major Crops in British India, 1891–1946

(per cent per annum)

| Foodgrain | Growth rates | Non-foodgrain | Growth rates |
|---|---|---|---|
| Rice | −0.09 | Cotton | 1.30 |
| Wheat | 0.84 | Sugarcane | 1.30 |
| Jowar | 0.05 | Tobacco | 0.03 |
| Bajra | 0.72 | Groundnut | 6.26 |
| Maize | 0.02 | Jute | 0.27 |
| Ragi | −0.37 | Tea | 2.74 |
| | | Indigo | −6.19 |

Source: Blyn, *Agricultural Trends in India*, Appendix Table 5A.

(v) Among food-crops, by far the most important source of stag-nation was rice. Wheat yield was growing. Among coarse grains, the picture is not uniform.

(vi) Regional experiences varied sharply. Bengal suffered a much greater decline than any other region, or the rest of British India together. Greater Bengal had below-average growth rates in both food and non-food crops output, in yield per acre, and in yield per capita (see Table 3.4). In rice, yield per acre in Bengal fell sharply, whereas that in Madras increased.

(vii) Until the First World War, food output grew more rapidly than population, which suggests an increasing availability of food

### TABLE 3.4
### Per Capita Output and
### Growth Rates of Output in Major Provinces, 1891–1946

*(trend growth rates in per cent per annum)*

|  | Growth rates, output of all crops | Per capita foodgrain output (tonnes) | |
|---|---|---|---|
|  |  | *1891* | *1941* |
| Greater Bengal | −0.45 | 212 | 147 |
| Rest of British India | 0.82 | 160 | 168 |
| United Provinces | 0.42 | 123 | 130 |
| Central Provinces | 0.48 | 207 | 149 |
| Bombay–Sind | 0.66 | 195 | 152 |
| Madras | 0.98 | 146 | 163 |
| Greater Punjab | 1.57 | 140 | 201 |

*Note:* 'Rest of British India' is a simple average of the rates of the other five major provinces.

*Source:* Blyn, *Agricultural Trends in India,* Appendix Table 5A.

### TABLE 3.5
### Relationship between Agricultural
### Output and Population Growth Rates, 1891–1946

*(per cent per annum)*

|  | *1891–1916* | *1921–1946* |
|---|---|---|
| Population | 0.44 | 1.12 |
| All crops | 0.84 | 0.34 |
| Foodgrain | 0.61 | 0.13 |
| Non-foodgrain | 1.66 | 1.08 |

*Source:* Blyn, *Agricultural Trends in India,* Appendix Table 5A.

per head. In the interwar period, population growth rate accelerated and food output growth rate decelerated. This meant a decline in food availability per head (see Table 3.5). The situation was the most acute in Bengal, where food output declined at an annual rate of about 0.7 per cent during 1921–46 and population grew at an annual rate of about 1 per cent in the same period.

These seven findings boil down to two basic conclusions. First, primarily commercial crops experienced more growth than primarily subsistence crops. That is, commercialization and growth in agricultural productivity were positively correlated. Second, while agricultural growth rate was small on average, there were significant regional differences. In fact, the main source of agricultural stagnation was the crisis in interwar Bengal.

## Investment and Technology

There is only scattered information available on investment in agriculture. Macroeconomic data (see Chapter 7) suggests that the scale of such investment was small, though possibly growing. Investment in irrigation is more well-documented, because this was a major area of government expenditure. The basic data is presented in Tables 3.6 and 3.7. Table 3.6 shows that acreage irrigated as percentage of cropped area increased from 12 to 22 per cent between 1885 and 1938. This expansion occurred mainly due to government canals and in private wells. Canal construction, in fact, started from the early-nineteenth century. The percentage of irrigated area was almost certainly much less than 12 around 1820.

TABLE 3.6
Area Irrigated, 1885–1938

| Area irrigated by | (million acres, excluding Burma) | |
| --- | --- | --- |
| | 1885–6 | 1938–9 |
| Canals | | |
| Government | 6.90 | 24.41 |
| Private | 0.94 | 3.53 |
| Tanks | 4.38 | 5.87 |
| Wells | 8.74 | 13.21 |
| Total irrigated | 23.09 | 53.73 |
| Total cultivated | 185.09 | 243.58 |
| Irrigated/cultivated area (%) | 12.4 | 22.1 |

Source: India, Statistical Abstracts for British India, Calcutta, various years.

Both canals and wells were concentrated in three regions, Punjab, Madras and western UP. In all three regions government and private investment had begun before 1885. And in all three, expansion continued after 1885. Table 3.7 compares the three provinces with the rest of British India. The above-average increase in wells in Madras and UP suggests that canals and wells were complementary investments, rather than substitutes. Usually, government canals encouraged a change in cropping pattern and raised the value of land. That in turn stimulated private investment in the form of wells. In the rest of British India, systems other than wells and canals were relatively more significant. To understand how government and private investment in irrigation were related with agricultural growth, we need to look into the development of markets for crops that these investments made possible to produce.

TABLE 3.7

Irrigated Area as a Proportion of
Cultivated Area in Major Provinces, 1885–1938

*(percentages, 'British India' excludes Burma)*

|  | 1885–6 | 1938–9 | % increase in irrigated area due to | |
|---|---|---|---|---|
|  |  |  | Government canals | Wells |
| Punjab | 29.3 | 57.4 | 95.5 | 9.3 |
| Madras | 24.1 | 23.5 | 49.6 | 18.6 |
| UP | 19.3 | 26.6 | 57.0 | 37.2 |
| Rest of British India | 6.0 | 12.5 | 31.3 | 10.7 |

*Note:* The last two columns may add to greater than 100 if acreage under other systems shrinks.

*Source:* India, *Statistical Abstracts for British India*, Calcutta, various years.

The basic set of agricultural implements changed little during British rule. There was a tendency towards the use of more iron in place of wood. This led to better quality irrigation equipment and better ploughs in some areas. But their diffusion remained limited. Nevertheless, other than canal and well irrigation, some significant technological changes did occur. Carts were used for transportation more commonly. In the case of wheat and cotton, improved varieties of seed played an important role in increasing productivity. This was the result of the establishment of a chain of agricultural research stations by the Government of India. These were staffed by scientists rather than bureaucrats, as had been the practice with experimental farms before. These stations, especially the one at Pusa, identified superior wheat strains by selecting from among hundreds of indigenous varieties. These new seeds became very popular.[6]

## EXPANSION IN MARKETS

During the period 1857–1947, there were significant changes in the demand and supply of crops, their marketability, and in the composition of landed classes. These processes had begun before 1858. They gathered strength in the latter half of the nineteenth century.

### Product Market

Commercialization can be defined as a process where peasants start producing primarily for sale in distant markets, rather than to meet their own need for food, or to sell in local markets. In the latter case it is the subsistence needs of a small local community of peasants that decide what and how much is grown. The terms 'distant markets' or 'long-distance trade' in the rest of this chapter refer to export as well as Indian markets accessible mainly by the railway system. Increasing production for sale in such markets led to commercialization.

Markets and trade in agricultural goods existed on a large scale in fairly organized forms in the pre-British period. But the market expansion in the British period marked a quantitative and a qualitative break. The quantitative aspect will be discussed later. There were three main qualitative changes.

(i) Before British rule, product markets were constrained and subject to serious imperfections given multiplicity of weights and measures, backward and risky transportation systems, and extensive use of barter. British rule weakened these constraints. By doing so, it enabled closer integration of global, regional, and local markets.

(ii) Export became a major source of demand. The post-1858 commercialization signified India's integration in to world trade.

(iii) In the post-1858 period, there was accelerated development of land, labour and financial markets.

### The End of the Earlier Commercialization

The earlier phase of commercialization (see Chapter 2) was based on indigo and opium trade in eastern India—these were no longer

---

[6] For a descriptive account of early agricultural research, see M.S. Randhawa, *A History of Agriculture in India*, Indian Council of Agricultural Research, New Delhi, 1983, Chs. 27, 34–7.

lucrative after 1860. Between 1850–90, indigo cultivation first shifted from Bengal to Bihar and eastern-UP districts, and thereafter declined generally. The reason for the shift was the Indigo Revolt in Bengal in 1860. Farmers protested against the forced and extortionate cultivation of the crop mainly by the European planters. Further west, indigo cultivation had a more voluntary character. It was stimulated in the UP by the spread of canal irrigation. It persisted until the 1870s, when the newly discovered mineral dyes began to reduce the usage of the indigo dye. Opium was never very remunerative because of government controls on prices.

Two other Bengal exportables, cane sugar and silk, also experienced decline. Cane sugar was an export item of districts in Bihar. Exports encouraged cultivation in the first half of the nineteenth century. This sugar was priced out of the world market by beet sugar after 1850. However, the local market for cane sugar grew and hence sugarcane cultivation did not disappear. Silk production on a small-scale by part-time farmers was an important export trade from Bengal until the late-eighteenth century. But throughout the nineteenth century it suffered a decline in quality and competitiveness *vis-à-vis* other Indian, European, and East Asian silks. One reason for this decline was weakness in industrial organization. In the eighteenth century, many European firms had invested large sums of money in this industry and trade. Most of them withdrew in the early nineteenth century. Thereafter, the production and trade came to be dominated by a large number of persons of small resources. Individually, they had little money to invest in improving the industry.

A much bigger wave of commercialization based on cotton, wheat and in a small way rice, had already begun in the late eighteenth and the early nineteenth centuries. Cotton and wheat were both lucrative commercial crops. After the 1850s, export of both products expanded greatly, and the trade was augmented by oil-seeds, tobacco, groundnut, and sugarcane.

## Demand and Supply Factors Behind Commercialization

The world demand for food and raw materials expanded substantially with the Industrial Revolution in Europe from the early nineteenth century. Steam shipping from the second quarter of the nineteenth century was a major stimulus to trade, as it enabled European buyers to access South Asian supplies far more quickly and cheaply than before. The opening of the Suez Canal in 1869 brought down shipping costs between Europe and India. The railways, by reducing transportation costs, increased foreign demand for certain crops that India was well-suited to produce thus encouraging changes in cropping pattern.

Export market was not the only area of expansion. Commercialization involved many crops that were sold mainly in the domestic market. The railways integrated markets and brought pockets of excess supply and excess demand closer together. Industrialization within India created a demand for food and raw materials in the industrial cities. In fact, the very process of production of non-foodgrain or 'cash crops' made the peasants who specialized in such production dependent on foodgrain trade.

On the supply side, agricultural production was stimulated by downward revision of revenue rates in the *ryotwari* areas. Such revisions occurred at different times in different regions. But they bunched in the second quarter of the nineteenth century, which many officers saw as a period of reform after what had been a period of too heavy a revenue burden. More generally, since the monetary burden of revenue was not revised quickly, commercialization and rising prices from the 1850s led to a decline in the real revenue burden. We can capture part of this decline for the period 1895–1925. The nominal revenue burden in all areas was more or less constant, whereas agricultural prices had doubled, implying a 50 per cent fall in real revenue burden. The railways, again, played a crucial and dynamic role. Road transportation was slow, risky and costly, especially over long distances and difficult terrain. River transportation was relatively cheap. But it was available for limited time in a year over small areas. The railways did not have these problems. Large-scale irrigation systems such as canals made waste-lands cultivable and increased cropping intensity (that is, reduced fallow) in areas where rainfall was limited.

A supply-side factor that further aided the production of commercial crops was induced changes in agricultural practices and technology, through canal and well water and seeds.

The Extent of Commercialization

It is not possible to precisely quantify the scale of commercialization. However, the following facts do give some indication.

(i) Export in value increased enormously (by about 500 per cent) between 1870 and 1914. Non-manufactured goods accounted for 70–80 per cent of the exports from India.

(ii) The unprecedented trend in agricultural prices of consistent rise led contemporary writers and administrators to infer that there was a sustained excess demand for Indian goods. In part, the increasing price trend was a worldwide phenomenon, fuelled by a steady monetary expansion after new sources of precious metals were discovered. Indian prices moved in response to this world trend because the Indian economy became more open than it had been before.

(iii) Area cropped increased in most regions in the period 1870–1920, usually led by wheat, cotton, oilseeds, sugarcane and tobacco cultivation.

(iv) Rents in nominal and real terms increased.[7]

(v) Scale of credit transactions increased. Credit indicates production for exchange. Production for subsistence does not require credit except in times of distress.

(vi) Scale of land transfers increased and so did the price of land.

(vii) Migration of former agricultural labourers out of agriculture increased.

(viii) Finally, limited statistics suggest that such indices of transportation and rural trade as the number of carts at work increased substantially in this period.

The price and trade series are the simplest indices to handle. Using this data it is possible to build a rough chronology of commercialization.

Phases of Commercialization
Reliable price series of agricultural goods are available from 1861.[8] In the nineteenth century the trend was a rising one, though it was broken frequently by severe fluctuations due to harvest failure. The first episode of increase in prices occurred during the 1860s with the cotton boom, which ended in a crash in the late 1860s. The 1870s were good for trade and saw sustained rise in prices led by cotton exports. There was also a general increase in exports with the opening of the Suez Canal. The early 1880s saw a depression in foreign demand, a result of a depression that affected the world economy. But from about 1885 until the end of the 1920s prices were rising more or less continuously. Price levels at 1928 were about three times what they were in the mid-1870s.

---

[7] See the readings listed under 'land market' at the end of the chapter.

[8] Regional and scattered price data exist for periods before that. One such series covers 1823–70. It shows no sustained trend in prices, but extreme fluctuations, and possibly a depression during 1845–55. See K. Mukerji, 'Price Movements in India between 1823 and 1871', *Artha Vijnana*, 5(4), 1963.

After 1920, conditions began to turn adverse with depressed international trade, and the start of a rapid deceleration in land-man ratio. By the early 1920s, world agricultural markets had begun to face persistent over-supply and price depression. In India, major cash crops faced stagnant or falling prices, though cotton was temporarily free of crisis. The agricultural depression was one factor among many that led to the Great Depression in 1929–32. This, again, was a worldwide event. But it was allegedly intensified in India by adverse macroeconomic policy. It upset not only the product market, also the rural credit market. Peasants who were already indebted faced rising real value of debt. There was probably a fall in real wages and living standards for agricultural labourers for a brief period (see Chapter 7 for a fuller discussion of the event). 1920s, thus, were a watershed in external market conditions. Also, by this time, good quality arable land was beginning to become scarce with accelerating population growth.

The peak of commercial expansion in India can be dated at 1860–1925. Between these years value exports increased by about six times, and prices about three times. The greatest developments in infrastructure occurred in this time. Marketing and financial institutions also developed and matured; the Depression upset, broke up, and altered some of these institutions.

Changes in Cropping Pattern

During Blyn's period of study, 1890–1946, there was little change in cropping pattern (see Table 3.8). The share of non-foodgrains in acreage cropped increased marginally between 1891–5 and 1935–9. It fell during the Second World War, as war demand greatly increased food prices, and consequently rice cultivation.

TABLE 3.8
Acreage Cropped, British India, 1891–1946

|  | | | | (annual average) |
|  | 1891–5 | | 1941–6 | |
| Crops | Million acres | Percentage of all crops | Million acres | Percentage of all crops |
| --- | --- | --- | --- | --- |
| Rice | 66.0 | 37.3 | 74.1 | 36.0 |
| Wheat | 21.9 | 12.4 | 26.4 | 12.8 |
| Jowar | 20.9 | 11.8 | 22.1 | 10.7 |
| Gram | 11.1 | 6.3 | 15.1 | 7.3 |
| Bajra | 11.7 | 6.6 | 15.1 | 7.3 |

| Crops | 1891–5 | | 1941–6 | |
|-------|--------------|----------------------|--------------|----------------------|
| | Million acres | Percentage of all crops | Million acres | Percentage of all crops |
| Barley | 5.2 | 2.9 | 6.7 | 3.3 |
| Maize | 5.1 | 2.9 | 6.3 | 3.2 |
| Ragi | 4.4 | 2.5 | 3.4 | 1.7 |
| Total Foodgrain | 146.0 | 82.5 | 169.0 | 82.0 |
| Cotton | 9.6 | 5.6 | 11.6 | 5.6 |
| Sugarcane | 2.9 | 1.6 | 3.6 | 1.7 |
| Jute | 2.0 | 1.1 | 2.5 | 1.2 |
| Groundnut | 0.4 | 0.0 | 5.6 | 2.7 |
| Oilseeds | 12.5 | 7.0 | 11.1 | 5.4 |
| Indigo | 1.4 | 0.8 | 0.05 | 0.0 |
| Total Non-foodgrain | 30.4 | 17.2 | 36.5 | 17.7 |
| All Crops (including others) | 177.0 | 100.0 | 206.0 | 100.0 |

Note: Oilseeds include rape, mustard, sesamum, and linseed.
Source: Blyn, *Agricultural Trends in India.*

Except for the rise of groundnut cultivation, all other important changes in cropping pattern had occurred before 1890. From provincial data we know that definite shifts did occur towards cash crops before 1890. The three main crops to have gained in acreage were cotton, wheat and sugarcane. Sugarcane did not occupy large area, but it added much greater value per area than most other crops.

Three Major Cash Crops

Cotton is an old crop in India, and was once cultivated widely. Before 1850, there had developed an internal and an external market for the raw cotton of western India. The export market shifted from China to Britain in the early nineteenth century. With this change, Bombay's business as a port town began to grow rapidly.[9] Still, the importance of Indian cotton for the British textile industry was as yet limited. The East India Company and important figures in the Lancashire mill industry tried to develop India as a major supply base for raw cotton. But they were not very successful because the quality of Indian cotton was not suitable, and Lancashire capitalists were rather uneasy about trading with Indian farmers. The 'Cotton Famine' of 1861 forced this trade upon them.

When the American Civil War broke out, supplies of cotton from

[9] Amalendu Guha, 'Raw Cotton of Western India: Output, Transport and Marketing, 1750–1850', *IESHR*, 9(1), 1972.

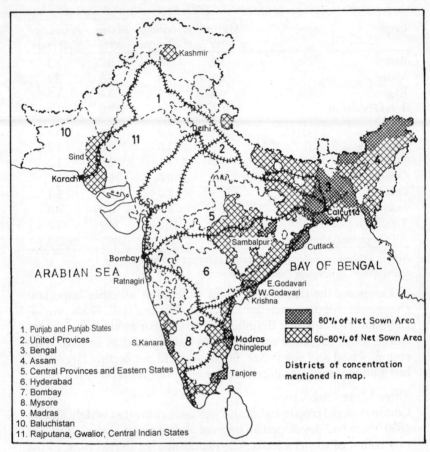

1. Punjab and Punjab States
2. United Provices
3. Bengal
4. Assam
5. Central Provinces and Eastern States
6. Hyderabad
7. Bombay
8. Mysore
9. Madras
10. Baluchistan
11. Rajputana, Gwalior, Central Indian States

80°/. of Net Sown Area

60-80°/. of Net Sown Area

Districts of concentration
mentioned in map.

MAP 3.1:  AREAS OF RICE CULTIVATION

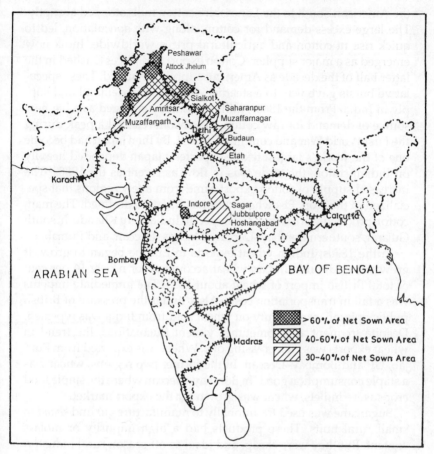

MAP 3.2: WHEAT AREAS

the American South to the Lancashire cotton mills stopped abruptly. The large excess demand for cotton, along with speculation, led to quick rise in cotton and agricultural prices worldwide. India now emerged as a major supplier. Cotton export and prices crashed in the latter half of the decade as American supplies resumed. These speculative bursts gave way to a steadier expansion in demand and supply in India. From the 1860s, mills in Bombay emerged as a big new source of demand for raw cotton. This boom reached a peak during the First World War and continued after it. By then Japan had become one of the world's largest textile exporters. Japan depended heavily on Indian cotton, the trade was in flow as recent as the 1980s. The increased supply of cotton export came from a few regions that specialized in the crop. Elsewhere cotton cultivation declined. The main cotton producing areas that developed in India were Khandesh, south Gujarat, southern Bombay–Deccan, Madras–Deccan, and Punjab.

In the 1870s, Indian wheat exports to Europe began to grow. It grew so rapidly that Indian wheat accounted for nearly 14 per cent of total British import of wheat about 1883. The immediate impetus was a fall in transportation costs. Also, under the pressure of British public opinion, export duty on wheat sold from India was repealed. Despite frequent and sometimes violent fluctuations, the trend in wheat exports was an increasing one. Wheat was exported from Punjab, UP and Bombay–Deccan. In the former two regions, wheat was a staple consumption good. In Bombay–Deccan where the staple food crops were millets, wheat was grown for the export market.[10]

Sugarcane was used traditionally to manufacture *gur* and *khand* in small rural units. These products had a high impurity or molass content. But they were cheap, and ideal as off-season rural industry. These traditional products came in competition with modern factories making refined white sugar from cane. But in colonial India, neither did white sugar become widely popular, nor did the method become internationally competitive (see also Chapter 5). The traditional products survived. However, within the traditional products, a great technological advancement had taken place with the introduction of the two-roller mill to crush cane in 1874, in place of the wooden mortar and pestle. The popularity of the more efficient crushers led to a rapid growth in the manufacture of *gur* and *khand*, and in turn, expansion in the area under sugarcane. A further impetus for sugar-

---

[10] A literal definition of 'millets' is cereal plants with small seeds. In the Indian context, millets stand for a range of relatively drought-resistant, dryland foodgrains that are consumed locally.

cane cultivation came from tariff protection given to the modern sector of the industry. The main regions where sugarcane was cultivated were, UP (which had over half of the total area under cane in the 1930s), Punjab, Bihar and Bengal. These four provinces accounted for 90 per cent of *gur* and nearly all of the *khand* production.

Regional Experiences

*Punjab:* Prior to the mid-nineteenth century, Punjab was largely dry consisting of vast 'wastes' that supported pastoralism but little cultivation. Between 1867 and 1892 cultivated area in Punjab increased by about 50 per cent. This was made possible by expansion in canal irrigation in the three major Doabs encircled by the Jhelum and Sutlej rivers. From about 1880, British engineers built large perennial canals tapping the waters of the five rivers, which turned vast tracts in the Doabs earlier sustaining only the most basic forms of pastoralism into arable land. In the same period, the length of canals expanded from 1569 miles to 12,368 miles, road length nearly doubled, and railway mileage grew fourfold. Blyn's data shows that between 1890 and 1920, agricultural production increased, and the main source of output growth was expansion in area cropped. In that respect, Punjab was not different from the rest of India in the late nineteenth century. The difference was that, in Punjab uncultivable wastes had been made arable, whereas in the rest of India, cultivable wastes were brought under the plough. After 1921, the conversion of wastes reached its limits. By then Punjab agriculture had benefited decisively from successful plant breeding experiments in wheat and cotton, so that productivity continued to increase. Lyallpur was one of the sites where superior strains were developed. These were popularized by private merchants.[11] While the Doab expanded its wheat and cotton production, the relatively drier areas of southwest Punjab (present-day Haryana) specialized in livestock, dairy and fodder crops.

*Western India:* Poor soil and unreliable rainfall had made most of western India a basically millet-growing region oriented to subsistence agriculture. Two exceptions were south Gujarat where cotton was for long an important cash crop, and Konkan where mainly paddy was grown. The railways altered the economic geography of western India. By connecting Bombay with the potentially cotton

---

[11] On the role of seeds (and canals) on Punjab's agricultural growth, see Carl E. Pray, 'Accuracy of Official Agricultural Statistics and the Sources of Growth in the Punjab, 1907–47', *IESHR*, 21(3), 1984.

growing regions, mainly the dry interior areas having black soil suited for cotton, it stimulated cotton cultivation in the latter. At the same time, poor communications and the absence of railways left the rice-based Konkan out of the new commercial network. Cultivated area increased by about 67 per cent between 1843 and 1873 in Bombay–Deccan.[12] Cotton led the increase, but there was no decline in foodgrain area or availability. Thereafter, total cultivated area grew slowly. But the area cropped under cotton, tobacco, sugarcane and spices increased. The main cotton growing regions in western India were the southern parts of Bombay–Deccan, south Gujarat and Khandesh. Tobacco was grown in Central Gujarat, groundnut in Satara, and sugarcane along the new Nira canal system southeast of Pune. The only major government irrigation scheme in Bombay, the Nira river area later developed into a major concentration of sugar manufacturing. A number of towns supported markets for cotton, and eventually some of them grew into sites where cotton spinning mills were started and migrant handloom weavers settled in. Sholapur is the most important example of these changes.

*Eastern India:* Unlike Punjab or western India, Bengal did not see major changes in cropping pattern. It remained paddy-based. There were only marginal shifts, such as the decline of indigo and the rise of jute and sugarcane. Rice itself, however, had an old long-distance trade that now expanded and changed direction. The main railway lines that connected the interior agricultural districts with the ports or market towns were more or less completed between 1854 and 1885. The pre-railway transportation system consisted of overland or riverborne trade. Overland traffic was costly and slow especially because of the large number of rivers. Water transport was impossible during almost eight months of the year because of low water level or poor navigability of many of the major rivers. These eight months included important harvest seasons. The railways quickly drew trade away from the rivers, and apparently increased the volume of trade. The extent of commercial production and the direction of trade changed in the period from the 1850s to the 1880s. The period saw moderate population growth in eastern India as well as rapid increase in the size of new population clusters based on non-agricultural activity. These included Calcutta itself, the Raniganj mining-industrial area, Serampur industrial area, and north Bengal and Assam plantations.

---

[12] Sumit Guha, *The Agrarian Economy of the Bombay–Deccan 1818–1941*, Oxford University Press, Delhi, 1985, p. 58.

These were new and concentrated sources of demand for rice. Elsewhere in India, specialization in non-food crops had increased the demand for import of foodgrains from other regions, including Bengal. Rice was also exported to other British colonies. Despite these large and growing markets, it is not clear that the supply or production of rice also grew at the same pace. Trade, doubtless, did grow. In the eastern districts, from the 1850s, demand from the newly established jute mills near Calcutta, and demand from jute mills elsewhere in the world stimulated jute cultivation. Like indigo, jute was exported, and the trade was controlled at the top by European firms. But unlike indigo, jute cultivation was entirely voluntary, and had no role for coercion.

*Coastal Madras (North), or Coastal Andhra:* Canal irrigation expanded in the delta districts, Godavari and Krishna between 1847 and 1852. High tax burden, transport bottlenecks and other problems initially restrained the commercial potentials of paddy, the main crop. As these constraints eased, long-distance trade in paddy began to expand. Canals encouraged diversification into oilseeds, sugarcane, tobacco, turmeric, chillies and plantains. Cultivated area increased significantly in the second half of the nineteenth century. Agrarian expansion stimulated grain trade and credit markets. These activities were concentrated in towns that rapidly grew in population and economic importance. They included Vijayawada, Eluru, Rajahmundry, and Vizagapatam. Markets and transportation systems also enabled regions within coastal Andhra to specialize. An example of extreme specialization is Guntur district where the bulk of India's tobacco crop came to be grown.

*Madras–Deccan:* By contrast with the coast, southern Andhra or Madras–Deccan was a region of scanty rainfall and low-fertility soil. This region was periodically ravaged by famines. Though poor in resource endowments and high in risks of cultivation, the region did include large black soil tracts on which railway connection with Bombay had an effect very similar to that in the southern Bombay-Deccan. There were shifts in cropping pattern and direction of trade away from millets to cotton, oilseeds, and fodder crops. Between 1871 and 1921, prices, acreage, road mileage, and the number of carts for transportation expanded in Bellary district, and there were signs of greater price integration between regions.[13]

[13] Bruce L. Robert, 'Economic Change and Agrarian Organization in 'Dry' South India 1890–1940:A Reinterpretation', *MAS*, 17(1), 1983. We may mention in the passing that the effects of commercialization on peasant welfare in Madras–Deccan has been a

*The Upper Doab:* In present-day western UP and Haryana, like Punjab and Coastal Andhra, a dense network of canals was constructed in the nineteenth century. In UP the irrigation channels increased from 4751 miles in 1871 to 16,136 miles in 1921. Farmers shifted to higher-valued crops such as wheat and sugarcane and increased area and yield. Other crops to have benefited from canal irrigation were barley and maize. Indigo and sugarcane were cultivated over smaller areas, but they were significant for the regional economy. Export of foodgrains was not made from the Doab on a large scale before the 1870s. From that decade it quickly became an important trade. Agents of European grain-exporting companies were based in the major trading-cum-financial towns that also became connecting points of railways, road, and river routes. Examples include Mirzapur, Farrukhabad, Lucknow, Kanpur, Allahabad and Agra. The railways and new roads connected the smaller towns in the interior (that had large weekly or biweekly spot markets) with these large towns where markets were permanent and trade was based on long-term contracts. Indigo became an important cash crop in the Doab from the 1860s. Owners of indigo factories were usually *zamindars*, who contracted with other cultivators to produce indigo and sell to them at a pre-agreed price. Sugarcane was already a commercial crop and sugar a major product in local trade in the Doab–Rohilkhand region during the Company's rule. The growth of canals and transportation gave this crop a great stimulus from the 1860s. Sugar mills and small refineries (*khandsari*) rapidly grew in number, many were owned by the local *zamindars*.

*Central India:* Major railway lines connecting the Central Provinces and Berar with Bombay, Calcutta and northern India were completed between 1860 and 1880. The impact of the railways on trade and cropping pattern of a region where nothing but the most primitive roads existed was dramatic. From 1860, trade, prices, acreage, rentals and scale of land and credit transactions increased.[14] The expansion was concentrated in two regions—the wheat exporting Narmada valley with Jabalpur and Sagar at its centre, and cotton exporting Berar with Nagpur at its centre. Berar emerged as the destination of

debated topic. In one view, ecology and the need to make large investments in land for cultivating cash crops intensified inequality and led to the dominance of a few 'magnates' over the countryside. In another view, new opportunities enabled upward mobility of the small peasants. See contributions by David Washbrook, C.J. Baker, Bruce Robert, and D. Rajasekhar cited in the readings at the end of the chapter.

[14] N. Benjamin, 'The Trade of the Central Provinces of India (1861–1880)', *Artha Vijnana*, 15(4), 1978.

one of the largest streams of internal migration, farm labourers from Chhattisgarh.

*Tamil Nadu:* Tamil Nadu consists of several agro-ecological regions. In the coastal 'wet' districts (mainly Tanjore and Chingleput), paddy was of overwhelming importance.[15] This region resembled Bengal and coastal Andhra in cropping pattern. In the drier interior districts (Salem, Coimbatore, Trichinopoly), coarse millets were initially the most important crop. In the first half of the nineteenth century, large canal irrigation projects were constructed on some of the major rivers, and extensive road building was also undertaken. Canal water was mainly concentrated in Tanjore, which was situated on the Cauvery delta and was a rice-growing district. On this foundation, interregional trade expanded in traditional commodities such as rice and garden crops. The dry regions of Tamil Nadu included tracts with black soil suited for cotton. The demand for raw cotton produced in Tamil Nadu—mainly in Coimbatore, Ramnad, Madurai and Tirunelveli districts—increased from the 1830s and nearly exploded after the 1860s. Raw cotton trade introduced new marketing and financial systems. It was a major source of livelihood in small towns where cotton was processed and packed for export. In the interwar period, cotton improved its position as a cash crop because of the growth of a mill textile industry in Madras and Coimbatore. The second most important cash crop was groundnut, grown extensively in North and South Arcot. The export market for groundnut grew with the expansion of modern food processing industry in Europe. Commercial expansion and rising prices steadily reduced the real burden of taxation. When added to the increased profits from cotton exports, this factor encouraged private investment mainly in the form of irrigation wells. Wells became the main irrigation system in Coimbatore and Madurai districts, and played a key role in the post-independence green revolution in Tamil Nadu.

## Land, Labour and Credit Markets

### Land Market

Sale of land increased dramatically in all regions of India in the nineteenth century. Where data exists, the proportion of mortgaged land

---

[15] The terms 'wet' and 'dry' have often been used as a rough way of distinguishing ecological zones in Tamil Nadu. 'Wet lands' generally mean the lands which have assured irrigation water either by canals or by irrigation wells and therefore do not directly depend on rainfall in that area, whereas dry land agriculture is basically rain fed cultivation.

in cultivated area can be seen to have increased. Land prices also increased as far as one can measure. Until about 1850, there were two main forces driving this growth of a land market. These were, the newly defined property rights, and revenue defaults that resulted from unusually high revenue demand. From the 1860s, commercialization, rising land prices, and increased demand for credit, became active in bringing more land into the market.

In the Permanent Settlement areas, a market for land in the sense of *zamindari* titles developed in the early nineteenth century itself. After a long rise, prices for *zamindari* titles began to fall from the 1860s. This was possibly an outcome of decreasing share of the *zamindar* in agricultural income as rents failed to keep pace with prices.[16] From the last quarter of the nineteenth century another dynamics was added. Market for land in the sense of occupancy tenant rights began to develop after the 1885 Bengal Tenancy Act. This made it possible for *zamindars* to put up peasant holdings for sale on default of rents.

A section among British bureaucracy and a section of historians held the view that the increased sale of land passed ownership rights to non-cultivating classes. The British authorities especially in Punjab were very worried that persons of money-lending castes were acquiring control over land. The current consensus on this question is that the actual extent of such transfers remained rather limited. Further, in the Permanent Settlement areas, sale of *zamindari* titles made little difference to who controlled land at the local level. Those in real control of the products of land after the rents were paid were usually the *jotedars*, or superior tenants (see also section on Effects of Market Expansion).

Tenancy or Market for User Rights

Land was sometimes cultivated by someone who did not own it, but leased it. Such practices, or 'tenancy' generally, increased in the colonial period. This increase may not all have been real. In part, it may reflect a shift from customary to formalized tenancy relations.[17] Customary tenancy was not always recognized or recorded as tenancy

---

[16] The stability of the Bengal *zamindar's* economic power is a subject of some debate. A contribution on this theme, arguing the *zamindars* did not experience significant decline in economic power until the 1930s, is Akinobu Kawai, *Landlords and Imperial Rule: Change in Bengal Agrarian Society, c. 1885–1940*, 2 vols, Institute for the Study of the Languages and Cultures of Asia and Africa, Tokyo, 1986–7. This view has been debated.

[17] Marcia Frost suggested this possibility to me.

in the modern sense. To customary tenancy we shall come back in a moment.

Increasing incidence of tenancy could have arisen from four sources. First, commercialization increased the return on good land, and therefore, the demand for land. Some of this demand arose from peasants who owned insufficient land, and were willing to lease in more. Their expected profits exceeded rents. Second, many landlords did not live in the village or were otherwise not interested in cultivation. Bengal *zamindars* are an example. They could lease out part of their estate on which they had direct control. Third, with increased inequality in land-ownership, the rich farmers tend to have more land than they can cultivate and the poorer ones less than they can cultivate. A market in user rights can then develop between them. Fourth, as population growth exceeded the growth in available arable land, poorer quality lands came into cultivation. Those who owned such land might have wanted to lease in the more productive land for survival.

In *zamindari* areas, the second condition was the main reason for extensive and increasing tenancy. In other areas, the extent of tenancy was less than in eastern India. But it was increasing due to commercialization. Where Brahmin landowners continued, cultivation was often leased out.[18] One difference between these two areas was in tenancy legislation. Because tenancy was more visible in the *zamindari* areas, tenants received more government protection there. In *ryotwari* areas, by contrast, there was far less protection, and the laws were somewhat loaded in favour of the proprietor.

Increasingly from the 1860s, the revenue system changed its objective from consolidation of property rights to protection of cultivator's rights. This was done by means of tenancy acts instituted in all the major provinces. The main thrust of these acts was to (a) fix the rents, (b) secure the right of cultivation for the 'occupancy *ryot*', generally defined as a cultivator who could prove to have been cultivating a particular plot of land for at least 12 successive years, and (c) in some regions, define rights below that of the occupancy *ryot*. These rights, in turn, became more easily saleable after these laws.

Tenancy came to be associated with poverty and insecurity. While British rule recognized proprietary rights on land, there was massive and universal confusion over 'sub-proprietary' or layers of tenancy rights. Many such rights were customary in nature. Only a part of

---

[18] For an example, see Yanagisawa, *Century of Change*, Ch. 4.

these customary rights, the British understood and legalized after much hesitation. As a result, secure tenancy rights, or occupancy tenant rights were rare. Below these superior rights, insecurity of rights to cultivate a plot was extreme—higher in the new regime, and almost certainly increasing over time.

Credit Market

Credit transactions in the village increased though the trend was not a smooth one. It was subject to disruptions caused by harvest fluctuations, and long commercial cycles. Commercialization increased the demand for working capital credit and sometimes consumption loans for several reasons.

(i) Compared to production for subsistence, commercialization expanded scale of production because markets outside tended to be bigger than the local market. Thus, commercial production needed more investment.

(ii) At least in the case of some peasants, the decision to produce non-food crops meant that the peasant had to buy food from the market rather than meet subsistence needs from own farm. To buy food before harvests the peasant needed to borrow.[19]

(iii) Payment of rent and revenue in cash rather than in kind resulted in loans taken to meet these payments. Loans might also need to be taken for payment of taxes because sometimes tax-collection did not necessarily occur after the harvest.

(iv) Cash crops needed finance because they were traded over long distances. In other words, they needed more investment in marketing.

(v) Commercialization increased the demand for relatively high cost inputs. Sugarcane, cotton and tobacco require water and nutrients. Therefore, they need greater investment in land preparation (levelling, ploughing, and hence cattle and implements), irrigation (more and deeper wells, more buckets, etc.), and fertilizers. Cotton crop on black soil was not too water-intensive, but needed heavy ploughs and many bullocks. These crops not only needed more investment in money, but also in time. They stood on the field longer than most foodgrains and thus required longer waiting period between investment and sale of crop.

At the same time, supply of credit increased for four reasons. First, the railways, growth of market towns, and new profit opportunities,

---

[19] In most cases, though, the decision to produce non-food crops did not mean a total or even significant substitution of food for non-food crops, but only a small substitution.

increased the mobility, migration, settlement, and enterprise of persons of trader–moneylender castes. Second, the creation of property rights in land and investments in irrigation increased the collateral value of land. Third, legislation concerning credit contracts gave the creditors much greater power to recover loans. Earlier, debt recovery was often resolved by local politicians, village officers, and simple balance of power between the individual lender and groups of peasant debtors. In the British period, the courts and new laws made repayment a legal obligation. Fourth, in the Permanent Settlement areas especially, but to some extent everywhere, rent as a source of income declined in importance for political–administrative reasons. Those who could tried to augment their rental income with income from moneylending.

That the growth of product and credit markets occurs together in a mutually dependent way is by itself neither surprising nor alarming. And yet, in the larger part of Indian economic history scholarship, credit has become a symbol of exploitation. Credit could certainly make the rich richer. For, money acquired new uses and money was universally scarce. But in fact, in both the British period and in historical scholarship, it has been repeatedly suggested that credit did far more. It made the poor poorer. It led to a serious dislocation in agrarian society and possibly to even agricultural stagnation. We shall deal with this argument more fully in the section on Explaining Growth and Stagnation.

## Labourers

In 1952, Surendra Patel concluded (on the basis of census data) that the proportion of agricultural labourers in rural population had increased during the nineteenth century.[20] Consequently he concluded that the British rule had had an adverse impact on the Indian economy. Labourers increased by two processes. He argued that the precolonial Indian village was a relatively egalitarian community that produced its own subsistence, and exchanged food for other goods with village artisans. British rule, by means of 'forced commercialization', broke up this system and created a class of agricultural labourers (see also Chapter 1 and section on Explaining Growth and Stagnation in this chapter). At the same time British commercial policy led to 'de-industrialization' which reduced many artisans to the status of agricultural labourers.

[20] Surendra J. Patel, *Agricultural Labourers in Modern India and Pakistan*, Current Book House, Bombay, 1952.

This simple but influential story is now known to be a myth. Dharma Kumar's classic work argued that in South India, 'members of certain castes were already by and large agricultural labourers at the onset of British rule'. On the basis of this correlation between caste and labour status, she estimated the minimum strength of agricultural labourers at that time. '[T]he estimate shows that the group was sizeable so that it cannot be held that landless labour was virtually created by British rule'.[21] A great deal of subsequent research and revival of interest in older works unearthed evidence pointing towards the existence of forms of attached labour that continue to the present day from pre-colonial times.[22] Later work on occupational structure questioned the very census data on which Patel's thesis was based.

Having said that, it cannot be denied British rule did affect the labourers deeply. It is possible that the incidence of agricultural labour may indeed have increased, though its scale is disputable. This appears plausible from the persistent weakness of the 'small peasant' (see sub-section on 'standards of living'). As for real wages, there was probably no change at all (see 'standards of living of agricultural labourers'). But conditions of employment and the social context of employment changed for the better. Many types of customary barter systems by which labourers worked on their employers' fields tended to break down, because both parties could gain from going to a spot market for labour.[23] In pre-colonial India, or even during the early British rule, landless labourers came from the lower castes whose primary duty was to perform agricultural labour. Many were 'attached' to land, that is, they were something like serfs. In certain cases in South India, they were actually saleable as slaves. In the colonial period serfdom and attached labour generally declined. The customary bondage of agricultural labour castes to land decreased. From the early twentieth century the social status of the depressed castes improved.[24] The element of compulsion in their employment

---

[21] Dharma Kumar, *Land and Caste in South India*, second edition, Manohar, Delhi, 1992 (first published by Cambridge University Press, Cambridge, 1965), p. xxxvii

[22] See 'Introduction' in Gyan Prakash (ed.), *The World of the Rural Labourer in Colonial India*, Oxford University Press, Delhi, p. 15.

[23] For an example, see Neeladri Bhattacharya, 'Agricultural Labour and Production: Central and South-east Punjab', in K.N. Raj, N. Bhattacharya, S. Guha, S. Padhi (eds), *Essays on the Commercialization of Indian Agriculture*, Oxford University Press, Bombay, 1985.

[24] See Haruka Yanagisawa, *A Century of Change. Caste and Irrigated Lands in Tamil Nadu 1860s–1970s*, Manohar, Delhi, 1996.

weakened. The imposition of various forms of social dictates, such as enforced dress codes and codes of conduct with respect to upper castes, was less strict. The length of the working day came down quite substantially. Migration within and outside agriculture increased. The possibility of migrating to the cities and to other British colonies led to diversification of occupational choice.

The decline of attached labour was partly induced by the widespread exit of these castes from agricultural labour. They entered plantations, mines, urban services, public works and government utilities. The change was partly due to the entry into labour of small peasants and tenants who experienced impoverishment. The religious conversion of tribals and many among the depressed castes, especially in South India, were a symptom and a cause of their exit from forced or attached labour in the villages.

The net result was increasing casual labour in place of attached labour and the creation of spot markets for labour. The correlation between agrarian labour and formerly menial castes did not disappear, but it did not remain as strong. The employment relationship became more explicitly contractual.

## EFFECTS OF MARKET EXPANSION
### Standards of Living: The General Picture

In the last quarter of the nineteenth century, average standards of living definitely improved. The conclusion is confirmed by the best available national income and per capita income statistics for this period, especially by trends in three indices, area cropped, yield of specific crops, and population. As Table 3.1 showed, real national income grew at 1.23 per cent between 1882 and 1898, and per capita income at 0.78 per cent per annum. Moni Mukherjee's estimates show that real national income grew at 1.76 per cent and per capita income at the rate of 1.23 per cent per annum between 1865 and 1885.[25] In this period, a rise in income derived mainly from rise in agricultural incomes. While this dataset has many problems, its basic conclusion, that there was significant growth in total and per capita income in the late nineteenth century, has not so far been empirically challenged. But three important qualifications need to be added to this picture.

Conditions almost certainly turned adverse in the interwar period. Per capita real income did not grow at all between 1900 and the 1940s.

[25] Moni Mukherjee, *National Income of India*, Statistical Publishing Society, Calcutta, 1935, Table 2.6, p. 65.

Total agricultural income was growing very slowly almost throughout this long period. Levels of living did not improve, and the poorer
sections of the agricultural population faced harder conditions in the
1920s and the 1930s. Such long reversal can be explained by circumstances that made the 1920s a watershed—slowdown in public investment in land and infrastructure, exhaustion of good land, rise in
population growth, and worldwide depression. As good land became exhausted and investment slowed down, productivity reached
its limits at the prevailing technology.

Growth in standards of living, therefore, varied over time. It was
also variable between classes and regions. For example, few writers
would be prepared to argue that the 'small peasant' or the labourer
was prospering in the twentieth century. A broad definition of 'small
peasant' is one who farmed land mainly with family labour, did not
have much surplus over subsistence, and did not have capital needed
to either invest in land or sell at more competitive markets. Many
among the small peasants did gain in the nineteenth century. But
these benefits were small, not easy to hold on to during famines and
periods of low income, and were probably disappearing from the
interwar period onwards as population began to grow faster. The
situation with the labourers was not very different, as we shall see in
the next section. Further, the Permanent Settlement areas like Bengal
experienced only limited prosperity.

Markets, clearly, were a necessary condition for economic improvement, but not a sufficient one. What caused persistent stagnation? We
shall return to this question later in the chapter in the section 'Explaining Growth and Stagnation'.

## Standards of Living of the Labourers

While agricultural labourers experienced social emancipation, commercialization did not lead to substantial improvement in their real
wages. The annual average of the agricultural real wage index calculated by Mukherjee (1890 = 100) stood at 93 during 1871–3, 99 during
1878–82, and 96 during 1896–1900. In the long run, money wages
adapted well to the rising trend in prices. In the short run, the index
fluctuated a great deal. Price fluctuations were not adjusted quickly
by change in money wages and led to severe fluctuations in real
wage. Thus, the middle years of the great famines of the nineteenth
century saw a steep fall in real wages.

This is the overall picture. The regional picture shows greater variation. There is reason to believe that labourers may in fact have

experienced an improvement in the major cash crop growing regions. Ian Stone has suggested this for Upper Doab.[26] Cash crop production meant increased demand for labour with increases in cropped area and/or labour intensity. Signs of material prosperity for the rural population can in general be seen in Punjab too. Even small peasants in an impoverished region such as Bengal, when engaged in major cash crops, gained in income and wealth.[27]

The picture becomes confusing for the period 1900–20. In coastal Andhra, there is evidence suggesting that real wages in the 1920s were higher than that in the 1900s.[28] In districts (especially in Madras) where commercialization combined with large net emigration, there were signs of a rise in wages.[29] For Bengal, the K.L. Datta Committee on prices suggested a rise in real wage between 1891 and 1911.[30] For Bombay–Deccan, Sumit Guha found no trend, Neil Charlesworth found stable real wages but some improvement in working conditions, and Sunanda Krishnamurty found stable or falling wages after 1903.[31] For Madras–Deccan, Bruce Robert found roughly stable wages between 1890 and 1920.[32]

After 1920, however, most studies find the onset of a declining tendency. Money wages fell sharply during the Great Depression. In some cases real wages also fell. Atchi Reddy has shown this for the southern coastal Andhra, and Chaudhuri for Bengal.[33] Dharma Kumar's conclusion seems valid, that 'the agricultural labourers probably felt the effects of the pressure of population after 1921 more keenly than any other group'.[34] Cases of upward economic mobility of former agricultural labour castes are rare if not unknown.

[26] Stone, *Canal Irrigation*, Ch. 8.

[27] Omkar Goswami shows this for the jute economy of Eastern Bengal, *Industry, Trade, and Peasant Society: The Jute Economy of Eastern India 1900–47*, Oxford University Press, Delhi, 1991, pp. 81–2.

[28] K. Atchi Reddy, 'Wages Data from the Private Agricultural Accounts, Nellore District, 1893–1974', *IESHR*, 16(3), 1979.

[29] Dharma Kumar, 'Agrarian Relations: South India', in *CEHI 2*, pp. 238–9.

[30] B.B. Chaudhuri, 'Agrarian relations: Eastern India', in *CEHI 2*, p. 172.

[31] Guha, *Agrarian Economy*, Table 5.9; S. Krishnamurty, 'Real Wages of Agricultural Labourers in the Bombay–Deccan 1874–1922', *IESHR*, 24(1), 1987; Neil Charlesworth, 'Trends in the Agricultural Performance of an Indian Province: The Bombay Presidency, 1900–20',in K.N. Chaudhuri and Clive Dewey (eds), *Economy and Society: Essays in Indian Economic and Social History*, Oxford University Press, Delhi, 1979.

[32] 'Structural Change in Indian Agriculture: Land and Labour in Bellary District, 1890–1980', *IESHR*, 22(3), 1985.

[33] K. Atchi Reddy, 'Wages Data', and Chaudhuri, 'Agrarian Relations: Eastern India', p. 173.

[34] Kumar, 'Agrarian Relations: South India', p. 239.

Why did agricultural labourers fail to attain a general and substantial improvement in wages and earnings? This question is central to the problem of persistent poverty in South Asia. Two general answers are possible. First, labour was in surplus, and increasingly so due to population growth. Second, while social oppressions weakened, such oppressions did not disappear quickly. Caste and status differences persisted, and were strongly correlated with economic opportunities. The rich tended to come from middle or upper castes, the poor tended to come from castes that had performed manual labour for generations. Commercialization in that case tended to strengthen the former and weaken the latter. Landed groups commanded labour at artificially low cost. The labourers remained subject to obligations to supply labour cheaply. In Peter Robb's expression, economics 'reinforce[d] subservience'.[35] Such situations were probably not the rule. But that economic and social power could get correlated and significantly weaken the poorer groups in some regions cannot be disputed. Bihar is one such example.

## Inequality of Incomes

In the nineteenth century, real income in agriculture was increasing, and there was no change in real wages. It is clear that the level of non-wage incomes was increasing. What did non-wage income consist of? The bulk of it probably represented the earnings of the 'small peasant', that is, one who relied mainly on the labour of his family. Such earnings cannot be defined as 'profit' or 'wage'. The smaller the land owned, such earnings tended to be supplemented more often with pure wage-work. The 'small peasant' tended to have just enough land for subsistence, though many did manage to sell some surplus to long-distance trade in the nineteenth century. At another end, there was a different type of composite earnings. There were rich peasants who controlled enough land to sell substantial quantities and to have to hire in labourers. They also usually had better access to credit, or were creditors themselves. Profits, rents and interests were often united in the composite earnings of the rich peasant.

Can we infer trends in income distribution from description of changes in the nineteenth century? That the level of wages was constant and the level of non-wage income increased, suggest that personal income distribution became more unequal in the nineteenth

---

[35] 'Peasants' Choices? Indian Agriculture and the Limits of Commercialization in Nineteenth Century Bihar', *Economic History Review*, XLV(I), 1992.

century. It does not suggest whether or not shares of wage and non-wage incomes in national income changed. For, the shares depend on these levels as well as on the numbers in each class. We cannot be quite sure of the population size of each class. We also cannot say how the earnings of the two types of mixed earners—small peasant and rich peasant—were changing. From qualitative evidence, it seems fair to say that the small peasant gained in a limited way, and the rich peasant gained substantially until 1900.

After 1900, real income in agriculture grew slowly. Real wages showed either no change or a fall. These facts suggest that the non-wage incomes as a whole may not have changed very much after 1900. However, qualitative evidence suggests that the small peasant faced progressively harder times, and the rich peasant continued to gain, if at a reduced rate. This is a hypothesis yet to be tested.

## Land-ownership and Class Structure

Marxist historians and economists have proposed a variety of 'polarization' theses, which suggest that inequality in land-ownership increased during British rule. One version owes to Patel (cited in the sub-section on 'Labourers'). Another is the 'forced commercialization' thesis which suggests that the title to land tended to pass from the peasants to the capitalists in the course of commercialization. Increase in labour and tenancy was read as a sign of polarization. The polarization thesis cites a larger debate over the experience of the middle peasantry during development of capitalism in agriculture. For Russia, V.I. Lenin argued on the lines of polarization and disintegration of middle peasantry, on the grounds that the risk of commerce would be too much for the middle peasants to take. A.V. Chayanov, however, argued for a broad stability of the small peasants' hold on property based on two counteracting factors—the cheapness of family labour, and a high rate of reproduction and population growth in family farms. It is fair to say that the Indian evidence rejects both polarization and peasant stability as general models. Their validity in specific contexts cannot be ruled out, and is yet to be fully tested.

The polarization thesis has been tested with quantitative data. The general conclusion is that there is little basis to suggest that inequality in land-holdings increased during the colonial period.[36] At least three

---

[36] Dharma Kumar, 'Land ownership and Inequality in Madras Presidency', *IESHR*, 12(2), 1975; H. Fukazawa, 'Agrarian Relations: Western India', pp. 200–2. See, for a discussion on other regional evidence, 'Introduction', in Yanagisawa, *Century of Change.*

authors found a decline in inequality in Madras–Deccan.[37] One of them explained it by the possibility of landless persons acquiring cultivable wastes in the interwar period.[38] That does not mean that there was no change in the pattern of land-ownership. Nor does it mean that inequality in incomes, a much harder thing to measure, did not increase. The qualitative evidence on land-ownership tends to be sensitive to caste, region, and period.

Generally, the older groups of rich people underwent a change in composition, and possibly, downward mobility. In the pre-British period, land-ownership or control over land had a strong correlation with high social or ritual status. In turn, social status had a correlation with powerful administrative offices held in the villages. These correlations weakened everywhere in the colonial period, though they did not disappear totally. There was a decline of old nobility and hereditary elites, and the power of the *Brahmin* as land owner. The decline of the *Brahmin* as land owner is perhaps best illustrated in various parts of south India. In the wet regions of Tamil Nadu, farms declined in size. Members of both lower and upper castes emigrated to the plantations and towns. At the same time, certain non-Brahmin castes increased in landed power.[39]

Such a picture of dynamism and mobility of the middle peasants seems to be a general one. Almost everywhere farmers from peasant stock who grew cotton, sugarcane or wheat on plots of land sufficiently large to buy them enough food and leave a profit grew richer. They also became less dependent on the moneylenders, and even began to lend themselves. Unlike some members of the upper castes, they were willing to farm themselves instead of being content with rental income. Unlike peasants with very small holdings they had better capital resources. These resources were sufficient land, livestock, carts for transportation, better and more implements, and superior access to credit. In Punjab and Upper Doab the jat peasantry,

[37] Kumar, 'Land-ownership and Inequality'; D. Rajasekhar, 'Commercialization of Agriculture and Changes in Distribution of Land-ownership in Kurnool District of Andhra c.1900–50', in S. Bhattacharya, S. Guha, R. Mahadevan, S. Padhi, D. Rajasekhar, G.N. Rao (eds), *The South Indian Economy*, Oxford University Press, Delhi, 1991, pp. 99–103; Bruce Robert, 'Economic Change and Agrarian Organization'.

[38] Rajasekhar, 'Commercialization of Agriculture'.

[39] Yanagisawa, *Century of Change*; On Madras–Deccan, see D. Rajasekhar, *Land Transfers and Family Partitioning*, Oxford and IBH and Centre for Development Studies, Trivandrum, 1988. Tests with data on other regions may bear out Yanagisawa's hypothesis that, if the *Brahmin* landowners are excluded, inequality may have increased in the colonial period.

the Vellalas in Tamil Nadu, the *jotedars* or large tenants with superior rights in western and northern Bengal, the Kanbi Patidars of south Gujarat, the rich Reddy farmers in Madras–Deccan, the Maratha peasants and Saswad Malis in the Mahrashtra sugarcane belt, and counterparts of these groups from various other regions illustrate this process of consolidation of the middle peasantry as dominant cultivators. The process was not a smooth one. Famines and the Great Depression caused reversals—but these were temporary reversals that did not upset the trend. These rich peasants created by commercialization sometimes originated in the old landed elite. Such has been argued for some of the *jotedars* of Bengal. More commonly they were of peasant castes theoretically ranked below the elites. But they usually claimed high social status. Some like the Malis in the western sugarcane areas were ranked even below peasant castes.

After independence, this class of relatively wealthy peasant communities created by colonial rule made successful attempts to control and shape local and national politics. The Green Revolution gave further stimulus to accumulation and political ambitions. In studies on political economy of independent India, they have been variously called 'commercial peasantry' (by Donald Attwood), 'the class of rich farmers' (Pranab Bardhan), and 'bullock capitalists' (Lloyd and Susan Rudolph).[40]

Such people, however, were not very numerous. In general land and capital were both scarce resources, and becoming scarcer with population growth. Further, while British rule recognized proprietary rights on land, sub-proprietary or layers of tenancy rights below occupancy were legally ill-defined, neglected, and insecure. Secure tenancy rights were rather rare. Those in possession of land, capital, as well as ownership or occupancy rights were even rarer.

What happened to the mass of the peasantry who did not own enough capital? The answer here is complex, regionally as well as temporally variable. Small peasants obviously suffered during famines and slumps. Famines hit them hard both by impoverishing them economically and by depleting the population of working males.[41] Despite the high risks they faced, there is no evidence that the small peasants were getting poorer in the nineteenth century. Many with small land-holdings did share in the profits from cash crops. Baker finds evidence that in dry Madras, many peasants formerly engaged

---

[40] See David W. Attwood, *Raising Cane. The Political Economy of Sugar in Western India*, Oxford University Press, Delhi, 1993, Ch. 1, for a discussion.

[41] See, for example, Rajasekhar, 'Famines and Peasant Mobility'.

in subsistence agriculture on small plots of land realistically hoped to get rich by groundnut cultivation.[42] Charlesworth wrote about frantic attempts by the small peasants to grab even a small piece of the most fertile lands available for sale.[43] This trickle-down of commercial profits leading to acquisition of small plots, in turn, leading to fragmentation of holdings, was probably quite a general phenomenon. Yanagisawa has made the point, that in the wet districts of Tamil Nadu the nature of investments in land and local infrastructure enabled more intensive cultivation in small plots.[44] Guha points out off-farm earning opportunities that the small peasants of western India could use. Small peasants also tried to hold on to their land stubbornly and did not lose them easily.

The general picture seems to change in the twentieth century. Upward mobility from a small-holding base becomes rarer and more difficult. Small peasants were constrained from improving their income by the small size of holdings each family could control, continuous subdivision due to population growth, insecurity of tenancy, high risks of cultivation, limited capital resources, and rising prices in the early twentieth century. Those among them who were net buyers of food from the market and had limited opportunities of making money from rural industry and trade, lived in the threat of losing their land when the harvest failed. The distinction between the proprietor, the tenant, and the labourer, became blurred at the lower end. The first often competed with the second for actual control over the land. And the second could make ends meet only by becoming a part-time labourer.[45]

## Famines and Food Security

Commercialization had a short-term and a long-term effect on food available for consumption within India. Export of foodgrains from India increased in the colonial period. Did these exports reduce domestic food availability during periods of bad harvests, and thus

[42] Baker, An Indian Rural Economy, Ch. 3.

[43] Neil Charlesworth, Peasants and Imperial Rule: Agriculture and Agrarian Society in the Bombay Presidency, 1850–1935, Cambridge, 1985, p. 299.

[44] Haruka Yanagisawa, 'Elements of Upward Mobility for Agricultural Labourers in Tamil Districts, 1865–1925', in Peter Robb, Kaoru Sugihara, Haruka Yanagisawa (eds), Local Agrarian Societies in Colonial India, Curzon Press, Richmond, 1996.

[45] David Washbrook describes these distress–induced movements between labour and small peasanthood in 'The Commercialization of Agriculture in Colonial India: Production, Subsistence and Reproduction in the "Dry South"', c.1870–1930', MAS, 28(1), 1994.

increase the intensity of famines? That is, did foreign trade increase starvation, hardship and mass mortality? There is a view that it did.[46] Sections of the British bureaucracy, on the other hand, held that foreign trade stabilized consumption. For exports increased only when domestic prices were low, that is, when good harvests had created a surplus over consumption needs. And exports fell when prices were high.

In the long run, commercialization could encourage or force the production of cash crops, thus reduce the availability of food stock at home, and make famines more frequent and more severe. The railways induced change in cropping pattern, which could have a similar effect. Famines could also increase in their severity if it is argued that average consumption was already so low at the beginning of commercialization, that even slight fall in this level led to a demographic catastrophe. If inequality increased due to commercialization, given an unchanging and low consumption level, the poor could be pushed in these ways too close to starvation. Is the view that markets and the railways intensified famines well-founded?

From a demographic point of view, the nineteenth century famines, especially the great famines of 1876–7 and 1896, were indeed devastating events. Millions of people perished during both these calamities. But there are at least two problems with the view that such mortality derived from commercialization. First, to suggest that there was a man-made or 'colonial' element in the impact of the nineteenth century famines requires it to show that these famines were more severe in effect than those before. Now, there is a complete absence of benchmarks with which the nineteenth century famines can be compared. Famines arose from agriculture's dependence on the monsoon. This dependence was no smaller in pre-British times than during British rule. There is no way of knowing how frequent and how severe famines in pre-British times were relative to those in the British times, or what role food stocks played in mitigating the effects of the pre-British famines. A priori, it is hard to believe that the great nineteenth century famines were exceptions in terms of severity. In any case, such an inference cannot be tested. On the other hand, it is clear

---

[46] This view was articulated by some Indian bureaucrats and nationalist writers, such as K.L. Datta and R.C. Dutt, shortly after the last great famine, 1896–8. It was popularized by such later writers as B.M. Bhatia, *Famines in India*, Bombay, 1951, pp. 14–21. Major regional studies also hinted at similar effects, for example, Elizabeth Whitcombe, *Agrarian Conditions in Northern India*, Vol. 1, University of California Press, Berkeley, 1972, p. 75.

that famines due to harvest failures became rare after 1900, which suggests a positive correlation between food security and economic changes in the colonial period, unless proven otherwise. The most critical positive change in this regard was market integration via the railways.

A second problem with the view that colonialism intensified famines is that the substitution of food for non-food crops was rather limited in colonial India. At independence, more than 80 per cent of the acreage cropped was engaged in food production. The percentage was surely higher about 1800, but it is hard to suggest that the extent of the shift was large enough to increase the occurrence of famines. .

What does historical scholarship say about the likely effects of commercialization on food security? As for the short-term effects of commercialization, or the effect of food exports on famines, Martin Ravallion has shown that foreign trade had a mitigating rather than an intensifying effect on food availability at home.[47]

As for the long-term effect of commercialization, we have already seen that food availability probably increased in the nineteenth century (Tables 3.1 and 3.5). Real wages did not fall in the nineteenth century. So there was no significant change in the purchasing power of the poor. It has been argued that in western India, commercialization did not lead to cash crops substituting food crops. Both expanded together. For Bombay Presidency as a whole, McAlpin has argued that markets and infrastructure increased food security and reduced the incidence and impact of famines. Ian Derbyshire has made the same point about eastern and western UP.[48] For several regions, it has been shown that irrigation reduced the chances of severe crop failure, and thus reduced the impact of famines. These are, coastal Andhra, the Upper Doab, and the sugarcane zone along the Nira canals.[49] Irrigation, in turn, encouraged non-food crops. These effects followed

---

[47] 'Trade and Stabilization: Another Look at British India's Controversial Foodgrain Exports', *Explorations in Economic History*, 24 (4), 1987.

[48] Neil Charlesworth, *Peasants and Imperial Rule*; M.B. McAlpin, *Subject to Famine: Food Crises and Economic Change in Western India, 1860–1920*, Princeton University Press, Princeton, 1983, Ch. 7; I. Derbyshire, 'Economic Change and the Railways in North India, 1860–1914', *MAS*, 21(3), 1987.

[49] A. Satyanarayana, 'Expansion of Commodity Production and Agrarian Market', in David Ludden (ed.), *Agricultural Production and Indian History*, Oxford University Press, Delhi, 1994, pp. 188–9; Ian Stone, 'Canal Irrigation and Agrarian Change', in David Ludden (ed.), *Agricultural Production and Indian History*, Oxford University Press, Delhi, 1994, p. 134; Attwood, *Raising Cane*, p. 41.

not only from local increases in production, but also from easier movement of crops across areas that the railways had made possible. A sign of such market integration was that prices tended to be equalized between regions.[50]

## Market Organization

Fukazawa has suggested, in connection with cotton in western India, what is possibly a generalizable point about market organizations. Compared to local markets dealing in subsistence crops, in long-distance trade in cash crops, spot markets were often bigger in size, more competitive, had standardized weights and measures, and enabled the sale of larger lots. Not all, but some peasants did have the ability to reach these markets and sell their crops here. They got better prices and the benefits of a more efficient market.[51] In the case of production for subsistence such an option did not exist. Markets were far more fragmented and localized.

Commercialization of the product market stimulated land, labour and credit markets, encouraged urbanization, and stimulated rural industry. It led to the growth of towns that had large spot markets and settlements of merchants-cum-financiers. From the interwar period, these towns saw growth of small-scale industries such as rice and oil mills, cotton gins, jute presses, and sugar mills (see Chapter 4).

### EXPLAINING GROWTH AND STAGNATION

Why was the growth rate of agricultural production and productivity so low in colonial India? Was stagnation a result of British rule? The most influential view in India holds that stagnation did result from British rule. This view has several roots. In the nationalist discourse represented by Romesh Dutt, the factor most responsible for stagnation was high revenue demand. But this explanation cannot be valid beyond the 1870s after which the real revenue burden steadily fell. In a Marxist historiography tradition, commercialization was forced by revenue demand. Thereafter, by leading to widespread indebtedness, it enriched mainly the non-cultivating rural classes such as the moneylenders. This thesis needs to be dealt with in some detail, both because of its wide popularity, and also because it is factually based.

---

[50] See, for example, Satyanarayana, 'Expansion of Commodity Production', p. 208.
[51] H. Fukazawa, 'Agrarian Relations: Western India', in *CEHI 2*, p. 200.

## Forced Commercialization

Between 1875 and 1900, a powerful official opinion argued that the peasantry had become so deeply and persistently indebted that it was losing ownership and control over land to moneylenders who were alien to the local society. The peasants became tenants and labourers in the process. An event that shaped such views was anti-money-lender riots in Poona and Ahmednagar districts in the summer of 1875. Almost no lives were lost but in a few dozen houses belonging to Gujarati and Marwari (but interestingly no Maratha Brahmin) moneylenders, property and account books were burnt. With the memory of the mutiny still fresh in their minds, officials panicked and far more was read into these disturbances than they deserved.

In one modern view, the 'Deccan riots' resulted from increased economic and political power of the moneylenders and the threat of peasants losing their land.[52] Punjab was another region where a section of the bureaucracy believed that widespread dispossession of land had been going on. Open or dormant peasant hostility to the moneylender was quite widespread in northern and western India in the last quarter of the nineteenth century. Land transfer by itself can increase inequality and cause peasant unrest. That it can also lead to lack of growth is an idea added by the post-independence left–nationalist historiography (Chapter 1). This school sees in money-lender power a negative force.

The story outlined in Surendra Patel's work on labour is an early statement of the left–nationalist view. The need to pay revenue or rent in cash had forced peasants all over India to cultivate cash crops in place of food crops in the nineteenth century. But cash crop production was not profitable enough, so the peasants had to borrow. They borrowed from professional moneylenders, mortgaging their land. A debt trap started, and peasants tended to be dispossessed of their land. The moneylenders were reluctant to invest in land improvement, so that agricultural backwardness persisted.[53]

In a celebrated paper published in 1973, Amit Bhaduri gave this vision of debt-led misery a theoretical grounding.[54] In particular, Bhaduri explains why the moneylender may be reluctant to make

[52] Ravinder Kumar, *Western India in the Nineteenth Century*, Routledge and Kegan Paul, London, 1968.

[53] Patel, *Agricultural Labourers*, pp. 48–63.

[54] 'A Study in Agricultural Backwardness under semi-Feudalism', *Economic Journal*, March 1973.

productive investment. The moneylender can be seen as the owner of the land, which is tilled by a landless peasant. Between them they share the crop by an agreed ratio. The former earns an income by giving consumption loans to the peasant. If the moneylender makes productive investment, the total output of land will increase and the peasant will get more income. In that case, he may not need to borrow any more, and the moneylender will lose interest income. Bhaduri suggests that fearing this loss, the moneylender will not make productive investment. Bhaduri later applied this theory to explain agricultural backwardness in colonial Bengal and post-colonial eastern India. The argument is that the Permanent Settlement in Bengal introduced layers of 'merchants and moneylenders' between the *zamindars* on the one hand and the peasants with generally inferior rights on the other.[55]

Bhaduri's theory has serious analytical flaws.[56] The most serious flaw is that the theory does not explain why the landowner will not make productive investment even if the profits from doing so exceed the interest lost. These theoretical problems need not concern us here. Does the historical argument that debts caused stagnation stand up to evidence? That the scale of indebtedness grew over time is, of course, no proof of the thesis that credit caused stagnation and misery. All commercial production needs working capital credit. There is no question that a great deal of debts in colonial rural India reflected this normal need for capital. Further, increased credit transactions, if driven by the creditworthiness of the borrower, is a sign of prosperity and not poverty of the peasants. This is a point that Malcolm Darling had made about growing indebtedness in Punjab.[57] So, the mere scale of indebtedness says nothing about whether credit generates growth or stagnation.

That credit caused backwardness can be tested by answering the following five questions. To believe it did cause backwardness would require a 'yes' in answer to each of these five questions.

Was commercialization 'forced' by revenue or rent demand?

[55] 'The Evolution of Land Relations in Eastern India under British Rule', *IESHR*, 15(1), 1976.

[56] The most critical of these were pointed out by Ashok Rudra. See the discussion in Sumit Guha, 'Weak States and Strong Markets in South Asian Development, c. 1700–1970', *IESHR*, 36(3), 1999. See also, Tirthankar Roy, 'Modelling History', a review of Bhaduri's essays on agrarian backwardness, *EPW*, 34(48), 1999.

[57] See Sugata Bose, 'Introduction', in Bose (ed.), *Credit, Markets, and the Agrarian Economy of Colonial India*, Oxford University Press, Delhi, 1994.

- Were loans taken mainly for payment of revenue or rent?
- Was there a 'moneylender' class in rural India?
- Was there large-scale dispossession?
- Did moneylender ownership of land cause agricultural stagnation?

Let us consider these five questions one by one.

Was commercialization forced or voluntary? There is some basis to suggest that cash crop production was induced by British policy. This is especially plausible for the period 1800–60. In this period, the use of power in influencing crop choices was often explicit, and the revenue burden was excessive in the *ryotwari* areas. However, along with the push from revenues, the pull of higher profits was always intermixed, and it is impossible to say which was the stronger motive before 1860. A further problem in testing whether or not commercialization was forced by revenue demand is that, both revenue collection in cash and local markets in food and non-food crops dated before the colonial period. Yet neither had led to commercialization in the scale that it did in the mid-nineteenth century. There is no inevitable correlation between the two. There must be other factors responsible for commercialization. Profitability is the most obvious.

B.B. Chaudhuri has questioned the idea that commerce was forced even during the period 1800–60. The context is eastern India, the region usually cited as the main example of forced commerce.[58] Citing indigo, opium, sugarcane and jute, Chaudhuri argues that (a) the notion of 'force' is naïve and unrealistic, (b) debt was neither a universal burden nor of similar scale everywhere, and (c) the practice of treating debts uniformly as evil confuses ordinary working capital loans with occasional consumption loans. A great deal of the debts was simple working capital essential for production to take place at all. These loans were given for reasons unrelated to exploitation, and could not have the effects the theory read in them.

After 1860, that is in the second and bigger phase of commercialization, the revenue burden as an influence on crop choices became increasingly weak, and the profit motive stronger. How do we know that the profit motive was an important influence on crop choices? For the early twentieth century, such an inference has been supported by statistical work showing a positive correlation between acreage

[58] B.B. Chaudhuri, 'The Process of Agricultural Commercialisation in Eastern India During British Rule: A Reconsideration of the Notions of "Forced Commercialisation" and "Dependent Peasantry"', in Peter Robb (ed.), *Meanings of Agriculture*, Oxford University Press, Delhi, 1996.

cropped and relative prices of crops. Farmers responded to prices in the way profit-maximizing producers are expected to.[59] What does this prove? First, this rejects the hypothesis that cash crops were produced only to pay revenue or interest. Cash crops were produced also or primarily because they were the more profitable crops. Second, by responding to price (profit) signals in this way, production of cash crops is likely to have led to an increase in value-added. It is possible that the capitalists captured most or all of the increase in value-added. The rich may have become richer. But that does not mean the poor got poorer. For, total income had increased.

It is possible to argue that those who gained from the process, such as rich farmers, forced small farmers and tenants to produce cash crops even if the latter did not profit by that shift. David Washbrook made a similar point about Madras–Deccan.[60] There is no way of testing if anyone actually lost by looking at the acreage–price correlation. The argument that the small peasants did suffer direct coercion and loss seems to exaggerate the power of the rich farmers. Such a proposition is denied by a host of counter examples. The acreage–price correlation disputes any inference that agriculture as a whole was worse off by the decision to produce the more profitable crop.

Were loans taken mainly for payment of revenue or rent? Loans taken to meet revenue demand did occur, especially in the mid nineteenth century in *ryotwari* areas. In periods of falling prices, again, such a tendency could be seen. The Deccan riots of 1875 occurred at such a time shortly after the cotton boom of the 1860s had ended. But such conditions were not general or persistent. From about the 1870s the real revenue burden was decreasing.

Was there a distinct moneylender class in rural India and did it control production? It is true that roughly until the third quarter of the nineteenth century, non-cultivating creditors were visible in many regions of India. They included Marwaris, 'Banias', Chettiars and other assorted trading–financier castes. They did increasingly control trade and own land. But the distinctness of a moneylender

[59] Dharm Narain, *The Impact of Price Movements on Selected Crops in India 1900–39*, London, 1965; Goswami, *Industry, Trade, and Peasant Society*, Ch. 3; Omkar Goswami and Aseem Shrivastava, 'Commercialization of Indian Agriculture: What Do Supply Response Functions Say?', *IESHR*, 28(3), 1991; Satyanarayana, 'Expansion of Commodity Production', p. 197.

[60] 'Economic Development and Social Stratification in Rural Madras: The Dry Region 1878–1929', in Clive Dewey and A.G. Hopkins (eds), *The Imperial Impact*, London, 1978. See also, Bruce Robert, 'Economic Change and Agrarian Organization in "Dry" South India, 1880–1940', *MAS*, 1983.

class, and the extent of their power over land, both declined over time in nearly all regions.

In the long run, rural credit came mainly from landowners or superior right-holders. Commercialization created rich peasants and consolidated dominant cultivators. It is they, and not persons of moneylender castes, who commanded the credit market. In some cases, moneylenders themselves turned landowners and became indistinguishable in behaviour or identity. The general situation bears out Eric Stokes's conclusion on the Narmada Valley, 'no real distinction could be observed between agricultural and non-agricultural classes'.[61] Even where a moneylender class can be distinguished, their power to influence the terms of transaction were often limited, a point made in the context of Punjab by Bhattacharya and Bombay by Guha.[62] There is evidence that the poorer cultivator often preferred to deal with the professional moneylender rather than with the rich peasant. For the moneylender's terms tended to be more custombound than that of the rich peasants, and the rich peasant had a variety of means to enforce repayment.[63]

Was there large-scale dispossession by moneylenders? The answer is a clear 'no'. Despite an initial surge in moneylender ownership of land, the actual extent of such ownership remained rather small, usually less than 10 per cent of cultivated land.[64] The professional moneylenders were outsiders, and did not necessarily want to own land. They sometimes preferred to give unsecured loans rather than loans on land mortgage. They were not always prepared to take on the risks of cultivation. For when they did, their investment became subject to agricultural fluctuations. To these factors was added legislation making transfer of ownership difficult. The two key legislations were the

[61] 'Peasants, Moneylenders and Colonial Rule: An Excursion into Central India', in Sugata Bose (ed.), *Credit, Markets, and the Agrarian Economy of Colonial India*, Oxford University Press, Delhi, 1994.

[62] Neeladri Bhattacharya, 'Lenders and Debtors: Punjab Countryside, 1880–1940', in Sugata Bose (ed.), *Credit, Markets, and the Agrarian Economy of Colonial India*, Oxford University Press, Delhi, 1994; Guha, 'Weak States and Strong Markets'.

[63] Whitcombe, 'Agrarian Conditions in Northern India', Vol. I, p. 168. Eric Stokes suggested further that in UP, agrarian backwardness tended to be negatively correlated with the existence of moneylenders as a distinct class, 'Dynamism and Enervation in North Indian Agriculture: The Historical Dimension', in David Ludden (ed.), *Agricultural Production and Indian History*, Oxford University Press, Delhi, 1994, p. 50.

[64] Guha, *The Agrarian Economy*, pp. 146–7 on Deccan; Nariaki Nakazato, 'Regional Patterns of Land Transfer in Late Colonial Bengal', in Peter Robb, Kaoru Sugihara, Haruka Yanagisawa (eds), *Local Agrarian Societies in Colonial India*, Curzon Press, Richmond, 1996 on Bengal, are two examples.

Deccan Agriculturists' Relief Act of 1879 and the Punjab Land Aliena-
tion Act of 1901. Generally, the professional moneylender tended to
retreat from the rural credit business after 1900 as a result of these new
laws.

Did moneylender ownership of land cause agricultural stagnation? If 'moneylenders' cannot be defined as a distinct class, and if
professional moneylenders did not own land to a large extent, obviously this explanation of agricultural stagnation or persistent poverty
does not work. Amit Bhaduri has argued that the rich peasants who
own land may prefer to stick to 'usury' rather than productive investment, for whatever reason. Such a process cannot be generalized for
any part of India. For, the rich peasants were a product of the cash
crops, and cash crops saw higher, not lower, growth in productivity.
Credit, commerce, inequality, and growth were positively correlated
in rural India. This is the inescapable conclusion from regional histories of commercialization. But it is testable with more statistical data.

What, then, caused the Deccan Riots and similar peasant resent-
ment about the moneylender? Charlesworth suggested that the significance of the Deccan Riots was exaggerated. I.J. Catanach too sees
it as an event not as serious as was once thought.[65] More generally,
Eric Stokes suggested that such outbursts were 'a symptom' of something other than real dispossession.[66] There was an agrarian distress.
But it was a temporary one and caused by a variety of factors, including high revenue demand, falling prices, and a sense of political
deprivation.

We have seen that the growth rates of agricultural output varied
greatly over space. We have also seen that agricultural growth did
occur in nineteenth century India, but it probably slowed down in
the twentieth century. The argument that macroeconomic changes
unleashed by colonial rule were responsible for stagnation does not
go very well with these differences over time and between regions.
Explanations of stagnation must be able to distinguish between regions. These must also explain why growth occurred at all. One possible approach would be to look at differential resource endowments.

[65] Neil Charlesworth, 'Myth of the Deccan Riots of 1875', MAS, 6(4), 1972; I.J. Catanach, Rural Credit in Western India 1875–1930, University of California Press, Berkeley,
1970, Ch. 1.

[66] Stokes, The Peasant and the Rāj: Studies in Agrarian Society and Peasant Rebellion in
Colonial India, Cambridge, 1978, cited by Sugata Bose (ed.), Credit, Markets and the
Agrarian Economy of Colonial India, Oxford University Press, Delhi, 1994, p. 11. See also
the re-interpretation of Deccan riots by Neil Charlesworth, Peasants and Imperial Rule,
Ch. 4.

## Resource-endowments

Water and land are both scarce resources in India. Agricultural growth in the nineteenth century derived, apart from steady expansion in markets, from the increased supply of these resources. Labour is a complex resource. Population growth and increased labour supply is a positive factor if there is unutilized arable land, and/or it is possible to use land-improvement techniques that need relatively more labour.[67] In the absence of either of these conditions, population growth can have a negative effect. For example, fall in land–man ratio can lead to inferior land being used. Fragmentation of holdings and smaller per capita holdings reduce the individual peasant's access to capital. Thus, population growth can slow the adoption of land-improvement techniques that require relatively more capital rather than labour. Scarcity of land tends to raise rents relative to profits and can squeeze the peasant who does not have secure ownership right on land.[68] Population growth was moderate between 1882 and 1921. But it was steadily high and accelerated after 1921.

Expansion in output was driven mainly by expansion in cropped acreage between 1885 and 1921. Increase in the supply of labour was a positive factor because unutilized resources existed and cash crop production increased labour requirements. But by 1920, land had become scarce and good land scarcer still. Investment in canals and wells, which had made wastes cultivable, slowed down. Technological change in seeds or in agricultural practices was limited in effect to a few regions and crops. After 1920 population growth induced steady fall in land-man ratio. The resources—water, land and people—were unequally distributed across space, owing to both natural and man-made factors. Do these inequalities explain regional disparities in agricultural growth?

A first look at India's rainfall map and a broad division of agricultural-ecological zones (Table 3.9) suggests two non-controversial hypotheses.

[67] Marcia Frost has shown, in the spirit of Ester Boserup, the creative ways peasants in Kheda district of British Gujarat adapted to increase in population densities, revenue demand and changes in relative prices of crops, in the early nineteenth century, 'Population Growth and Agrarian Change in British Gujarat, Kaira District, 1802–58', PhD dissertation, University of Pennsylvania, 1995.

[68] For a discussion of these issues and the related literature, see Vasant Kaiwar, 'Property Structures, Demography and the Crisis of the Agrarian Economy of Colonial Bombay Presidency', in David Ludden (ed.), *Agricultural Production and Indian History*, Oxford University Press, Delhi, 1994.

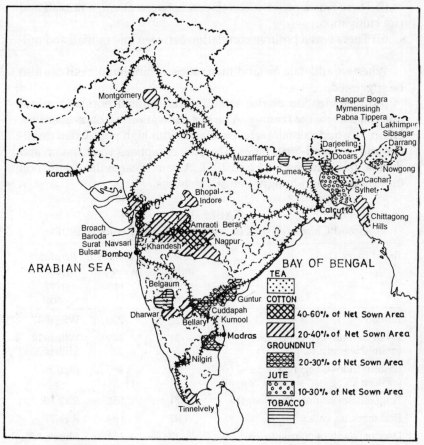

MAP 3.3: COTTON, GROUNDNUT, JUTE, TOBACCO, AND TEA

(i) There was a positive correlation between average rainfall and rice cultivation.

(ii) There was a positive correlation between low rainfall and millets.

When we add data on land-man ratios, a third hypothesis can also be suggested.

(iii) Combination of rice with assured rainfall normally meant mitigated impact of famines. Also rice cultivation is labour-intensive. Hence rice and rainfall were associated with high population densities and low land–man ratios. The only exceptions were Assam and Burma. But between 1901 and 1931, Assam became the destination for hordes of land-hungry Bengali peasants.

TABLE 3.9
Broad Characteristics of Agriculture and Ecology, 1901

| Broad zones | Mean annual rainfall (inches) | Population per square mile | Percentage share of cropped area |
|---|---|---|---|
| Punjab | 20 | 200 | Wheat 47 |
| Western Indo–Gangetic plains (mainly western UP) | 31 | 409 | Wheat 24 Millets 35 |
| Eastern Indo–Gangetic plains (eastern UP, Bihar, western Bengal) | 48 | 490 | Rice 59 |
| Bengal delta (mainly Bangladesh) | 71 | 552 | Rice 80 |
| Brahmaputra valley | 92 | 84 | Rice 73 |
| Deccan (south of Narmada, east of the Ghats, including Mysore plateau and part of Hyderabad) | 30 | 151 | Millets 57 Pulses 17 |
| Gujarat | 27 | 182 | Millets 52 |
| West Coast (Konkan and Malabar coasts) | 104 | 334 | Rice 75 |
| South India (mainly interior Tamil Nadu) | 33 | 259 | Millets 50 |
| East Coast South (Coastal Tamil Nadu and Nellore) | 48 | 359 | Rice 50 |
| East Coast North (Krishna–Godavari delta) | 52 | 229 | Rice 65 |

Source: Based on a table printed in the *Census of India 1901*, Vol. 1, Part I (report), Calcutta, 1901, p. 190.

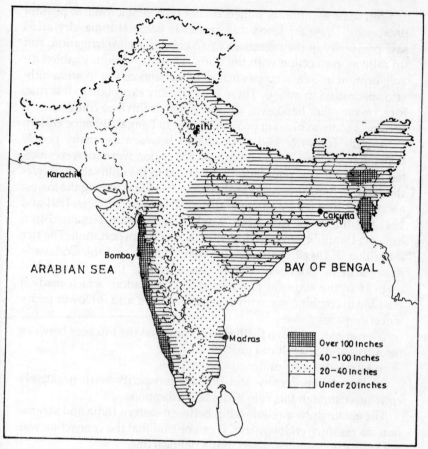

MAP 3.4: RAINFALL (ANNUAL)

With some exceptions, millets do not represent a route to peasant prosperity. These are low-value grains. In colonial India, dry areas saw prosperity in the presence of two conditions: (a) irrigation, and (b) railway connection with the ports. These conditions enabled diversification into cash crops such as wheat and cotton in areas hitherto specialized in millets. There is hardly any exception to this rule. Rice, on the other hand, was a high-valued grain. Rice could in itself become a route to peasant prosperity. But in Bengal, Bihar or eastern UP income from rice had to be shared between too many people dependent on land. Further, parts of this region were so overexploited about 1901 that population growth led to the cultivation of inferior land. In Bengal, acreage cropped per head was among the lowest about 1891, and fell by an unparalleled 80 per cent between 1891 and 1941. Of the major rice areas, Konkan and Assam remained in a low-level equilibrium trap, for want of good transportation. The rice areas that did well commercially were Tanjore and the Godavari–Krishna delta. Both shared two characteristics that distinguished them from the stagnant rice regions: (a) irrigation, which made it possible to combine rice with dry-season crops, and (b) lower population densities.

We can now add two further hypotheses on the linkages between resources and agricultural growth.

(iv) Irrigation was uniformly productive.

(v) Population density and peasant prosperity were negatively correlated, though this rule had a few exceptions.

The above drew a relationship between eastern India and stagnation via resource endowments. It can be said that the connection was not primarily resource-based, but a political one.

## Class-structure

For private investment in agriculture, it is necessary that the classes that benefit from such investment command money and political power. For, money and power are needed to mobilize resources that are scarce and carry risks. This condition did not materialize everywhere to the same extent.

How did class structure matter in agricultural growth? The question has been driven by the 'stylized fact' that stagnation seems to be correlated with *zamindari* settlement, whereas dynamism seems to be correlated with *ryotwari*. Many historians have made the point that in stagnant regions those who benefited from the allocation of property rights were not interested in innovation, investment and risk-taking. Eric Stokes' essay on the contrast between eastern and western UP is perhaps the most well-known example.[69] Parts of the forced commercialization literature also made a similar point. The broad regional contrast in the structure of rural power is described here.[70]

The coastal areas where colonial rule first established itself—eastern UP, Bihar and Bengal—practised agriculture based on abundant rainfall. These regions had highly fertile land capable of sustaining dense populations, well-developed foreign trade, and a relatively hierarchical society. Land in these areas could sustain high rents, and thus a prosperous rent-earning class. There were great economic and social inequalities between the landed or rent-earning classes on the one hand and those who did not have enough or any land on the other. The former, furthermore, were rarely of peasant castes. By contrast, the interior areas annexed later—such as Punjab, Sind, Deccan or Upper Doab—were drier, more sparsely populated, and cultivated relatively more drought-resistant coarser grains and pulses. Peasantry here was less hierarchical, kinship units were powerful, and these units tended to control land collectively. Farming here co-existed with extensive pastoralism.

In the former areas, the definition of property rights generally strengthened the already privileged minority. In the interior, the definition of property rights strengthened the farming communities and those among the pastoralists who became settled farmers. Stokes made the point that in densely populated areas a rent-earning group was already distinct and powerful. Therefore, the direct cultivators normally had inferior rights to land. The British made alliances with these powerful groups by the *zamindari* settlement. It perpetuated their power and blocked the way for basic restructuring in rural society. By contrast, in regions of insecure agriculture where 'land was plentiful and hands few', the individual or *ryotwar* settlement was the natural choice.[71] In these areas, the land revenue system could allow middle peasant groups to become rich by accumulating the profits of agriculture.

In all regions, commercialization of agriculture benefited peasants

[69] Stokes, 'Dynamism and Enervation'; David Ludden, 'Introduction', in Ludden (ed.), *Agricultural Production in Indian History*, Oxford University Press, Delhi, 1994.

[70] I shall follow a recent restatement by David Ludden.

[71] Stokes dwelt especially on the Jat *'bhaichara'* communities in the Upper Doab where land was held and revenue paid collectively by peasant kinship units in a village.

as well as those earning an income from rent, trading profits, or interest. In the coastal areas, the benefits weighed more heavily in favour of groups that did not cultivate land directly, such as the *zamindars*. In the *ryotwari* settlements, a section of the peasantry tended to benefit the more. These areas were thus prepared for higher levels of private investment in land.

Where the upper castes retained superior rights, social oppression joined hands with rent seeking. This is what happened in large parts of rural Bihar. In Chota Nagpur, poor resources, poor communication, high population density and oppression over small peasants and labourers by *zamindars* and superior tenants, combined to produce poverty and stagnation.[72] Here, property rights merely armed the old and new oppressors with legal weapons. Usually, such examples of stagnation arose in subsistence agriculture. These were regions that traded little and felt little of the liberating effects of markets.

## COMMON PROPERTY RESOURCES

### What were Common Property Resources?

The economy of the countryside was not exclusively the economy of settled agriculture. Settled agriculture existed alongside a very large population of hunter-gatherers, pastoralists, shifting cultivators and fisherfolk. These occupations lived on resources available in common, such as forests, grasslands, or water. Peasants themselves depended on these common resources for fuel, building material, raw material for rural industry, medicines, grazing grounds, and subsistence during famines.

In the pre-British period, the right to the use of uncultivated common land within easy access to the village tended to be decided jointly by dominant peasants in the village. Where the areas were large and the population that used the commons not settled near these lands, the rights tended to be customary in nature periodically negotiable with the local rulers. Examples were nomadic pastoralist communities that traversed the grasslands in north and south India.

### Changes During British Rule

In the nineteenth century, the commons began to disappear and access to them became increasingly difficult. Some broad statistics on

---

[72] See, for example, Detlef Schwerin, 'The Control of Land and Labour in Chota Nagpur, 1858–1908', in D. Rothermund and D.C. Wadhwa (eds), *Zamindars, Mines and Peasants*, Manohar, Delhi, 1978.

land use patterns are available. Common lands can be measured by the extent of forests, and uncultivated wastes available for cultivation. Wastes not so available usually represent area for residential purposes, water bodies, etc. These data suggests (a) slight fall in the area under uncultivated wastes available for cultivation between 1885 and 1921, (b) increase in the area under cultivation including current fallows, and (c) increase in the area under forests. However, this data is suspect for a number of reasons. The total figure was obviously underestimated in 1885. The area under forests almost certainly reflects not the area under actual forests, but the area under the forest department, or area officially defined as forests. Nevertheless, even this data suggests one indisputable fact. Since no significant change in total area occurred after 1921, per capita availability of the commons began to shrink. Setting aside official statistics, the total area under wastes and forests (if Burma is excluded) is likely to have fallen in the latter part of the British period.

TABLE 3.10
Land-use, 1885–1938

| | | | (million acres) |
| --- | --- | --- | --- |
| | 1885 | 1921 | 1938 |
| Cultivated area (including current fallow) | 186 | 254 | 258 |
| Uncultivated area | 98 | 90 | 94 |
| Uncultivated area not available for cultivation | 59 | 66 | 68 |
| Forests | 49 | 101 | 101 |
| Total area (net of states and Burma) | 391 | 511 | 521 |

Source: *Statistical Abstracts for British India*, Calcutta, various years.

In the British period, access to common resources declined steadily. This was connected with 'sedentarization' and 'peasantization' of those communities who primarily depended on the commons. They settled as farmers, which is what government policy aimed at implicitly or explicitly.

There were several factors that led to this change.

(i) The British redefined their political relationship with pastoralist communities and often imposed new taxes on them. In regions located near areas of conflict such as Punjab, some pastoralist communities not believed to be sufficiently loyal fell victim to these conflicts.

(ii) Various forms of joint rights on the use of the commons were either not understood or ignored. These were replaced by private property. This led the dominant cultivators to try to enclose and subdivide common lands wherever they could. In Bengal, the *zamindars* imposed restrictions on the use of forests within their domains. In some cases they implemented these restrictions brutally. This was one of the grievances that led to the Santal Rebellion in western Bengal in 1855.

(iii) Large canal irrigation systems crisscrossed and broke up grazing grounds and converted some of them into cultivable land.

(iv) Population growth led to encroachment on forests and grazing grounds.

(v) The government reserved access to forests. There were two reasons behind this. Forest produce, especially timber, increased immensely in market value and the government wanted to earn a rent from the exploitation of such resources. But there was also a conservation motive. This arose from a sense that the traditional forms of forest use such as shifting cultivation or unregulated timber extraction might endanger the forests.

(vi) With the decay of customary rights to the commons, a problem arose that is well-known in the economic theoretical literature as 'free riding' and the 'tragedy of the commons'. In short, individuals began to encroach on the commons wherever policing was lax, without regard to depletion of the stock of resources.

The closure of access to the forests and enclosures for private or collective use had a number of economic effects, some of which are not well-researched. Regional studies hint at a disappearance of occupations, problem of inadequate subsistence, and problems for agriculture. Also, with the bureaucratization of forest management, a whole variety of tensions developed between the government and the forest-dwellers over such issues as abuses of power by petty officials, loss of rights of collection of forest products, collective responsibility for damage, etc.[73]

That politics, market, laws, population, and fiscal policy reduced the quantity and quality of the commons is a story that varies little in content between different regions of India. But regional experiences do vary in terms of the prehistory of access, economic uses, and forms of adaptation. The task before the economic historian who might wish to capture these divergences can be summed up in three questions.

[73] Richard Tucker, 'Forest Management and Imperial Politics: Thana District, Bombay, 1823–87', *IESHR*, 16(3), 1979.

- What kind of customary institutions controlled the use of the traditional resources?
- What were the economic uses of the commons?
- How did the population adapt to declining access to traditional resources?

In agrarian history, the whole story has been told marginally. In recent years, a large and growing literature on 'environmental history' has explored major aspects of this transition, especially the impact of policy on the pastoralists, populations dependent on the forests, and on water usage. This literature has recognized that in pre-British periods, agriculture, forests and pastoral zones were bound together in a complex way. This interdependence was not just an economic one. It was sustained culturally and politically through a network of customary or natural rights that survived change of regimes until the nineteenth century.

The plains of the Punjab and sub-Himalayan North India have been studied rather more intensively in this literature so far, and will be taken up for brief 'case-studies' in the rest of this section.

## Some Regional Experiences

Punjab[74]

In Punjab, initially 'unclaimed' wastes were abundant both outside village areas, and within them under joint management of village proprietary bodies. The region had abundant if poor quality land, and natural conditions that led to a large pastoral population. These people migrated along traditional routes that crisscrossed the open grass land.

The basic aim of British revenue policy was to maximize revenue per unit of land. This policy forced the authorities to try to bring village wastes under cultivation or reserve these for the use of cultivators, and to reserve the 'open wastes' outside the village areas for the government. Accordingly, village boundaries were demarcated and access to the open wastes prohibited. Some of these vast open wastes were later used to resettle cultivators in the canal colonies. The village wastes were divided among proprietors according to their

---

[74] See Minoti Chakravarty-Kaul, *Common Lands and Customary Law: Institutional Change in North India over the Past Two Centuries*, Oxford University Press, Delhi, 1996; Neeladri Bhattacharya, 'Pastoralists in a Colonial World', in David Arnold and Ramachandra Guha (eds), *Nature, Culture, Imperialism. Essays on the Environmental History of South Asia*, Oxford University Press, Delhi, 1995.

ancestral shares, and specifically prohibited from being used by primarily pastoralists.

The pastoral population faced closed access to both their traditional routes and old grazing grounds. A few continued within the new regime. But large numbers settled down as peasants and small-scale traders. Many turned to wage labour. The wastes declined in scale. The length of the fallow was reduced. There was a disturbance of the balance between cultivation and livestock breeding, which may have intensified the effect of famines in some areas. 'Customary laws' on the use of the commons were not totally ignored. For the British wished to respect traditional authority as far as possible. But these 'laws', not being coded, were so badly misinterpreted that the traditional authority declined anyhow.

At the same time, the economic context changed rapidly. Canals increased the productivity of land. The railways extended markets. All kinds of public works were major consumers of the produce of the waste, from timber to rubble. Population growth and migration reduced the supply of cultivable land. The commons were either reserved or turned into farms. Within the village, the decline of traditional authority and increasing competition for land led to partition and enclosure of the village commons, as well as to 'free riding' or overuse of the commons that remained.

## Uttarakhand Forests[75]

The forests of the western Himalayas were earlier used by a large migratory pastoral population, as well as by the peasants who lived on small plots of hillside lands between the forests. In fact, as the elevation increased, agriculture alone became less capable of sustaining lives. It had to be combined with animal husbandry, mining, trade, and extraction of diverse resources from the forests. Ramachandra Guha suggests that the village community decided on some loosely defined norms of access to and usage of the forests. This interpretation has been questioned. Chetan Singh suggests that such communities had been generally rare, and were created by the colonial state's attempt to define customary property rights in wastes.

In any case, the access to the forests became difficult or impossible after the rulers decided to conserve forest resources and collect rents

[75] Ramachandra Guha, *The Unquiet Woods: Ecological Change and Peasant Resistance in the Himalaya*, Oxford University Press, Delhi, 1989; Chetan Singh, *Natural Premises: Ecology and Peasant Life in the Western Himalaya 1800–1950*, Oxford University Press, Delhi, 1998.

from them. The most important such resource was timber. Competing claims on forests, such as those of the pastoralists, were marginalized. Together, the destruction of forests and conservation efforts that focused on the more profitable types of trees changed the very nature of the forests. Property rights in wastes in this region too underwent changes during British rule. Customary rights were replaced by individual property rights and restriction of access to what lay beyond.

## SUMMARY AND CONCLUSION

Despite the great diversities within India, and the intense debates about the effect of British policy and effects of markets, a few processes stand out. To understand them better we need to make three crucial distinctions: (a) between the periods, 1860–1920 and 1920–39; (b) between regions that produced a large quantity of the most lucrative cash crops and regions that did not, and (c) between peasants with secure property rights over large enough land and those without such assets.

The overall picture was one of increasing demand for agricultural goods during 1860–1920, with a slowdown thereafter. This increased demand was met by expansion in area cropped, developments in long-distance trade networks, and improved infrastructure. In the nineteenth century, increased crop output led to increased incomes. In the twentieth century, growth rates in total output and income were smaller.

In both periods, agricultural growth varied greatly between regions. Stagnation characterized eastern India and those with poor endowments of water and infrastructure. In the rest of India, growth rates were generally positive and nowhere significantly low. Available evidence suggests that average standard of living did improve in cash crop growing regions in the period 1860–1920.

Evidence from most areas indicates growing prosperity and economic-political power of 'rich peasants'. Real wages of the agricultural labourers changed little in the long run. The small peasants too did not appear to be doing well in the period 1930–39. There are two possible ways of explaining increasing income inequality implied in this description. First, factor-endowments were changing against labour and in favour of capital. 'Capital' in this case included both working capital and good land in sufficient quantity under superior title. Second, caste-based dominance of the landed people over the landless continued, and became an instrument to get hired labour cheaply.

## The Starting Questions

Let us now return to the two central questions. What caused agricultural stagnation? Why did the colonial patterns of growth and stagnation persist in post-colonial India?

In left–nationalist historiography, commercialization as such or British policy in particular is seen as detrimental to the Indian economy. But that perspective is inadequate. For, commercialization was clearly a stimulus for agricultural growth. This is seen from (a) the generally higher growth rates in productivity of the major cash crops, (b) the broad association between regions producing cash crops and regions experiencing growth in output, and (c) signs of increased incomes in the nineteenth century. What, then, caused stagnation? In the colonial period, the growing and the stagnant regions were distinguished by a set of features. Of these, two stand out as especially important. These are the structure of rights to land, and resource endowments. In answer to the second question, impetus for growth and stagnation became long-lasting because class structure and resource endowments cannot be changed easily or quickly.

There were also constraints on further growth in all regions of India. These constraints came into play after 1920. First, the world market was in depression after the mid-1920s. Second, there was technological inertia. Expansion had been driven by increased supply of land and water. When the rate of increase in the supply of land and water slowed down, growth stopped too. Further bursts in output expansion in the better endowed regions had to await the green revolution in the 1970s.

Formalized property rights in land and expansion of markets jointly initiated a process of destruction of the common lands. The British rule restricted access to the uncultivated commons out of the rather contradictory combination of motives—earn a rent from the resources, and protect the resources. A range of occupations dependent on the commons disappeared or were forced to a difficult adaptation. Economies of regions where forests supplied subsistence were disrupted, and the close interdependence of cultivation and common lands disturbed.

In left–nationalist historiography, a major example of the detrimental effects of markets relates to small-scale industry. In the chapter that follows, this subject will be taken up. It will be argued that one lesson of the present chapter, that commercialization generated economic growth but resource endowments restricted its scope, applies to the history of small-scale industry as well.

## ANNOTATED READINGS

A comprehensive bibliography on Indian agriculture in the British period will be unmanageably long, and is not necessary for the student. For such a listing, see the 'Bibliographical essay' in David Ludden, *An Agrarian History of South Asia*, Cambridge, 1999. The list that follows contains representative works on the major themes. It is not expected that the student will read all of these, or where whole books are cited, that s/he must read the whole book. It is strongly recommended that the student read (a) the articles cited, and (b) parts of the books cited. Which parts are essential readings have been indicated. Where no such indication is given, the student is recommended to read the introduction, conclusion, and anything else depending on specific doubts and interests.

### Trends in Agricultural Production

George Blyn, *Agricultural Trends in India, 1891–1947: Output, Availability, and Productivity*, University of Pennsylvania Press, Philadelphia, 1966. Sumit Guha (ed.), *Growth, Stagnation or Decline? Agricultural Productivity in British India*, Oxford University Press, Delhi, 1992. Introduction is essential reading, other chapters optional.

### Expansion in Markets

General Sources
The four articles, by Eric Stokes on agrarian relations in northern India, B. Chaudhuri on eastern India, H. Fukazawa on western India and Dharma Kumar on south India, in *CEHI 2*, are essential readings.

Regional Studies
*Northern and Central India:* Elizabeth Whitcombe, *Agrarian Conditions in Northern India*, Vol. 1, University of California Press, Berkeley, 1972, Introduction and Ch. II. Ian Stone, *Canal Irrigation in British India*, Cambridge, 1984, Ch. 8 (on the effects of canals upon standards of living and the regional economy). D.E.U. Baker, *Colonialism in an Indian Hinterland. The Central Provinces 1820–1920*, Oxford University Press, Delhi, 1993, Chs 3–5. Imran Ali, *Punjab under Imperialism, 1885–1947*, Oxford University Press, Delhi, 1989. A.H. Siddiqi, 'Nineteenth

Century Agricultural Development in Punjab: 1850–1900', *IESHR*, 21(3), 1984. Laxman Satya, *Cotton and Famine in Berar, 1850–1900*, Manohar, Delhi, 1997.

*Western India:* Neil Charlesworth, *Peasants and Imperial Rule. Agriculture and Agrarian Society in the Bombay Presidency, 1850–1935*, Cambridge, 1985, 'Introduction' and 'Conclusions' are essential, the rest of the book recommended. Sumit Guha, *The Agrarian Economy of the Bombay–Deccan 1818–1941*, Oxford University Press, Delhi, 1985, Chs III–V. M.B. McAlpin, *Subject to Famine: Food Crises and Economic Change in Western India, 1860–1920*, Princeton University Press, Princeton, 1983, Ch. 7. Donald W. Attwood, *Raising Cane: The Political Economy of Sugar in Western India*, Oxford University Press, Delhi, 1993, especially Chs 2–7. Jan Breman, *Of Peasants, Migrants and Paupers: Rural Labour Circulation and Capitalist Production in West Asia*, Oxford University Press, Delhi, 1985, pp. 14–25, Chs 4, 5. Marcia Frost, 'Population Growth and Agrarian Change in British Gujarat, Kaira District, 1802–58', PhD dissertation, Economics, University of Pennsylvania, 1995.

*Eastern India:* B.B. Chaudhuri, 'Growth of Commercial Agriculture in Bengal' in David Ludden (ed.), *Agricultural Production and Indian History*, Oxford University Press, Delhi, 1994. Sugata Bose, *Peasant Labour and Colonial Capital: Rural Bengal since 1770*, Cambridge, 1993, the whole book. These two works exclude Assam, present-day Bihar and Orissa. On these regions important works exist directly or indirectly touching on the themes of markets, property rights, struggles around property, regional economy, growth and stagnation. A short selection would include Amalendu Guha, 'Assamese Agrarian Societies in the Late Nineteenth Century: Roots, Structures and Trends', *IESHR*, 17(1), 1980. P.P. Mohapatra, 'Aspects of Agrarian Economy of Chotanagpur 1880–1950', PhD dissertation, Jawaharlal Nehru University, New Delhi, 1990, and J. Pouchepadass, *Land, Power and Market: A Bihar District under Colonial Rule, 1860–1947*, Sage Publications, New Delhi, 2000. Studies in the agrarian and regional history of north Bengal and Assam have explored the relationship between plantations and agriculture. A selection of such works, notably that of Ranajit Das Gupta, will be cited in Ch. 6.

*Southern India:* A. Satyanarayana, 'Expansion of Commodity Production and Agrarian Market' in David Ludden (ed.), *Agricultural Production and Indian History*, Oxford University Press, Delhi, 1994. G.N. Rao, 'Canal Irrigation and Agrarian Change in Colonial Andhra: A Study of Godavari District, c. 1850–90', *IESHR*, 25(1), 1988.

G.N. Rao, 'Transition from Subsistence to Commercial Agriculture: A Study of Krishna District of Andhra 1850–1900', *EPW*, 20(25–6), 1985. Bruce L. Robert, 'Structural Change in Indian Agriculture: Land and Labour in Bellary District, 1890–1980', *IESHR*, 22(3), 1985. G.N. Rao and D. Rajasekhar, 'Commodity Production and the Changing Agrarian Scenario in Andhra: A Study in Interregional Variations, c. 1910–47' and D. Rajasekhar, 'Commercialization of Agriculture and Changes in Distribution of Land Ownership in Kurnool District of Andhra (c. 1900–50)' in S. Bhattacharya et al (eds), *The South Indian Economy: Agrarian Change, Industrial Structure, and State Policy c. 1914–47*, Oxford University Press, Delhi, 1991. G.N. Rao and D. Rajasekhar, 'Land-use Pattern and Agrarian Expansion in a Semi-arid Region: Rayalaseema in Andhra 1886–1939', *EPW*, 29(26), 1994. David Washbrook, 'The Commercialization of Agriculture in Colonial India: Production, Subsistence and Reproduction in the "Dry" South, c. 1870–1930', *MAS*, 28(1), 1994. C.J. Baker, *An Indian Rural Economy, 1880–1955: The Tamilnad Countryside*, Oxford University Press, Delhi, 1984, Ch. 3. Haruka Yanagisawa, *A Century of Change: Caste and Irrigated Lands in Tamil Nadu 1860s–1970s*, Manohar, Delhi, 1996, 'Introduction'. David Ludden, *Peasant History in South India*, Princeton University Press, Princeton, 1985, Ch. 5. M.S.S. Pandian, *The Political Economy of Agrarian Change. Nanchilnadu 1880–1939*, Sage Publications, New Delhi, 1990.

### Land Market

Chaudhuri, 'Eastern India', *CEHI 2*, pp. 98–109, and the other three *CEHI 2* essays on major regions. Sumit Guha, 'Agricultural Rents in India c. 1860–1960', in M. Hasan and N. Gupta (eds), *India's Colonial Encounter. Essays in memory of Eric Stokes*, Manohar, Delhi, 1993; and 'The Land Market in Upland Maharashtra 1820–1960', *IESHR*, 24(2–3), 1987. Jacques Pouchepadass, 'Land, Power and Market: The Rise of the Land Market in Gangetic India', in Peter Robb (ed.), *Rural India. Land, Power and Society under British Rule*, second edition, Oxford University Press, Delhi, 1992. Nariaki Nakazato, 'Regional Pattern of Land Transfer in Late Colonial Bengal', in Peter Robb, Kaoru Sugihara, Haruka Yanagisawa (eds), *Local Agrarian Societies in Colonial India: Japanese Perspectives*, Curzon Press, Richmond, 1996.

### Credit Market

'Introduction' and all the essays (except Ranajit Guha's essay) reprinted in Sugata Bose (ed.), *Credit, Markets and the Agrarian Economy*, Oxford University Press, Delhi, 1994. This book contains examples of works (such as Shahid Amin) illustrating the role of rural credit in agrarian backwardness. See also Sumit Guha, 'Commodity and Credit in Upland Maharashtra 1800–1950', *EPW*, 22(52), 1987.

Labour
Dharma Kumar, *Land and Caste in South India*, second edition, Manohar, Delhi, 1997, Introduction. All the essays in Gyan Prakash (ed.), *The World of the Rural Labourer in Colonial India*, Oxford University Press, Delhi, 1994.

### Effects of Market Expansion

The four essays in *CEHI 2* have discussed peasant and landowner mobility. See also the 'Introduction' of Yanagisawa, *A Century of Change*, for discussion of the literature on inequality in land-holding. Relevant regional studies have been cited in the text.

### Explaining Growth and Stagnation

For a survey of the arguments relating to the adverse role of rural credit, see Sugata Bose, 'Introduction', in Bose (ed.), *Credit, Markets and the Agrarian Economy*. Of the statements of the forced commercialization thesis, the following is sufficient: Amit Bhaduri, 'Evolution of Land Relations in Eastern India under British Rule', *IESHR*, 15(1), 1976. Specific criticisms of 'forced commercialization' include B.B. Chaudhuri, 'The Process of Agricultural Commercialization in Eastern India During British Rule: A Reconsideration of the Notions of "Forced Commercialisation" and "Dependent Peasantry"', in Peter Robb (ed.), *Meanings of Agriculture*, Oxford University Press, Delhi, 1996; Chiranjib Sen, 'Commercialization, Class Relations and Agricultural Performance in Uttar Pradesh: A Note on Bhaduri's Hypothesis', in K.N. Raj et al (eds), *Essays on the Commercialization of Indian Agriculture*, Oxford University Press, Delhi, 1981; Omkar Goswami, *Industry, Trade and Peasant Society. The Jute Economy of Eastern India 1900–1947*, Oxford University Press, Delhi, 1991, Section 3.2.

### Common Property Resources

'Introduction' in David Arnold and Ramachandra Guha (eds), *Nature, Culture, Imperialism. Essays on the Environmental History of South Asia*, Oxford University Press, Delhi, 1995. Ramachandra Guha, *The Unquiet Woods: Ecological Change and Peasant Resistance in the Himalaya*, Oxford University Press, Delhi, 1989. Neeladri Bhattacharya, 'Pastoralists in a Colonial World', in Arnold and Guha (eds), *Nature,*

*Culture, Imperialism.* Minoti Chakravarty-Kaul, *Common Lands and Customary Law. Institutional Change in North India over the Past Two Centuries,* Oxford University Press, Delhi, 1996. Chetan Singh, *Natural Premises. Ecology and Peasant Life in the Western Himalaya 1800– 1950,* Oxford University Press, Delhi, 1998. Sumit Guha has studied the variable and complex relationship between forests and people in *Environment and Ethnicity in India 1200–1991,* Cambridge, 1999, Ch. 8. This interaction took a specific course in the British period when communities primarily living on the forests tended to become peasants.

# 4

# Small-scale Industry

During the colonial period, employment was shrinking in some segments of manufacturing, whereas it was rising in others. In the most widely held interpretation, 'large-scale industry', to be defined shortly, was expanding, and 'small-scale industry' was in decline in competition with large-scale industry. This view has been questioned recently. It can be shown that small-scale industry as a whole was a dynamic sector. But certain segments and certain forms of industrial organization within it were in decline. The trend derived to a lesser extent from competition with large-scale industry, and to a larger extent from growth of markets and competition within small-scale industry itself.

Standard histories of Indian industrialization deal mainly with a type of firms described as 'modern industry' or 'large-scale industry' Large-scale industry can be defined by three basic characteristics, relating to technology, organization, and government regulation.

(i) Large-scale industry used machinery and steam-powered technology. It was the relatively more capital-intensive sector in manufacturing.

(ii) It was organized in large factories sometimes employing several thousand persons, rather than in small factories or in 'households'. Households are defined as units where members of the owner's family are the main workers.

(iii) These large factories satisfied the official definition of a 'factory' This definition has changed over time. Today it applies to any unit employing 10 or more workers and using electricity or 20 or more workers and not using electricity. Once such a unit is registered officially as a 'factory', it becomes subject to government regulations under the Factories Act concerning the wages and welfare of the workers. A unit officially registered as factory can sometimes escape implementing these regulations. But overall, the Factories Act has quite strongly influenced employer-employee contracts inside large factories in India.

In contrast to large-scale industry, in numerous industrial firms in India neither machinery, nor large factories, nor government regulations played significant roles. These formed the relatively more labour-intensive component in manufacturing. We call this sector 'small-scale industry'. The present chapter will deal with small-scale industry. Large-scale industry will be dealt with in Chapter 5.

A long chapter devoted to small-scale industry represents a break from the mainstream treatment of Indian industrialization.[1] The mainstream has either ignored or been very sketchy about small-scale industry, despite the fact that about 90 per cent of the industrial work-force at independence was engaged in small-scale industry. The mainstream has dealt primarily with large-scale industry. Such a focus can only be explained through biases induced by theories of industrialization, that is, by views about what should happen in India rather than what actually happened. In particular, there is an implicit belief that industrialization and economic growth necessarily mean employment of machinery and wage labour. What did not use machinery was backward, marginal, in decline, and incapable of generating economic growth. This belief has many roots. The Marxists' preoccupation with technological change is one of them. A full chapter on small-scale industry is partly in recognition of their quantitative importance. But it is also a critique of the mainstream world-view. The chapter will suggest that small-scale industry was capable of generating economic growth in the colonial period. In that respect, the chapter suggests that the experience of the small-scale industry must be a central theme in any economic history of India.

How did small-scale industry change in terms of scale and organization? How have these changes been explained? The chapter will try to answer these two questions. The first section of the chapter will define types of industry a little more precisely, and discuss the relationship between these types. The second section presents a statistical outline of industrialization in the long run, with special reference to different types of industry. The rest of the chapter is divided into six

---

[1] See, for example, the first three works cited in the readings list of Ch. 5.

sections—the first five deal with 'traditional' small-scale industry, and the last with 'modern' small-scale industry. We begin by defining these two terms.

## TYPES OF INDUSTRY DEFINED

Industry types were defined above by using three criteria—technology, organization and regulation. Small-scale industry can be divided further based on a fourth characteristic, vintage. Large-scale industry was a product of the Industrial Revolution, and its growth in India was partly a result of colonial India's economic relationship with Britain. For the majority of the small-scale industry firms, on the other hand, the products and technologies dated before the colonial period. An example is handloom weaving of cloth. This set of enterprises can be called 'traditional' small-scale industry. There were, however, a few small-scale firms modern in origin. Compared to large-scale industry, these were units of smaller scale usually unregulated. However, and compared to traditional industry, these were usually of recent vintage, used machinery to a greater extent, and had higher average scale. We can call this type, 'modern small-scale industry'. In the interwar period, a significant growth of modern small-scale industry took place, examples being foundries, cotton gins, jute presses, edible-oil extraction, rice mills, flour mills, etc. Table 4.1 summarizes the main characteristics of the three types of industry.

The term 'modern' can be misread, and needs to be qualified. The dividing line between traditional and modern small-scale industry was not a very sharp one. Most types of modern small-scale industry, in fact, supplied old products. Thus, grain milled by machinery and that milled by hand were both meant for the same consumers, but supplied by different technologies. Sometimes, however, new technology led to a new product altogether, for example, machine-milled rice was often seen as a distinct product from hand-pounded rice, and in some cases, involved different grains. In many cases, money made in a traditional small-scale industry tended to be invested in starting firms that were bigger in scale, technologically more developed, and more capitalized. These would tend to be classified as 'modern small-scale industry' by our definition, even though the difference in terms of vintage between modern and traditional in this case would be rather inappropriate. The example of handloom weavers who set up small factories equipped with power-driven looms is perhaps the most suitable.

The dividing line between small-scale and large-scale was a little sharper. But they too had close interlinkages. Large-scale industry supplied raw materials to small-scale. Workers often moved between them. And small-scale industry workers and entrepreneurs sometimes learnt their skills and acquired new ideas by working in large-scale industry. The former could even buy secondhand machinery from the latter. Most obvious examples of such interrelationships can be found in textile manufacturing.

TABLE 4.1
Different Types of Industry

| | Large-scale industry | Small-scale industry | |
| --- | --- | --- | --- |
| | | Modern | Traditional |
| Organization | Factories with several hundred workers and supervisory staff | Factories with usually less than 100 workers | Household and small factories |
| Technology | Modern machinery, use of steam-power, electricity | Limited use of machinery | Hand-tools |
| Regulation | Regulated by the Factories Act, and other acts governing employment and management | Some regulated, some not | Usually not regulated |
| Vintage | Colonial | Colonial | Pre-colonial |
| Examples | Cotton mills, jute mills, steel, sugar, paper, etc. | Foundry, rice and flour mills, oil mills, weaving factories with power-driven looms | Handloom weaving |

## LONG-TERM PATTERN OF INDIAN INDUSTRIALIZATION

This section will outline the most important features of Indian industrialization in the long run, and discuss the scale and organization of traditional and modern small-scale industry in that context. The focus will be on the colonial period, but the post-independence period will also be analysed to provide a perspective to what happened before. This analysis will use exclusively, data on employment derived from the censuses. Occupational statistics in India are available from 1881 (see also Chapter 9), but the level of detail and the definition of work and workers changed so significantly between the early censuses, that it is not easy to create reliable time-series using censuses before 1911. Having to start from the 1911 census is a major limitation in the case of traditional and modern small-scale industry, which saw important changes in the nineteenth century. But it is not a major limitation if we look at large-scale industry, which was a very small sector until the interwar period.

There is another problem with employment data. Industrial units can differ significantly in terms of the productivity of labour, partly due to differences in capital-intensity and partly due to differences in efficiency. In other words, two units with identical employment can generate different levels of income per head. That is, the share of any one type of industry in employment can be quite different from its share in incomes generated by industry. The share of large-scale industry in real income was in fact higher than its share in employment. Income data by sector, however, is not as detailed as employment data. This chapter, therefore, restricts itself to employment data.

Industrial employment data are available from two main sources —the census which gives total employment in industry, and the statistics on officially registered factories, which give employment for these registered factories. On the one hand, large-scale industry dominated employment in registered factories. On the other, employment outside the registered factories was located mainly in traditional small-scale industry. The problematic category is modern small-scale industry, which straddled both the 'factory' and non-factory categories. It is fair to assume that most modern small-scale industry firms did not register themselves. In the analysis that follows, employment in registered factories will be treated as employment in large-scale industry. Employment outside the registered factories will be treated as employment in small-scale industry.

Table 4.2 presents an overview of industrial employment in India since 1911. It shows that while both industrial and total employment has grown, the growth in the former has been rather slow and fluctuating. Measured in terms of the share of industry in total employment, India is not significantly more industrialized today than a century ago. But this conclusion needs to be qualified. The share of industry in national income has grown steadily despite stagnation in employment share. An important conclusion of Table 4.2 is that industrial employment declined during 1911-31. This decline derived mainly from a decline in small-scale industry employment. To this finding we shall return.

TABLE 4.2
Total Employment and Industrial Employment, 1911–91

| | Industrial employment (millions) | Total employment (millions) | Percentage share of industry in total employment |
|---|---|---|---|
| 1911 | 17.5 | 148.9 | 11.8 |
| 1921 | 15.7 | 146.4 | 10.7 |
| 1931 | 15.6 | 153.9 | 10.2 |
| 1961 | 20.0 | 188.7 | 10.6 |
| 1971 | 17.1 | 180.7 | 9.5 |
| 1981 | 25.1 | 242.0 | 10.4 |
| 1991 | 28.7 | 306.0 | 9.4 |
| *Annual rate of growth in per cent* | | | |
| 1911–31 | −0.6 | | |
| 1961–91 | 1.2 | | |
| 1981–91 | 1.3 | | |

Table 4.3 shows that large-scale industry was, and remains, a relatively small contributor to employment generated in the economy. The overwhelming majority of Indian industrial workers was occupied, and continues to be occupied, in small-scale industry. However, the share of large-scale industry in real income from industry is higher. The share increased from 15 per cent in 1900 to about 40 per cent in 1947. The share of large-scale industry in employment grew slowly in the colonial period, rather rapidly between 1951 and 1971, and has been declining after 1971. Such a tendency is driven by demand for and supply of labour in large-scale industry, a subject that awaits more research.

Employment in small-scale industry fell before independence. It grew at a very small rate after independence. Since independence, the censuses collect data separately for household industry and non-household industry. If we exclude the employment in registered factories from non-household employment, we get employment in those units that are not officially recognized as factories and yet employ wage labour. We then have a distinction between two types of small-scale firms—households, and unofficial or informal factory. In the period 1961–91, there has been a shift from the households to the informal factory, or a conversion of the former to the latter. The conclusion is, the low rate of growth in employment does not imply overall stagnation, but a shift from firms that use less productive and less specialized labour to firms that use more productive and more specialized labour. For, most household workers work in industry only part-time. Clearly, such a shift can reduce total employment, and yet raise the productivity of labour.

TABLE 4.3

Industrial Organization, 1911–91

*(employment in millions, percentage of industrial employment in brackets)*

| | Large-scale industry | Small-scale industry | |
| --- | --- | --- | --- |
| | | In family-labour oriented units | In wage-labour oriented units |
| 1911 | 0.88 (5) | n.a. | n.a. |
| 1921 | 1.57 (10) | n.a. | n.a. |
| 1931 | 1.57 (10) | n.a. | n.a. |
| 1961 | 3.00 (15) | 12.00 (60) | 5.00 (25) |
| 1971 | 5.47 (32) | 6.33 (37) | 5.31 (31) |
| 1981 | 7.78 (31) | 7.78 (31) | 9.54 (38) |
| 1991 | 8.32 (29) | 6.89 (24) | 13.78 (48) |
| *Annual rate of growth in log per cent* | | | |
| 1911–31 | 2.9 | | |
| 1961–91 | 3.4 | –1.8 | 3.4 |
| 1981–91 | 0.7 | –1.2 | 3.7 |

*n.a. implies that adequate data is not available.*

*Source: Census of India, various years; Statistical Abstracts for British India, Calcutta, various years; Statistical Abstracts for India, Delhi, various years.*

We cannot test directly whether or not such a shift had been underway in the colonial period. But there is indirect evidence suggesting that it had. Firstly, women's participation in industrial employment dropped (see Table 4.4). Secondly, labour productivity in small-scale industry increased. In the most popular view, the decline in women's participation in industry is a reporting error (see 'de-industrialization' below). However, a different view can be suggested. Women's participation in industry used to be strongly correlated with the strength of the family as a producer. Women in India tended to work, and still prefer to work from their own homes. Women work in factories to a very limited extent because special legislation concerning night-duty and maternity benefits tend to discourage employers. Also, there are negative social attitudes towards women working in collective workshops. Thus, in household industry today, women occupy about half the jobs. Likewise, about half of women's industrial employment is inside homes. Clearly, if household industry declines, women's participation in industry will fall. A decline in women's participation can mean a decline of the household as type of producer. An increase in labour productivity also suggests organizational (and possibly technological) change within small-scale industry.

There are two probable reasons behind the decline in household industry. First, certain industries operating only from households were disappearing. Second, the household lost out in competition with other more efficient organizations. Two centuries ago, when markets and competition were far more limited than they are today, households were a stable organization. But from the colonial period, commercialization pitted the households against superior organizational forms, and the former is losing out steadily. We shall explore these reasons more fully in the section on 'dissolution of traditional systems'.

TABLE 4.4
Women's Employment in Industry, 1911–91

|  | 1911 | 1921 | 1931 | 1961 | 1971 | 1981 | 1991 |
|---|---|---|---|---|---|---|---|
| Percentage share of women workers in industrial employment | 34.3 | 32.1 | 29.7 | 27.3 | 12.9 | 14.8 | 16.5 |

Table 4.5 shows that large-scale industry was concentrated in two provinces, Bombay and Bengal. This geographical locational aspect will be discussed further in Chapter 5. Both these British provinces were relatively less important in small-scale industry. In the colonial period, nearly half the employment in small-scale industry was in the United Provinces, Punjab and Madras. Thus, the growth of large-scale industry and the experience of small-scale industry involved different regions. And likewise, the manufacturing histories of different regions in India involve quite different types of enterprise.

After 1947, western India (former Bombay) and eastern India (former Bengal) developed a contrasting pattern of industrialization. Western India significantly increased its share of small-scale industry employment after independence. The roots of this growth go back to the interwar period. Eastern India by contrast, remained less important in small-scale industry employment, and declined in respect of large-scale industry employment.

TABLE 4.5
Industrial Location, 1931

|  | Large-scale industry | | Small-scale industry | |
|---|---|---|---|---|
|  | Employment (millions) | Percentage share of province/state | Employment (millions) | Percentage share of province/state |
| Madras | 0.13 | 8.2 | 2.38 | 17.0 |
| Bombay | 0.38 | 23.9 | 0.69 | 4.9 |
| Bengal | 0.44 | 27.9 | 0.93 | 6.7 |
| United Provinces | 0.10 | 6.3 | 3.04 | 21.6 |
| Punjab | 0.04 | 2.8 | 1.61 | 11.5 |
| Bihar and Orissa | 0.06 | 4.0 | 1.29 | 9.2 |
| Central Provinces and Berar | 0.06 | 3.8 | 0.69 | 4.9 |
| Hyderabad | 0.03 | 1.9 | 0.80 | 5.7 |
| Mysore | 0.02 | 1.5 | 0.27 | 1.9 |
| Total (including other regions) | 1.57 | 100.0 | 14.03 | 100.0 |

TABLE 4.6
Industrial Composition, 1921–81

|  | (percentage share in total industrial employment) | | | |
|---|---|---|---|---|
|  | 1921 | 1931 | 1961 | 1981 |
| Textiles | 25.7 | 26.2 | 32.7 | 29.6 |
| Food, drink, tobacco | 10.5 | 9.4 | 15.4 | 16.2 |
| Hides and skins | 2.0 | 2.0 | 4.0 | 1.9 |
| Metals and machinery | 11.4 | 11.1 | 13.5 | 9.9 |
| Chemicals | 3.7 | 3.9 | 1.6 | 3.0 |
| Wood, stone, glass | 10.1 | 10.4 | 10.9 | 9.5 |
| Total | 100.0 | 100.0 | 100.0 | 100.0 |

By far the most important industry in India was textiles (see Table 4.6). One in every four workers was employed in textiles. Next in importance were food processing, metals, wood products and hides and skins. We can conclude from this pattern that industries intensive either in natural resources (cotton, metals, minerals, animal substances) or labour, dominated the composition. As we shall see in Chapter 5, the dominance of textiles was a feature of large-scale industry too. Generally speaking, the high resource- and labour-intensity characterized large-scale industry as well. However, large-scale industry arose only when mechanical options were available at all.

The discussion on employment size and organization boils down to two main facts.

(i) Overall employment in small-scale industry declined in the colonial period, and grew slowly thereafter.

(ii) There has been a growth of wage-labour, or increasing commercialization of labour, in small-scale industry. The key signs of this are, rising labour productivity, decline of households, and decreasing participation of women.

Any general interpretation of industrial change in India must be able to explain both these facts. We now deal with some of these general interpretations.

## PERSPECTIVES ON SMALL-SCALE INDUSTRY: DE-INDUSTRIALIZATION

'De-industrialization' is an argument that British India, which started with a large and well-developed manufacturing tradition, saw a decline in its traditional industry during the colonial period and a consequent fall in employment and income, and that the large-scale industry that grew in its place did not compensate for the great loss.

The Industrial Revolution in the nineteenth century deeply affected small-scale industry in India. Trade between India and the world increased dramatically, and products of the mechanized textile industry in Britain began to compete with handmade yarn and cloth in the Indian market. What was the net effect of this globalization? 'De-industrialization' suggests that the net effect was negative. At 1750, India supplied nearly a quarter of the world's manufacturing output. By 1900, India supplied less than 2 per cent. There was, thus, a relative decline in India's position in world industry. A relative decline does not mean an absolute decline as well, for between these dates the total scale of world industry output had grown enormously. In fact, the 'de-industrialization' suggests that there was also an absolute fall in industry in India.

The theory lays down five propositions.

(i) Small-scale industry declined in India.

(ii) It declined because of technological obsolescence, that is, it declined because hand-tools had to compete with machinery, and lost the competition.

(iii) It was British machinery that competed with Indian tools.

(iv) This battle was imposed on India by Britain's commitment to free trade as an engine of growth.

(v) Closer economic relationship with Britain did create some large-scale industries in India. But this creative role of globalization did not compensate for the destructive role. One of the reasons why large-scale industry did not grow enough is that, it was a kind of implant rather than an extension or evolution of Indian traditional industry.

To sum up, de-industrialization means a decline in traditional small-scale industry that (a) derived from technological obsolescence against British goods, (b) was sustained by colonial policies, and (c) remained uncompensated by new enterprise. The term makes an explicit contrast between Britain, which experienced *industrialization*, and her major colony India, which experienced de-industrialization, at the same time and due to the same set of causes, namely, trade and technological change.

The theory had two distinct roots. The first is an Indian nationalist tradition represented by R.C. Dutt, Dadabhai Naoroji and somewhat later by Jawaharlal Nehru. The second root is the Marxist theories of imperialism.[2] In the postwar period, both these schools were revived in history, development studies, and Indian historiography. In this last scholarship, de-industrialization became a part of what we have called the left-nationalist paradigm on colonial India (see Chapter 1).

De-industrialization is difficult to test. Any decline in any industry cannot be called de-industrialization. It is the total effect that counts, and the data for measuring that total effect is non-existent. Why is the total effect crucial? It is crucial because a decline in industry due to technological obsolescence always has a beneficial side. When more efficient and productive suppliers drive out less productive ones, one outcome is a fall in price of the good or service in question. Such a change benefits consumers and raises total demand, even if it

---

[2] Karl Marx saw England fulfilling a 'double mission' in India, one destructive and the other creative. The destruction of industry was an example of the former role. The railways built with foreign capital were an example of the latter. Lenin and other early theorists of imperialism explored the latter role, which they felt would become stronger as export of capital from rich to poor countries became inevitable for the survival of capitalism in the west. A postwar scholarship, led by Andre Gunder Frank, argued that such forms of globalization further retarded the poorer countries.

hurts the less productive suppliers. In cotton yarn and shipping, two major examples of obsolescence, this positive effect was present and significant. Now, de-industrialization is a bad thing only if these gains were smaller than the costs arising from fall in employment. The proponents of de-industrialization do not usually consider this problem. In what follows, we shall examine the evidence for or against a narrower hypothesis, that small-scale industry declined in colonial India, and that the decline was derived from competition with British goods. In other words, we shall test only the propositions (i) and (ii) above.

Three types of evidence can be cited for or against de-industrialization. These relate to (a) technological obsolescence, (b) industrial employment, and (c) national income. There is an apparent problem in using any of these evidence to test de-industrialization. Relevant quantitative data begins to become available from the end of the nineteenth century. It may be suggested that de-industrialization commenced from the early nineteenth century, and that it slowed down from the late nineteenth century, so that available quantitative data are irrelevant to its test.

If de-industrialization is defined as a general process of technological obsolescence, then such an assertion is invalid. Technological obsolescence is an irreversible process. If small-scale industry became obsolete by 1850, it must become even more obsolete by 1900, because the pace of technological progress is always faster in the machinery-using industry compared with the tool-using ones. So, later evidence should reflect the same process as earlier evidence.

In one sense such an assertion can be made. It is possible that obsolescence was not a general process, but confined to certain sectors of small-scale industry, whereas other sectors did not compete with British industry. Further, the former not only declined in competition with British industry, but the process of decline was completed in the early nineteenth century, before the census data begins. The textile example seems to illustrate such a hypothesis. Cotton spinning by hand and partly handloom weaving declined in competition with British goods, a decline that occurred between 1820–80. On the other hand, in data after 1880, we see a substantial stability in handloom weaving. But what happened to cotton textiles cannot be generalized into small-scale industry in general. In the early nineteenth century, Britain herself was semi-industrialized. Its only major manufactured export to India was cotton textiles. Textile was an exception, and cannot be generalized into a story about industrial decline due to technological obsolescence brought on by British competition. An earlier decline in industry therefore is a weak hypothesis.

## Technological Obsolescence

Cotton spinning by hand is a clear example of propositions (i) and (ii) above. Studies by Amiya Kumar Bagchi, M.J. Twomey, and a number of other writers prove that a decline in cotton textile industry in the nineteenth century took place.[3] Trade data is a clear evidence of such a decline. The scale of the decline is open to question. Bagchi suggests that the share of industry in total employment in gangetic Bihar came down from as high as 18 per cent about 1820 to as low as 8 per cent in 1901. These employment figures have been disputed. These relied on the questionable statistics collected by Buchanan–Hamilton in the early nineteenth century, and could not be adjusted for the presence, even predominance, of non-specialized and under-employed labour among the textile work-force.[4] Twomey adjusted for this problem, and still found a large enough decline in labour time. It is almost certain that the bulk of this decline occurred in spinning.

Spinning by hand, however, is more or less the only example of a major traditional industry that became extinct due to competition from imported British goods. Other examples exist, such as indigenous shipping and ship-building that declined in competition with steam-ships. But their scale is uncertain or minor.

Within textiles, handloom weaving presents a curious case. Handlooms declined in nineteenth century. In 1833 India imported about 46 million yards of British cloth. In 1887, India imported 2100 million yards, which was the maximum that imports reached. The size of the cloth market about 1887 was possibly 3300 million yards. The market share of imports was about 65 per cent. In 1833, it was no more than 5 per cent. In short, the market share of handlooms in domestic cloth consumption may have decreased from 9 to 35 per cent in 50 years, production approximately from 2500 to 1000 million yards.

This is neither disputable, nor surprising. What is surprising is that after the 1880s, handloom cloth production and labour productivity were continuously rising for the next 50 years. Now, the productivity

---

[3] See the readings list at the end of the chapter.

[4] Marika Vicziany, 'The De-industrialization of India in the Nineteenth Century: A Methodological Critique of Amiya Kumar Bagchi', *IESHR*, 16(2), 1979; J. Krishnamurty, 'De-industrialisation in Gangetic Bihar during the Nineteenth Century: Another Look at the Evidence', *IESHR*, 22(4), 1985.

per hour of a handloom was only about 15–20 per cent that of a power-driven loom. Why was handloom cloth being sold along with mill cloth, despite such an unbridgeable gap in productivity and costs of production? Over time, the handlooms benefited from a number of improved tools. Amiya Kumar Bagchi, somewhat implicitly, explained their survival by these improvements.[5] But in fact, these changes together were incapable of bringing handloom productivity anywhere near the productivity of a power-driven loom. Morris D. Morris suggested that the handlooms survived because total market for cloth expanded in nineteenth century India.[6] This suggestion has been attacked by the left-nationalist school, for the wrong reasons. The school argued that total market could not have expanded. That assertion is wrong, and Morris is right on this point. There is sufficient evidence that national income did grow in the late nineteenth century (see Chapters 3 and 7). A more basic objection to Morris is that, growth of markets does not explain survival of the handloom, given unbridgeable productivity gap between the handloom and the power-driven loom.

So, how did the handloom survive? A recent scholarship on the industry has explored the most acceptable answer, market segmentation. Handlooms and mills had comparative advantages in different types of cloth. Many consumers preferred to buy the cloths that the handlooms were better able to make. These markets experienced commercialization, capital accumulation, and eventually new investments. In this view, the new tools were the effect, and not the cause, of survival. To sum up, the textile experience, had two aspects—competition with large-scale industry as in spinning, and segmented markets between small-scale and large-scale industry as in handloom weaving.

In several other industries, there was a yet third type of situation. Competition from imports and large-scale industry were of little importance outside cotton textiles. But quite often, new firms that used slightly improved tools and slightly higher capital-per-worker replaced manual labour. For example, old manual processes of grain milling by women inside peasant families changed to mechanized processing inside small and seasonal factories, wooden mortars for

---

[5] *Private Investment in India 1900–39*, Cambridge, 1972. See also the section 'Deindustrialization' in Irfan Habib, 'Studying a Colonial Economy without Perceiving Colonialism', *MAS*, 19(3), 1985.

[6] 'Towards a Reinterpretation of Nineteenth-Century Indian Economic History', *IESHR*, 5(1), 1968.

crushing sugar changed to iron rollers, old ways of warping threads for handlooms by the wives and daughters of weavers gave way to beam-warping inside factories, or old ways of cleaning cotton gave way to new ones. Why did such shifts happen? Why were new organizations and new tools being adopted within small-scale industry? The key process was commercialization of the products of small-scale industry. This point will be developed further on.

To sum up, small-scale industry experienced mechanization in a far more complex way than de-industrialization suggests. Products of British mechanized industry replacing Indian hand-made goods, was more exceptional than the rule. Two other situations were more general. The first was market-segmentation, when large-scale and small-scale industry did not compete at all, but served different markets and produced different goods. And the second was the emergence of firms within small-scale industry that differed from older type of firms both in organization and in capital-intensity.

## Census Employment Statistics

Census data on aggregate employment have been used as the major and clinching evidence supporting de-industrialization. What do these data show? The censuses tell us that industrial employment declined steadily and sharply, between 1881 and 1931. It declined from about 20 million to 13–15 million, while at the same time, employment in agriculture increased from 71 to 100 million. The percentage of workers in agriculture increased from 62 to 71, and that in industry declined from 18 to 9. The decline in industrial employment was concentrated in small-scale industry. Does this suggest a big decline in small-scale industry and a ruralization of employment? There are two sets of critique suggesting that it does not. The first questions the statistics, and the second questions the interpretation to be drawn from it.

Detailed work by Daniel and Alice Thorner suggests that these shifts in occupational structure were probably spurious and arose from several problems with the census definitions (see Chapter 9 for more details). In their reconstruction, occupational structure hardly changed between 1881 and 1951. This basic finding has not been seriously questioned in subsequent work.

However, this finding rests, among others, on one argument about women's employment that is questionable. Women's participation in industry declined dramatically in the census period, as we have seen. If women's employment data is excluded, occupational structure shows rather little change. If women's employment data is included, the share of industry in work-force shows a fall. The Thorners suggest that the trends in women's industrial work arose from a reporting problem, and therefore, they should not be given too much credence. Women who were mainly engaged in household duties and marginally in commercial production tended to be classified as workers, in their view. In other words, there was a possible overestimation of women workers in the earlier censuses.

Now, the point that the tendency of declining participation of women in industry is purely a reporting problem is a questionable assumption, because the decline has been a very long-lasting one. It occurred over nearly a century. If this decline is even partly a real one, how can it be explained? The explanation we favour is decline in household industry in competition with units using mainly wage-labour.

Let us now consider the second critique of employment data, which does not dispute a decline in employment, but questions what it means. Does decline in employment mean technological obsolescence? Not entirely, because employment declined in a number of industries where no serious competition with machinery was in existence (such as dress and toilet, wood, ceramics, construction). Does decline in employment mean technological obsolescence of Indian goods in competition with foreign goods? Not necessarily, for as noted by J. Krishnamurty in 1967, a fall in industrial employment could have resulted from more capital-intensive new producers driving out less productive suppliers within Indian industry.[7] How do we test this? If incomes in industry increased, even as employment fell, that could mean rising capital intensity within Indian industry. Let us, then, see what the income data tell us.

## National Income [8]

National income data suggests that total and per worker real income in industry grew at significant rates (in the range 1.5–2 per cent per year) between 1901 and 1947. Several authors have explained this by rising capital-intensity. In this view, what we see in census and

[7] 'Changes in the Composition of the Working Force in Manufacturing, 1901–51: A Theoretical and Empirical Analysis', *IESHR*, 4(1), 1967.

[8] The national income data used here come from S. Sivasubramonian, 'National Income of India, 1900–1 to 1946–7', PhD Dissertation, Delhi School of Economics, Delhi, 1965; and his 'Revised Estimates of the National Income of India, 1900–1 to 1946–7', *IESHR*, 34(2), 1997.

income statistics is the beginning of a large-scale substitution of labour by machinery within India.[9] Usually, this hypothesis is meant to suggest that Indian large-scale industry replaced Indian small-scale industry. Such a thesis is counterintuitive, because it suggests that what happened in India was no different from what happened in the advanced stages of industrialization in Britain. And it is unrealistic because large-scale industry engaged a tiny percentage of industrial employment (4–6 per cent) in the early twentieth century. With such marginal weight in employment, it is not credible that it could compensate for the decline in small-scale industry even in income.

When we look at national income data more closely we see strong signs that in fact real incomes increased within small-scale industry as well. More surprisingly, income per worker probably increased at a faster rate in this sector than in large-scale industry.[10] Evidence of productivity increase is strong also in specific industries like handloom textiles, tanning, and metal work. In textiles, real value-added unquestionably increased, and in all of them, output indicators show growth whereas employment indicators show stagnation or fall.[11]

What does this finding mean? It partly confirms Krishnamurty's hypothesis that decline in employment reflected, not decline in demand, but rise in capital-intensity. The important qualification being

[9] See, for example, Deepak Lal, *The Hindu Equilibrium, Cultural Stability and Economic Stagnation in India 1500 BC–1980*, Oxford University Press, Delhi, 1988, p. 186. W.J. Mac-Pherson seems to have been the first to make the capital-intensity critique about de-industrializtion, in an essay published in A.J. Youngson (ed.), *Economic Development in the Long Run*, George Allen and Unwin, 1972.

[10] S. Sivasubramonian, 'Revised Estimates'. Total income calculations for small-scale industry in this paper, and Sivasubramonian's earlier work done in 1965, rest on two sets of data. The first is census employment in industry (also includes construction) outside official factories. The second is an average wage index for the small-scale sector, derived from a large number of wage and earning estimates for different occupations, time-points, and types of worker. When we say that total income increased despite a fall in employment, it means the income estimates show increase in real terms. This income series has problems, but the problems are not so bad as to call into serious question the conclusion of a rise in income per worker in small-scale industry. The finding that 'small-scale industry' experienced productivity growth of the order that Sivasubramonian finds it did has surprised other commentators on Indian National Income, such as Alan Heston and Angus Maddison. But no alternative method or estimate has been used that can upset this result. In the essay cited, Sivasubramonian has defended the finding with additional qualitative evidence.

[11] For evidence, see the discussion in Sivasubramonian, 'Revised Estimates', pp. 127–9; Tirthankar Roy, *Traditional Industry in the Economy of Colonial India*, Cambridge, 1999, Ch. 2.

added here is that such rise occurred within small-scale industry. The rise in productivity was partly a result of technological change, and partly a result of organizational change. Signs of organizational change such as decline of the household we have seen already. Why did tools and organizations change? Where did that capital come from? Answers to these questions will follow in the next section.

To sum up this long critique of 'de-industrialization', the main points are restated. De-industrialization explains employment decline by technological obsolescence due to competition between British goods and Indian goods. This is an unsatisfactory explanation for four reasons.

(i) It generalizes from only one example, cotton spinning by hand.

(ii) There were several sectors where employment fell despite absence of significant competition with machinery.

(iii) De-industrialization is inconsistent with productivity and income growth within small-scale industry.

(iii) De-industrialization cannot explain changes in industrial organization such as rise in wage-labour or decline in women's labour. We need an alternative theory to explain how employment can decline in traditional industry and yet there can be rise in productivity and organizational change.

There is an alternative, which starts from two premises. First, British machinery and Indian tools were generally not competitive. By and large, the latter made labour-intensive consumer goods for which there was no imported mechanized alternative available. Or such alternatives were not profitable because capital was relatively costly in India. Secondly, small-scale industry changed not due to external competition, but due to internal competition. From these premises, we can suggest an alternative story, which I shall call 'commercialization'.

PERSPECTIVES ON SMALL-SCALE INDUSTRY:
THE COMMERCIALIZATION THESIS

The period of the book is a period of commercialization in India. Long-distance trade expanded and regional markets integrated on an unprecedented scale due to, mainly, three factors—foreign trade, modern transport and communication, and the definition of contract law and private property rights. The effects were dramatic, and well researched for agriculture (see Chapter 3). It is not so well-recognized that small-scale industry was also transformed by commercialization.

Production for subsistence, production under various types of non-market and barter distribution arrangements such as *jajmani*, and production for local, rural, periodic and other spot markets declined in favour of production on contract for distant markets. New marketing systems arose. These were located in big cities or at key railway points. This rise in long-distance trade had three types of effects—increased competition, changes in industrial organization, and changes in technology.

(i) Commercialization increased competition within small-scale industry. In textiles, leather, metal-work, etc, we see numerous cases of small remote manufacturing traditions decaying from the late nineteenth century because either they were not known for good quality products or were located too far from marketing and transportation networks. At the same time a few large agglomerations emerged, these became concentrations of production, trade, capital, and labour. Artisans migrated in increasing numbers. These migrations created or extended markets in labour and capital, and encouraged the hiring of labour.

(ii) Industrial organization changed for several reasons. First, long-distance trade and new marketing systems had made information and working capital essential resources. These were scarce resources. The small number of capitalists who had access to these resources expanded scale of business, could take closer control of the manufacturing process, and sometimes make technological experiments and improvements. Capitalists and labourers became more clearly distinguishable. So did employer–employee relationships. Second, competition among manufacturers led to increased specialization and division of labour. There are two major examples of specialization. Formerly, many rural artisans performed agricultural labour on the side, such as tanners and coarse cotton weavers in many regions. Such part-time industrial activity generally declined whereas specialized artisans survived. Another example is the decline of household industry in favour of small factories employing wage-labour. The family as a production unit had certain advantages, but it also had disadvantages, such as it could not specialize enough, or could not be supervised closely enough. It is this competitive decline of the family that explains the long downward trend in women's participation in industry. For women formerly used to work in industry mainly as members of the household. When the household declined, women workers exited industry, and were replaced by male hired labour. Women are returning now to the factory, not because the household is coming back, but for other factors that influence women's participation in the factory.

(iii) Small-scale industry also began to use better tools in the colonial period. We know little about the extent of this change, and about its contribution to growth of productivity. What we do know is that the new innovations did not get used simply because they were available, but because commercialization had created wealth among the artisans who could afford to buy them.

The de-industrialization perspective can explain decline in employment, but not rise in productivity. Commercialization can explain both decline in total employment and rise in productivity.

The commercialization perspective is only a general approach, and need not exactly fit the experience of every industry. As a general approach it has the merit of explaining a wider range of facts than the de-industrialization thesis. It is thus a more realistic approach. But we need to keep in mind that each industry had its own somewhat unique history, shaped by its particular technology and the nature of its connection with the precolonial economic and social system. It is necessary to have some idea about these specific aspects, as well as the general tendency. The section that follows presents brief studies of some major industries.

## EXAMPLES OF TRADITIONAL INDUSTRIES IN TRANSITION
### Cotton and Silk Weaving

Scale

In the interwar period, possibly 3 to 3.5 million persons were engaged in the cotton, silk and wool spinning-weaving industry. The mills employed about 10 per cent of this total, the rest used mainly hand-tools and were organized in households or very small factories.

From the late nineteenth century, it is possible to estimate the scale of production of handloom cotton cloth based on quantities of mill-made and imported yarn that was left over after use by the mills. Handlooms accounted for about 25 per cent of the cotton cloth produced annually in the first half of the twentieth century. Market-share of handloom cotton cloth was roughly stable between the 1890s and the 1930s. The total production of handloom cotton cloth expanded by about 30 per cent between 1900 and 1939. Throughout this period, total cloth consumption was growing marginally, and Indian cloth was steadily substituting imported cloth. In cloths made of silk and other fibres, handlooms dominated. Taking all fibres together except wool, in the 1930s handlooms' market-share in total cloth consumption in value may have been about 50 per cent.

The number of handlooms was roughly stable in the first half of the twentieth century at around 2 million. Rising production and constant loomage suggest that the productivity and the capacity of the looms increased. This can be independently confirmed. Estimates of real wages and earnings in handloom weaving suggest great variation between more skilled and less skilled weavers. But there was no sign of a sustained downward trend. National income data, in fact, suggests a slow increase in wages.

Conditions of Demand

At least parts of the cotton textile industry were highly commercialized even before British rule (see Chapter 2). These segments supplied mainly to foreign trade. From the first quarter of the nineteenth century, this foreign trade declined, and British cloth began to compete with Indian cloth even in Indian markets. Some commercialized cloth thus disappeared. But some other cloths that were not heavily traded before became commercialized during the colonial period.

Cotton textile is the most important example of a craft threatened by steam-powered technology. The threat came from Lancashire from the 1820s until the prewar decade. Thereafter, the competition came mainly from the cotton spinning-weaving mills in Bombay and Ahmedabad. The power-driven loom is much faster than a handloom. Why, then, did the handloom survive at all? We have seen the answer already. It survived because it was more efficient in certain types of traditional clothing.

As far as one can judge, in the mid-nineteenth century, two types of cloth faced very keen competition from foreign or Indian mill-made cloth. The first was 'coarse-medium' cotton cloth, and the second, printed and bleached cotton cloth. By contrast, (a) cloths that used very coarse or very fine cotton yarn, (b) cloths that used complex designs woven on the loom, and (c) cloths that used non-cotton yarn partially or wholly, tended to use the handloom. The types (a) and (b) tended to be so labour-intensive that the mills did not enter them by choice. The mills did not want to use non-cotton fibre like silk or rayon because that would mean under-utilizing their cotton spinning capacity. The most important example of a handloom speciality, one that is still made on a handloom, is a sari with a designed border. In 1930, there were many more such cloths. Turbans, bordered dhotis, checked and striped lungies, were also common handloom items. By contrast, the mills dominated shirting, suiting, dhotis and simple saris, basically, any cloths that could be woven in long sheets with very simple designs.

Even as handlooms faced competition in certain categories, in those classes where it had a comparative advantage consumption grew in the early twentieth century. The increased consumption derived partly from increasing purchasing power of those rural regions that produced lucrative cash crops. It also derived from changes in clothing habits. For example, the depressed castes of south India began to wear a greater quantity and finer types of clothing from the turn of the century.

In handloom cloth, especially silk, long-distance trade was not new. But trade almost certainly increased in extent in the second half of the nineteenth century. Imported and mill-made cloth had destroyed many local weaving traditions. Thus it had reduced local transactions of cloth in rural markets or seasonal fairs where weavers and consumers often dealt directly. At the same time, wholesale trade increased. Similarly, long-distance trade in yarn, dyes, silk and gold-thread—all major raw materials for the handloom industry—became more extensive and more organized from the 1870s when these materials began to be imported or made in the mills. Handloom cloth also used these systems. Quite often the wholesale traders in textile raw materials came from weaver backgrounds.

The Supply Side

About 1860, the usual unit of operation in weaving was the household. Inside a weaving household, one would generally see adult men working as weavers, adult women on winding and sizing operations, and children as assistants in both weaving and winding. By and large the family remained the usual unit in handloom weaving during and after the colonial period. But there was a noticeable expansion in handloom factories from the interwar period. These factories employed mainly migrant labour, and were established by persons who had made money in the relatively new trades in cloth, yarn, dyes, zari, or silk. They generally used improved tools and were concentrated in major textile towns of western India.

Capital and labour involved in the handloom industry became increasingly mobile. There was migration from rural regions towards new points of trade, and towards the railways and spinning mills. The most important example is a migration into textile towns in western India such as Sholapur, Malegaon, Bhiwandi, Burhanpur and

Surat. The weavers came from depressed or overpopulated regions like eastern UP and the Hyderabad state.

Many new types of invention in handloom weaving became available for wide usage in the twentieth century, largely due to the efforts of provincial governments in popularizing these instruments. It will not be wrong to say that this was the only significant example of government policy in promotion of traditional and modern small-scale industry. On the other side, the increasing wealth and knowledge of capitalist weavers and increasing certainty of their markets, made them more willing to try out new tools. The traditional loom was set up in a pit dug up in the living room of a weaver's home. The shuttle was thrown by hand across the width of the loom. From this system, there was change towards (a) the fly-shuttle loom, where the shuttle was moved much faster by ropes and pulleys, and (b) a type of loom mounted on wooden frame. The frame loom took up much less space, could weave longer lengths of yarn, and thus, became very popular with the handloom factories. The systems of preparing warp for the loom also changed. The use of a warp beam was popularized, with the effect that longer lengths of thread could now be woven. Warp preparation was previously a side activity of women in weaving localities. This form of collective labour was replaced by the warping factory. Another major example of technical improvement was the synthetic dyestuff.

A final stage in this process of endogenous technological change was the 'powerloom' factory. From the frame loom, the idea of a power-driven frame loom was a small step. Power-driven looms were constantly being discarded at scrap rates by the mills. So buying such a loom and reconditioning it to fit the weaver's factory shed was not expensive. Relatively well-off weavers started to replace handlooms by power-driven looms in products where such a switch was possible. The first such looms in India appeared in handloom towns about 1900 and were run with fuel oil. They spread much faster from the 1930s when many such towns received electricity. These looms, of course, were run with power. By 1940, there were about 15,000 such looms, some in cotton, and some in silk and rayon. These had been started by persons of handloom background. The ground had thus been prepared for what was to become in the next few decades India's largest industry.

Through these changes and through the handloom factory, weaving and processing separated out as tasks, and thus specialization and division of labour increased in comparison to the household.

Stages of Development

The period 1800–60 saw a net decline in textile employment. The export market for cloth began to wane from about 1800. Decline in cotton spinning began from the second quarter of the nineteenth century. It was speeded up only after the railways connected the ports with the interior, that is, the 1860s and the 1870s. The competitive decline of handloom weaving probably followed similar dynamics.

In the period 1860–1900, the railways intensified competition for handloom cloth, and the two famines of the Deccan plateau caused great disruptions for industry. As against this, there were factors at work that clearly favoured the weaver. Commercialization of agriculture improved purchasing power and extended trade in cash crop regions. Better demand was favourable for both handloom and mill-made cloth, and recreated and sustained trade networks. Spinning mills started coming up in cotton growing regions. The towns and regions where handlooms would later concentrate were beginning to acquire their comparative advantage in textiles. Western India and Tamil Nadu were most important from this perspective. The last 30–40 years of the nineteenth century were thus characterized by changes in consumption, trade systems and commercialization of handloom cloth.

The First World War, by creating an acute shortage of yarn, was a major disruption for the weaving industry. However, the interwar period was again one of growth. More importantly, this was also the period when most types of changes in organization and technology occurred. Migration into textile towns, which had seemingly begun in a trickle from as early as the mid-nineteenth century, had by the 1920s increased in scale. The powerloom factory began to spread towards the end of the interwar period.

## Leather

Tanning of hides and skins became a major export item in the late nineteenth century. From the 1870s down to the Great Depression, it remained a major export. Thereafter, the export of tanned hides and skins fell, but increasingly, tanned hides were being used as inputs by local leather manufactures, and the export of such manufactures began to increase. Today, leather is one of South Asia's most important manufactured exports. Much of the industry is built up on a foundation of skills, expertise, and capital accumulated during the colonial period.

Tanning was originally a rural craft practised under conditions of extreme servitude. It was mainly an occupation of groups of people who were part-time agricultural labourers. They were very low in the caste hierarchy, and had little bargaining power in dealing with their main customers, the peasants. This description applies with some variations to the main tanning caste of north India, the Chamars, which was also the most numerous caste in north India. In most places hides were bartered for grain. But the terms of the barter were adverse for the hide suppliers. The grain-share of the leather artisans was much smaller than their share in population. The usual organization in rural tanning was either a single household, or a kind of collective labour not ordinarily seen in other crafts. The tanning locality was set a little apart from the main village where the village was a large one. In this locality, men, women and children worked together in jointly owned pits.

The export market concentrated hide trade in Kanpur, Madras, Bombay and Calcutta. And the superior quality demanded by foreign consumers of Indian hides encouraged the establishment of factories in these cities owned by hide merchants. These developments first of all weakened the rural barter system. For anyone who had access to hides now wanted to sell it to an exporter. It also weakened servitude by encouraging leather artisans to migrate to the cities in large numbers. They were re-employed as factory labourers in the merchant-owned urban tanyard. In the course of this change, flaying, tanning and leather-manufacture—which were often performed by the same person formerly—separated out. Division of labour and specialization increased thereby. The old customs did not completely vanish, but often persisted in the tannery in the form of direct or indirect hierarchy between workers and supervisors, and could permit poor working conditions inside the factory. But the factory was a substantially newer and a freer system of work.

## Woollen Carpets, Engraved Brass-ware, Shawls

In north Indian towns patronage of pre-British local rulers had led to the growth of a number of highly skilled crafts. This was so especially in the heart of the former Mughal empire, in towns such as Delhi, Agra, Amritsar, Lahore, Multan, Srinagar, Lucknow, Moradabad, Farrukhabad, Benares, and others. The most important among the skilled crafts were woollen carpets, engraved brass-ware, wood carving, ivory carving, jewellery, decorated pottery, shawls, etc. These were urban crafts, and had participated in long-distance trade even before the nineteenth century. But, by and large, the reason for which they existed was the consumption of the rich persons of these towns. In some cases they were made inside factories owned by these powerful customers.

In the colonial period, many of these rich customers became impoverished. But at the same time, these products began to be exported as well as traded over longer distances within India. Woollen carpet is a major example of export, one that survives as an important handicraft export from South Asia. Other examples of shift from local to long-distance trade are Moradabad's decorated brass-ware and Srinagar's shawls. Less important examples are, Benares brocades, Saharanpur wood-carving, Khurja pottery, Lucknow silk-cotton embroidery, Farrukhabad prints, and many others.

One result of commercialization was increasing competition between craft towns. In this competition, many towns that had the industry on a small scale, that were located too far from new trade routes, or that did not produce good quality products disappeared. The industry came to be concentrated in fewer places where most of them can be found today.

Industrial organization did not change very dramatically in the colonial period. These crafts were practised either in households, or more commonly, in workshops where a male master–artisan worked with his apprentices, usually young boys. If in leather and weaving, there was a tendency for factories to grow, in the skilled crafts, the household and the apprenticeship system survived. In these crafts, training on the job was very important. The artisans wanted to preserve skills and limit access to skills to a small trusted group of people. The old institutions served these functions well.

As elsewhere, in these crafts too, new types of merchants appeared and they wanted to take control of production. What emerged was a variety of contractual systems between the households or master–artisans on the one hand, and the merchant on the other. One example is Agra and Amritsar carpets, where European and American carpet traders started factories in the interwar period. In these factories, several master–apprentice teams came and worked. They were not really the owners' employees, but contractors who brought their own work-teams to the factory. Such two-stage three-party contracts —between the merchant and the master, and master and apprentices—were often known as *karkhanadari* in northern India. Given that a clear employment contract did not often exist in these factories, they were not factories in the modern sense.

## Weaving of Wool

Weaving of woollen garments and blankets was largely a rural and nomadic occupation and almost as dispersed as cotton handlooms in the mid-nineteenth century. Wool was produced and largely woven by the shepherds themselves, because both sheep-rearing and domestic labour were relatively cheap. Sheep-rearing was cheap because commons and wastes were plentiful, and because it provided the shepherd with plenty of free time. Arable land was frequently used as pastures for sheep flocks because such a practice improved fertility of the soil. However, the quality of such home-grown wool was rather poor.

From the end of the nineteenth century, formal or informal closures of the commons and wastes reduced the supply of home-grown wool as well as the locally woven blankets and garments. Long-distance trade in both wool and woven products expanded. Sheep-rearing relocated towards areas that could support better breeds and easier grazing conditions. The railways played a role in deciding which regions would specialize in woollen weaving. Thus, Rajputana specialized in wool production, whereas United Provinces and Punjab developed as major weaving centres. At the same time, imported better-quality woollen garments altered tastes and introduced new standards. Consumers increasingly moved away from the coarse rural blankets. They preferred finer products made in new weaving establishments in the cities using traded wool. Competition from urban weaving and depletion of pastures brought about a separation between spinning, weaving and the rearing of sheep. Specialization increased in this way.

The largest of the new establishments were two European factories in Kanpur and Dhariwal. These at first supplied woollens to the army, but gradually catered to urban civilian demand as well. From the start these factories had to receive their raw material not from the neighbourhood but from far away. Similarly, Muzaffarnagar and Bijnor in UP and Panipat and Ludhiana in Punjab developed handloom–powerloom complexes in blanket weaving. The railways enabled these towns to develop as points from which finer blankets were exported towards Bombay and Calcutta. These new towns received great encouragement during the First World War. The Munitions Board began to contract out orders in these cities for blankets and smaller articles. Many cotton weavers in these cities shifted to wool, and the existing woollen manufactures expanded and diversified.

## Utilitarian Crafts: Blacksmiths, Potters, Carpenters

The major occupation of blacksmiths and carpenters in the colonial period was to supply and repair agricultural implements. As a result, carpenters and smiths often belonged in the same caste but different sub-castes. Usually, they were found in close proximity. There is evidence from north India that members of the most important black-smith caste, *Lohar*, cultivated land and performed agricultural labour quite routinely. During the colonial period, a new demand expanded in cutlery, metal tools, machine-parts, and durable consumer goods. Small factories were started to manufacture these items. Towns specializing in such goods expanded their industries. In general, the most important location of such new enterprise was the suburbs of the big cities, where the major demand arose. Many blacksmiths by tradition entered these flourishing factory enterprises. To the extent they became full-time blacksmiths, specialization increased.

The north Indian potters, *Kumhars*, were also known to perform rural labour. They were adversely affected by the growing demand for metal utensils, the rather poor quality of their pottery, and the difficulty of long-distance trade in the average earthenware articles. The vessels of mass consumption were flimsily made, given the force of a custom that frowned upon re-usage of earthenware. The only segment where superior skills could be seen were the objects of art. These were made by specialized town potters. Their industry needed more expensive kilns. Towards the end of the period of study, this sector diversified into ceramic tools and components, which is now one of its major outputs.

A similar movement also characterized the carpenters. The furniture industry as we know it today developed from the colonial period. The very nature of interior decoration and furnishing that urban Indians consider standard today was a product of cultural contact with the British. The industry developed initially by drawing in artisans who were engaged in supplying traditional rural demand. The furniture industry was concentrated in towns and cities that had a large number of people willing to buy new types of furniture. The urban industry was mainly factory-based. Thus, in the course of adapting to a new demand, there were increasing specialization, urban migration, and changes in organization in favour of larger city-based workshops.

## Stages of Development

For industries other than handloom weaving, it is harder to generalize on chronology. The following time-division seems to be largely valid. First, in the prewar period the central process underway was commercialization and long-distance trade. Second, the First World War came as a major break, in some cases negative and in others a positive one. And third, in the interwar period the organizational changes can be most clearly seen to be happening.

### LABOUR IN TRADITIONAL SMALL-SCALE INDUSTRY

## The Basic Tendency: Growth of a Labour Market

As we have seen in the section on employment statistics and the industry studies above, one of the most fundamental long-term tendencies in traditional small-scale industry has been the increasing employment of hired labour, or the growth of a labour market. In this section, this tendency is examined more closely.

## Factory Labour

The tendency was most visible in situations where a rapid growth of factories took place. In this context, the word 'factories' means a shed where a large number of workers gathered. Such sheds were not usually registered officially as factories. Factories in this loose sense grew in traditional small-scale industry in four circumstances. First, they appeared in towns that received a large number of migrants, such as handloom weaving in Sholapur. Second, factories appeared in industries that were relatively less skill-intensive, such as tanning of hides and skins. Third, factories appeared in industries that partially mechanized, two examples being the zari industry in Surat and processing of yarn prior to weaving. Finally, in some skilled crafts of northern India where merchants set up large sheds where master-artisans came with their teams of apprentices to work factories developed. Such sheds, however, did not really employ wage labour in the strict sense. Carpet weaving furnished one example, which we will revisit in a later section.

Migration of artisans is intimately connected with the growth of factory labour. From the last quarter of the nineteenth century, there is record of steady and large-scale migration of artisan groups to industrial towns. Some of them gave up their craft to become general labour. Some entered the mills. Still others only relocated their craft near sources of raw material and market points. Employment was typically generated in factories in these towns.

## Traditional Systems of Work:
## Family Labour and Apprenticeship

In the skilled crafts there was no explicit 'labour market' in existence. Also, in the absence of migration or technological change, wage labour developed to a limited extent. As the skill-intensive industries commercialized, merchants assigned or contracted out work to producers who worked in traditional firms. These firms recruited labour without full-fledged hiring.

This happened in broadly two ways. Firms using mainly family labour employed workers from within the family, and masters hired apprentices. The family–firm and the master–apprenticeship system were the two general pre-factory systems of production that survived the colonial period, and participated in long-distance trade and industrialization. Both these institutions were especially tenacious in the skilled crafts. For here they performed the important tasks of training children in these skills and restricting access to skills. In the relatively unskilled crafts the traditional institution tended to decay more quickly. In both examples of traditional institution, children were employed. But as long as they were employed within the family, within the master–apprenticeship system, or within localized limited hiring, children worked without the existence of an explicit market for the services of child labour.

The family–firm and domestic labour were usual among Hindu artisans, the apprenticeship system among the Muslim artisans. The latter was most clearly visible in the towns of western UP. Generally, master–apprentice systems involve a system by which masters can control the graduation of apprentices into masters, and thus, into potential competitors. There is an important contrast between medieval Europe and India. The former had the standard historical paradigm of apprenticeship where the authority of masters was exercised via near-formal institutions, the guilds. Guild in the sense of a corporate distinct from public authority was almost non-existent in India. What seems to have existed in its place was an ideology of competence. The *ustad*, as masters were generally called, was a powerful term in the north Indian urban craft milieu. The term still retains much of its aura.

The most well-documented example of apprenticeship comes from carpet weaving. Interestingly, this industry was found mainly in large factories owned by carpet merchants in cities like Amritsar, Agra and Srinagar in the interwar period. We have seen that the relationship inside the factory was not an employer–employee relationship, but a putting-out one. The common work-shed may have arisen out of a need for supervision by the merchants.

## Other Systems

There were two major combinations of family labour and master–apprenticeship. The first one can be called domestic–collective work, and the second inter-family apprenticeship.

All over India, women were often found working in collectives inside someone's home or in common spaces inside a village populated by artisans. North Indian embroidery, especially Lucknow chikan, is the most famous example of the former. An informal kind of apprenticeship may have been involved in such work. But we know rather little about that aspect. Warping of thread before it goes into the handloom was done, and continues to be done in some regions, by women and girls in a common area shaded by trees inside the weavers' village. This is an example of the latter type of domestic–collective work.

Secondly, in industries and regions where the mainstay was family labour, children were available for hire in neighbourhood firms. Such hiring necessarily involved boys. It often led to near-formal apprenticeship such as that in carpets. N.G. Ranga wrote about such a system in south Indian silk weaving. His respondents explained apprenticeship system in the same terms as a school, a learning and disciplining institution. The loom was meant to discipline unruly children of one's professional comrades, boys who would otherwise grow into 'disorderly youth and men, predisposed to drunkenness and brawls'.[12]

## Dissolution of Traditional Systems

As we have seen, family labour declined in the long run. The apprenticeship system as described above also became rare after 1947. What were the factors behind their weakening? Six hypotheses can be offered, some of them could be seen at work in the colonial period itself.

(i) As supply of labour increases relative to capital, investment funds become less easily available. Loss of access to capital is a reason why the average family finds it difficult to survive.

[12] N.G. Ranga, *Economics of Handloom*, Taraporevala, Bombay, 1930, p. 110.

(ii) As trade expands and markets integrate, production concentrates in towns that have strong comparative advantage over their competitors. This agglomeration encourages migration, migrants tend to be males rather than families, further encouraging break-up of the family.

(iii) The needs for division of labour and specialization are served less efficiently inside a family.

(iv) Surplus labour available for industrial employment increasingly originates among groups, like small peasants, that did not have prior experience in industry and thus had no prior ties with traditional employment institutions.

(v) With increasing division of labour, craftsmanship has become less important, and with it the family firm or the apprentice system has lost one important reason for their existence, the training function.

By a simple extension, each one of these factors can be applied to explain the decline of the master–apprenticeship system in northern India.

The above was also a result of competition between household and other systems of work relying on wage labour. The sixth reason for the dissolution of the household stemmed from unequal job opportunities of men *vis-à-vis* women. When new opportunities arose for some members of the family, the whole family's occupational profile changed, forcing the other members to adjust as well. Samita Sen's recent research has shown that when men get factory jobs, women previously employed in paid work, tend to withdraw and specialize in domestic duties.[13] A similar process may have been at work inside artisan families, but we know rather little about it. When the family was the producing unit, women performed specific tasks, such as spinning, food-processing, embroidery, etc. as support services. When these began to be replaced by factories, machinery, or male labour, women were rendered unemployed. But that, in turn, must have forced the males of the family to look for more remunerative alternatives.

## Child Labour

The decline of households and old-style apprenticeship suggests that traditional industries in India witnessed a transition from social contract to unregulated labour markets in the context of employing

---

[13] See Ch. 5 ('labour') for a fuller discussion and references.

children. Carpet weaving supplies perhaps the best-known example. The Partition witnessed large-scale migration of carpet *ustads* from India to Pakistan. The old factories were practically destroyed. But the industry did not disappear. In fact, it prospered greatly after the Iranian revolution of 1979. After the revolution, the major source of Persian carpets in western markets became uncertain, and the consumers turned to South Asia for replacement. Labour laws in India made the survival of children in the factories unsustainable, but tolerated it in practice when not too visible. The result was a retreat of carpets into small and rural factories. The major concentration in India came to be the relatively rural complex of Mirzapur–Bhadohi area in eastern UP. The workshops were owned by peasant castes, and they began to recruit employees from one of the most densely populated and impoverished agrarian zones, eastern UP and north Bihar. Child labour was justified by citing the carpet tradition. But, in reality, children were no more employed in carpets as part of a master–apprenticeship system. They were not students or prospective masters, but merely a form of cheap labour. Their young age reflected not studentship, but the extreme vulnerability of the eastern Indian labour in general.

## CAPITAL IN TRADITIONAL SMALL-SCALE INDUSTRY
### Sources of Capital

Small-scale industry in general had little or no contact with the formal banking sector. It had very little contact even with the informal money and capital markets. The main form of working capital finance seems to be trade credit, as it is even today.

Producers and merchants often devised their own systems of informal finance. One such system was the north Indian *baqi*. A worker–apprentice had an account with the master–employer. Wages were added on the credit side and loans or withdrawals on the debit. The account was cleared on certain festive days. Some such implicit banking was more or less universal in the urban crafts. Similar systems developed in dealings between the producers and merchants as well.

There is evidence that it was easier to raise fixed capital loans in certain towns than in others. Surat, a major textile centre, was apparently an example where employers and traders in the zari industry routinely gave loans to their contractors for purchase of machinery. How such practices evolved and why they were customary in certain towns are not clear.

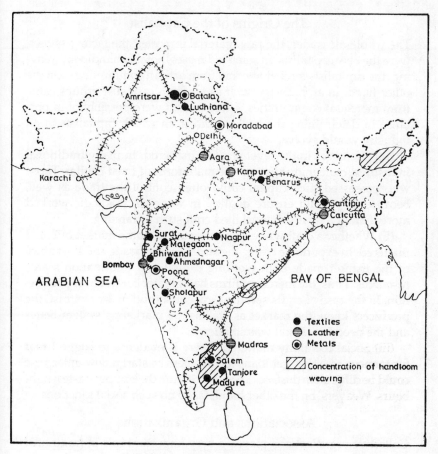

MAP 4.1: SMALL-SCALE INDUSTRY

## The Origins of the Capitalist

The wholesale trader, the raw material importer, the factory owner, were the new capitalists. In some industries, notably handloom weaving, the capitalists tended to come from artisan communities. On the other hand, in an industry such as tanning, capitalist groups came from merchant communities. Three factors were possibly of importance in determining the background from which capitalists in an industry would evolve.

(i) Differences in the level of skills mattered. In many traditional industries, craftsmanship was the main form of fixed capital. Those who possessed such capital could often control the trade as well, because they could ensure quality. In weaving, this logic worked more than in a relatively unskilled craft such as tanning.

(ii) Whether a craft was export-oriented or home market oriented mattered. In exportable crafts, the larger scale of trade and the nature of the market made both working capital and information scarce resources. Thus, the merchant firms had greater control over production. In the case of crafts serving local consumption, by contrast, the producers knew the market as well as the marketing system better and the need for capital was smaller.

(iii) Social hierarchy mattered. There is evidence to suggest that for tanners, to either get loans for business or start a new enterprise could be difficult in the face of resistance from their upper-caste neighbours. Weavers, on the other hand, faced no such social sanctions.

## Associations and Organizations

Collective organizations played a very important role in traditional small-scale industry. This role was multi-faceted. For example, masters needed some system of control over the graduation of their apprentices into masters and thus into potential competitors. Insiders needed to control the entry of outsiders into the craft. Where both employers and workers belonged in the same community, conflicts over industrial relations could be kept in check by strengthening the sense of belonging to a community. Further, any business needs an infrastructure—mainly supply of credit and insurance. Where these markets are undeveloped or beyond the access of a particular business group, these functions tend to be provided by a collective organization. In medieval and late-medieval Europe, the artisans' and merchants' guilds performed some of these functions. In India, a formal association such as the guild was rare. Nevertheless, caste and community associations did develop systematically to take care of some of these needs.

## MODERN SMALL-SCALE INDUSTRY

A big question mark in Indian industrial history concerns modern small-scale industry. The little that we can say by way of a general history of modern small-scale industry can be organized in the following way:

(i) *Period of Growth:* Modern small-scale industry in the sense we use the term was practically non-existent before 1900. But factories with a little machinery and less than a hundred workers each became conspicuous in the 1930s. Their growth, in fact, accelerated in the interwar period.

(ii) *Industry Groups:* Modern small-scale industry concentrated in textiles, food-drink-tobacco, wood, and ceramics. Many were seasonal.

(iii) *Scale:* The broad groups, food-drink-tobacco and wood-stone-glass, accounted for about 20 per cent of factory employment in 1931. Based on this fact and using rough estimates, about one-third of factory employment can be expected to have been located in small factories with some usage of machinery.[14]

(iv) *Origin:* A segment among them, such as the powerloom factories, operated in old products. They represented advanced forms of traditional small-scale industry. Others were of new origin in terms of capital and labour, though not necessarily in terms of markets.

(v) *Location:* The growth of modern small-scale industry dispersed registered factories beyond the main mill towns such as Calcutta or Bombay to clusters located all over India. Generally, they were located near raw material sources. However, some of these clusters were also located close to big cities. An example is tanning in Dharavi, which is now a part of Bombay. Another example is engineering and metal-working firms such as foundries in Howrah, near Calcutta. Why did such industry cluster around big cities? One reason is that the use of machinery depended on the diffusion of cheap electric power. Power was not widely diffused in the 1930s. Further, these new firms usually sold products via marketing networks that were very urbanized. Leather was exported, and therefore, benefited from

[14] This estimate qualifies the earlier equation between 'registered factory' and 'large-scale industry'. The equation is convenient for reading employment data but not very realistic. A large proportion of the 'factories' was small-scale.

being close to a port. Sometimes their markets were concentrated. For example, the engineering firms supplied cast iron tools, machine parts and consumer goods to urban users including the government and the mills. Cotton gins had business transactions largely with the Bombay mills. Finally, nearly every small firm used the railways and very many used the telegraph. In short, while modern small-scale industry was more dispersed than large-scale industry, it retained an urban, sometimes a big-city, bias.

Little research exists on these enterprises except to a limited extent on Madras and modern Kerala. Who set up these factories? Who worked in them? Where were they located? What was their most active period of growth? What markets did they serve? What kind of management did they have? None of these questions have been answered satisfactorily.

Since many of these factories were seasonal, and did not satisfy the official definition of a 'factory' perfectly, they periodically went in and out of factory statistics. Factory statistics is a rather poor guide on the scale and growth of such factories. Nevertheless, it is a good guide on certain qualitative aspects, especially location. Table 4.7 lists the major regional–industrial clusters as seen from factory statistics. Some of the districts that figure in Table 4.7 later grew to become major industrial clusters employing hundreds of thousands of workers each. The industries listed in the first column still form the core activities in some of them. Some others have, however, diversified from these roots.

TABLE 4.7
Regional Clusters of Factories other than Large Mills, c. 1939

| Industry | Districts of major concentration |
| --- | --- |
| Gins and presses | Towns all over Khandesh and Bombay–Deccan,[*] Berar, Broach–Baroda, Bellary, Coimbatore |
| Rice and oil mills | Krishna–Guntur–East Godavari, Coimbatore, Madurai, Tanjore |
| Bidi | Singhbhum, North Arcot, Malabar, Nasik–Ahmadnagar, Guntur |
| Handloom[**] | Sholapur, Malabar |
| Silk mills | Surat, Bangalore |
| Saw mills | Nagpur, Jabalpur, Malabar |
| Tannery | North Arcot, Bombay suburbs |
| Shellac | Manbhum (Purulia) |

| Industry | Districts of major concentration |
|---|---|
| Tiles, kiln | Malabar–Quilon–South Kanara, Barnala–Bhatinda–Patiala |
| Glass | Agra–Firozabad |
| Cashew and coir | Quilon, Alleppey |
| Brass and aluminium | East Godavari |
| Engineering workshops | Krishna, Ludhiana–Jullundur, Kanpur–Lucknow–Meerut, Howrah |

\* Includes the cotton growing districts in the southern part of the Bombay Presidency, notably, Bijapur, Dharwar, Belgaum, Sholapur, and Ahmadnagar.

\*\* Handloom factories were widespread in the urban weaving complexes all over the country, but in Malabar and Sholapur, they represented the principal organization in weaving.

Source: Reproduced from T. Roy, 'The Pattern of Industrial Growth in Interwar India', *Journal of Indian School of Political Economy*, 6(3), July–September, 1994.

In major regional and agrarian histories, the growth of modern small-scale industry in agriculturally developed areas has been touched upon briefly. Examples are, canal colonies in the Punjab, coastal Andhra, Upper Doab, Tamil Nadu, and the sugarcane belt on the Nira canal system in Bombay.[15]

C.J. Baker's work in particular is important because it suggests two hypotheses on this growth, which may have general validity. First, classes allied with land and having investible surplus moved into industry in some regions. They did so due to a combination of factors. One was agricultural commercialization in the last quarter of the nineteenth century. In Punjab, coastal Andhra, Tamil Nadu, Nira valley, and Khandesh, prosperity based on rice, wheat, sugarcane and cotton induced many farmers to set up cotton gins, sugar mills, rice and oil mills. The other factor was a fall in relative return on land from the interwar period, as agriculture became less profitable than before.

In another variation of the relative-returns view, the accent falls on finance capital. As elsewhere in the world, the depression of the 1930s brought on a crisis of inadequate liquidity, as real debt volumes increased and incomes fell. With the crash of agricultural prices land lost its worth as collateral. This forced liquidation of gold and silver assets, and relocation of capital from rural to urban sectors. Via

[15] See the brief references to industry in the works of Imran Ali, A. Satyanarayana, Ian Stone, and D.W. Attwood, cited in the Ch. 3 readings list; and the works of C.J. Baker and H. Yanagisawa cited in the readings list of this chapter.

banking, some of this rural capital moved into industry. Both these hypotheses are conjectural. But they are supported by the fact that the major expansion in small factories, at least in Tamil Nadu, occurred in the 1930s and the 1940s.

In a recent criticism of these hypotheses, Haruka Yanagisawa has pointed out that the growth of such factories in Tamil Nadu began about 1910s, well before agricultural prices became depressed and the financial relocation effect of the Depression could be felt. One major source of the growth of such rural factories was increased demand for their products. For example, the rice mills initially made 'parboiled' rice for export to Southeast Asia. Increasingly, local consumers began to replace the export market. Cheapness and better quality of the parboiled rice, and consumption of rice by people who formerly ate coarser foodgrains were the major reasons. A similar set of circumstances encouraged a growth in factories engaged in groundnut oil extraction and beedi making.

## CONCLUSION

Commercialization transformed traditional small-scale industry and created modern small-scale industry in colonial India. A key feature of the transition was changes in industrial organization, especially increasing use of wage labour in place of family labour. The labour market emerged slowly, out of two traditional institutions, the family and the master–apprenticeship system. The decay in these institutions in the long run owes to many factors which include migration, new entry in capital and labour, and reduced role for craftsmanship. Altered circumstances in which children and possibly women are employed in small-scale industry can be understood better in terms of this framework of a shift from traditional institutions to markets for casual labour.

The experience of traditional small-scale industry in colonial India can be compared with eighteenth century Europe and twentieth century East Asia. In all the three, a form of industrialization occurred that was based on utilizing labour more productively, rather than on replacing labour by machinery. The underlying process was commercialization and modernization of traditional small-scale industry. Such a process resulted in capital accumulation on a small scale, though not necessarily accompanied by rapid increases in average incomes. In the course of this transition, there was a persistence of traditional organizations in the short run. But underneath that stability, a movement towards casual labour market slowly began. In one respect, colonial India was different from the other cases. In Europe, large-scale industry had indirect roots in small-scale industry. In India the two developed side by side and were very different from each other.

In studies on Indian industrialization, there has been an implicit bias on large-scale industry. At first sight, such accent may seem unjustified by the latter's small share in industrial employment. However, large-scale industry did play a transformative role far exceeding what its share in employment might suggest. It is to this role that we now turn.

ANNOTATED READINGS

## De-industrialization and Commercialization

For statements—classic and modern—of de-industrialization and the origins of underdevelopment, see the discussion in Bipan Chandra, *The Rise and Growth of Economic Nationalism in India*, People's Publishing House, New Delhi, 1966, Chs II and III, and Amiya Kumar Bagchi, 'De-industrialization in India in the Nineteenth Century: Some Theoretical Implications', *Journal of Development Studies*, 12(2), 1976.

On empirical tests of de-industrialization see Bagchi, 'Deindustrialization in India'; M.J. Twomey, 'Employment in Nineteenth Century Indian Textiles', *Explorations in Economic History*, 20(3), 1983; Marika Vicziany, 'The De-industrialization of India in the Nineteenth Century: A Methodological Critique of Amiya Kumar Bagchi', *IESHR*, 26(2), 1979.

For work on occupational structure touching on de-industrialization, see '"De-industrialization" in India, 1881–1931', in Daniel and Alice Thorner, *Land and Labour in India*, Asia Publishing House, New York, 1962; Alice Thorner, 'The Secular Trend in the Indian Economy, 1881–1951', *Economic Weekly*, 14(28–30), special number, 1962; J. Krishnamurty, 'Occupational Structure', in *CEHI 2*.

The 'commercialization' perspective is illustrated in T. Roy, *Traditional Industry in the Economy of Colonial India*, Cambridge, 1999, Ch. 2.

## Handloom Weaving

Brief descriptions can be found in references to industry in the four essays of *CEHI 2*, on regional economies. These are T. Kessinger on north India, S. Bhattacharya and B. Chaudhuri, both on eastern India, V.D. Divekar on western India, and Dharma Kumar on south India.

For a discussion of statistical estimates of size and growth of the industry, see Tirthankar Roy, *Artisans and Industrialization: Indian Weaving in the Twentieth Century*, Oxford University Press, Delhi, 1993, Chs 2, 3.

On demand, market, consumption, see Roy, *Artisans and Industrialization*, Ch. 4, Haruka Yanagisawa, 'The Handloom Industry and its Market Structure: The Case of the Madras Presidency in the First Half of the Twentieth Century', *IESHR*, 30 (1), 1993. On industrial organization, see Douglas Haynes, 'The Logic of the Artisan Firm in a Capitalist Economy: Handloom Weavers and Technological Change in Western India, 1880–1947', in Burton Stein and Sanjay Subrahmanyam (eds.), *Institutions and Economic Change in South Asia*, Oxford University Press, Delhi, 1996. For regional studies—Sumit Guha, 'The Handloom Industry of Central India: 1825–1950', *IESHR*, 26(3), 1989; Peter Harnetty, 'De-industrialization Revisited: The Handloom Weavers of the Central Provinces of India, c. 1800–1947', *MAS*, 25(3), 1991; Konrad Specker, 'Madras Handlooms in the Nineteenth Century', *IESHR*, 36(2), 1989. Impact of events—J.G. Borpujari, 'Indian Cottons and the Cotton Famine, 1860–65', *IESHR*, 10(1), 1973; Douglas Haynes, 'Urban Weavers and Rural Famines in Western India, 1870–1900', mimeo, 1996.

## Other Industries

Brief descriptions can be found in references to industry in the four essays of *CEHI 2*, on regional economies (cited above). Roy, *Traditional Industry*; J. Krishnamurty, 'De-industrialisation in Gangetic Bihar in the Nineteenth Century: Another Look at the Evidence', *IESHR*, 22(4), 1985; D.R. Gadgil, *Industrial Evolution in India in the Recent Times*, Oxford University Press, Delhi, 1971.

## Capital and Labour

Douglas Haynes and Tirthankar Roy, 'Conceiving Mobility: Weavers' Migrations in Precolonial and Colonial India', in *IESHR*, 36(1), 1999; Tirthankar Roy, 'Capitalism and Community: A Study of the Madurai Sourashtras', *IESHR*, 34(4), 1997; Haynes, 'Weavers' Capital and the Origins of the Powerlooms: Technological Transformation and Structural Change among Handloom Producers in Western India, 1920–1950', *Past and Present*, forthcoming; Roy, *Traditional Industry*, Ch. 2.

# Modern Small-scale Industry

C.J. Baker, *An Indian Rural Economy: The Tamilnad Countryside*, Oxford University Press, Delhi, 1984; Haruka Yanagisawa, 'The Growth of Rural Industries in Tamil Nadu and their Domestic Markets, 1900–1950', in T. Mizushima and H. Yanagisawa (eds), *History and Society in South India*, Tokyo University of Foreign Studies, Tokyo, 1996; K.P. Kannan, *Of Rural Proletarian Struggles: Mobilization and Organization of Rural Workers in South-west India*, Oxford University Press, Delhi, 1988, pp. 55–69. On the origins of the powerloom weaving industry, see Haynes, 'Weavers' Capital', and Tirthankar Roy, 'Development or Distortion? Powerlooms in India 1950–1997', *EPW*, 33(16), 1998.

# 5

# Large-scale Industry

In Chapter 4, 'large-scale industry' was defined by three basic characteristics—technology, organization, and government regulation, that is, use of machinery, large factories, and the imposition of the Factories Act. Large-scale industry in India was a fairly recent development; a product of India's economic contact with Britain. In cotton and jute, the idea of a mill, the technical knowledge, the equipment, a portion of the capital, and some of the engineers first came from Britain. Higher capital-intensity and adherence to the British precedence led to ways of organization that did not exist before. The very notion of laws regulating factory work or company management was new.

Large-scale industry employed a rather small proportion of the industrial workforce, but its contribution to income was quite large. The qualitative contribution of large-scale industry to urbanization also far exceeded its small share in employment. Large-scale industry gave rise to cities such as Calcutta or Bombay. It shaped urban labour markets. It encouraged the growth of infrastructure, such as railways, ports, laws, banks, and technical schools. It familiarized a part of the urban population with machinery, automation, and new management systems. It was also a significant force behind the modernization of services, especially trade and finance. As in industry, the general picture in the services was that of a small formal sector emerging from a vast backdrop of informal and traditional enterprise. As in industry, the overall socio-economic impact of the modern service sector was substantial when compared to its low scale of operations.

The present chapter will deal with various aspects of large-scale industry in terms of production, sources and constraints on growth, and socio-economic significance. The chapter is divided into eight sections: statistical outline, phases in the growth of large-scale industry, major forms of large-scale industry, labour, finance, entrepreneurship, management, and large-scale industry in the princely states. In a concluding section, some general issues will be discussed.

## STATISTICAL PROFILE

Taking the officially registered factory as the definition of large-scale industry, such industry accounted for about 5 per cent of industrial employment in British India at 1891. This percentage increased to about 11 by 1938. The share of large-scale industry in real income generated by industry increased from about 15 per cent in 1900 to 45 per cent in 1947. The princely states together had a smaller size of factory employment. From that small base, employment increased quite rapidly between 1921 and 1938 (see Table 5.1). Including the Indian states, the share of large-scale industry in total industrial employment at 1938 was about 12–13 per cent.

### TABLE 5.1
Employment in Factories, 1891–1938

|      | Total employed in British India | Percentage employed in British India | | | Total employment for the Indian States |
|------|------|------|------|------|------|
|      |      | Men | Women | Children | |
| 1891 | 316,815 | 80.2 | 13.8 | 6.0 | n.a. |
| 1901 | 468,956 | 79.5 | 14.6 | 5.9 | n.a. |
| 1921 | 1,266,395 | 79.8 | 14.8 | 5.4 | 129,968 |
| 1938 | 1,737,755 | 85.3 | 14.1 | 0.6 | 299,003 |

*Source: Statistical Abstracts for British India, Calcutta, various years for Tables 5.1–5.4.*

We have seen that women's participation in industrial work declined (see Chapter 4) significantly between the censuses. Inside both the cotton and the jute mills, women's participation declined in the first half of the twentieth century. However, there was no change in women's participation in total factory employment (see Table 5.1). This possibly suggests that in smaller-sized factories there was an increase in women's participation. If so, the trend needs to be studied further. The decline in women's role in the larger factories has been studied in recent works on industrial labour. The theme will be taken up in this chapter in the section on labour.

The most dramatic change in the age–sex composition of factory labour was a sharp fall in employment of children, the fall occurred mainly over 1928–36 due to the implementation of some provisions of the Factories Act. The Royal Commission on Labour in India (1931) had a singular impact on child labour in factories. Children were replaced by adult men.

Factory employment in the colonial period was overwhelmingly dominated by the textile industry (see Table 5.2). Textiles consisted of cotton and jute spinning and weaving mills, cotton gins and jute presses that were primarily seasonal activities, and a few isolated large firms in wool and silk spinning and weaving. Next in importance was food processing—this included mainly smaller firms like rice mills, oil mills, sugar refining, and tobacco products. Chemicals, metals and machinery represented capital and intermediate goods. Their share in employment was small. Metals and machinery, was a very heterogeneous group that consisted of firms ranging from small repair shops to organizations like Tata Steel.

TABLE 5.2
Industrial Composition, 1921–81

*(percentages)*

| Industries | Share in factory employment | | | | Share in total industrial employment | | | |
|---|---|---|---|---|---|---|---|---|
| | 1921 | 1931 | 1961 | 1981 | 1921 | 1931 | 1961 | 1981 |
| Textiles | 41.6 | 44.8 | 30.8 | 16.2 | 25.7 | 26.2 | 32.7 | 29.6 |
| Food, drink, tobacco | 7.2 | 12.5 | 18.9 | 16.7 | 10.5 | 9.4 | 15.4 | 16.2 |
| Hides and skins | 0.9 | 0.5 | 0.5 | 0.8 | 2.0 | 2.0 | 4.0 | 1.9 |
| Metals and machinery | 4.6 | 3.0 | 9.5 | 12.6 | 11.4 | 11.1 | 13.5 | 9.9 |
| Chemicals | 2.6 | 3.3 | 3.7 | 6.5 | 3.7 | 3.9 | 1.6 | 3.0 |
| Wood, stone, glass | 7.1 | 3.5 | 1.3 | 2.2 | 10.1 | 10.4 | 10.9 | 9.5 |
| Total | 100.0 | 100.0 | 100.0 | 100.0 | 100.0 | 100.0 | 100.0 | 100.0 |

This pattern, interestingly, changed after 1947. The textile industry increasingly shifted out of large factories, but its overall dominance continued. Like textiles, wood, stone and glass is a group that seems to have shifted out of large-scale to small-scale industry. Machinery and chemicals, on the other hand, have risen significantly in importance within factory employment.

Where was large-scale industry located? Table 5.3 reveals a feature already outlined in Chapter 4. This is the exceptionally high concentration of factory employment in two provinces, Bombay and Bengal. These provinces did not have large shares in industrial employment as a whole. Nor was industry quantitatively very important in their local economies. Yet, they dominated large-scale industry in India. The attraction of Bombay and Calcutta derived from a number of factors. They were major ports and centres of transportation. Both cities had developed as points of export trade in the early nineteenth century. Calcutta had a concentration of European settlement. The two provinces, moreover, had conditions suitable for cotton and jute production. In the interwar period, the cotton industry had spread out and new industries had expanded. These tendencies reduced the share of these two provinces in factory employment. In general, the share of factory in industrial employment rose in the colonial period, from about 5 per cent in 1911 to about 10 in 1931. In Bombay and Bengal, this rise in the share of large-scale industry was more rapid than it was elsewhere.

TABLE 5.3
Location of Large-scale Industry, 1911–31

|  | Percentage share of the province/state in factory employment | | Percentage share of factory in industrial employment for each province/state | |
|---|---|---|---|---|
|  | 1911 | 1931 | 1911 | 1931 |
| Madras | 7.5 | 8.2 | 2.4 | 5.3 |
| Bombay | 29.9 | 23.9 | 21.6 | 36.5 |
| Bengal | 36.8 | 27.9 | 19.2 | 32.8 |
| United Provinces | 6.3 | 6.3 | 1.8 | 3.3 |
| Punjab | 3.8 | 2.8 | 1.9 | 2.7 |
| Bihar and Orissa | 2.7 | 4.0 | 1.8 | 4.8 |
| Central Provinces and Berar | 5.4 | 3.8 | 5.9 | 8.3 |
| Hyderabad | n.a. | 1.9 | n.a. | 3.8 |
| Mysore | n.a. | 1.5 | n.a. | 8.3 |
| Total | 100.0 | 100.0 | 5.0 | 10.4 |

Did infrastructure or business culture differ significantly enough between British India and the princely states to tell on the presence of large-scale industry? The data on the states are not very detailed. But, as far as we can gather, share of the two kinds of territories in industrial employment did not change very much, and the two were quite comparable by most indices except one (see Table 5.4). British India had a higher share of factory employment in industrial employment as a whole. But this is an effect of Bombay and Bengal being part of British India. The rest of British India and the princely states were very similar in the structure of industrial employment.

TABLE 5.4
Industrial Employment, 1911–31:
Comparison of British India and the Indian States

|  | Percentage share in industrial employment | | Percentage share in total employment | | Percentage share of industry in total employment | | Percentage share of factory in industrial employment | |
|---|---|---|---|---|---|---|---|---|
|  | 1911 | 1931 | 1911 | 1931 | 1911 | 1931 | 1921 | 1931 |
| British India | 75.5 | 77.1 | 75.5 | 75.8 | 11.5 | 10.4 | 12.1 | 10.8 |
| Indian States | 24.5 | 22.9 | 24.5 | 24.2 | 12.6 | 10.3 | 3.3 | 4.7 |
| Total | 100.0 | 100.0 | 100.0 | 100.0 | 11.8 | 10.4 | 9.9 | 9.3 |

Note: Factory data for states is not available for 1911 or earlier.

## STAGES OF INDUSTRIALIZATION

Growth of large-scale industry in India went through several stages. From the point of view of historians, the issues are different for each stage. A convenient time division is the following: (a) 1850s to 1914 or the prewar period, (b) the First World War and consequent shifts in policy, (c) 1920 to 1939 or the interwar period, with special reference to the Great Depression of 1929–30, and (d) the Second World War.

## The Pre-war Period

Historians of the nineteenth century often ask two questions. Where did the capital invested in large-scale industry come from? Why did such investments begin from the middle of the century? The capital came partly from foreign investment and partly from internal accumulation in the wake of the first wave of commercialization in India. The growth of India's trade with China after the East India Company's monopoly in India–China trade ended (1834–5) was a significant episode. Bombay and Calcutta benefited from the exceptional growth of foreign trade in the next twenty years that followed. These were the cities where large-scale industry first appeared— capitalizing on trading profits and the enterprise of the communities which dominated foreign trade.

A simple answer to the second question should list the following facilitating events that occurred in the middle of the nineteenth century. In a general way, the nineteenth century saw the rise of large-scale industry the world over, and especially in parts of Europe and North America. India was a resource-rich colony of the 'first industrial nation', and was naturally a potential candidate for industrialization by 1850. Given Britain's own stage of industrial maturity, the 1850s was a decade when the prevailing mood was to look for profitable business opportunities abroad. Steam ships and telegraph brought the continents much closer than before. The Suez Canal was at the crest of this infrastructural leap. A key episode in the transition from trade to industry was the American Civil War (1865) which cut off supplies of American cotton to Britain's textile industry. Indian cotton was suddenly in great demand. The resultant boom in cotton prices created great profits. A part of these profits wiped out in a subsequent crash. But after a few years of lull, trading profits returned to the constructions of cotton mills in western India. An obsession for investing in tea developed about the same time in Calcutta and a rush for gold gripped Madras. These too ended in a crash that forced many small companies to close shop. But all three booms had left a permanent imprint on the Indian industrial scenario. The companies that had been formed quickly had stimulated the local stock exchanges and popularized the notion of joint-stock companies. Partly as a cause and partly as an effect of these first steps into large-scale industry, company laws were being legislated about this time. Finally, depreciation of the rupee in the second half of the century (see Chapter 7) encouraged exports.

By far the most important large-scale industries in this period were cotton and jute spinning and weaving. One was based in Bombay and Ahmedabad, and the other in Calcutta. The history of these cities, therefore, dominates any discussion of large-scale industry in the prewar period. And conversely, prewar industrialization tells us a great deal about the history of these cities. Another important theme of this period is the growth of infrastructure and institutions. To these themes we shall return.

## First World War

The war diverted the resources of the belligerent nations into producing war supplies. India was not directly at war, but Britain was—this had two contradictory effects. On the one hand, given the worldwide shortage demand for goods made in India greatly increased. But on the other, machinery, raw materials, spares or chemicals earlier imported by Indian industry either from Britain or from her enemy country Germany, stopped. Thus, while there was excess demand for Indian goods, there were also constraints on their supply. Some industries encouraged from this situation as net gainers while others lost on the whole. An example of industries that were badly affected by supply constraints is handloom weaving, which relied on English yarn. Examples of industries that gained are steel, jute and cotton mills. By the third or fourth year of the war, there was widespread shortage-induced inflation which benefited the existing producers. The supply constraints eased somewhat as the war progressed.

By the end of the war, industrial production had expanded, and conditions were ripe for starting new industries and making new types of products in the old ones. The war, together with growing nationalist discontent, had also induced a change in government policy. Until the war, the government followed a policy of non-intervention in the promotion of industries. Thus, purchase of industrial goods for defence, railways or administrative use was earlier heavily dependent on Britain. This dependence created sudden shortages of these goods in India during the war. It also justified a criticism that the government was indifferent even hostile to Indian entrepreneurship. Such a view was being voiced every year since 1905 in a forum called the Indian Industrial Conference.

After the war, the government began to look towards local sources and talked about promoting such sources. Three events that represent this shift in attitude are the establishment of the Indian Munitions Board (1918), the Indian Industrial Commission (1916–8), and the Indian Fiscal Commission (1921–2). The Fiscal Commission sanctioned the use of protective tariffs for industrial promotion, provided the protected industry had 'natural advantages' that made it capable of eventually competing with foreign goods without protection. Between 1923 and 1939, 51 cases were appraised for suitability of demand for protective tariffs. In 11 of these cases, tariffs were raised.

These included salt, heavy chemicals, magnesium chloride, sericulture, plywood chests, gold thread, iron and steel, cotton textiles, sugar, paper and paper pulp, and matches. The Industrial Commission stressed the government's responsibility in matters of technical and scientific advancement. It listed the industries that the government could promote directly or indirectly. These possibilities were partly realized in the two decades that followed, though the financial capacity of the government was a severe constraint on what it could do directly in the matter of industrial promotion. After 1921, the main responsibility of industrial development passed to the ministers in the provinces, and the provinces were even more financially constrained.

## The Interwar Period

The first half of the 1920s and the second half of the 1930s were relatively good for industry and trade worldwide. In India, large-scale industry expanded and diversified in this period. Industries such as sugar, iron and steel, cement, matches, paper, and wool, were established and expanded. In this process of growth and diversification, tariff protection to some industries was crucial. Much of this expansion occurred in cities other than Bombay or Calcutta (where labour movement had become stronger). Also, infrastructural facilities such as railways and electricity had extended into the interior making it possible for industries to be located close to points of supply of raw material. New factories thus came up around Coimbatore, Kanpur, Madras, Jamshedpur, etc.

Within older industries such as cotton and jute mills, the interwar period saw both the start of new firms in new locations and crises in old firms. Competition within textiles and steel was keener in this period than ever before. In textiles, competition came not only from Japan but also from many new mills that were started in small towns away from Bombay. In steel, worldwide capacity building expanded much faster than new demand. In jute, Indian capacity grew faster than world demand. The result in each case was low or fluctuating profits combined with adverse factors specific to these industries. The demand for tariff protection arose largely from this crisis. But tariffs alone could not solve the problem. Some of the industries had to make innovations in technology and management.

Between 1925 and 1935 economies the world over were in various stages of mild or deep depression. Capacity in some industries worldwide had expanded too fast. This included steel, paper, sugar and cement. Competition from Japan was keen across all textiles. Indian industry faced both cheap imports and falling world prices. The Indian nationalists convincingly argued that the rupee was an overvalued currency in these years, making competitive imports cheaper than they ought to have been. The competition from Japanese textiles was especially keen, and was possibly aided by the then prevailing exchange rate policy. An overvalued exchange, however, is likely to have had contradictory effects. If rupee was indeed overvalued it made import of machinery that much cheaper and may have been a stimulus for investment. The Great Depression (1929–30) hurt industries that were mainly selling abroad, such as jute. The state of other key Indian industries hit by excess capacity in the world was alleviated to an extent by tariff protection in the 1920s.

If we look not at specific industries but at industry overall, the Depression did not have a very deep impact. While the Depression was severe in the USA and parts of Europe, its effect on Indian industry was much less serious. Real income from industry hardly changed in the depression years. Trends in wages in these years suggest that money wages in India were quite flexible. Thus, one of the reasons behind the severity of the Depression and one around which Keynes built his theory of short-term fluctuations, downward rigidity of money wages, did not hold good for Indian industry by and large. The Depression did have a deep impact on financial markets in India. As prices fell, debtors experienced an increased real burden of debt. There was a great deal of transfer of mortgaged assets and sale of assets that would otherwise not have come to the market. In a general way, banking seems to have benefited from such transfers making credit flows to large-scale industry easier.

## Second World War

Qualitatively, the effects of the Second World War were very similar to those of the first. Again, excess demand and supply constraints developed and consequently, prices soared. But Indian industry in 1939 was much more diversified and better equipped to further diversify than in 1914. Thus, real growth of industrial incomes was greater and diversification into new industry wider during the Second World War. However, in one sense the Second World War was far more stressful—it led to a massive scarcity of food, the main 'wage good', and was thus a bad time for the labourer and labour-intensive occupations. The plantation sector suffered because of this and possibly industry did too to a lesser extent.

Throughout these decades, two conditions faced by large-scale industry were almost constant in their presence. First, large-scale industry continued to depend on imports of capital goods and manufactured inputs such as electrical machinery, transport equipment, heavy and fine chemicals. Second, it continued to depend on foreign technicians. They were paid about twice the salary of an Indian available for the same job. This dependence reduced over time at different rates across the major industries. Significant change came only after independence with protection for the capital goods industry, and large government funding of higher and technical education.

## MAJOR INDUSTRIES
### Cotton Mills

The first steam-powered factory making cotton yarn appeared near Calcutta around 1817 or 1818. This venture, like a few others in western and southern India, was set up by an European. But these firms did not succeed. In 1854, a Parsi merchant of Bombay, C.N. Davar, started the first successful cotton mill. The idea attracted other merchants of Bombay, many of them already engaged in cotton and textile trade. By 1865, there were 10 mills, the majority in Bombay. In the next few years, a boom and a crash shook up cotton export from western India. When the dust settled, a furious expansion of the mill industry began. At 1880, there were 58 mills with an employment of about 40,000. With a few exceptions, these mills and nearly 80 per cent of the workers in them were located in Bombay and Ahmedabad. By 1914, the number of mills had risen to 271 with an average daily employment of about 260,000. The two cities now contributed only about 60 per cent of the employment.

Between 1870 and 1914, cotton mills were mainly selling yarn to handloom weavers in India and China. In both these markets, they competed successfully with British yarn in the coarser varieties. But they found it difficult to compete in yarn of the finer varieties. Indian mill-made yarn thus hastened a process that had begun since the 1820s, the gradual destruction of hand-spun yarn in cotton. Thus, the main source of the explosive growth of Indian mill industry was not an expansion in the total market. The mills grew by replacing coarser British yarn, and hand-spun yarn, which was again, mainly coarse. Later in this period the tables turned on the Indian mills with the capture of the Chinese market by Japanese mills.

Towards the end of the prewar period, the mill industry spread out wider. Any small town that had cotton trade, a railway connection, and preferably a handloom industry, became an attractive location for a spinning mill. Such a town would have a ready market, cheaper raw material, and wages that were lower than those in Bombay. For these reasons, Kanpur, Madurai, Coimbatore, Sholapur, Nagpur developed as important mill centres. None, however grew into mill towns quite as large as the two pioneers. These 'up-country' mills not only paid lower wages than in Bombay or Ahmedabad, they could down size wages if necessary more easily than mills established in the older towns.

The loss of the China market and keener competition at home forced the mills of Bombay to make important changes in the interwar period. First, they started weaving their own yarn much more than before—the substitution of British cloth by Indian cloth, therefore, accelerated. Second, they tried to spin and weave finer yarn. Third, they tried to save on labour costs. This last change intensified industrial unrest. For some mills that were already poorly managed, these changes were not enough to bail them out. Thus, the interwar period saw unemployment, labour unrest, technical and managerial reorganization, demand for tariffs, intensification of nationalist sentiments among millowners, and the beginnings of bankruptcy in many of Bombay's cotton mills.

## Jute Mills

Jute is a natural fibre grown mainly in southern West Bengal and Bangladesh. It is used as raw material for sacking cloth. The demand for sacks increased enormously in the nineteenth century in direct proportion to the volume of international trade. Until the 1870s, Bengal raw jute was processed into sacking outside India, mainly in Dundee in Britain, and somewhat later in Germany. But already by then, mechanized jute spinning and weaving had started near Calcutta. George Acland's mill of 1855 was the pioneer. In a short while, the Indian industry grew to hold a virtual monopoly in the world. As in cotton mills, the first fifteen years of the industry faced unstable conditions and slow growth. After 1870 expansion was rapid. Between 1869 and 1913, number of mills increased from 5 to 64, and employment from possibly about 5000–10,000 to about 215,000. Until the First World War, the industry was entirely owned and managed by Europeans, which made Calcutta's business environment quite different from Bombay's.

The industry ran into rough weather in the interwar period. The world demand for sacking was growing less rapidly than in the pre-war period or during the war. Internally, the industry was trying, unsuccessfully, to set up a cartel. India being a virtual monopoly, the jute industry could ask for high prices in periods of excess demand and get away with it. But such tactics attracted new firms that hoped to gain more market by not joining the cartel. Old firms often tried to devise rules to restrict their output, but very often failed to gain cooperation. The result was excess production, unstable profits, and increased competition. The situation in jute was not unique. Many industries worldwide at that time were trying to deal with depressed markets by forming cartels and cutting production rather than by becoming more efficient producers and cutting costs. Where the industry consisted of many types of firms, old and new, small and large, such attempts tended to break down because of internal conflicts. Those who stayed out of the cartel, in that case, grew faster than those who stayed in. In jute, the former consisted of small Indian entrepreneurs whereas the older firms represented the more established and organized British capitalists. Eventually, the failure of jute cartel invited the Government of Bengal to impose production limits. But, as in Bombay, a large part of the industry was doomed already for having delayed technical improvements.

## Other Industries

Besides cotton and jute mills, the prewar history of large-scale industry in India is a history of a few isolated firms. In the late nineteenth century, two large wool mills were started in Kanpur and Punjab, a match unit started in south India, a large paper mill started near Calcutta, and two leather manufacturing firms were started in Kanpur. These ventures had two things in common—they were all European firms, and they were all dependent on government demand or demand from the European residents in India. Naturally, the demand being so narrow, there was no scope in these industries for more such firms.

The most outstanding industrial achievement of the prewar era was the Tata Iron and Steel Company. It began as a firm in 1907, and started production from 1911. Tata Steel owed its existence to its founder J.N. Tata's persistence and vision. The firm of the Tatas was established in textiles and had a considerable brand name in Bombay. The Tatas were also the largest steel importers into India and knew the trade well enough to be confident of being able to produce steel at lower cost. The establishment of the firm was preceded by almost twenty-five years of exploration and research into the supply of key raw materials in the region where it was finally set up. These raw materials were coal, iron, limestone, manganese and water. Tata Steel, however, shared with the other large factories of this period, their dependence on government demand.

The war gave a great boost to any industry that had a war-related usage and that did not rely heavily on imported raw material. Steel, cotton, paper and jute did exceptionally well, though in steel the government fixed prices during the war. The manufacture of Portland cement had begun. New investments had been planned during the war both in old and in new industries, and these began to take shape after 1920. Tata Steel carried out its first major expansion between 1925 and 1935. Several new firms in cement manufacture were started during 1920–35. The Titagarh paper mill was joined by another large European firm.

All these industries faced falling prices from the late 1920s. They coped with this situation in different ways. In cement, there was amalgamation of smaller firms to create the Associated Cement Companies with better control on prices. The pressure on the government to grant tariff protection became strong. After 1925, steel and paper received protection. In paper, tariffs alone did not help, for India used raw materials such as *sabai* grass or straw that had become relatively costly after Europe switched to the cheaper material, wood pulp. The Indian industry, therefore, had to progressively shift to bamboo pulp. It had to adapt not only in terms of methods of production, but also in location of the factories, which tended to shift near sources of bamboo. Tariff protection was also given to manufacture of refined sugar. This was in response to a worldwide fall in cane prices that threatened to ruin Indian cane-growers unless a local sugar industry grew to use their product. A local industry did grow between 1919 and 1935. But it grew so rapidly that soon there was excess capacity. The older firms in the industry coped with excess capacity in the same way that jute mills coped with their crisis at the same time. That is, they formed cartels and sought government help to protect the cartel from the entry of new firms. They, however, succeeded in this venture to a limited extent.

## LABOUR

In a narrow quantitative sense, labour is a surplus resource in India, and there is no evidence that any industry faced a problem of inadequate supply of labour in the long run. Nevertheless, deeper analysis of the history of labour supply and its attendant problems suggests that just abundance of a resource does not necessarily ensure smooth supply.

Factory labour was a new form of employment in India in the middle of the nineteenth century. Growth of factory labour represents a shift from rural and traditional occupations such as agriculture and the crafts to modern ones such as mechanized industry. Most workers in large-scale industry were immigrants into cities like Bombay or Calcutta. There were changes in the nature of work, workplace, habitats, and lifestyles. Historians of Indian labour have asked what this shift meant to the employers and the workers. Did it improve income and welfare of the workers? How different were these worlds? Before we get to these questions, it is necessary to look at some of the basic facts about factory labour.

All large-scale industry involves a hierarchy of workers on the factory floor. Usually, a distinction can be made between those with formal and/or extensive on-the-job training in technology, and those without such training. The trained workers can, in theory, have complete knowledge of the technological operation of the factory as a whole. That is, they can operate a variety of machines, operate a single machine for a variety of purposes, and repair or replace machinery if necessary. The untrained group is either capable of performing particular mechanical tasks, or general manual labour inside the factory. This distinction is obviously not a watertight compartmentalization in that there are many types of workers whose skills lie in the intermediate category between the two extremes. But by and large, the highest-paid and the lowest-paid workers on the floor can be distinguished in this fashion. The employment contract is also varied between these groups. Till today, skilled workers tend to be permanent employees and unskilled ones consists of a large proportion of casual or temporary workers. Some mobility between these groups is possible. Unskilled labourers could acquire skills and be treated as skilled labour. But in the main, these groups are recruited separately and come from different backgrounds.

Until well into the interwar period, skilled workers in cotton, jute, steel, and other large-scale industries comprised of a significant percentage of foreigners, followed closely by Hindu literate upper castes with high school education. Unskilled workers, on the other hand, came mainly from agrarian and artisanal castes with little or no education. This divide within the labour force is an important feature of

Indian labour, and was not present to the same extent in other industrializing economies.

Most labour histories deal with the relatively unskilled labour, because they were dominant in number and for them the change from past occupations and lifestyles was more dramatic than for the technicians and engineers. There is no clear sign that the recruitment of unskilled labour was a serious problem in any industry. And yet, the mills did use special systems of recruitment in some cases. For example, the cotton mills until the interwar period relied on 'labour contractors' who undertook to gather together a number of workers usually from areas where the contractors had personal connections. They sometimes even managed the workers at the factory floor. The contractor was an important figure in the Bombay cotton mills, where he received commission for his services both from the mills and from the workers whom he gave employment. The contractor's power over the workers increased in times of excess supply of labour and a shortage of work. But, in such times, the mills needed his services less acutely, and could cut him out altogether. Such a situation arose in Bombay in the interwar period. An important factor behind the labour unrest in Bombay during that time was the vulnerable position of the contractor, and his resistance to the mills. In jute, by contrast, this kind of intermediary was much less powerful.

Mill workers tended to come from certain regions—mainly the Konkan, the Deccan, and UP in the case of cotton mills, and north Bihar, eastern UP and Orissa in the case of jute. These streams of migrants fell into the larger pattern of internal migration in colonial India consisting of two main flows. The first went from north to east. The second went from south to west. What were the pull and push factors behind this migration? Why did large-scale industry tend to employ migrants rather than the locals? Lalita Chakravarty suggests that the 'reserve price' of labour was very low in the source regions because of poor agricultural conditions.[1] Local agrarian labour usually earned more that the migrants did in their home regions. She also suggests that the migrants did not necessarily gain very much by coming to the mill town because the employers used a number of tactics to keep their wages and bargaining power low. Employment through an intermediary, what she calls 'labour-lordism', was one such non-market institution of power (see also 'migration: internal' in Chapter 9).

[1] 'Emergence of an Industrial Labour Force in a Dual Economy—British India, 1880–1920', *IESHR*, 15(3), 1978.

More recent work on migration suggests two difficulties in apply-
ing this model. First, migrants came from all strata of rural society.
They were not necessarily the poorest classes. In both Bombay and
Calcutta, there were many individuals who owned land back in the
villages they came from. They were usually adult males, who had left
their families in the villages to look after the rural work. Their families
migrated only if rural resources got exhausted. City work was neither
a total break from, nor a clear alternative to, rural work. Such migrations can be viewed as a diversification in the portfolio of occupations
for the working family as a whole. The purpose could be to augment
family incomes, reduce and spread risks, and retain a toe-hold in the
rural economy.[2] Secondly, migration was 'segmented'. That is, migrants of specific backgrounds moved into specific occupations.[3] This
makes suggesting a general explanatory theory difficult. Nevertheless, there are two things that all migrants did share. The first was
the knowledge of new economic opportunities and second, acquain-
tance with individuals or systems in specific channels of migration
that could actually bring them into the city.

The share of women in the cotton and jute factories declined.
Women tended to be replaced by migrant males. In both cotton and
jute, the fall in the proportion of women was especially rapid during 1928–40. Employment legislation made special provisions for
women, such as maternity benefits and prohibition of night work.
These often discouraged employers when male labourers were available for the same work.[4] Samita Sen has recently argued that, with
the increase in migration, there was also a change in perceptions of
women's work.[5] Women workers became disadvantaged in the urban labour market by new perceptions of their familial role. They
were meant to stay at home and look after the rural occupation of the
family. With increasing withdrawal from paid and so-called men's
work, women's contribution tended to get devalued.

Employment legislation (Factories Act) and trade union legislation
(Industrial Disputes Act) evolved slowly during the colonial period.

---

[2] Such types of migration have been described in Rajnarayan Chandavarkar, *The
Origins of Industrial Capitalism in India: Business Strategies and the Working Classes in
Bombay, 1900–40,* Cambridge, 1994, p. 9; Samita Sen, *Women and Labour in Late Colonial
India: The Bengal Jute Industry,* Cambridge, 1999, Ch. 1.

[3] Arjan de Haan, 'Migration in Eastern India: A Segmented Labour Market', *IESHR*,
32(1), 1995.

[4] Chandavarkar, *Origins of Industrial Capitalism,* p. 96.

[5] *Women and Labour,* 'Introduction'.

They began in the nineteenth century, but were widely known and somewhat effective only in the interwar period. By then, the major political parties had begun efforts at organizing factory labour which the government repressed because movement for workers' rights sometimes got identified with anti-colonial struggles and sentiments. Nevertheless, trade union membership jumped from a negligible 100,000 in 1927 to 400,000 in 1938. The political situation, legal developments, popularity of trade unions, and crisis in some of the older industries such as the Bombay cotton mills, combined to generate a spate of strikes in the interwar period. No industry remained untouched by this burst of industrial disputes, but Bombay was especially disturbed. As a result of this episode, Bombay witnessed greater involvement of the government in labour legislation and dispute settlement. Also, labour militancy became a part of the tradition of Bombay's cotton textile industry.

What did the shift from traditional to modern sector mean for those who underwent it? First let us see what it might mean economically. There was a wage-hierarchy at the shop-floor, and those nearer the top could usually enjoy a lifestyle better and more secure than that in the village. The average wage was usually better than agricultural labourer's earnings anywhere in India. But it was usually not sufficient to bring the workers' families into the cities. Most earned an income too little or too insecure to think of settling in the city in the long-term and giving up connections with land and agricultural labour. Based on these facts, historians have tended to characterize factory labour in the big city as 'unfortunate human beings'.[6] But this is a somewhat biased assessment. The city-dwellers never suffered the threat of famine in the way the rural population, and especially the lowly-born within them, did. Caste oppression and caste as barrier to entry in new jobs was a weaker force in the cities. For individual workers, the opportunities of occupational and income mobility were far greater in the cities than in the villages. The evidence of this is the upward trend in mill wages in the early twentieth century, though there were differences across places and over time (see Table 5.5). On the other hand, neither peasant incomes nor agricultural wages seem to have been growing in the same period. In this sense, there was a distinct improvement in the economy of the people who came to large-scale industry.

[6] Dipesh Chakrabarty, *Rethinking Working-Class History*, Princeton University Press, Princeton, p. 11.

TABLE 5.5

Average Real Wage in Large-scale Industry, 1900–44

*(annual average)*

| | Bombay cotton textile mills 1934 = 100 | Ahmedabad cotton textile mills 1951 = 100 | Calcutta jute mills 1951 = 100 |
|---|---|---|---|
| 1900–4 | 45.2 | 37.8 | 64.0 |
| 1910–14 | 51.6 | 39.0 | 057.0 |
| 1920–4 | 66.2 | 47.4 | 53.0 |
| 1930–4 | 109.4 | 88.0 | 61.8 |
| 1940–4 | 106.0 | 95.2 | 74.0 |

*Sources:* K. Mukerji, 'Trends in Real Wages in Cotton Textile Mills in Bombay City and Island from 1900 to 1951', *Artha Vijnana*, 1(1), 1959; 'Trends in Real Wages in Jute Textile Industry from 1900 to 1951', *Artha Vijnana*, 2(1), 1960; 'Trends in Real Wages in Cotton Textile Industry in Ahmedabad from 1900 to 1951', *Artha Vijnana*, 3(2), 1961.

What did the shift mean in cultural terms? In Marxist writings on labour and labour history, a question often asked is, how well does a 'preindustrial' and 'precapitalist' population acquire an 'industrial' mentality. The latter is defined in terms of disciplined use of time and the sense of belonging in a homogeneous working class rather than in castes, communities, regions, etc. There is not much dispute among historians that Indian labour in large-scale industry did not as a rule see themselves as a homogeneous class in the way trade unions expected them to. Dipesh Chakrabarty is the most well-known writer to have argued against a 'class'-oriented approach.[7] The social and ethnic divisions among the labourers remained powerful. Adaptation to factory discipline happened in an imperfect way. The falling short of the working class ideal can be seen as a continuity of the peasant-like habits of the mind into the factory floor and urban life.

Recent contributions in labour history suggest a somewhat different view. These works do not make strong distinctions between 'rural' and 'urban', 'pre-industrial' and 'industrial', both in the cultural and in the economic spheres. Rural connections were rarely given up, but maintained because they served an important purpose of mitigating the suddenness and shock of the transition. Workers in- variably fashioned new identities, adjusted to the new environment, and

[7] *Rethinking Working-Class History.*

developed new friendships and social connections, based upon notions they brought from places of origin.[8]

## FINANCE FOR INDUSTRY

Capital for industry was severely and perpetually scarce in India. Industrial investment cannot expand without a well-developed system of credit. Credit comes from three sources: banks, the capital market, and household savings. A modern banking system was almost non-existent in 1850, and developed slowly thereafter. The major government-supported banks of the period were extremely conservative about choosing clients. The largest of the modern banks was the Bank of Bengal. Its clients were mainly the local British firms. An implicit ethnic preference may have influenced their operations, as Amiya Bagchi has suggested.[9] The rest of the banking sector had very limited reach. It was always plagued by risks, instability, and a rather high frequency of failure. Further, unlike German or Japanese banks, the Indian banking companies followed the English tradition and supplied only working capital and not fixed capital. Fixed capital could be, and was, raised in the capital market. But the share bazaar was a rather small and insignificant institution. It was also plagued by several episodes of speculation. The amount invested in shares even by the end of the interwar period was a minuscule percentage of estimated savings in the economy.

In both Bombay and Calcutta, share market trans- actions had a highly speculative bias that surely discouraged the risk-averting small investor. In both cities, a great deal of the daily business in the stock exchanges was done, based on the differences in borrowed money, without compulsory settlement of profits or losses in short-term transactions. This feature, to quote R.S. Rungta, was a 'sure sign of speculation as well as disaster'. Disaster, because it could lead to widespread failure of payments, bankruptcy, and loss of public confidence. Rungta explains the speculative propensity in ethnic terms, by the presence of Marwaris in this market.[10] But in fact any resource in short supply (such as capital or information) might encourage

---

[8] For example, see the works by Chandavarkar, Sen, and Joshi cited in the readings list.

[9] *The Evolution of the State Bank of India, Vol 2: The Era of the Presidency Banks, 1876–1920*, Alta Mira Press, Walnut Creek, and Sage Publications, London and New Delhi, 1997.

[10] *The Rise of Business Corporations in India 1851–1900*, Cambridge, 1970, p. 211.

speculation and 'rent-seeking' unless a good regulatory system is in place. The people who did business in the stock exchanges were very skilful and talented, but they were not the kind to command the trust of the general public.

Such a situation of persistent scarcity of capital led to some distortions, and some innovations. Shortage of fixed capital led to under-capitalization of the businesses that depended on bank finance. New industrial investment in India followed certain dynamics, which have not completely disappeared even today. Fixed capital being in short supply, there was a tendency towards over-capitalization during booms. That is, machinery was purchased only at the time of rising prices, at the high prices. For, only such times provided the investors with ready means of payment. In normal times, there was under-capitalization. That is, there was great carelessness about cash reserves and depreciation allowance.[11] During downturns, that condition could push otherwise healthy businesses to the wall. This vulnerability was increased by the fact that most Indian firms tended to pay excessive dividend in times of boom to generate investor confidence. Generating reserves was a lesser priority. On the more innovative side, Indian companies tried to popularize preference shares and debentures. Debentures were a moderate success. Also, mills of Bombay and Ahmedabad developed a dependence on public deposits. This was a useful source of funds, but a rather costly and insecure one (see also 'distortions in the financial system' in Chapter 6).

Many developed countries, in fact, started with an underdeveloped financial market, but developed one with a combination of government intervention and private enterprise. One source of capital market development in continental Europe was the vast investments made in railway construction in the nineteenth century. In India, the capital market was not only undeveloped, but also fragmented. London, and not Bombay, supplied a great deal of such capital, including all of railway investment.

Given this implicit high cost of capital, it is not surprising that the pioneers in large-scale industry came almost entirely from communities that had specialized in trading and banking activities. Only they could raise money easily compared with, say, the artisans or farmers. There was an almost perfect correlation between hereditary

[11] See, for example, P.S. Lokanathan, *Industrial Organization in India*, George Allen and Unwin, London, 1935, p. 214; Rungta, *Rise of Business Corporations*, pp. 213–4; the discussion in Indian Tariff Board, *Cotton Textile Industry Inquiry*, Vol I, Calcutta, 1927, chapter on 'Internal Causes of the Present Crisis'.

traders-bankers and large-scale industry. By and large, fixed capital in large-scale industry came from own sources of funds, or from borrowings from within a small set of people known to each other.

## ENTREPRENEURSHIP

### Pre-history

Generally speaking, the situation with hereditary trade and banking in the mid-eighteenth century was as follows. In the north, that is in the Delhi and Agra area, Punjab, Rajasthan and Sindh, the Khatris, the Lohanas, and to a smaller extent the Bhatias, were the dominant trading groups. Their counterparts among the Muslims were the Khojas and the Parachas, said to have been converted Khatris. They were prominent as financiers of local trade and banking. They were engaged in the overland trade with Central Asia and Afghanistan. And they occasionally took part in local administration. As an extension of their trading activity, they migrated to distant regions within and away from India. But none played an important role in maritime trade. In the west, Gujarat was one of the most urbanized and commercialized regions of India at this time. Hindu and Muslim trading communities in Gujarat and Saurashtra conducted not only inland trade, but also maritime trade between the Gujarat coast of India and the Persian Gulf, Arabia, Africa, Malabar. Until the advent of the Europeans in the Indian Ocean, they also conducted trade with Southeast Asia. It is said that Muslim Gujarati traders initiated the conversion of Indonesia to Islam. The relatively less commercialized Maharashtra region drew its capital and enterprise mainly from Gujarat. In the south, two prominent trading communities were the Telugu-speaking Komatis and the Tamil-speaking Chettis. Although primarily inland traders, the Chettis became actively involved in Burma and Malaya trade after these territories came under the control of Britain. In the east, the role of the Bengali trading caste in the region's business has been rather marginal. Bengalis do figure in accounts of eighteenth and nineteenth century trade, not as a community but as collection of individuals drawn from both trading and non-trading backgrounds. These individuals successfully helped or collaborated with European capitalists. Europeans were always especially active in the eastern Indian trading world, though north Indian professional traders had systematically begun to immigrate into Bengal from the eighteenth century.

The most important element in Indian business during the ascent of British power was the 'broker' of European trading firms. They were Indian agents who mediated between artisans, local merchants and the European firms. Employment of Indian agents was a practice that all European firms routinely followed. In some cases such agents started as or eventually became some sort of partners. This was the background from which the early-nineteenth century Bengali business enterprise arose. Such partnerships can be found in all areas of India where European traders were active. One important example is the Parsis. Parsis were traditionally not traders or financiers, but artisans, carpenters, weavers, and ship-builders. Their entry into trade was largely a result of their contact with the Europeans as brokers.

The scale of operations of some of the Indian trading firms was truly enormous and multinational, but the number of such big firms was not large. Trading firms frequently performed some banking services. There were also specialized banking houses or *pedhis*. These performed the money-changing service (converting one currency to another), provided and cashed bills of exchange or *hundis*, lent to governments, and occasionally took up revenue contracts. Such activities brought business firms and rulers closer to each other. Yet, there are not many examples of business firms taking a close control of or interest in political matters. There are not many instances where trading and banking firms became involved in industry before the nineteenth century, whether as direct producers or as financiers. Artisans remained distant from professional traders and bankers. The latter did finance industry in the case of exportable goods such as textiles in certain regions. But these industries were more exceptions than the rule. Commercial and financial capital, thus, found relatively little use outside commerce and banking. A great deal of trading and banking profits went into the purchase of idle assets such as gold jewellery, such spiritual assets as building temples, construction of ghats in Kashi, or charity and relief during famines.

## Western India

In 1850, on the eve of the rise of large-scale industry in India, Parsis were the most prominent community engaged in the trade of the two principal exportable goods from the western coast, cotton and opium. Among other communities similarly engaged were the Khojas, the Bhatias, the Gujarati traders and bankers with their base in Ahmedabad, and the Bombay-based Baghdadi Jews. Several of them had some history of collaboration with Europeans. Some had withdrawn from more active maritime trade as European firms based in London took control. The owners of the first cotton mills came from these communities, and partially from European trading houses dealing in cotton. The pioneering names among cotton millowners included Petit, Wadia and Tata (Parsis), Currimbhoys (Khojas), Sassoons (Jews), Khatau, Gokuldas, Thakersey (Bhatias from Kutchch), and Greaves Cotton, W.H. Brady and Killick Nixon (European houses). The origin of Ahmedabad's mill industry was more rooted in Hindu and Jain business. Among the prominent names, Sarabhais and Lalbhais were Jain traders already prominent as *pedhis*. The combination of cotton textiles and cotton trade was an advantageous one.

## Eastern India

In Calcutta, and largely north and south India, Europeans dominated large-scale industry. Among the early pioneers there were some speculative and reckless individuals who did not survive long. But eventually, industry based in Calcutta came to be controlled by reputed 'managing agency' firms. These were already engaged in import-export trade, banking and insurance. Interestingly, while Indian business entered large-scale industry (cotton) that competed with British goods directly, the main sphere of European large-scale industry was in such goods that did not compete with British goods. Examples are jute (along with tea and coal), and engineering industries that supplied machinery and spares to the other industries and to the government. Either the decision by European traders not to compete was a conscious one. Or it was advantageous for them to belong in the trading world that centred itself in London. In both these senses, European enterprise in large-scale industry can be called a product of the British Empire. The large British firms in Calcutta's manufacturing were, Andrew Yule (jute, tea, coal, paper, engineering), Bird and F.W. Heilgers (jute, coal, engineering, limestone), Mc-Leod–Begg–Dunlop (jute, tea, railways), Jardine–Skinner and George Henderson (jute, tea, engineering), Octavius Steel (tea, electricity), Shaw Wallace (tea, coal), Gillanders–Arbuthnot (jute, tea, coal), Macneill–Barry (jute, coal, electricity), Martin–Burn (coal, wagon, dockyard, cement), Balmer–Lawrie (coal, paper, engineering), and Kilburn (tea, coal, engineering). Smaller groups included Kettlewell–Bullen, McKinnon–Mckenzie, Thomas Duff (all three in jute). Two other large houses, Williamson–Magor and Duncan Brothers, mainly owned tea estates.

Supplying European firms raw materials were Indian traders

based in Calcutta, chiefly the Marwaris. Throughout the eighteenth and the nineteenth centuries, the Marwaris had steadily dispersed from their original home in Rajasthan and resettled themselves in new business towns as moneylenders and revenue-farmers. From that base they began to enter trade. Most of the prominent Marwari houses of the city had migrated to Calcutta during the last quarter of the nineteenth century. The history of prominent Marwari houses such as Birla, Badridas Goenka, Bansidhar Jalan, H.P. Poddar, Ramkrishna Dalmia, Babulal Rajgarhia and others suggests that their main interests about 1900 were in jute baling, mining, *zamindari*, and import agency. By the end of the interwar period, these firms had entered the jute industry in a major way. On a smaller scale they entered sugar, paper, cement, construction, and share-brokerage.

Their position as insiders in the stock market, and the small holdings of many of the British managing agents in the firms they controlled, enabled the Indians to effect a series of takeovers of foreign firms in the 1950s and the 1960s. The British owners themselves found the changed political climate uncongenial. This was so especially because, in the stock market manipulations, the Indians received implicit support from the ruling politicians. Several other firms, therefore, were voluntarily sold to Indians. In the business legends of Calcutta, this rather sudden and near-total transfer of ownership is widely held to be a reason behind the progressive bankruptcy of these firms. Most of them were subsequently managed badly, owned by persons having little regard for efficiency, and were robbed of cash. A detailed scholarly history of the transfer is yet to be written.

Historians have asked why European entrepreneurs dominated Calcutta. For the Indians with money, *zamindari* could be a safe and attractive option when rising prices began to reduce the real burden of taxation. However, since industry continued to attract foreign capital, surely it was lucrative too. Besides, not everyone with capital could afford to buy a *zamindari*. Why, then, did more Indians not enter industry?

A.K. Bagchi has suggested that the Europeans were politically stronger than Bengali business and could prevent entry. Europeans in Calcutta did behave in a clannish way on many occasions. But to develop this closeness into a theory about their supremacy in business faces at least three counter arguments. First, it cannot be tested. After 1850, there were very few cases of even attempted entry by the Bengalis into manufacturing. How do we tell for sure whether those who did not enter industry were unwilling, incapable, or obstructed? Secondly, if the Europeans obstructed the Bengalis, how do we explain that many Marwari firms overcame such tactics and successfully turned industrial from the interwar period? There must be factors at play that can overcome barriers to entry. Thirdly, in the 1840s, Bengali large-scale enterprise suffered a crippling blow. That episode had nothing to do with European power in Calcutta. The episode suggests that there might have existed inherent shortcomings in Bengali enterprise.

Pursuing that line of thought, one weakness is obvious. Nearly all the Indian business groups of that time saw business as their hereditary profession. They had developed rules of cooperation that could sustain them in business despite great political and economic adversities. The Bengalis did not see themselves this way, and barring a few exceptional castes and sub-castes, had evolved no such rules. They were not a business community in that sense. Their's was basically an agricultural population that briefly toyed with business due to the prospect of European collaboration in foreign trade. To stand on their own feet in business, they needed what the Marwaris or the Parsis had, that is, a strong cooperative community. The fact that they lacked such a community was one reason why they were pulled down so badly in 1847. It could also be a reason, or the one reason, why they left industry altogether thereafter.

## Southern India

In south India, interestingly, the pioneers in large-scale industry did not come from the traditional business communities, but from agrarian background. Unlike Bombay or Calcutta, Madras offered narrower scope for collaboration between Indian and European capitalists. Consequently, the response of the Chettiars (Chettis) to the new economic opportunities in the nineteenth century was quite unique. They went overseas. Capital accumulated in these foreign operations did flow into manufacturing before the First World War, but on a limited scale. In the interwar period, the Tamil Nadu region witnessed vigorous industrialization, mainly based on small-scale industry. Two large-scale industry complexes also came up around Coimbatore and Madras. The main source of capital here was the savings of the rich cotton farmers-cum-traders. Cotton farming and trade, indeed, played a pivotal role in early industrialization in all the regions of Tamil Nadu. Major Chettiar groups entered industry in the 1930s, after setbacks during the Depression and unconducive

political developments in Burma. By then, the composition of entrepreneurs had become quite diverse.

## MANAGEMENT

Historians have described two kinds of management, informal and
formal. The traditional Indian business firm typically functioned from
within the family and community. The firm and the joint family were
frequently indistinct entities. Just how the firm drew strength from
family relationships is a complex question. Trust is essential to all
forms of business. Its importance increases in a situation where laws
and systems of settlement of disputes are immature, and distribution
of information is not uniform so that a party better-informed may be
tempted to cheat the one less informed. One way of dealing with this
situation is for businesspeople to develop personal connections and
networks. Family relations and common identity ensured that trust
would rarely be betrayed. For such acts could invite social sanction.
Such commonality of roots also resulted in easier access to support
facilities such as supply of credit, comfort of travel, profit-sharing and
apprenticeship. Thus, any Marwari immigrant from Rajasthan to Calcutta in the nineteenth century could hope to be helped by the community at Calcutta not only in physical survival but also in building
a career. Sometimes, belonging to a community or family helped in
keeping trade secrets. In this sense the community could behave like
a 'guild'. Finally, being an insider in a business community made the
choice of occupation of a young person relatively easy. Many social
histories of business communities in India and elsewhere have made
the point that economic success was strongly rooted in the ability to
create a cooperative community.

The causal connection between 'community-feeling' and actual
cooperation is not easy to interpret. In older writings, caste or family
tended to be seen as inherently cooperative. But caste or family does
not necessarily imply emotional homogeneity. It is better perhaps to
treat the cooperative community as an innovation. Caste was used
for this purpose wherever necessary, when for example mutual support was needed to keep monopolistic control on a trade, or survive adversities. When such needs reduced, the community-ties also
weakened. Thus, in the more developed and cosmopolitan environment like that of Bombay, occupational affiliations and chambers of
commerce were more important than familial connections.

As for formal management systems, corporate management was

a new concept in the mid-nineteenth century India. It was, therefore, the field of many experiments and repeated legislation. Until 1850, partnership was the general form of ownership-cum-management. This made raising finance and management difficult and clumsy. Limited liability was formally recognized in the first Companies Act of 1850, but it was not until the 1860s that its coverage became comprehensive. The period 1860–5 saw a boom in company formation and share markets. The crash that followed exposed their organizational weaknesses. The Bombay stock exchange was organized in 1875, and began to attract small investors. The 1870s saw a revival of company formation. New legislation also brought stability. In this situation, new paradigms in management began to take roots. The most important of such institutions was the 'managing agency' system.

In this system, the Directors or representatives of the owners of a company contracted a firm to manage that company for a fee (or increasingly commission on sales). The idea of a management contract originated in the insurance business in India in the early nineteenth century. It survived the 1840s depression that destroyed many of the firms that had used this system. By the 1870s it changed form to some extent and became established in large-scale industry, mining and plantations. Strangely, many practices associated with the operation of the system remained outside legislation until 1956.

Why did such a system originate? One obvious answer is the following. Scarcity of managerial talent led to a few firms managing other people's businesses. But this theory does not fit the facts. For, frequently the managing agent was also the promoter of a new firm. R.S. Rungta suggests that the system initially became popular because the financiers of a new firm came from a small group of rich but busy merchants.[12] They wanted to try a new idea but did not have the time to implement it themselves. So, when a managing agent firm proposed an interesting idea, they gave it money, but contracted the management to the proposer, and kept a close watch upon the affairs of that company. They could do so because both the proposer-cum-manager and the financiers formed a small club.

The situation changed when limited liability became popular and many small investors bought shares of a new company. The substantial body of owners now had no personal or direct control over the managing agent, nor could they be well-informed about what might

[12] *Rise of Business Corporations*, p. 252.

go on inside the company. This information gap enabled mismanagement and fraud. When such a thing happened and a company went bankrupt, shareholders could rarely recover their money or change the laws. Even when the owners were a small group, the contract could be manipulated to enrich the agents who routinely and illegally speculated in commodity trade in goods and raw materials in which the company was involved. Such speculation was often against the company's interests. Why, despite these serious and frequent abuses, did the system continue?

Clearly because it served a persistent need. Generally, Indian firms found it very hard to meet their fixed and working capital requirements out of paid-up share capital, and had to rely heavily on loans and public deposits. A large part of these loans, the owners or the managing agent firms themselves supplied, but substantial percentages came from banks and the public. Loans require a guarantor, and deposits require the borrower to be a trusted and reputed name. The managing agents served these functions. Given limited information about the capacity of individual managers or reliability of individual owners, management tended to concentrate in reputed, branded and publicly visible firms.

Nevertheless, the system became redundant in the mid-twentieth century. A much simpler institution, the holding company, could perform the controlling functions of a managing agent. As the capital market matured and became broad based, brand names shifted from the managing agent firm and settled on business families and combines. The separation of owners and managers had become a more real one in quite a few firms. In 1970, the managing agency system was formally abolished.

## LARGE-SCALE INDUSTRY IN THE PRINCELY STATES

The growth of large-scale industry showed very similar trends in the princely states and British India. In both, the really significant growth occurred during the interwar period. The industrial composition was similar; thus, in Gwalior, Indore, Baroda and Hyderabad, cotton textiles dominated large-scale industry. Like British India, in Indore and Gwalior, enterprise and capital mainly originated from north Indian mercantile communities such as the Marwaris.

There were several characteristic traits of large-scale enterprise in major states which need mention:
First, in the larger states such as Mysore, Hyderabad and Travancore, the government played, or wanted to play, an active role in initiating

industrialization. The history of state encouragement to industry in Mysore is of particular significance because debates about state policy in Mysore became the point of conflict between two basic approaches to industrial policy then current in provincial circles. One of these focused on adapting traditional industry to modern markets and consumption pattern. This is closely identified with the name of Alfred Chatterton, a Director of Industries in Madras and briefly in Mysore. The other focused on starting large-scale industry, especially capital and intermediate goods, under state sponsorship. It stressed the need to make new technology, organization and management more popular. This approach was closely identified, in the case of Mysore, with the Prime Minister (Diwan) M. Viswesvaraiya. After independence, the Government of India itself pursued such an approach to industrialization.

Second, in the large and resource-rich southern states, natural resources played a major role in shaping the composition of modern enterprise. The textile industry was present in the three larger states, Hyderabad, Travancore–Cochin and Mysore. But each had its own specific types of resource-intensive enterprise. Coal mining, tobacco manufacturing and cement were important in Hyderabad, and gold mining, steel, sandalwood oil and soap factories in Mysore. In Travancore–Cochin, the major forms of modern enterprise were plantations of tea, rubber and coffee, and agricultural-processing industries such as coir and cashew.

Third, in several of the princely states, specific local communities had significant presence in the ownership of large-scale industry. They included, the Kanbis in Baroda, a landed group, and the Syrian Christian community of Travancore–Cochin, prominent in the region's commerce, finance, industry and plantations.

Fourth, the role of foreign capital was insignificant in the north Indian states, and relatively weak in Hyderabad (if the railways and the colliery are excluded). In Mysore, foreign capital was not important in industry but the Kolar gold-fields, the single largest modern enterprise in Mysore, was foreign-owned. On the other hand, in Travancore foreign capital was important. Plantations and agro-processing had a significant foreign presence.

Fifth, consistent with the nature of their industries, the states varied in the importance of long-distance trade in their economies. In this respect, Travancore was a case in point. The Travancore economy was significantly more export-oriented than most parts of British India and the states, a fact helped directly by the long seafront of the

state and indirectly by its rich maritime tradition. Of the other major states, Baroda was well-connected to the port in Bombay by the railways. But nearly all the others were land-locked, and had no comparable history of long-distance commerce.

## THE SIGNIFICANCE OF LARGE-SCALE INDUSTRY

What did large-scale industry contribute to industrialization and economic development in India?

Let us define industrialization as a rise in the share of industry in employment, and define development as sustained rise in average income. Let us then define two types of industrialization. Industrialization based on large-scale industry is capable of generating rapid increase in labour productivity, and therefore, in average income. It does so by means of capital-intensive technology and efficient organization of resources. It is possible to think of a contrasting kind of industrialization based on small-scale industry. Small-scale industry tends to be much more labour-intensive. Such industrialization can create employment in industry. But it is not capable of generating economic development, because labour productivity cannot grow rapidly in these activities.

In reality, many developed countries in the early stages of industrialization did in fact start on a small scale, that is, they sold labour-intensive goods. But sooner or later, they reached a point where labour was scarce relative to capital, and there was upward pressure on wages. Industry was encouraged to replace labour by capital, become more efficient in the use of labour, and shift increasingly towards capital-intensive large-scale industry. From this point on, average incomes began to rise rapidly. In development literature, this transition is sometimes called a change from 'extensive' to 'intensive' growth regime.

Let us evaluate the Indian experience in this context. Large-scale industry did develop in India, but in a limited way. Therefore, the potential of large-scale industry to generate economic development was also limited. Why was the scale of capital-intensive modern industry restricted?

If we look at the profile of large-scale industries that did develop, we realize that the main reason behind them being established in India was low cost of raw materials. Almost all the major forms of large-scale industry, cotton and jute mills, sugar, leather, woollens, cement, tobacco, even steel, not to mention rice or oil mills, depended

most critically on the abundance of their basic raw material, cotton, jute, raw hides, coal, iron, limestone, grains, seeds, etc. If India had not been well-endowed in natural resources, she was not likely to have seen any of these industries.

Further, since capital was costly in India, it is not likely that Indians would have developed the machinery used in these mills on their own. The Industrial Revolution reduced cost of machinery and facilitated the spread of knowledge the world over. Indians could simply buy this knowledge instead of having to develop the technology from a scratch. As a result, corresponding to the raw material advantage, the capital cost disadvantage became weaker, and large-scale industries using these raw materials could develop. Only such large-scale industry developed in India in the colonial period that required: (a) simple borrowable machinery, and (b) natural raw material that were found in abundance in the country.

Further to the discussion on the magnitude of presence of large-scale industry in India, Morris D. Morris has argued that the home market was small and in a number of industries could not support more than one or two factories. But this is true only of such special industries that supplied to the government, such as steel. As a general theory, it has several problems. For example, we need to ask why Indian industry could not expand by exporting. The answer, obviously, is that given the high cost of capital relative to labour, capital-intensive industry as such would be relatively costly and uncompetitive. In the second variant of the limited-market argument, Amiya Bagchi has pointed out that the home market was shared by Indian and imported manufactures, and that the colonial government did not protect Indian industry from low-cost imports. The argument is based on the theory that there are economies of scale and learning in industrial production. The Indian firms that were high-cost initially could become low-cost in the long run if they were allowed to grow under protection. But the applicability of this logic in India is disputable. Again, we need to remember that the cost of capital was relatively high in India. It is not credible that in a capital scarce situation, capital-intensive industry as such could become competitive in the long run just through protection. That the Indian government did give protection after independence only to create a high-cost and globally inefficient capital-intensive industry is a further proof of this statement.

There can be a third answer to the question, why large-scale industry was so limited in India. This is based on factor-endowments

and relative resource costs. Let us remind ourselves that the basic resource condition of the Indian economy—scarcity of capital relative to labour and raw material—was not conducive to wide use of machinery. What did develop were those industries that (a) processed raw materials abundantly available in India, and (b) could readily import machines and technicians. If we ignore this small segment, the general situation was exactly as the prevailing resource conditions would permit—a vast labour-intensive industrial sector housed in homes or small workshops. Large-scale industry was an exception in India created by the unusual combination of the richness of India's natural resources and the availability of a menu of technologies invented by India's closest trade partner, Britain. Small-scale industry represented the rule, the normal pattern of industrialization given India's resource costs and availability.

Nevertheless, as we have mentioned in the beginning of this chapter, the share of large-scale industry in employment is not an adequate index of its contribution. An important contribution of the large-scale industry was the progressive modernization of the services sector. The next chapter deals with organized banking. It also deals with mines and plantations. Together with large-scale industry, mines and plantations formed an integrated network of trade, finance, capital, and in some ways, even labour. In Calcutta's business world especially, the three were almost inseparable.

## Annotated Readings
### Major Industries

There are three main works on the history of large-scale industry in India: Amiya Kumar Bagchi, *Private Investment in India, 1900–1939*, Cambridge, 1970; Rajat K. Ray, *Industrialization in India: Growth and Conflict in the Private Corporate Sector, 1914–47*, Oxford University Press, New Delhi, 1982 (paperback), and Morris D. Morris, 'The Growth of Large-scale Industry to 1947', in *CEHI 2*. Of these three works, the most convenient read is Morris, which also covers the pre-1900 developments. The student can begin with this article, but switch to the others if interested in details on particular industries or times. For industry surveys, the following overviews are more recent and of high quality. (1) Jute: Dipesh Chakrabarty, *Rethinking Working-Class History: Bengal 1890–1940*, Princeton University Press, Princeton, 1989 (also printed by Oxford University Press, Delhi, 1989), Ch. 2, and Omkar Goswami, *Industry, Trade and Peasant Society. The*

*Jute Economy of Eastern India 1900–47*, Oxford University Press, Delhi, 1991, Section 2.1. (2) Cotton: Rajnarayan Chandavarkar, *The Origins of Industrial Capitalism in India*, Cambridge, 1994, Ch. 6. (3) Sugar: Sanjaya Baru, *The Political Economy of Indian Sugar*, Oxford University Press, 1990, Chs II and III.

## Labour

The general surveys by Morris and Bagchi are adequate to begin with. On migration, Chandavarkar, *Origins*, Ch. 4; Arjan de Haan, 'Migration in Eastern India: A Segmented Labour Market', *IESHR*, 32(1), 1995; Ranajit Das Gupta, 'Factory Labour in Eastern India: Sources of Supply', *IESHR*, 13(3), 1976; Lalita Chakravarty, 'Emergence of an Industrial Labour Force in a Dual Economy—British India, 1880–1920', *IESHR*, 15(3), 1978. On debates about what industry meant to a semi-rural population, see Chandavarkar, *Origins*, Ch. 1, Chakrabarty, *Rethinking*, Ch. 1, and Samita Sen, *Women and Labour in Late Colonial India: The Bengal Jute Industry*, Cambridge, 1999, Ch. 1. See also Chitra Joshi, 'Bonds of Community, Ties of Religion: Kanpur Textile Workers in the Early Twentieth Century', *IESHR*, 22(3), 1985.

On women, Sen, *Women and Labour*, Ch. 1.

For straight factual accounts of the Indian trade union movement and development of labour legislation see the historical portions of V.B. Karnik, *Indian Trade Unions, a Survey*, Manaktala, Bombay, 1966; Sunil Kumar Sen, *Working Class Movements in India, 1885–1975*, Oxford University Press, Delhi, 1994.

## Finance

R.S. Rungta, *The Rise of Business Corporations in India, 1851–1900*, Cambridge, 1970, Ch. 11. Read also the Introduction of Amiya Kumar Bagchi, *The Evolution of the State Bank of India, Volume 2: The Era of the Presidency Banks, 1876–1920*, Alta Mira Press, Walnut Creek, and Sage Publications, London and New Delhi, 1997.

## Entrepreneurship

There are many works on Indian enterprise, biographies of industrialists, European entrepreneurs, and the relationship between businesspeople and the colonial government. It is not necessary to produce a comprehensive list here. The general histories above give an adequate picture of specific industries. The classic survey of enterprise on the eve of British rule is D.R. Gadgil, *Origins of the Modern*

*Indian Business Class: An Interim Report*, Institute of Pacific Relations, New York, 1959. A useful survey is 'Introduction', in Rajat K. Ray, *Entrepreneurship and Industry in India: 1800–1947*, Oxford University Press, Delhi, 1994, and the articles by Ashok Desai (on Parsis), Thomas Timberg (on Marwaris), Amiya Kumar Bagchi (on Europeans of Calcutta), and Omkar Goswami (more specifically on Europeans and Indians in Calcutta jute) reprinted in the same volume. Finally see Dwijendra Tripathi (ed.), *Business Communities of India*, Manohar, Delhi, 1984, especially the essays by Amalendu Guha on Parsi Sheths, Raman Mahadevan, 'Entrepreneurship and Business Communities in Colonial Madras, 1900–29', J.S. Grewal, 'Business Communities of Punjab' and Dwijendra Tripathi, 'Class Character of the Gujarati Business Community'

## Management

Rungta, *Rise of Business Corporations*, Chs 11–12.

## Significance of Large-scale Industry

The discussions cited are from Morris, 'Growth of Large-scale Industry', Bagchi, *Private Investment*, Ch 1. See Ray, 'Introduction' for a survey of these discussions.

# 6

# Plantations, Mines, and Banking

After agricultural and industrial employment are taken into account, about 15–20 per cent of the work-force remains to be categorized. In this context, it is possible to discuss further three types of occupations. Though not numerically the largest, these were relatively homogeneous, comparatively modern, and therefore better documented. These three sectors are plantations, mines and the organized financial sector consisting of banks and insurance companies. Along with large-scale industry these sectors were a product of India's economic contact with Britain via trade and investment. All three sectors were relatively new in the organization of firms, their markets, and marketing systems. And yet, all three adapted in varying degrees to conditions in India. Thus, the production organization of plantations and mines adapted to the kind of manual labour available. In banking, the nature of the clients influenced the operations and performance of banks. This duality, of a modern industry, run by Western capital in most cases, adapting to local conditions, is a constant theme of the literature that has developed around these activities. The present chapter will give a descriptive account of these three sectors and suggest how this dichotomy affected the developmental potential of these activities.

Within plantations and mining, it is possible to narrow down to two specific sectors without significant compromise on coverage. At 1921, plantations and mines together employed about 1.1 million persons. The vast majority of them were employed in eastern India. This figure represents less than 1 per cent of total employment but nearly one-third of employment in modern sectors. Plantations employed 821,000 persons. Of this number, 748,000 or 91 per cent were employed in tea production alone (coffee and rubber employed another 7 per cent). Mines employed 268,000 persons, of whom 182,000 or 68 per cent were employed in coal. The other 32 per cent were spread over many types of minerals; the largest in employment being gold (8 per cent) and mica (7 per cent). Coal was the oldest form of modern mining enterprise dating back to the early nineteenth century. Among others, iron and manganese owed their growth to the more recent iron and steel industry. The history of the oil wells of Burma is of some interest because it was the subject of a nationalist critique of British rule. Exploration and industrialization greatly diversified this list of minerals of commercial interest by 1940. But individually the new minerals employed too few people to merit separate discussion.

The chapter is divided into three parts. These deal with plantations, mines, and banking and insurance respectively. The first part is almost exclusively about tea, the second about coal, and the third mainly about banking.

## TEA PLANTATIONS
### Early History

When the East India Company lost its monopoly in China trade in 1833, it turned to India for supplies of tea. Assam, which had become part of British India in 1825, had the ideal climate and topography for tea plantations. Efforts began to develop plantations in Assam. The first Indian tea was cultivated in a government experimental farm and arrived in England in 1838. Based on its popularity, the Assam Company was formed the following year taking over the government farms. Also in 1838, the government set up rules for leasing out land to plantation companies. These terms were very liberal, and in some cases liberalized further over time. The 1860s were a period of cotton mania in Bombay, and a tea mania in Calcutta. The liberal terms of land-use rules and visions of fabulous prosperity encouraged the tea boom. The boom did not last long. For lack of good labour, experience, transportation, good land, and of course poor quality of tea all turned the boom around rather rapidly.

Although plantations continued to expand in Assam, the period

1840–70 was not a profitable one for the industry. Transportation to and from the ports at Calcutta and Chittagong was a major problem. The cheapest mode of carrying bulk goods was steamers along the Brahmaputra. But this service was uncertain and infrequent. A railway connection was necessary. The terrain was inhospitable in the earlier years and needed extensive investment in forest-clearing. Most importantly, labour was not locally available.

A series of railway projects connected Calcutta and Chittagong with the tea districts of Sylhet, Cachar and upper Assam, in the 1880s. The steamer service was expanded in the same decade. The Suez Canal had meanwhile increased the demand for Indian tea by reducing transportation costs and time of delivery. With these developments, area under tea gardens expanded rapidly from 154,000 acres in 1880 to 337,000 acres in 1900. The number of workers in tea increased from 184,000 to 665,000 in this period. Gardens came up in the Darjeeling hills and the Dooars region in north Bengal. Nearly 75 per cent of tea land in India was by then located in Assam. Tea was by far the largest item of traffic from Assam to Calcutta. The share of Indian tea in Britain's market increased from 7 per cent in 1868 to 54 per cent in 1896.

The pace of growth slowed down in the following decade. But remained impressive. Acreage expanded to 502,173 in 1901, and to 715,000 in 1921. No significant growth in acreage was possible after that. During the 1890s, quality improved and costs of production came down. About this time, tea plantations started in south India. Tea was already being grown in the Nilgiri mountains. It was extended to the Wynaad and the Kannan–Devan hills in north Travancore. South India accounted for a large part of the acreage expansion in this period.

The First World War brought some minor problems for the industry in shipping and packaging, but it was otherwise a period of rapid growth in market. The 1920s were again a prosperous period. Price fluctuations, however, were a problem. From the end of the war, the international tea trade cartel became more powerful. In particular, the London-based Indian Tea Association had begun to exercise controls on the volume of production from time to time, to match world supply to world demand and thus stabilize prices and profits. These actions were resisted by the south Indian planters and the Dutch East Indies planters. Price fluctuations continued to occur. The most serious episode occurred in 1931, during the Great Depression. The international tea trade cartel became more powerful in the 1930s after this episode. The Second World War was a period of growth in demand. But the 1940s also saw a massive inflation in food prices. Tea being a labour-intensive industry, procuring food for the labourers became a major problem for the bigger gardens.

## Capital and Marketing System

Tea sales were made through auctions at Calcutta and London. The participants were 'broker' firms who sampled, inspected, tasted, and valued tea from the plantations. They brought tea to the auctions, and gave advances to the tea growers. There were very few broker firms in Calcutta. All were British concerns until independence.

Ownership of estates was also overwhelmingly European. The ethnic composition of ownership, in fact, was conducive to the creation of a cartel. Calcutta-based British managing agent firms controlled the majority of the estates and the largest of them. The major firms were, Andrew Yule, McLeod, Begg–Dunlop (merged with McLeod in the interwar period), Jardine–Skinner, Octavius Steel, Williamson–Magor, Shaw Wallace, Gillanders–Arbuthnot, Davenport, and Duncan Brothers. James Finlay controlled almost the entire crop of the Kannan–Devan hills. Bengali capitalists entered the industry quite early (in the 1880s), but never dominated it. The majority of them owned small gardens in the Dooars. Most Indian firms consisted of individual families rather than corporate firms. They did not have enough resources to invest in their estates, and usually operated at the poorer quality range aimed at domestic consumers. In one view, their limited and low-level operation resulted from European dominance in tea business as well as in politics.[1] Alternatively, European dominance in the business can be explained in terms of economic factors. For example, the export trade carried large economies of scale in production and marketing. European firms had better access to capital. However, the sphere of operations of the Indian firms expanded—by the 1950s they were a visible presence in the northeast where they formed a lobby distinct from that of the Europeans.

A more dramatic 'Indianization' of ownership took place in the 1950s and 60s with the sale and takeover of British firms by the prominent Marwari business houses in Calcutta. McLeod was captured by the Soorajmull–Nagarmull group, Octavius Steel went to the Goenkas, and Davenport to the Bajoria group. Among jute

---

[1] Ranajit Das Gupta, *Economy, Society and Politics in Bengal: Jalpaiguri 1869–1947*, Oxford University Press, Delhi, 1992, pp. 62–5.

companies owned by the same British firms, such sales and takeovers were more extensive. In tea they happened to a limited extent.

## Labour

In the Assam plantations, local labour was sufficient until 1860. Thereafter an increasing proportion of the workers were immigrants. Most of them migrated from Chota Nagpur and other districts of Greater Bengal during 1860–1900. They were recruited mainly by licensed labour contractors. They were sometimes called *arkattis*. Later, labour was also recruited directly by senior workers or *sardars*. Planters found the latter system preferable—it was cheaper, and the *sardars* tended to bring entire families over to the plantations.

The labourers came from backgrounds that were both socially and economically oppressed. Many were tribals or agricultural labourers who had little to lose by leaving their homes. And yet, migration to tea plantations involved considerable abuses. The *arkattis* painted an exaggerated picture of comfort to the labourers. The tea mania of the 1860s in particular produced an unscrupulous bunch of contractors— many of them Europeans. Contracts were drawn before the labourer could come to the garden and become familiar with the conditions. The labourers understood little of the terms of the contract, which legally bound them to work in the plantations for a certain period. This combination of a background of extreme poverty, asymmetric information, and the employers' greater legal power gave rise to a context of migration that had shades of slavery and oppression in it.

Until the railways started, the journey to the plantations was hazardous and led to many deaths. Sanitary conditions at the transit points were very poor. Not all the deaths, however, reflected the hardship of the journey. The migration was heavier during famines, when immunity to epidemic diseases was generally low. The plantations offered poor quality of life. The newly cleared forests, in particular, exposed the migrants to new parasites such as malaria. The death toll of migrants was very high, the work heavy, and escape was legally and practically difficult.

The wages of plantation workers were only slightly higher than the real income of agricultural labourers and usually less than those of factory or mine workers. From 1859, tea labour steadily came under legislation restraining their freedom to leave the garden. Laws that improved their working conditions came in place more slowly. These laws related to duration of contract, minimum wages, execution of contracts after and not before the labourer came to the garden, etc. Wages were piece-rated. There was provision for deductions if the plucking of leaves was of poor quality. Rules governing these decisions were generally absent or arbitrary.

The conditions, however, improved from about 1900. The death toll during the journey came down substantially with technological improvements in transportation. Country boats of the 1860s had given way to the railways in the 1900s. There was better medical care and sanitation. By the interwar period, abuses and human tragedy were more exception than rule. Tea garden labour was now a settled population that had lost much of its attachment with its place of origin. Conditions of work had improved. But these conditions depended on a 'free and easy relationship' between managers and labourers rather than legal protection for workers.[2] In the 1950s, with the stresses of the Second World War behind them and a new political attitude to labour working under European firms, new laws quickly came in place governing wages and other dues.

## Plantations and Development

Plantations had three important positive effects. First, they were a major and a better alternative to agricultural labour for a large number of people. Second, they generated externalities in the form of urbanization, creation of markets for rural produce, transportation, schools, hospitals, a local trade network that supplied material to the plantations, etc. Third, they generated profits that flowed back to and enriched almost all the major towns in Eastern India, such as Calcutta, Darjeeling, Siliguri, and Dibrugarh. The trades were also a source of public revenue.

On the other hand, the formation of the plantations entailed a violent uprooting of people. The violence was not necessarily an outcome of foreign rule. It originated in an information gap between rural labourers and urban merchants and their unequal access to legal resources. Plantation labour did not represent substantially more skilled work than agricultural labour. The labour colonies were replanted villages. And the workers lived at an unbridgeable social and economic distance from the managers and owners.

An organizational weakness of plantations in colonial conditions stemmed from the divided ownership structure. Europeans and Indians represented distinct capitalist groups. They rarely collaborated.

[2] Percival Griffiths, *The History of the Indian Tea Industry*, Weidenfield and Nicholson, London, 1967, p. 345.

Eventually, though the Indians operated on smaller scale and had weaker resources and capability, they emerged as the politically stronger voice.

## COAL MINING

### Early History

The Industrial Revolution was fuelled by coal, which was the main source of energy in running steam engines. India had substantial deposits of coal, but its wide usage had to await the growth of modern industry and transportation. During the rule of the East Indian Company there was some interest in developing the commercial extraction of coal. At that time, the main use of charcoal was in the smelting of metals by rural artisans. For the same purpose, the ordnance factories needed coal in larger quantities. Such coal was imported from Britain as the few attempts to use local coal did not satisfy the engineers. With the growth of steam ships in Indian waters the demand for local supplies strengthened. To meet this demand Calcutta's agency houses started small-scale mining operations in western Bengal. The Carr Tagore Company (see Chapter 5) acquired the only major colliery, Raniganj, in the 1830s. It started enterprises that could use this coal. After Carr Tagore failed, the colliery passed on to European hands. Inland transportation of this bulky commodity was, however, a serious problem. Rivers were not navigable throughout the year. Road transport was costly. Coal, therefore, continued to be mainly imported.

### 1850–1947

From the 1850s the situation took a dramatic turn. The railways connected Calcutta with the coal deposits in Raniganj in 1855. Barakar and Giridih were connected in the next 15 years and Jharia at 1893. By 1940, small railway lines connecting the mining towns with the main routes crisscrossed the Damodar river basin. Although smaller deposits were later discovered in central and southern India, the Damodar basin remained overwhelmingly important as a source of coal, with the result that almost the whole of India excluding Bengal had to bear heavy transportation costs of fuel. This was one factor that encouraged the exploitation of hydroelectric power in western India.

While the spreading rail network made the transportation of coal to distant users substantially cheaper, further railway expansion itself turned into a major source of demand for coal. Almost simultaneously, jute mills started in Calcutta—again major customers for coal. At the end of the First World War, the railways alone consumed about 30 per cent of total Indian production of coal. Modern industry, plantations and mining itself consumed about 25–30 per cent. Shipping and the Port Trusts took about 10–15 per cent, and small-scale industry and domestic users another 20–25 per cent. A substantial quantity was exported from India to Ceylon and Southeast Asia, replacing first British and later Japanese supplies.

1890–1919 has been described as the period of the 'coal rush' in eastern India. Output increased from 2.2 to 22.6 million tons. Number of workers in the mines of Bengal increased from 25,000 to 175,000. The mining business was very profitable. In some years it was exceptionally so. At 1860, domestic production of coal at 0.3 million tons exceeded imports (0.15 m). At 1947, India was a net exporter of coal with coal output at 30 million tons. Table 6.1 presents some figures on the growth of coal production.

The interwar period saw considerable fluctuations in prices and outputs. After 1920, exchange appreciation and a dull world market led to a fall in exports. The reputation abroad for the quality of Indian coal was not very good either. Conditions improved towards the end of the 1920s. But they again worsened due to the Great Depression. In the early 1930s many small collieries closed down and average dividends paid and rates of profits dropped substantially. The Coal Mining Committee of 1936 was a response to these problems. The Second World War saw another massive burst in profitability.

Table 6.1
Production of Major Minerals, 1891–1938

|  | 1891 | 1921 | 1938–9 |
| --- | --- | --- | --- |
| Coal (million tonnes): All India | 2.30 | 18.40 | 28.33[*] |
| Bengal, Bihar, Orissa | 1.92 | 16.18 | 23.00[*] |
| Iron ore (million tonnes): All India | 0.02 | 0.94 | 2.74 |
| Gold (million ounces): All India | n.a. | 0.39 | 0.32 |
| Mysore state | n.a. | 0.38 | 0.32 |
| Petroleum (million gallon): All India | 8.47 | 305.68 | 322.66 |
| Burma | 8.47 | 296.09 | 251.33 |

[*] Indian states.

Source: Statistical Abstracts for British India, Calcutta, various years.

## Capital

Who met the coal rush of 1890–1919? As in all Calcutta-based modern enterprises, in coal mining too foreign firms and joint stock companies were the main owners of capital in the prewar period. There was a close interlocking of jute and coal interests. This interlocking not only supplied the mines with a captive market, but also with railway wagons for transportation to other users at a time when wagons were in short supply. The railways favoured the European firms with wagons. They did so ostensibly because their coal was of better quality, but allegedly because of racial sympathies.[3] In 1914, ten large European managing agencies based in Calcutta owned almost all of the capital of joint-stock companies interested in coal. European firms supplied possibly over 80 per cent of the output. The main consumers were modern industry, shipping and the railways.

The role of the small, individually owned Indian firms who supplied the rest of the output was somewhat more significant in coal than in the mills and plantations. Their share was rising from the First World War. By 1947, they supplied about one-third of the total production. They mined low quality coal from shallow pits, did not use much or any machinery, and served mainly the domestic users of coal and small-scale industries. Some of the early Indian entrepreneurs owned *zamindari* estates in the area. *Zamindars* became involved in mining in varying degrees. The most well-known example perhaps is the Malias of Searsole near Raniganj. The prominent Indian names about 1913 were Bengalis who were former employees or merchants of the European companies. This group was instrumental in setting up an association of Indian colliers. It seems possible that the labour contractors in mining, again usually Bengalis, had also bought up or started a number of collieries. The Bengalis, however, were steadily replaced by the Marwaris in the interwar period.

At 1914, the coal mining interests were polarized in two camps, the Europeans belonging in the Indian Mining Association affiliated to the Bengal Chamber of Commerce, and the Indians organized under the Indian Mining Federation. The start of the latter association was provoked by the railways' alleged preferential treatment to European colliers. These associations not only worked as cartels, the latter in particular tried to popularize the use of coal in industries

[3] Ratna and Rajat Ray, 'European Monopoly Corporations and Indian Entrepreneurship, 1913–1922: Early Politics of Coal in Eastern India', *EPW*, IX(21), 1974.

where wood fuel was still being used. In the 1920s, both associations joined hands to resist labour militancy. Labour movements were causing problems at a time when the market was beginning to enter a depressed phase.

## Production and Labour

Even as late as the 1920s, the extraction technology was largely manual. Coal was cut, loaded, and hauled by hand, and wherever possible, not extracted from great depths. The technology was more primitive in smaller mines. The largest of the European mines did use electricity and steam power for hauling coal, for pumping out water from the mines, and for lighting pits. But electricity was an exception rather than the rule. This can be seen in the large coal usage in the mines themselves. In general, economies of scale were rarely utilized fully, and the tools were seldom of the most productive variety. The Indian mine labourer's average output was less than half that of the British miner, and one-fourth that of the Australian in the mid-1930s. Further, mines worked with very little regard for conservation and safety. Underground fires, subsidence, and accidents, were frequent.

The profits of the coal business were shared between landlords and colliers. The owners of the mine lands were the *zamindars* of the *jungle mahals*. By and large they were a rent-receiving luxury-loving class who held no interest in mining. They leased out land to the colliers and received a fixed rent, irrespective of the rate of profit. So they had no interest in productivity either.

Why did the colliers not invest more in improving the technology of mining? The answer lies, not in lack of profits but in the low wages at which coal labour was available. The mines hired experienced and educated personnel only for their small managerial cadre. Bulk of the labourers were hired by contractors at piece wages. They came from the poorest rural strata, and had few alternative opportunities to fall back on. Although a poor region in terms of resources and infrastructure, Chota Nagpur was nevertheless a densely populated area at the end of the nineteenth century. The conditions of servitude that characterized the rural proletariat are legendary. The existence of a cheap unskilled labour force on hire not only made mining costs unbeatably low in India, but also encouraged mining technology to remain as crude as possible. With labour unrest rising post the 1920s, the miners made sure that their work-practices were such as not to require a permanent or skilled labour force. The reliance on the contractor and piece-rates was a recruitment feature common to both mines and plantations. Wages, however, were higher in the mines and rose faster in mining until 1930. The contract system bound labourers to service on terms they little understood before agreeing to them. In this respect, mining and plantation labour were similar in the early days.

## Other Mines

Crude oil had been indigenously extracted and used in Burma for a long time. Modern oil wells owed their origin in the late nineteenth century largely to the government's keen interest in oil. The government was interested for several reasons. Firstly, the Crown had monopoly mining rights over the empire. Secondly, kerosene was becoming a household fuel and its regular supply was a matter of political concern. Thirdly, the Royal Navy was in need of oil. Oilfields at first existed only in Burma, with a small operation in Assam producing only a fraction of the total oil output. The mining contract in Burma was held by a British firm, the Burmah Oil. Non-British contenders for mining, such as Standard Oil Co. or Shell, were excluded by the government, which led some nationalist writers to accuse the government of favouring the British firm. G.G. Jones argues that the decision was influenced by the belief that Standard Oil was a predatory company with monopolistic propensities. This decision could be defended until 1905 when the government invested in exploration and surveys. After 1905, Burmah Oil's monopoly retarded such developments while a revenue tariff continued to give them some protection.[4]

Gold was mainly mined in southeastern Mysore. A European company leased in these mines and started a township in Kolar. Most workers were migrants of depressed castes, lowly paid, and casual. Their work contract was seldom to their advantage, drawn-up by their employers who had better access to legal information. The work was hazardous and could lead to diseases and accidents. Nevertheless, the enterprise generated considerable externalities. The image of plenitude and personal freedom of the mining town that drew migrants was well-founded. Wages in the mines were higher than agricultural wages. The consumption basket was bigger and more diverse. Entrepreneurial opportunities in the mining town were greater and social status distinctly less oppressed .

India has been one of the major producers of mica in the world.

---

[4] 'The State and Economic Development in India 1890–1947', *MAS*, 13(3), 1979.

The demand for mica increased worldwide along with the production of electrical and military aeronautics apparatus. However, the demand was not a steady one so that the prices and quantities fluctuated a great deal. Mica was mined in eastern India and in the Nellore district of Madras. A recent work on mica in Nellore shows how mining could become a lucrative, if a rather speculative venture. And yet it left little positive long-term effects on the local population or labour.[5]

## Mining and Development

Coal was an enterprise that fuelled modern sectors, attracted European capital, and was extremely profitable almost throughout the colonial period. Coal mining was a major source of non-agricultural income in eastern India. And yet, the potential of mining to generate broad-based economic development was limited. For, the mines used work practices that were largely traditional. They were traditional in the sense of relying on a large pool of surplus unskilled labour. The miners invested little on developing individual skills as the mines had no use for them . The labouring population in the mining districts lived a life that was hardly different from that of their rural brethren except for the fact that they did not face stark starvation. It is probable that if high profits had coincided at some point with a serious and persistent labour shortage, technology and wages might have improved. But that never happened. The region's accelerated population growth further ensured surplus labour and low wages. There was no incentive to change the dismal standards of labour and life on the mines. In other recent work on mining labour, the same duality of high profitability with pathetic working conditions reappear.

Having said that, mining did transform the local economies by creating considerable externalities. In the Damodar basin, the rural or semi-rural areas where the mines themselves were located, became dotted with small and large towns supplying white-collar workers and modern services such as banks, hospitals, and schools. The mining towns were a source of enterprise, with diverse job opportunities. They were less hierarchical than the migrant labourers' hometowns and villages. The region had a dense network of infrastructure, which suited limited state-sponsored industrialization.

[5] K. Das, 'Growth and Decline of Mica Mining Industry in Nellore, 1911–50', *IESHR*, 28(4), 1991.

## BANKING

Banking in colonial India can be divided into two broad segments —informal and formal. The informal sector consisted of private banking houses that were not legally recognized as either companies or banks. Formal sector banking in the colonial period had four constituents. These were the exchange banks, the Presidency banks, the Indian joint stock banks, and the cooperative credit societies. Foreign trade and remittance was handled by the group of foreign-owned exchange banks. The Presidency Banks and private joint-stock banks handled domestic trade and remittance in a small formal sector. Indian moneylenders, banking firms, and traders catered to the credit needs of a vast body of private individuals consisting of peasants, landlords and artisans producing for the local markets. The borders between these segments were not clearly defined. The exchange banks deposited a part of their balances with the Presidency banks. The Presidency banks and Indian moneylenders often financed the same business at two different stages, or were mediated by the *shroffs*. Nevertheless, in any occupation that did not concern foreign trade, remittances, or modern factories, the formal banking sector tended to have a marginal role. In terms of employment and income, such occupations probably dominated economic activity. Cooperative credit societies were started after the passing of the Cooperative Societies Act of 1904, which exempted cooperative societies from the Indian Companies Act. Rural credit societies increased in number and quantum of deposits rapidly. But at the time of independence 1947, this remained a very small segment of the banking sector, and not a very efficient source of rural finance either.

## Commercial Banking

### The Informal Sector

A great deal of the credit transactions in agriculture and small-scale industry was in the form of loans given by employers or merchants to actual producers against work-in-progress. In other words, the bulk of the transactions was individual trade credit and not banking as such. Professional moneylenders and bankers gave credit to a wider range of clients. They changed currencies and remitted money within and outside India. But they rarely accepted deposits from the public. In that sense, they did not serve as 'banks'. They had no function in savings or in the circulation of money between households and producers, but they did help money to circulate among producers.

Little concrete information exists about the history of informal credit in India. No data exists on the scale or the terms of credit.

## Exchange Banks

The failure of the agency houses in Calcutta (see Chapter 5) created a gap in financing foreign trade in India. Overcoming some resistance from the East India Company, foreign banks began to enter this field from 1853. These banks were based at the countries of origin, but they financed trade from and to India. Of the 17 exchange banks that remained at independence, 7 had their head offices in England, 2 each in the USA, Japan and Pakistan, and the others were based in France, Holland, China and Hong Kong. Four of these, including the Chartered Bank and the Grindlays, had the bulk of their business in India. The operation of the exchange banks was a matter of some controversy. As a group, they monopolized foreign trade financing. While the Indian private banks could in principle enter this market, they could not operate easily at the London end of the dealings. On the other hand, for reasons of security or easier communication, the majority of the clients of the exchange banks were foreigners themselves. Indian traders by and large found it difficult to do business with the exchange banks.

## The Presidency Banks

The three Presidency banks—the Bank of Bengal, Bank of Bombay and Bank of Madras—were all established between 1809 and 1843 with government participation in capital, and control on management. Of these, the Bank of Bombay failed in 1868, shortly after the cotton boom of Bombay. But a bank by the same name was started again. These banks performed five key functions. They (a) held the government's cash balances, (b) issued, in a limited way, and circulated currency notes, (c) discounted bills and securities, (d) advanced short-term working capital credit to private business, and (e) accepted deposits from the public. Being the government's banker, the Presidency banks had to operate under restrictions. Thus, they were not permitted to deal in foreign exchange, which was initially considered a risky business, and following Anglo–Saxon tradition, they did not supply long-term loans. They did, however, accept securities against advances. Thus, they can be seen to have stimulated the capital market in this way. In 1876, all three came under a single Act and a uniform set of regulations. In 1921, they were amalgamated to form the Imperial Bank of India. In 1947, the Imperial Bank was nationalized and renamed State Bank of India.

Indian Joint Stock Banks

Other than the Presidency Banks, joint stock banks in India, until the start of the Reserve Bank of India, had a history of booms followed by crashes. The first boom occurred in Calcutta in the early nineteenth century. The agency houses provided some small-scale banking services for the East India Company, private merchants, and the public. The crashes in the 1830s and 40s finished them off. The second boom occurred in Bombay in the 1860s, encouraged by cotton speculation and the recognition of limited liability. Again, most of the banks then started, later went into liquidation. A third boom originated from Calcutta in 1906 with the spread of the spirit of swadeshi. But Indian banks elsewhere, also profited from the nationalistic wave. In 1913–14, a few major bankruptcies led to a widespread crash of these banks.

In this rather awkward way, Indian joint stock banks as a whole expanded and the habit of banking spread among urban households. Until the end of the First World War, deposits held at the Presidency banks exceeded that held in the Indian joint stock banks. Thereafter, growth of deposits in Indian joint stock banks was far more rapid, despite periodic crashes of major banks (the biggest of which occurred in 1923). In 1947, the Indian banks together formed the largest segment in modern banking. The high risks of failure were a rather heavy cost that the public paid for such growth. It is probable that actual savings would have been much higher but for the high failure rate of Indian banks.

Two questions of analytical interest about this history are the following. Why did the Indian banks continue to grow rapidly despite the high risks? And why did they suffer from high risks? The former question can be answered by pointing out the limited physical reach of the Presidency banks, their conservative mentality, and the offer of high incentives by the Indian banks. The Presidency banks were slow to expand branches. They had almost no presence in smaller towns. Many such towns had considerable demand for credit due to agricultural trade. Being the government's banker, they were rather rigid, conservative, and complacent. They never tried hard to seek out business from the private sector. This complacency was somewhat shaken in the interwar period with the entry of a large number of joint stock banks.

The main clients of the Presidency banks were businesses connected with European enterprise in India and that small segment of Indian enterprise that the Europeans understood or could easily communicate with. Thus, the largest of the *shroffs*, the indigenous bankers, were also clients of the Presidency Banks. The Presidency Banks were not easily persuaded to lend money to small or medium-scale Indian business. Increasingly joint-stock banks were started by Indians to meet that need. Basically, a small Indian firm had little chance of being entertained by the Presidency banks. The number of such firms was growing rapidly, leading to a pervasive and acute excess demand for credit.

Indian banks, in their turn, were new and unknown firms. While they were less conservative about their clients, they had neither the brand name of the Presidency banks nor the image of high security that the government backing gave the latter. Thus, they felt that they needed to offer high incentives to attract deposits and borrowers. Furthermore, the absence of an explicit regulatory system or a central bank made them take undue risks. As it often turned out, they also made unrealistic commitments. In brief, they suffered from high risks of failure due to under-capitalization, inexperience, insider lending, adverse selection, and the absence of a lender-of-last-resort. Let us examine these problems in more detail.

The common features of the swadeshi banks started between 1906 and 1913 were small paid-up capital, boards of directors predominated by lawyers, and management by persons without any experience or knowledge of banking. They secured deposits by offering high rates. The Presidency banks lent only on the strength of very good securities which made it difficult for an average Indian business to borrow from them. There were simply not enough first-class securities around. The Indian banks were forced to lend on inadequate securities. To earn enough money on a high-cost capital, they lent to risk-taking businesses. In other words, they suffered from an 'adverse selection' problem. While the Presidency banks strictly confined themselves to working capital credit, the Indian banks did not necessarily thus restrict themselves. They responded to a genuine excess demand for fixed capital credit. But this business locked up money for long periods of time often on dubious mortgages. Many Indian banks were started by leading trading-industrial houses with a view to lending money borrowed from the public to the group's own businesses. This practice of insider lending is always subject to risks of default, because rules of repayment are rarely enforced in a strict way.

When a crisis of widespread default did strike, these banks were less able than either the Presidency banks or the exchange banks to tide over. The average Indian bank had very small capital to start with. Its deposit-base was tiny compared to any one of the Presidency banks or the average exchange bank. While their own reserves were small, the absence of a lender-of-last-resort pushed even slightly troubled banks quickly into liquidation. Usually, when a few banks are troubled by default, the banking system can remain stable if loans are available from the central bank to capitalize the troubled banks. Otherwise mild crises can create panic among depositors and snowball into major runs on all banks. This is what happened many times between 1913 and 1946.

## Evolution of a Central Bank

Though the Reserve Bank of India was established only in 1935, the idea of a central bank had a long pre-history. It was proposed for the first time in 1773 by Warren Hastings. The objective was to have a government's banker, to develop a competitor for the private moneylenders who then ruled the money market, and to resolve the chaos that arose from a number of currencies in circulation. A bank did result from this proposal, but was quickly closed down, probably as a result of conflicts within the Company, despite having made some profits in the few years that it was at work. Subsequently, the establishment of the Presidency banks took care of the most pressing need, that of a banker to the government.

There are basically four functions that a central bank is expected to perform: (a) banker to the government, (b) banker to other banks, (c) regulation of currency and money supply, and (d) management of foreign exchange. The Presidency banks (and the Imperial Bank of India after 1921) served only the first function. In addition, they operated as commercial banks. They did become bankers to other banks on a functional level. That is, they received deposit from other major banks, but not as a matter of obligation. Nor were they obliged to or expected to lend to other banks in times of crisis. The Presidency banks had little or no role in the pursuit of objectives (c) and (d). Until the establishment of the Reserve Bank of India, the third role was played by the finance department of the government.

The need for an institution to serve all the functions of a central bank was periodically restated, especially since the model of the Bank of England was in the minds of every influential voice on Indian finance. In the 1860s the proposal was briefly revived. It was shot down by the then viceroy Sir John Lawrence. His minute on the subject revealed that the government was not willing to accept the idea of a monetary authority independent of its influence. The proposal was revived again in the course of the 1898 currency reform committee. The Royal Commission on Indian Finance and Currency (1910) invited J.M. Keynes and Sir Ernest Cable to write a proposal for a central bank. Keynes was known to be strongly in favour of the idea. Until 1925 the government remained inert. The war and the exchange controversy diverted its attention. But perhaps more importantly, the idea of an independent monetary authority still faced substantial mental block.

The idea finally came on its own at the Currency Commission, 1926 and the Indian Central Banking Enquiry Committee, 1931. Both reports officially endorsed it, and recorded strong recommendation for it from influential witnesses. One of them was Sir Montagu Norman, the then Governor of the Bank of England. When the Reserve Bank finally started, one of its first tasks was to integrate what seemed a very fragmented and chaotic banking system. This was done neither suddenly nor completely. It was attempted in a series of steps, some of which were forced by circumstances such as subsequent banking panics.

## Banking and Development

How far did modern banking contribute to industrialization, savings behaviour, and economic stability? What conditions influenced banks' involvement with long-term or fixed capital credit? Was the nature of financial institutions responsible for India's limited industrialization compared to the developed world? Did colonialism shape these institutional factors?

### Growth of Banking Capital

Deposits in all commercial banks increased from Rs 125 million in 1870 to Rs 2,530 million in 1937. In 1870, the Presidency banks accounted for over 90 per cent of the deposits. By 1940, Presidency banks, exchange banks and other types of banks had roughly equal shares in total deposits. In real terms, deposits grew about twelve times. This was a significant order of growth, for it well exceeded the rate of growth in real national income. However, bank deposits accounted for no more than an estimated 10–15 per cent of financial savings about 1940. Bank loans financed an equally small percentage of capital formation. This limited reach of banks in ordinary people's lives was a result of two things, the conservatism of the European banks who confined their operations to the urban areas and to large-scale businesses, and the high risk of failure of Indian banks. These conditions need closer look.

Credit Rationing

Recent work on banking has highlighted what is known to be a basic condition of the industrial credit market, pervasive and acute excess demand and resultant credit rationing. Rationing was noted as early as 1918, in the report of the Indian Industrial Commission. One obvious problem was poor information. When the financier was a European officer of a Presidency bank, and the borrower was the Indian owner of a small firm, the creditworthiness of the client was neither taken for granted nor easy to establish. The managerial cadres in the Presidency Banks were heavily Europeanized. 'Asymmetric information' was pervasive in the dealings between the managers and their Indian clients. The problem also arose in the business of the exchange banks for the same reason. It appeared in the business of the Indian joint stock banks because their clients tended to be small and unreputed firms. Credit rationing led to a number of distortions in industrial financing.

Distortions in the Financial System and Behaviour

Credit rationing led to a shortage of fixed capital. The major banks did not lend for long periods. Financing expansion, new and unknown ventures tended to push the investor to high-cost sources. It discouraged the small firm from dealing with the large banks as they insisted on quality securities which none but the richest firms could offer. The system heavily discriminated against the 'middle-class industrialist'. Indians especially 'find it difficult to satisfy a bank'.[6] There was, thus, a divide within the modern banking sector, big banks dealt with big clients and small banks dealt with small and often unknown or unreliable clients.

Whether for big or small firms, long-term capital came from commercial accumulation and the capital market. But the capital market was fragmented. London, not Bombay, was the main market for securities. London was out of reach for most Indian investors, and securities floated abroad had a smaller impact on development of the capital market in India as compared with securities sold at home. The London market financed construction of the railways, a sector that played the role of a catalyst in the financial development of continental Europe but had no comparable impact in India. As we have seen, excess demand for capital and the element of implicit

[6] India, *Report of the Indian Industrial Commission 1916–18*, Calcutta, 1918, p. 213.

discrimination against small Indian firms encouraged the entry of weak, inexperienced, dishonest, and under-capitalized banks. The condition, in turn, increased risks of failure.

The shortage of fixed capital also led to under-capitalization of the businesses that depended on bank finance. As was mentioned in Chapter 5, short supply of fixed capital led to a tendency towards over-capitalization during booms with under-capitalization at other times. Investors had the means to buy machinery, only during a boom with rising prices. New firms were negligent about maintaining cash reserves and providing for depreciation.[7] Further, majority of the Indian firms paid dividends during a boom to secure investors. Given that the capital market was undeveloped or out of reach of most small investors, if banks did lend money for fixed capital, there was a tendency to take too much loan which was a much costlier way of financing fixed capital *vis-à-vis* shares. Thus, new ventures tended to be financially weak from the start.[8]

Shortage of capital led to dependence on new sources of finance that could be risky. For example, there was a high degree of dependence of Bombay and Ahmedabad mills on deposits from the public. Depositors had little commitment in the industry. As there were no banks or other institutions intervening between the mills and depositors, the latter 'were apt to be easily led away by any bazaar gossip'.[9] Scarcity made capital an object of speculation. Any artificial scarcity could generate rents. Furthermore, the fact that the joint-stock organization was not a product of gradual evolution in India, but introduced from outside, increased the scope for speculation. Insiders knew how to manipulate the share market—outsiders knew very little, and checks on the insiders were few. These conditions led to the first stock market speculations in Bombay, Calcutta and Madras. This speculative image of the stock market continued.

[7] See also discussion in p. 175 and references cited in footnote 11, Ch. 5.

[8] A citation describing how the typical 'swadeshi' enterprise began is a good illustration: 'Most industries are started in Bengal with inadequate capital. Where rupees 10 lacs are required, the promoters, as soon as they raise rupees 2 lacs, buy land, erect buildings, and then approach banks for loan to purchase machinery by mortgaging land and buildings. When the machinery arrives, it is hypothecated and further loan is raised to purchase more machinery. By the time manufacture starts the industry is heavily indebted'. 'Banking' in *Career Lectures*, Appointments and Information Board, Calcutta University, Calcutta, 1939, p. 229–30. This is a collection of popular lectures by persons established in commerce and industry in Calcutta, designed to make students more familiar with such vocations.

[9] Nabagopal Das, *Industrial Enterprise in India*, Oxford University Press, 1938, p. 9.

Turning to the depositors of the joint-stock banks, a point of interest is how far banks could induce a change in savings behaviour so as to make more funds available. Despite substantial increases in the scale of deposits, the aggregate rates of savings and investment remained very low and choice of assets remained largely traditional. Banks were limited in reach both as a saving and a credit institution. The riskiness of Indian banks played a major role in hindering the stride of modern banking.

Further, there is the problem of the informal sector. What type of institutions could supply long-term capital to, say, artisans or middle peasants? Modern banking had no role here. The informal sector moneylenders did not ordinarily lend for productive investments. The cooperative societies did not grow sufficiently to make a difference. In post-independence India, this problem has been addressed by government ownership of banks and government directives on the banks to lend to the informal sector. But this road has proven unproductive and wasteful.

## Insurance

The history of the insurance business is significant for several reasons. It made an early start when the Calcutta agency houses introduced it in the late eighteenth century. They mainly supplied marine insurance. Indian business enterprises of Calcutta were interested in insurance in this early phase. Insurance was also the originator of the managing agency system. While the agency houses collapsed, insurance business survived and continued to draw new entrants.

Commercial life insurance began in 1818 with the Oriental Life Assurance Co. of Calcutta (no relation of the company of the same name today). In 1823, the Bombay Life Assurance Co., and in 1829, the Madras Equitable Co. were formed. The idea of life insurance had come from London. In a country such as India with low life expectancy, it can be expected that insurance, though expensive, would become instantly popular. However, in the absence of reliable mortality tables for Indians, insurance remained confined mainly to the small European population resident in India. It took nearly half a century for Indian insurance providers to treat Indian lives as equivalent to Europeans in India. The Bombay Mutual Life Assurance Co. was the pioneer in this respect.

From a very small base, total stock of policy values increased rapidly after the 1870s. This was one business that remained more or less unaffected by the Great Depression. Per capita policy value increased from about Rs 0.37 in 1901 to Rs 7.81 in 1941. But both coverage, and average value were fractions of that in any developed country of that time. Besides limited reach, a major problem of the business was high mortality of companies. These problems were similar to that of the banking sector, and were probably related.

## Conclusion

Three general impacts of the mines and plantations need to be re-stated. These activities generated incomes for themselves and for the regional economies. They contributed to the working of a modern economy. And they affected the lives and labours of a million people directly employed by them. A large part of plantation and mine studies has been influenced by the labour experience and, while providing indispensable narrative histories, have tended to stress rather excessively the inequality of power in the relationship between these sectors and the local economies, and between labour and capital within these sectors. Migrant labour in plantations did work in an unequal environment. But they came from backgrounds that were usually far more insecure economically, and more degrading socially.

Commercialization and industrial growth depended on modern banking. Banks and insurance grew very rapidly in colonial India, especially after 1870. This growth was not really rooted in old banking tradition. It originated mainly in European enterprise, and partly in Indian mercantile enterprise. The growth occurred in an environment of pervasive capital scarcity and poor regulatory framework. Inevitably, the growth was characterized by high instability. This is probably the reason why, despite the rapid growth of banking capital, banking habits grew to a very limited extent.

Chapters 3–6 described production and occupations. We can now turn to the question of how the economic system as a whole, of which production was one component, worked.

## Annotated Readings
### Plantations

Percival Griffiths, *The History of the Indian Tea Industry*, Weidenfield and Nicholson, London, 1967. This readable and comprehensive history is more than 700 pages long. It is not expected that the student will read all of it, but s/he become familiar with the book. For a descriptive history of the plantations in south India, see S.G. Speer, *UPASI 1893–1953*, Coonoor, no date.

More analytical histories have seen the plantation sector together with the regional economies where they were located. In these works, there is an overwhelming accent on labour. For northern Bengal, see Ranajit Das Gupta, *Economy, Society and Politics in Bengal: Jalpaiguri 1869–1947*, Oxford University Press, Delhi, 1992, Ch. 4; and Virginius Xaxa, 'Colonial Capitalism and Underdevelopment in North Bengal', *EPW*, 20(39), 1985. For Assam, see Ranajit Das Gupta, 'From Peasants and Tribesmen to Plantation Workers—Colonial Capitalism, Reproduction of Labour Power and Proletarianisation in North East India: 1850s–1947', *EPW*, 21(4), 1986; R.P. Behal, 'Forms of Labour Protest in Assam Valley Tea Plantations, 1900–1950', *EPW*, 20(4), 1985; Ralph Shlomowitz and Lance Brennan, 'Mortality and Migrant Labour en-route to Assam, 1863–1924', *IESHR*, 27(3), 1990; Arjan de Haan, 'Migration in Eastern India: A Segmented Labour Market', *IESHR*, 32(1), 1995. On south India, Tharian George and P.K. Michael Tharakan, 'Penetration of Capital into a Traditional Economy: The Case of Tea Plantations in Kerala', *Studies in History*, 2(2), 1986; K. Ravi Raman, 'Labour under Imperial Hegemony: The Case of Tea Plantations in South India, 1914–46', in S. Bhattacharya et al (eds), *The South Indian Economy*, Oxford University Press, Delhi, 1991.

## Mines

C.P. Simmons, 'Indigenous Enterprise in the Indian Coal Mining Industry, c. 1835–1939', *IESHR*, 13(2), 1976. C.P. Simmons, 'Recruiting and Organizing an Industrial Labour Force in Colonial India: The Case of the Coal Mining Industry, c. 1880–1939', *IESHR*, 13(4), 1976. Henner Papandieck, 'British Managing Agencies in the Indian Coalfield', in D. Rothermund and D.C. Wadhwa (eds), *Zamindars, Mines, and Peasants: Studies in the History of an Indian Coalfield*, Manohar, Delhi, 1978. D. Rothermund (ed.), *Urban Growth and Rural Stagnation. Studies in the Economy of an Indian Coalfield and its Rural Hinterland*, Manohar, Delhi, 1978. Dilip Simeon, *The Politics of Labour Under Late Colonialism: Workers, Unions and the State in Chota Nagpur 1928–1939*, Manohar, Delhi, 1995, especially pp. 16–8, 23–30, 149–158. A.B. Ghosh, *Coal Industry in India*, S. Chand, Delhi, 1978.

## Banking and Insurance

A.G. Chandavarkar, 'Money and Credit, 1858–1947', CEHI 2. R.S. Rungta, *The Rise of Business Corporations in India, 1851–1900*, Cambridge,

1970. A.K. Bagchi, *The Evolution of the State Bank of India*, Vol. 2, Sage Publications, New Delhi, 1997, Ch. 2. G.R. Desai, *Life Insurance Business in India*, Macmillan, Delhi, 1973.

# 7

# The Macroeconomy

This chapter will be concerned with movements in macroeconomic variables such as national income, savings, investment, price indices, etc.. It will also explore the relationships between these variables, which can be seen as a way to describe the economy. Such descriptions can lead to better understanding of the causes behind growth and fluctuations. In that sense, the chapter is an application of basic macroeconomics. Further, they can be seen as a critique of colonialism. For colonial India, applied macroeconomics is a topic with political implications. These implications derive from two characteristics of colonial Indian economy. The first is the relatively low growth rate of national income. And the second is certain features of the macroeconomy that arose from India's status as a British colony. Nationalist writers drew a cause and effect relationship between the political status of the country and its economic performance. Historians too have had to deal with the question, does colonialism explain India's stagnation? The subject, however, is not a very popular one. Partly due to problems of data, and partly because the analytical language is not widely used, it has been confined to a rather small body of scholars.

The chapter is divided into five sections. The first presents a summary of the main facts about the economy of colonial India. What were the specific features of the colonial economy? How were these responsible for growth or stagnation? These two questions will be answered briefly in the first section, abstracting from a number of details that will follow in the rest of the chapter. The second section presents a statistical overview of the 'real' side of the economy. It deals with incomes, investment, balance of payments, and government transactions. The third describes the 'financial' aspect, analysing two interrelated processes of money supply change, and the determination of exchange rate. The fourth deals with fluctuations in prices and outputs. In the fifth and final section, two possible answers of the question—why India stagnated—will be suggested. At the end of the book, there is an appendix showing how a national accounting framework can be useful in analysing the economic performance of colonial India. The national accounts being no more than a set of definitions, can be described very simply without any prior knowledge of macroeconomics. Nevertheless, for an adequate understanding of this system, familiarity with the first chapter of a standard macroeconomics textbook is required.

## AN OVERVIEW:
## ECONOMIC STRUCTURE, GROWTH AND FLUCTUATIONS

### Structure

The economy of colonial India had certain distinct features, some of which characterized the world economy in the nineteenth century. For example, a greater degree of openness in respect of trade or investment, and closer link between money supply and balance of payments. Some others can be called typically 'colonial'. An example is the presence of large remittance abroad on the government account. And still others were specific to India. For example, the importance of agriculture in the national economy, risks and uncertainty of monsoon agriculture, and the Indians' craving for gold and silver.

### Openness

India was a more open economy in the colonial period, relative to what it had been in the eighteenth century, and what it became in the first 40 years of independence. Openness can be seen in trade relations, income and capital flows, government transactions and policy, and the monetary system. Total foreign trade (export plus import) expressed as a ratio of national income tends to be used as a measure of the commercial openness of an economy. This ratio increased from possibly less than 10 per cent in the 1860s to about 20 per cent by 1914. These percentages are comparable with that of rapidly growing economies. The ratio for Japan was over 30 per cent about 1914. In the United States, the ratio was 16 in 1880, but fell thereafter as the country attained industrial maturity.

Apart from trade, income and capital flows were also almost certainly larger in the colonial period than before or after. Until the Great Depression, there were two main sources of net receipt in India's foreign transactions—foreign trade and foreign investment. India's exports exceeded the value of imports. India received foreign investment in industry, commerce, and infrastructure. These two net receipts were balanced by three large items of net payment: purchase of gold and silver, remittances made by the private sector, and remittances made by the government.

Government transactions were intimately connected with the balance of payments. The government borrowed heavily abroad to finance its investment and other commitments in India. Repayment of these loans along with regular remittance on account of charges made by Britain on Indian administration was a large net payment item in India's foreign transactions.

Money supply in colonial India was mainly influenced by the balance of payments. This feature characterized many contemporary economies. It arose from the primary objective of monetary policy in that period to stabilize the exchange rate. The objectives changed to stabilization of prices and outputs after the Second World War under the influence of Keynesian macroeconomic thought.

While the economy was 'globalized' in so many ways, it was also very dependent on a purely internal source of growth and fluctuations—agriculture.

Agriculture as the Main Source of Domestic Demand
India was primarily an agrarian economy at the beginning and the end of the colonial rule. The main source of variability in national income was a purely internal one, the size of the harvest. The size of the harvest responded relatively less to demand and more to the quantity and timing of rainfall during the monsoons. In that sense, it was a variable more or less independent from the rest of the economy. Agriculture, or rather the interaction between agriculture and the rest of the economy, is the key to explaining growth and fluctuations in colonial India.

Policy
Formally, there was minimum direct government intervention in the economy. Stabilization of prices and outputs was meant to happen automatically. Economic growth was not seen as a goal that could be served by macroeconomic policy. Indirectly, of course, the actions and priorities of the government could be an important factor behind

growth. Stabilization in Britain's external account was usually in the minds of those who decided Indian affairs. When Indian interests and Britain's interests came in conflict, there was often an implicit or explicit intervention. Such a situation arose in the interwar period.

## Growth

Economic growth can be defined as sustained increase in total and per capita income for a sufficiently long period. Broader definitions would include various kinds of assets and the quality of life. Historically, economic growth begins to occur in the presence of sustained increase in demand for goods and services, and (a) availability of resources needed for expansion of supply of goods and services, (b) investment that enables expansion of productive capacity, and (c) increasing efficiency in the utilization of resources. The relative importance of these factors can vary.

Nearly all examples of rapid economic growth saw commercialization, and rapid growth in exports. Commercialization makes production market-oriented, and following Adam Smith, creates conditions for increased efficiency.

Empirical works on economic growth in the long run suggest a sequence whereby a poor country abundant in natural resources and labour starts by exporting resources. Later, with the exhaustion of resources, and increased savings and knowledge of alternative opportunities, it switches to export of labour-intensive manufactures. Further on, with exhaustion of surplus labour and further increases in savings and knowledge, it switches to capital-intensive industry. All three stages can generate growth in total income. But only the third—when capital-per-worker begins to increase and labour-productivity rises—implies growth in wages and in per capita incomes. The shift from the second to the third stage, therefore, is significant. That shift also requires limited or falling population growth rates so that surplus labour gets exhausted quickly. Further, the increased use of machinery or of capital-per-worker implies rising saving and investment rates in national income.

The pattern of growth in colonial India illustrates the first and the second stages of this model, though not the exact sequence of stages. In the nineteenth century, economic growth did occur. It was driven by India's integration in a rapidly growing world market mainly as supplier of goods intensive in natural resources or labour. Investment in irrigation and railways enabled the expansion in supply of land in a number of ways. Labour was not scarce. But as population was not growing rapidly, demand for labour probably grew faster than the supply of labour. On small-scale industry, commercialization had a contradictory effect, but on the average, small-scale industry experienced growth rather than decline.

In the first half of the twentieth century, agriculture and investments slowed down. The growth momentum in industry and certain services strengthened. But agriculture had a much larger weight in national income. Why did the nineteenth century dynamics of the economy weaken? First, resource-intensive growth had reached its limits with the exhaustion of the critical resource, land. Second, the world economy entered a depression from the mid-1920s. And third, due to accelerated population growth, the supply of labour was rapidly increasing relative to capital and resources. Economic growth needed investment for making better use of scarce resources such as land, and in such sectors as education and health that could create the pre-conditions for lower population growth and develop human capital by enhancing the capability of the average worker.

Rates of investment were always low in colonial India. Further, the share of investment in government expenditure, and the ratio of public investment in national income both declined in the last 50 years of British rule. Why were these rates low and decreasing? One available answer is that, colonialism imposed financial burdens on the government. Alternatively, we can explain low rates of private investment through adverse structural features, such as high risks and uncertainty.

TABLE 7.1
Measures of Economic Growth, 1891–1938

|  | 1891 | 1921 (Base) | 1938 |
|---|---|---|---|
| Real National Income |  |  |  |
| Total | 70 | 100 | 126 |
| Per capita | 78 | 100 | 82 |
| Agriculture | 67 | 100 | 100 |
| Industry | – | 100 | 175 |
| Infrastructure |  |  |  |
| Acreage irrigated | 52 | 100 | 123 |
| Railway mileage per capita | 51 | 100 | 110 |
| Postal articles handled per capita | 27 | 100 | 57 |
| Real value of telegraphs sent per capita | 55 | 100 | 83 |

| | 1891 | 1921 (Base) | 1938 |
|---|---|---|---|
| Employment | | | |
| Factory | 25 | 100 | 137 |
| Total | 80–85 | 100 | 105–110 |
| Foreign Trade | | | |
| Real value of export | 76 | 100 | 96 |
| Real value of import | 72 | 100 | 95 |
| Financial Development | | | |
| Real value of bank deposits | 29 | 100 | 183 |
| Resources | | | |
| Cultivated land (million acres) | 56 | 100 | 103 |
| Production of coal (million tonnes) | 11 | 100 | 156 |
| Population | 89 | 100 | 153 |

*Sources:* The table collates data presented and discussed in the other chapters.

Thus, colonial India illustrates the strengths and limitations of economic growth based on intensive use of natural resources and labour. The initial impetus and its weakening are both outlined in Table 7.1 with the help of a number of indices. It shows that agriculture and the physical infrastructure progressed in the nineteenth century but the rate of growth fell in the interwar period. There was no exact cut-off date, but 1921 demonstrates this slowdown well enough. The only sectors where growth continued in the interwar period were industry and financial services.

## Fluctuations

The location of India in the tropics makes it exceedingly drought-prone. The prospect of devastating famines once every few years was inherent in India's ecology. Hence, not only did high risk discourage investment by making the returns uncertain, but also, available saving were often used up in coping with calamities. A major form of savings in India was gold and silver jewellery. This preference for precious metals reduced savings available for productive investment. This behaviour can be interpreted as a response to risks. Other financial assets fluctuate in real value given the price fluctuations that climatic factors cause. Gold and silver might be seen as more stable assets.

Prices (and real wages) in colonial India fluctuated a great deal. India functioned under currency regimes that made money supply sensitive to the balance of payments. But real incomes depended primarily on harvests. Harvests were extremely weather-sensitive, and the weather was unreliable. This points to an inherent and chronic maladjustment between money supply and the transactions demand for money. Episodes of very rapid inflation were usually periods when a bad harvest coincided with buoyant trade demand, so that a decline in demand for money coincided with an increased supply of money. Similarly, the Great Depression saw contraction in money supply because of trade depression, even as domestic demand for money did not decline.

India was not exceptional in this instability. Even in the 1930s, most colonial economies in Asia and Africa possessed neither central banks, nor governments explicitly concerned with domestic stabilization. Many colonies were agrarian economies constantly under the threat of harvest-induced fluctuations. The interwar period witnessed price and income fluctuations more severe than the world had seen before. In a world well integrated by trade and investment, these shocks quickly transmitted to regions ill-equipped to cope with them. It is probable that an unstable environment inhibited local enterprise.

## STATISTICAL OUTLINE

Although some estimates of India's national income before 1900 are available, reasonably reliable estimates begin from 1900. For the nineteenth century, only the foreign trade figures are reliable and fairly complete. This section, therefore, will deal mainly with data for the period 1900–47. Wherever possible, it will cite nineteenth century estimates and compare them with the twentieth. In most cases, the period 1900–14 is more or less similar to the latter half of the nineteenth century. But between the pre-war and the interwar periods, there were major differences. The First World War, in other words, was a macroeconomic 'structural break'.

It is not necessary to go into the details of how the various national income estimates are arrived at or how many different estimates there are. It is sufficient here to mention that alternative figures arise mainly from alternative estimates of agricultural production, a subject that has been dealt with in Chapter 3. The latest figures come from an article published in 1997 by a major contributor in this field, S. Sivasubramonian. This article will be the main source of national income figures used in this chapter. However, the student of the subject ought to be aware of the assumptions that are usually made in any calculation of India's national income in this period. The readings at the end of the chapter will cite some of the works that discuss estimation procedures.

## National Income

What we usually have as India's national income is the expression Gross Domestic Product or GDP + net factor income from abroad + taxes, that is, national income inclusive of taxes. This is the variable we shall be dealing with in this section. Tables 7.2 and 7.3 summarize the basic statistics of national income. From Table 7.2, two conclusions can be drawn. First, in 1900–47 national income grew. Second, it grew at a rate less than 1 per cent per annum. By the best estimates available, nineteenth century did see higher growth rates. In the twentieth century, the 1 per cent growth in National Income translated into a growth rate of per capita income (0.1 per cent) that was near zero. The rate was not only too slow to ensure rapid improvements in living standards but also to be comparable to growth rates of post-independence India, or selective international rates.

At 0.1 per cent per year, it would have taken India centuries to double the average standard of living. Post-independence India has seen higher rates as Table 7.2 shows. The post-1950 period is perhaps not a fair comparison. Productive capacity has grown worldwide so enormously in the last 40–50 years that the world today is used to much higher growth rates than in the past. However, even the past standards of the rest of the world were higher. In the peak periods of the Industrial Revolution, Britain's real national product grew at well over 2 per cent and average income at over 1 per cent. A rate such as the latter was common to most parts of the industrializing world in the late nineteenth and early twentieth centuries. These countries began from income levels that were higher than India's in the mid nineteenth century. Japan is often compared with India because their standards of living were similar in the mid-nineteenth century. From that time until the beginning of the Second World War, Japan's average income grew at a rate that was 5–10 times that of India. Such massive disparities in rates of growth derived partly from India's slower growth of total income, but it also reflected the fact that population was growing at rates that were dissimilar. India's population was beginning to accelerate in the twentieth century, at a time when population growth rate was beginning to fall in most of these countries or stabilize at about 1 per cent per year. In Japan, population growth rate was higher and accelerated, but it fell quickly within 15–20 years after the war.

TABLE 7.2
National Income at 1948–9 Prices, 1900–5 to 1992–5

(annual averages)

|  | National income | | Exponential growth rates over the period (%) | |
|---|---|---|---|---|
|  | Total (Rs billions) | Per capita (Rs) | Total | Per capita |
| 1900–5 | 43.4 | 228 |  |  |
| 1942–7 | 51.5 | 239 | 0.9 | 0.1 |
| 1992–5 | – | – | 4.0[*] | 2.0[*] |

[*] Growth rate over 1950–51 and 1992–5

Source: S. Sivasubramonian, 'Revised Estimates of the National Income of India, 1900–1 to 1946–7', IESHR, 34(2), 1997; Statistical Abstracts for India, New Delhi, various years.

## The Composition of National Income by Sector of Origin

Table 7.3 shows that growth rates of real income were unequal across sectors. India was primarily an agrarian economy throughout colonial rule. Agriculture was growing slowly in the early twentieth century. Industry and the services grew at much higher rates. A great deal of the explanation of India's slow overall growth turns on the question why agriculture was growing slowly. The issue has been discussed in Chapter 3. One immediate reason is the low levels of investment in the economy, to which we shall return.

TABLE 7.3
National Income by Sector, 1900–90s

|  | Percentage contribution to national income at current prices | | | | Exponential growth rates over the period, constant prices (%) | | |
|---|---|---|---|---|---|---|---|
|  | Primary | Secondary | Tertiary | Net income from abroad | Primary | Secondary | Tertiary |
| 1900–4 | 66.0 | 12.0 | 23.5 | −1.5 |  |  |  |
| 1942–6 | 53.3 | 14.5 | 32.3 | −0.2 | 0.4 | 1.4 | 1.7 |
| 1992–5[*] | 34.5 | 24.0 | 41.5 | – |  |  |  |

[*] Net Domestic Product
Source: See Table 7.2.

It is necessary to discuss the experience of the secondary and the tertiary sectors in a little more detail. There are three main components within the secondary sector—mining, large-scale industry and small-scale industry. Large-scale industry grew at rates over 4 per cent per year. The much larger small-scale industry grew at less than 1 per cent. Within the tertiary sector, the contribution of government administration grew at over 2 per cent per year. The two other major components—commerce and transport, and real estate—also expanded quite rapidly at rates of about 1.5 per cent. Thus, there were three powerful positive forces driving the non-agricultural sector. These were, industrialization, government administration, and long-distance trade. The most important negative force here was the slow growth of real income in the small-scale industry. As Chapter 4 argued, the overall small growth rate can be misleading as it conceals the fact that small-scale industry had both growing and declining segments in it.

It needs to be noted that net income from abroad was steadily negative. This component consisted of payment of interest, dividend, pensions, salaries, etc. to foreigners. There were a large number of foreigners working in India who received part of this income for services without which a modern economy would not function in India. However, whether all of this payment was justified or not is a debatable question, to which we shall return.

## Composition of National Income:
### Types of Goods and Services

National income can be seen as an aggregate of consumption goods, capital goods, net export, and goods and services purchased by the government sector (see Table 7.4). For a long-term comparison, similar sets of figures for two periods after independence are also shown in the table. Here, there are three interesting lessons to be learnt about how economic structures of colonial and independent India differed. First, colonial India was a more open economy and a significant net exporter compared to India in the 1970s. The contrast reduced after the mid-1980s with the economic reforms that again encouraged exports. Second, in respect of private investment and government expenditure, colonial India was more backward than independent India. Finally, colonial India was characterized by very high proportion of consumption in national income. This has been decreasing over the decades. All poor countries share this feature.

TABLE 7.4

Components of National Income, 1900–90s

|  | 1901–13 | 1930–9 | 1940–6 | 1970–5 | 1990–6 |
|---|---|---|---|---|---|
| National income | 100.0 | 100.0 | 100.0 | 100.0 | 100.0 |
| Net export of goods and services[a] | 3.4 | 1.4 | n.a. | −0.7 | −0.7 |
| Investment | 6.9 | 9.3 | 7.3 | 18.3 | 24.6 |
| Purchases by the government[b] | 5.4 | 3.5 | 4.3 | 8.9 | 10.8 |
| Consumption[c] | 84.3 | 85.7 | n.a. | 76.0 | 59.5 |

[a] The percentages for the colonial period use Sivasubramonian's revised national income estimates.

[b] For the colonial period, current revenue is taken as a proxy for expenditures in rupees, that is expenditures on goods and services produced in India.

[c] For the colonial period, calculated as a residual.

Sources: The other tables in this chapter for the colonial period, and Economic and Political Weekly Research Foundation, National Accounts Statistics of India, 1950–1 to 1996–7, Mumbai, October 1998 for the more recent periods.

## Foreign Trade

A key to understanding the tertiary sector growth is the trend in India's foreign trade. Foreign trade as a ratio of national income increased significantly from the late nineteenth century. The ratio of exports to national income is a rough measure of the importance of foreign trade for the economy. This was about 8–9 per cent over 1900–39, with a drop around the time of the Great Depression.[1] Total foreign trade (export plus import) expressed as a ratio of national income tends to be used as a measure of the commercial openness of an economy. This ratio increased from possibly less than 10 per cent in the 1860s to about 20 per cent about 1914. These percentages are comparable with that of rapidly growing economies (see 'openness' above). The growth of the tertiary sector reflected India's increasing openness. The fact that net export (export minus import) was steadily positive in colonial India has some significance in causal analysis of her economic growth or stagnation, as we shall see.

Both the composition and direction of India's trade underwent considerable change in the colonial period with the First World War as a watershed. As Table 7.5 shows, if the major items of export are

[1] It declined steadily from this level in post-independence India, to become about 3–4 per cent in 1980. The 'economic reforms' from the late 1980s had the effect of raising export's share in income back to about 8 per cent.

classified into three broad groups—purely agricultural or peasant exports, semi-processed natural resources, and manufactured goods —then the prewar period mainly saw a great burst of peasant exports. But in the interwar period, industrial capability improved in a number of ways and so did manufactured exports. The same tendency also altered the composition of imports in favour of machinery and intermediate goods. Limited tariff protection had been at work from the mid-1920s in the case of some industries. Import-substitution speeded up in these industries in the interwar period. The most important example was cotton textiles.

In the context of trade, India's dependence on the Chinese market declined sharply in the pre-war period (see Table 7.6). India's dependence on Britain as a market also declined in the pre-war period, but increased somewhat in the interwar period mainly due to preferential tariffs under the Imperial Preference Treaty (1921). India's dependence on Britain as a source of imports was almost total in the mid-nineteenth century, and changed relatively little until the First World War. In the interwar period, there was a sharp drop in Britain's share, and increase in those of Japan, USA, Germany, and Italy. The interwar period, in short, was one of diversification both in India's capability and in its trade partners.

TABLE 7.5
Composition of Trade, 1850–1935

*(percentages of total export or total import)*

|  | 1850–1 | 1910–1 | 1935–6 |
|---|---|---|---|
| Export |  |  |  |
| Agricultural (raw cotton, raw jute, foodgrains, seeds) | 26.2 | 55.0 | 29.5 |
| Semi-processed goods (indigo, opium, hides and skins) | 42.8 | 12.5 | neg. |
| Manufactured goods (tea, jute, cotton textiles) | 4.8 | 19.3 | 28.1 |
| Import |  |  |  |
| Cotton textiles | 40.5 | 33.5 | 15.3 |
| Machinery | neg. | 3.7 | 11.1 |
| Intermediate goods (mineral oil, metals) | 16.8 | 13.8 | 13.3 |

*Note:* neg. stands for negligible
*Source:* K.N. Chaudhuri, 'Foreign Trade and Balance of Payments' in *CEHI 2.*

The change in direction of trade reflected a bigger shift in regional trade pattern and industrialization. A recent scholarship has argued that in the early twentieth century, intra-Asian trade expanded while Europe's dominance in Asian trade reduced. The intra-Asian trade was based on the emergence of the modern cotton textile industry in Japan. A three-way cotton-oriented trade and division of labour between India, China and Japan emerged as a result. In turn, intra-Asian trade stimulated primary good exports from China and Southeast Asia.[2]

TABLE 7.6

Direction of Foreign Trade, 1850–1940

| | (percentages of total export or import) | | |
|---|---|---|---|
| | 1850–1 | 1910–1 | 1940–1 |
| Export from India to | | | |
| Britain | 44.6 | 24.9 | 34.7 |
| China | 35.0 | 9.2 | 5.3 |
| Japan | neg. | 6.4 | 4.8 |
| USA | neg. | 6.4 | 13.9 |
| Import to India from | | | |
| Britain | 72.1 | 62.2 | 22.9 |
| China | 8.6 | 1.8 | 1.8 |
| Japan | neg. | 2.5 | 13.7 |
| USA | neg. | 2.6 | 17.2 |

Note: neg. stands for negligible.
Source: See Table 7.5.

## Saving and Investment

Sustained economic growth requires a sufficiently high proportion of investment in national income. Investments are financed partly from domestic savings in bank deposits and securities, and partly from foreign investment inflow. Deposits and securities, however, were not the popular form of assets in which Indians saved. A substantial part of savings consisted of hoarded-up precious metals. In addition, a smaller part of the savings went as investments abroad, and as purchases of government bonds in India.

What is a sufficiently high rate of savings and investment may be

[2] See Kaoru Sugihara, 'Patterns of Asia's Integration into the World Economy, 1880–1913', in C. Knick Harley (ed.), *The Integration of the World Economy, 1850–1914*, Vol 2, Edward Elgar, Cheltenham, 1996.

debatable. But there cannot be any debate over the fact that these rates in colonial India were very low indeed. Net capital formation and savings was 2–4 per cent of national income in the first half of the twentieth century (Table 7.7). In the same period, the ratio increased dramatically from about 8 to 18 per cent of national income in Japan. In some industrialized countries such as the United States it declined. But it declined to a level that was many times that of India's ratio. Table 7.7 also reveals some other adverse features of capital accumulation in India. These are the rather low proportion of investment in machinery, the small percentage of investment in agriculture, and the declining share of the government in aggregate investment. A curious feature is the rather high proportion of depreciation or replacement expenditure (note the difference between gross and net capital formation).

Private foreign investment was a rather small fraction of the total foreign investment or total capital formation. It went through three distinct phases. In the late nineteenth century, it was mainly confined to railway construction. By the 1880s and the 1890s, industrial investment dominated and railway investment had slowed down. The major sectors where money flowed were tea, jute, and mining. A great deal of this money was in the form of portfolio investment. That is, it was in the form of shares floated and held in Britain by individual investors. This pattern began to change in the interwar period. Portfolio investment tended to be replaced by direct investment in subsidiaries of foreign firms. The Anglo–Indian firms tended to be replaced by multinational firms. And the old products tended to be replaced by new and relatively technology-intensive ones. In one view, the waning ability or willingness of the Anglo–Indian firms in doing business in India reflected the promise of a change in the political environment. In another view, it was influenced by tariff protection and the attraction of a protected home market.

Table 7.8 presents data on savings. The point to note in this table is the proportion of national income that went to the purchase of gold and silver. In the early part of the twentieth century the proportion was about as large as that of other forms of saving. In the normal course, and in any good agricultural year, Indians purchased gold and silver in large quantities. Among the few exceptions in colonial period to this normal behaviour were, the years of the Great Depression and the two World Wars. During the wars, gold import was restricted legally. Just after the depression there was net export. The difference between metals and other forms of saving is the following.

All other forms of saving were essentially lending by savers to potential investors, but those who bought precious metal hoarded it. Except to a limited extent when metals were mortgaged against loans, they did not generate new investment. Thus, precious metals were a form of 'leakage' from funds available for productive investment.

TABLE 7.7

Estimates of Investment, 1901 to 1946

|  | 1901–13 | 1930–9 | 1940–6 |
|---|---|---|---|
| *Per cent of gross capital formation*[a] | | | |
| Gross capital formation | 100.0 | 100.0 | 100.0 |
| Construction | 61.2 | 67.5 | 70.2 |
| Machinery | 29.8 | 29.2 | 28.5 |
| Agriculture | 2.0 | 3.5 | 4.6[b] |
| Other | 27.8 | 25.7 | 23.9 |
| Inventory | 9.0 | 3.3 | 1.4 |
| Public sector | 32.7 | 22.2 | 18.0 |
| Private Sector | 67.3 | 71.8 | 82.0 |
| | | | |
| *Per cent of national income*[d] | | | |
| Gross capital formation | 6.93 | 9.35 | 7.30 |
| Net capital formation[c] | 4.00 | 2.84 | 2.12 |
| Public investment[e] | 2.23 | 2.08 | 1.32 |

[a] This is defined as domestic investment plus foreign investment inflow. In fact, the 1901–13 figures relate to 'total' capital formation, whereas 1940–6 ones relate to 'domestic' capital formation. However, by this time, inflow of foreign capital had become a trickle.

[b] 'Rural' in the source.

[c] Net capital formation is gross minus depreciation.

[d] The national income (Gross National Product) figures used are different from Tables 7.2, 7.3 above. But the resultant differences in the ratios are small, usually less than 0.5 per cent.

[e] The important study by M.J.K. Thavaraj estimates a slightly lower percentage for all three periods. The differences are small, and its source is not immediately clear. The difference could be due to (a) deliberate exclusion of transfer of assets between private and public sectors in Thavaraj's estimates, or (b) the national income figures used. The rather crude income figures generally included the Indian states, whereas the public investment figure did not. See his 'Capital Formation in the Public Sector in India: A Historical Study, 1898–1938', in V.K.R.V. Rao (ed.), *Papers on National Income and Allied Topics*, Allied Publishers, 1962.

*Source:* Raymond W. Goldsmith, *The Financial development of India, 1860–1977*, Yale University Press, New Haven and London, 1983, Tables 1–10 (p. 20) and 2–9 (p. 80).

TABLE 7.8

Estimates of Saving, 1901–46

|  | 1896–1913 | 1930–9 | 1940–6 |
|---|---|---|---|
| *Per cent of national income* | | | |
| Financial saving* | 2–3 | 3.2 | 3.3 |
| Net accumulation of gold and silver | 1.5 | –1.5 | 0.0 |

* Financial saving consists of deposits and securities with the private sector, foreign investment outflow, and purchase of government bonds in India.

Source: Goldsmith, *Financial Development*, pp. 21–2 and 80.

## Public Finance

Government expenditure must be matched with government revenue to obtain a balanced account. There were two main types of government expenditure in British India—expenditure in India and expenditure abroad. The two most important types of government's expenditure abroad were pensions paid in sterling to retired employees, and interest on public debt raised in London. The government could finance its expenditure by three means. The first was current revenues; 70–80 per cent of current revenues was raised in taxes. The second was borrowings from abroad, and the third, borrowings at home. We can write:

Government expenditure = expenditure in India + expenditure abroad

= Government's receipts

= current revenue (mainly taxes) + borrowings abroad + borrowings in India

The detailed composition of government revenues and expenditure will be discussed in Chapter 8. Table 7.9 in this chapter describes only the broad pattern of public finance in the first half of the twentieth century. A few points in this data are noteworthy. The government borrowed quite heavily to finance its expenditures, both in the London money market and also in India. These borrowings peaked at the time of the World Wars. There were two types of securities sold by the British government. One was denominated in sterling, and the other denominated in rupees. In the nineteenth century, the main buyers of both were Europeans. Some had associations with India and some did not. The holders of rupee securities were more likely to be Europeans residing in India. But over time, the proportion of Indian banks and Indians increased among the buyers of rupee securities. Also, over time, there was increasing reliance on the Indian money market by the government. The London borrowings as a proportion of national income peaked in the last quarter of the nineteenth century. These loans were raised to finance wars and railway construction in India. By 1900–13, military compulsions were much weaker, and railway investment was beginning to decline. After the Great Depression, net borrowings in London steadily declined, but the government's debt in the form of rupee securities increased.

An interesting feature reflected by Table 7.9 is the declining share of investment in government expenditure, and the declining ratio of public investment in national income. The three main heads of investment were, railways, irrigation, and roads and buildings. Of these three items the first was the largest. But its share in gross investment fell from 51 per cent in 1898–1913 to 27 in 1930–8. Irrigation was a small item of expenditure (11–16 per cent in this period). The share of roads and buildings increased from 31 to 46 per cent. But there was a net decline in public investment–national income ratio.

The two most important items in remittance on the government account were, as we have mentioned, pensions and debt service.

TABLE 7.9

Receipts and Payments on the Government Account, 1901 to 1946

| | 1901–13 | 1930–9 | 1940–6 |
|---|---|---|---|
| *Per cent of national income* | | | |
| Current revenue | 5.39 | 3.50 | 4.26 |
| Net capital receipts | | | |
|     Net issue of rupee debt | 0.22 | 0.49 | 3.48 |
|     Net issue of sterling debt | 0.30 | −0.19 | −0.96 |
| Expenditure[*] | 5.91 | 3.80 | 6.78 |
|     Investment (from Table 7.7) | 2.21 | 2.08 | 1.32 |

[*] Calculated by summing items on the receipt side.

*Source:* Based on Goldsmith, *Financial Development*, Tables 1.21, 1.22 (pp. 39–40), 2.29, 2.31 (pp. 112–5).

## Balance of Payments

Balance of payments is a statement of the external transactions of a country. Receipts in foreign currency must equal payments in foreign currency for a zero balance. There were four main heads of external transactions in British India. These were (a) net export, (b) net capital movement, (c) net export of gold, and (d) net factor receipts from abroad. Net capital movements consisted of net private investment from abroad and net borrowings by the government. Net factor receipts consisted of net factor receipts on the private account, and net factor receipts on the government account. Of course, some of these four items could be negative and others positive such that when added up they totalled zero.

The basic pattern of balance of payments is shown in Table 7.10. The table covers the period for which detailed balance of payments estimates exist. However, the pattern for the 1920s is not very different from the pattern that existed in India before the First World War. Until the Great Depression, two items, net commodity export and net investment, usually attained positive values. The three other items, net export of gold and silver, net receipt of remittances by the private sector, and net receipt of remittances by the government, were usually negative.

TABLE 7.10
Balance of Payments, 1921–39

|  | 1921–9 | 1930–9 |
|---|---|---|
| *Per cent of national income* | | |
| Net export of goods | 3.0 | 2.0 |
| Net export of treasure | –1.3 | 1.4 |
| Net Private remittances into India | –2.7 | –3.3 |
| Net government remittances into India | –0.4 | –0.5 |
| Net capital movements* | 1.4 | 0.5 |
| Balance of Payments | 0.0 | 0.0 |

* Defined as net foreign investment inflow plus purchase of government bonds by foreigners. In this table, this item is estimated as a residual balancing item. This item requires some explanation on database. In India's external transactions, the most reliable data is available for commodity and treasure. Discharge of public debt in sterling is also reasonably correct. Banerji has estimated, within some margin of error, the factor payments series. There is no reliable estimate available for net investment by the private sector, and therefore, no reliable estimate available for net capital movements. In this table, net capital movements are calculated by simply adding the other four items (all the five items together should add to zero). But this figure is subject to the same margin of error that applies to Banerji's series on factor payments.

*Source:* A.K. Banerji, *India's Balance of Payments*, Asia Publishing House, Bombay, 1962, Tables V, XXVI and XXXVII; and national income figures from S. Sivasubramonian (see Table 7.1).

This basic pattern in the balance of payments changed towards the end of colonial rule. First, net exports declined. Second, there was a steady decline in factor payments, both on private and government accounts. The major reasons behind the decline were, withdrawal of

private foreign investment (which was an important part of the process historians call 'decolonization'), and retirement of sterling debts.
In the 1930s, gold imports fell and gold exports increased. Many
historians have seen in these gold exports a sign of distress of Indian
peasants during the Great Depression (more on this later). Irrespective of whether this reading is correct or not, the gold exports did
save Indian balance of payments in the 1930s. In this period, net
commodity exports fell but India's obligations on factor payments
remained high and negative. Without the gold exports India might
have defaulted on those obligations. In general, the long-term colonial pattern of balance of payments represented in 1921–9 figures
began to become weak and unstable after 1930 (see also Table 7.11).

TABLE 7.11
Structure of Balance of Payments,
Comparison of Early and Late Colonialism

|  | (Rs millions, annual average) | |
| --- | --- | --- |
|  | 1866–76 | 1930–9 |
| Net export of goods | 221 | 403 |
| Net export of treasure | –87 | 283 |
| Net private remittances into India[a] | –66 | –675 |
| Net government remittances into India | –130 | –111 |
| Net capital movements[b] | 61 | 100[c] |
| Balance of Payments | 0 | 0 |

[a] Both factor payments and private foreign investment for 1866–76; consists of only
factor payments for 1930–9.
[b] Only net change in government debt for 1866–76, both private foreign investment
and government debt for 1930–9.
[c] Derived as a residual.

Sources: A.K. Banerji, *Aspects of Indo–British Economic Relations, 1858–98*, Oxford University Press, Bombay, 1982, p. 157, and Banerji, *India's Balance of Payments*,
Tables V, XXVI and XXXVII.

Factor payments need a detailed description. As Table 7.12 shows,
there were some items that dominated net payments throughout the
colonial period. The most important was remittance by the government in the form of the payment of pensions to retired government
employees settled in Britain, payment for the use of the British army,
and increasingly, debt-service. In the nineteenth century, another
large item was dividend payments of companies that had constructed part of the railways in India. Payment on this account

increased from 9 per cent of net payments in 1860–1 to 40–50 per cent in the 1870s, the peak period of private railway construction. It dropped steadily thereafter. With the expansion of general private enterprise, remittance on private account such as interest and dividend payments by individuals or freight and insurance charges on imports increased over time. But the government account was always a major element in factor payments.

TABLE 7.12
Composition of Factor Payments, 1860–1939

| | *(percentage of total net payment)* | | |
|---|---|---|---|
| | *1860–1* | *1921–2* | *1938–9* |
| Main payment items: | | | |
| Freight, insurance, etc. on import | n.a. | 26 | 12 |
| Net railway dividend | 9 | 0 | 0 |
| Remittance by the government | 43[a] | 31[b] | 28[b] |
| Interest and dividend on private investment | 18 | 38 | 37 |
| Total net payment for services and non-commercial transaction | 100 | 100 | 100 |

[a] 'Home charges' as defined by Banerji.
[b] Consists of interest on public debt and pension payments only.
*Source:* Banerji, *Aspects of Indo–British Economic Relations*, Table 34 (pp. 168–9), and Banerji, cited under Table 7.10 above.

## MONEY SUPPLY AND BALANCE OF PAYMENTS

Money supply in colonial India was mainly influenced by the balance of payments. This feature characterized many contemporary economies. It arose from the primary objective of monetary policy in that period to stabilize the exchange rate. The objectives changed to stabilization of prices and outputs after the Second World War under the influence of Keynesian macroeconomic thought. Another difference between earlier and later monetary regimes is that, in recent times domestic stabilization has been maintained with intervention from central banks. But in the past, exchange rate stabilization occurred without significant role of any central monetary authority.

Behind such a policy, there worked a theory of automatic stabilization. Presuming that money supply responds to balance of payments, if a country experiences excess demand for its goods and services, its money supply should increase to the extent of the excess demand. The resultant inflation in the country will reduce demand for its exports and restore balance. Exchange rate need not change. All that is required is a system wherein money supply is linked to balance of payments. Similarly, if a country experiences poor demand for its goods and services, there should occur a deflation leading to a rise in demand for its exports.

In the interwar period, the theory of automatic stabilization began to break down. Its most significant weakness was that a country operating in such a system must have enough reserves (under gold standard, reserves mainly in the form of gold or currencies convertible into gold) to pay for its obligations when demand for its goods fell. If it did not have enough reserves it might need to raise its interest rates to attract capital from abroad. Both due to deflation (rise in real interest rates) and due to rise in nominal interest rates, the result could be a collapse of domestic investment. In theory, foreign investment attracted by high interest rates can compensate for the decline in domestic investment. But in practice, if every country follows a policy of attracting foreign investment to its domain none may succeed. This was, broadly, the situation that the developed world faced on the eve of the Great Depression.

By this time, many developed countries had started their own central banks, even though the objectives of monetary policy did not change very much yet. In India, a central bank with some freedom in deciding the objectives of policy had to wait until almost the end of colonial rule.

## The Silver Standard

From 1858 to 1893 the Indian rupee was a silver coin. Its supply could increase by one of two means. First, when foreign buyers of Indian exports or more often the exchange banks that financed foreign trade wanted to pay for their purchases, they could go to the Secretary of State in London and buy a draft by paying in pound sterling. Against this draft, known as 'council draft', rupee was paid by the government in India. The sterling that the Secretary received in London served an essential function. It was used to pay for factor services on government account. The second route was, the banks could buy silver, ship them to India, and get the silver minted into rupees at any of the government mints for a fee. Anyone in India could also take silver to the mints and get them coined for a small fee. Which of these two routes the exchange banks would take depended on two prices: (a) the price of silver in terms of sterling, and (b) the rupee–sterling exchange rate. If silver became cheaper while the exchange rate remained unchanged, banks would find it cheaper to buy silver rather than council drafts. The rupee-sterling exchange rate was basically stable. But it tended to fluctuate somewhat depending on the demand and supply of India's tradeable.

From the 1870s this system came under stress because excess supply of silver in the world led to a steady fall in the price of silver in terms of sterling. Silver was abundantly available because most countries had departed from silver standard for their currency and moved towards a gold standard. If the Secretary of State were to sell any draft, he had to depreciate the rupee, that is, offer more rupee for sterling. There were two implications of this move. The first was a possible inflation in India as import prices increased. The second was pressure on the government budget as government remittances would then require more rupees per sterling. The government did depreciate the rupee, but as the fall in silver prices continued the government was forced to stop the practice of allowing anyone to mint silver coins in 1893, reserving that right for itself. This move stopped a channel by which anyone other than the government was able to get rupee on demand.

## The Gold Exchange Standard

From about 1898, there was only one price that mattered—the rupee-sterling exchange. This was set at 1s–4d per rupee, the rate at which the Secretary of State sold drafts. The sterling itself was on a gold standard, that is, convertible against gold. The rupee was not convertible against gold but only against sterling. This system was known as the 'gold exchange standard'. In principle, money supply in India expanded when the Secretary of State sold council drafts, whether to finance export or new investment in India. Money supply contracted when the government converted its revenues into sterling and remitted them abroad. There was no immediate effect on money supply of net borrowings. The aim was to keep the exchange rate stable. In any market, if the price remains fixed the market must clear by quantity adjustments. That is, supply has to change every time demand changes. The government in India would occasionally release more rupees or withdraw more into reserves depending on its perception of how tight or easy the money market was in particular seasons.

In the period before the First World War, this system worked smoothly because there was always a surplus of export over import, and thus a steady supply of sterling relative to rupees. In 1906–7, the situation became adverse. A harvest failure led to a fall in export whereas imports continued to come in. Given that the demand for rupees fell, while the demand for sterling was strong, there were few takers for the council bills in London at the prevailing rate. If the government were to avoid the rupee depreciating, it needed to release as much sterling as traders and bankers wanted to pay for imports into India. This it did, reluctantly, by using resources of its currency reserves set up for such occasions. Also, 'reverse' council drafts were introduced, which were drafts sold in rupees but payable in sterling in London.

During the war, and especially in the interwar period, the monetary regime came under steady pressure from both economic and political fronts. The major threat to the system arose with inflation in silver towards the middle of the First World War. Given the exchange rate, such an event could cause rupees to disappear from the market on a large scale since the rupee was still largely a silver coin. Under the circumstances, a managed float of the exchange rate was introduced around 1917. There was immediate pressure to appreciate the rupee against sterling. But gradually, with the stability in silver prices and increasing usage of paper currency, the exchange rate became steadier. This switch in regime from fixed to a 'managed float' was not quite deliberate. It was more of an accident as the government took time to arrive at a rate that could be taken as the long-term equilibrium. In any case, the new regime did make currency growth fluctuations more regularized and manageable in terms of magnitude in the first half of the twenties. From 1926, exchange was again closely controlled to remain about 18d per rupee, the rate prevailing for the next several decades.

The period 1925–35 was one of great financial disturbance worldwide. The Great Depression was in many ways the immediate cause of these disturbances. But there were also long-term causes that involved the nature of international trade and payments in the interwar period. More on the Depression will follow later.

## Critique of Colonial Monetary Policy

There are two types of criticisms against the colonial Indian monetary regime. The first arose from contemporary Indian business and nationalist politicians and was related to the objective of holding the rupee–sterling exchange rate fixed at what the officials thought was the correct level. The nationalist critics alleged that the rupee tended to be systematically overvalued to implicitly subsidize government charges in sterling. Such a bias would have restricted export prospects, even though it might encourage the import of capital goods. The main evidence for inadequate supply of rupees was a steady decline in price level in the second half of the 1920s. Bureaucrats in charge of operating the system disputed the significance of this evidence.

A second criticism of the regime found expression in contemporary scholarly views on India, but took shape more explicitly in later research. India, like the rest of the interwar world, had a fixed or closely-controlled exchange regime. While the world retreated from fixed exchange rates during the Depression, in India, monetary policy remained more rigid. Moreover, the policy never compromised on India's external obligations on the government account—not even at the height of the Depression. This rigidity was decidedly 'colonial', and it contributed to the difficulty in depression adjustment in India.

Many historians believe that the basic aims of monetary policy in colonial India were connected not with India's welfare but with the stability of economic transactions between Britain and the rest of the British empire. In this sense, the monetary policy was 'colonial'. These aims were not always explicitly stated by the government itself, but they were quite openly discussed by several of the officers in charge of monetary policy.

One overwhelming objective was to keep the rupee–sterling exchange rate stable especially to prevent the rupee from depreciating. This was done in the interests of stable trade between Britain and India, and to provide the government some stability in its calculation of the remittances to be paid. A second aim was to restrain India's import of gold. India played a counter-cyclical role in the world economy. This role was mediated by the Indian desire for gold. In a world characterized by fixed exchange rates and gold as a main item of reserves, expansion in India or the world, led to India absorbing non-monetary gold at the expense of monetary gold elsewhere. During and after the First World War, Britain was faced with trade and liquidity problems at home and the fear that Indian gold appetite might upset Britain's own post-war adjustment process. Under these fears, the British authorities tried to restrain expansionary tendencies in India. In short, both the objectives implied a bias against economic expansion in India.

Yet another drawback of colonial monetary policy was that it was particularly inadequate in the task of stabilization of prices and outputs. This aspect drew the attention of only a few scholars and commentators, but they included such eminent names as J.M. Keynes.

## FLUCTUATIONS IN PRICES AND OUTPUTS
### Price Movements

Agricultural output was an independent variable swayed by weather conditions. For this reason, prices were extremely volatile in colonial India. Severe inflations, of the order of 20–30 per cent, were common. Usually these were followed quickly by an equally sharp crash. High volatility in prices can generate high volatility in profits and thus discourage investments. Why were prices so volatile? The fact that harvests were so dependent on weather is only a part of the problem. Partly, volatility derived from the interaction between monetary factors and harvest shocks.

India's monetary system kept a balance between demand for rupees from foreign trade and the supply of rupees. It did not leave any road open for traders and producers not involved with exports to get more rupees in hand if they needed to finance a purchase. In other words, this system was badly suited to serve demand for means of payment on behalf of purely internal commerce. Now, internal commerce was driven not only by foreign trade, but also by the size of the harvest. There was little flexibility in the monetary system to adjust to the needs of internal trade when the harvest was better or worse than average, the result was price fluctuation. A good harvest year needed more money to meet the increased transactions demand for money. But the foreign trade situation might lead to a deflation. A bad harvest year needed less money for transactions, but might see an expansion in money supply.

In a few episodes in the early twentieth century, such a conjunction of monetary and real pressures seemed to occur leading to greater price instability. For example, consider the three major inflations in the early twentieth century—1903–8, 1913–14, and 1919–20. Each of these was preceded by a major harvest failure. Real agricultural output declined by 7 per cent in 1902–4, by 15 per cent in 1906–7, by 14 per cent in 1910–13 (steady fall from a record crop in 1910), and by nearly 30 per cent in 1917–18. Prices began to rise due to the shortage of agricultural goods. In each case, buoyant export demand led to expansion in money supply. These two factors combined to generate very rapid spurts in prices. The Great Depression, when a trade contraction and monetary contraction coincided, was an example of the same kind of maladjustment.

## The Great Depression and India

Many scholars have seen this episode as the starkest example of how the gold exchange standard could harm India's economic interests. To see how, we first need a brief background on the depression itself.

The major industrial economies of the world experienced a downward shift in the demand for their goods and services in the first half of the 1920s. The sources of this contraction differed between the major economies. The demand curve shifted along an upward-sloping supply curve so that both prices and quantities fell. The extent of wage-price flexibility influenced the relative impact on prices and quantities. In general, wages and prices fell to a lesser extent than the quantities in most industrial economies around the time of the Depression. Thus, employment and output contracted quite severely.

As trade declined, there followed a universal monetary contraction. In general, this outcome was a consequence of the gold standard. Given gold-denominated fixed exchange rates, adverse trade or payments led to deflation rather than devaluation. Such a situation, if sufficiently serious, could also lead to a run on foreign exchange reserves, unless interest rates were increased to attract capital. Deflation is neutral on production and employment if monetary changes only alter absolute prices. But it affects production if there is a rise in interest rates. Interest rates (nominal, real, and expected) did rise with further contractionary effects. The Depression deepened, in the US especially, via banking panics that stemmed from a rise in the risk of defaults as the real value of debts increased, and from higher costs of intermediation. The panics themselves were a reflection of the peculiarities of the US financial system. But they shared one precondition with other economies, a general shortage of liquidity.

India shared two conditions with nearly all the other open economies that suffered the shock. First, there was a contraction in exports. And second, the gold exchange standard compelled deflation and real interest rates rose. But India's case differed in its monetary policy. Whereas the threat of deflation forced Britain, like several other economies, to leave the gold standard and devalue, India faced a depressed demand for its tradeables and an uncompromising obligation on account of remittances without the option of being able to devalue. Nationalist opinion in India pushed for devaluation. But British authorities were against it. They feared that devaluation would make the government of India unable to pay the foreign re-mittances due from it (see also Chapter 8).

The result was a steady and severe deflation, the effect of which was worsened by cuts in government expenditure. Rise in interest rates crowded out some private investment. Private debts and rents increased in value. As time went on, assets, land and gold, began to be sold. A great deal of rural unrest crystallized around debt and rent relief.

The really effective counter-deflationary measures did not come from the government. These were, the export of gold that reflated the economy to some extent, and widespread cuts in money wages that restored profitability. Both these adjustments were taking place in the first half of the 1930s. Both adjustments were stressful for a large number of people.

## Speculating the Causes of Stagnation

Why did colonial India grow so slowly? Before we seek the answers in macroeconomic relationships, we need to address the following issues:

(i) Why was the share of investment in national income small (see Table 7.7)?

(ii) Given that the government was in charge of investment in critical public goods such as schools, roads, irrigation, hospitals, etc., why was the government's share in investment small (see Table 7.7)?

(iii) Given that colonial monetary policy was more concerned about stabilization in Britain's external account than India's prices or outputs, did such a bias in policy actually depress aggregate demand and national income in India?

There can be two approaches to these questions. The first believes that colonialism was directly responsible for India's underdevelopment. The second blames India's economic structure. But as the government did not do enough to change the structure, it must share the blame to some extent. By far the most popular view is the first one. The second view is not only unpopular but also politically incorrect, for apologists of the empire tended to hold rather extreme versions of this view. Let us consider the substance of these arguments in more detail.

### Colonialism was Responsible

Politics can be seen to have suppressed private and public investment by means of several channels of 'leakage' of potential investment

funds. The most notorious was government remittance. We can con-
jecture two effects of a relatively large remittance abroad on the government account. First, given revenue, a larger remittance leads to
lower government expenditure within India. And second, for a given
net receipt of sterling from abroad, a larger remittance implies lower
capacity to import. The period was one when a great deal of the
machinery and raw materials needed by industry was imported.

There was also a problem with regard of financing government
expenditure. The British government had very limited capacity to
collect taxes. Its tax-structure adversely affected mass consumption
(see Chapter 8 on both these features). Given limited taxable capacity,
a larger remittance implied greater government borrowing abroad.
There was nothing as such wrong with government borrowing except that debt service in turn added to the burden of remittances.

In the late nineteenth and early twentieth centuries, nationalist
criticism of British rule in India focused on these payments abroad.
Payments on government account tended to be called 'drain' or 'trib-
ute' and seen as wasteful on the grounds that such resources could
be used to create productive assets in India. The most notable spokes-
man for the 'drain theory' was Dadabhai Naoroji.

While there is no question that factor payments on government
account contained a wasteful element, there is no convincing meas-
urement of how large it was. The nationalist writers' attempts to
measure it suffered from a serious logical flaw. Virtually any payment they called drain. But clearly not all forms of government remittance were wasteful. When the Indian government paid higher
salary to a European for work that an Indian could do for less, there
was a waste of resources. Many European bureaucrats were in fact
paid fantastic salaries for work that involved power but no great
talent. But when the government paid high salary to a European
engineer or a university professor who had technical skills not available in India, that expenditure was far from wasteful. In the nineteenth century, a great deal of government expenditure was in fact
incurred for services that India needed but could not supply on her
own. After all, the two countries were worlds apart in their technical,
scientific and managerial capabilities. Unless the justified and unjus-
tifiable payments, in the above sense, are measured separately, one
cannot judge how large the 'drain' was. This is virtually impossible
given the database. Not only did drain theorists not attempt this
separation, many including Naoroji himself were not even aware of
the logical problem.

Finally, nationalist writers of the colonial period and many historians of our own time have argued that the colonial *monetary* policy
depressed aggregate demand, (both investment and consumption),
and thus national income. This remains a plausible inference about
the effects of British monetary policy on India. But how large the
effect was, whether the effect was long-term or only became acute at
times like the Great Depression, are questions that remain open.

## Economic Structure was Responsible

Morris D. Morris mentions, in the context of industrialization, that
pervasive risk and uncertainty discouraged the average investor.
Morris focuses on risks that derived from poor information. India
was risk-prone in a more fundamental and more crippling sense.
Climatic risks, which made the size of the harvest and therefore national income, notoriously uncertain, might discourage productive
investment. The future was so uncertain that providing for it could
become inconsequential in individual decision-making. If harvests
happened to be excessive in one year, individuals were more inclined
to spend the extra income on sumptuous marriage feasts and jewellery rather than on irrigation or road-building. It is plausible that the
Indians' hunger for gold and silver originated as a response to risks,
perhaps as a form of 'precautionary' savings.

A second crippling structural factor was poorly developed institutions, especially financial, such as banks and insurance. Recent scholarship on banking history has shown that credit was in short supply
relative to demand in India. A modern banking sector did develop
in the nineteenth century. But its reach was limited to the European-
dominated formal sector. And segment of it was plagued by high
failure rate. Because of this, not only were savings relatively low but
also the fraction available for investors was small. This was adverse
for investors who were severely credit constrained, such as small-
scale industry (see Chapter 6).

Both these problems can be partly redressed by government expenditure. Investment in common property resources such as irrigation
and water management can be a means to reduce risks of cultivation.
Implicit or explicit government guarantee has played an important
role in the financial development of a number of developed countries
in the early period of their industrialization. However, public finance
in British India did not meet these needs. Either the government did
not diagnose the problems correctly, or its hands were tied by political
commitments.

Continuing the same story, colonial India also had certain microeconomic characteristics that might have retarded growth. The most important example is the import of gold and silver. Indians had a desire to posses precious metals the intensity of which had no parallel elsewhere in the world. Other things remaining the same, if gold import becomes larger, two effects can follow. First, savings usable for productive investment can fall. And second, imports, (a large component of which in colonial India was machinery), can fall. Both effects are adverse for investment and economic growth.

These two stories that hold as culprit, colonialism and economic structure respectively, are not mutually exclusive. It is likely that both types of factors were at work together, but it is impossible to measure their effects separately.

## CONCLUSION

Colonial India was characterized by low levels of saving and investment. Government investment was not guided by any explicit developmental objective, and was a declining proportion of national income in the twentieth century. The macroeconomy was in an increasingly disturbed state in the interwar period. Parts of the 1920s and the 1930s suffered from unstable and overvalued exchange rate and depression. Ironically, the interwar period was a favourable one for Indian large-scale industry, so that the political lobby demanding autonomy and more purposeful public investment strengthened. But that is a different story (see Chapters 5 and 8).

One particular aspect of colonial Indian macroeconomics that figured prominently in the foregoing discussion but did not receive sufficient space in this chapter, is the government's role in creating modern institutions and infrastructure. It is to this issue that we now turn.

## ANNOTATED READINGS
### National Income

The series used most frequently here can be found in S. Sivasubramonian, 'Revised Estimates of the National Income of India, 1900–1 to 1946–7', *IESHR*, 34(2), 1997. Extensive discussion of previous estimates, and problems of estimating various sectoral incomes can be found in the earlier work by this author, 'National Income of India, 1900–1 to 1946–7', PhD dissertation, Delhi School of Economics,

University of Delhi, 1965. National income estimates need to make several strong assumptions, and are subject to considerable margins of error. They also need to use several official statistical series on agricultural income as raw material. The reliability of this dataset is open to question. It is necessary, therefore, to know about alternative estimates of national income and the main reasons that they differ. See A. Heston, 'National Income' in *CEHI 2*, for a discussion, and Chapter 3 for a description of the problems of measuring agricultural output in colonial India.

For a broad comparative macroeconomic history, see R.W. Goldsmith, *The Financial Development of India, Japan, and the United States*, Yale University Press, New Haven and London, 1983.

## Saving–Investment

Bina Roy, 'Estimation of Capital Formation in India', PhD dissertation, Calcutta University, 1975, is the most authoritative work on the subject. But this work remains unpublished and is not easily accessible. The student may see R.W. Goldsmith, *The Financial Development of India, 1860–1977*, Yale University Press, New Haven and London, 1983, which contains a skilful integration of various macroeconomic databases into as complete a picture as one can get on colonial India. Roy's work is the primary source for Goldsmith's discussion of saving and investment. On foreign investment, see B.R.Tomlinson, 'Foreign Private Investment in India 1920–50', *MAS*, 12(4), 1978.

## Government

Goldsmith, *Financial Development*, is sufficient on the relationship between public finance and macroeconomics. More detailed works on public finance will be cited in Chapter 8. M.J.K. Thavaraj, 'Capital Formation in the Public Sector in India: A Historical Study, 1898–1938', in V.K.R.V. Rao (ed.), *Papers on National Income and Allied Topics*, Allied Publishers, 1962.

## Balance of Payments

On foreign trade, see the chapter by K.N. Chaudhuri, 'Foreign Trade and Balance of Payments' in *CEHI 2*. Although Chaudhuri's chapter has 'balance of payments' included in its title, it is superficial on factor payments and capital movements, and should not be consulted on these subjects. The most painstaking and detailed estimates of the complete balance of payments are available from the two books by A.K. Banerji, *India's Balance of Payments*, Asia Publishing House,

Bombay, 1962, and *Aspects of Indo–British Economic Relations, 1858–98*, Oxford University Press, Bombay, 1982. Banerji's work, however, is primarily statistical and can be heavy reading for the student. The best course would be to combine the present chapter with selected parts of Banerji where the most important items of external transaction are explained and estimated.

## Monetary Policy

Some standard works on the subject are, B.R. Tomlinson, *The Political Economy of the Raj, 1914–47*, Macmillan, London and Basingstoke, 1979; M. De Cecco, *Money and Empire*, Blackwell, Oxford, 1974, on pre-war India; G. Balachandran, *John Bullion's Empire: Britain's Gold Problem and India between the Wars*, Curzon Press, Richmond, 1996. A.K. Bagchi, *The Presidency Banks and.the Indian Economy, 1876–1914*, Oxford University Press, Delhi, 1989, Ch. 2, contains a good survey.

## The Great Depression and India

The subject has been touched upon in every significant work on India's interwar monetary history. See, for example, Tomlinson, *Political Economy*, and Balachandran, *John Bullion's Empire*. D. Rothermund, *India in the Great Depression. 1929–39*, Manohar, Delhi, 1992, is a more general review of the relationship between colonial policy and the Depression. Rothermund has researched the Depression in a number of works. A very useful book on the origins of the Depression in Europe and the USA, and its impact on a number of developing countries is his *The Global Impact of the Great Depression*, Routledge, London, 1996. Chapter 9 of the book deals with India.

## Debates about the Impact of British Rule

Banerji, *Aspects of Indo–British Economic Relations*, Chs 8–9, contains a survey of drain theory and its significance. Banerji's own views on the subject are debatable. Bagchi, *The Presidency Banks*, touches on the controversies surrounding government remittances. The works on the Great Depression cited above also deal with the biases and harmful aspects of colonial policy.

## National Accounts

Read United Nations, *A System of National Accounts*, New York, 1968, pp. 3–6 and Appendix B.

# 8

# The Role of the Government

The nationalist writers accused the colonial rulers of resisting policies that might benefit India and Indian enterprise, and pursuing those policies that benefited Britain.[1] There cannot be any dispute over the point that the British government had British economic interests in mind while ruling India. However, that does not necessarily establish the nationalist thesis. Imputing a one-point economic programme to the colonial regime simplifies the nature of the rule and ignores its internal contradictions. In the case of policies that aided freer trade or easier capital movements, British and Indian interests did not necessarily conflict. And, in many cases of government intervention, the motives behind specific policies and their actual effects were quite different.

Research on various aspects of policy suggests that the potentiality of colonial rule to modernize the Indian economy were constrained in two ways. The protection of the interests of the British economy was a precondition to any policy-making in India. Also, the nature of Indian society limited the government's ability and willingness to introduce radical changes. Remaining within these parameters, the British rule appears to have done far more than what its predecessor regimes and contemporary Indian regimes were able to do. But it did far less than what was needed for a 'big push' or what it possibly could if it were not bound by some of the imperial obligations.

The purpose of this chapter is to describe the government's contributions to economic development, and to point out where these

[1] See Bipan Chandra, *The Rise and Growth of Economic Nationalism in India*, People's Publishing House, New Delhi, 1966, pp. 190–3.

contributions fell short. The chapter is divided into five sections. The first answers two simple questions. What were the relevant policies? And who decided them? The second and the third sections deal with trade and government finance respectively. The fourth discusses public investment in infrastructure and institutions. The fifth describes government policy in the major princely states. A concluding section returns to the following general questions. Was there a specifically colonial element in these policies? Would India have been better off with a different set of policies?

## POLICIES AND POLICY-MAKING

Basically, policies that affect economic growth can be divided into two heads: state intervention in the working of markets, and investment by the government in infrastructure, institutions and welfare. Promoting industrialization by using protective tariffs is an example of the former. Investment in major forms of public goods such as education, health-care and sanitation are an example of the latter. Policies of the former kind control competition and gains from trade. Policies on government investment create capability of individuals and economic systems.

After 1858, Indian affairs were decided at three levels—the India Office at London headed by a Secretary of State who was a member of the British cabinet, the Viceroy who headed the government of India seated in Calcutta until 1911 and Delhi thereafter, and the provincial governments headed usually by Governors. These three levels of governance did not function in concert. Their priorities were different. Imperial priorities such as trade or defence were foremost at London. Calcutta was relatively more concerned with Indian finances. And the provinces were concerned with local developmental or welfare related issues. As and when British and Indian interests seemed to conflict, these three levels opposed each other. In the nineteenth century, the India Office won some major battles. But the balance tilted in favour of India in the twentieth century. This discord was at the heart of Indian policy-making as we shall see from time to time.

## TRADE POLICY

Until the First World War, trade between India and Britain was effectively free of tariffs. Free trade was a powerful ideology that influenced many colonial administrators. The idea also served the interests of the exporters of British manufacturers. In this group belonged the Lancashire textile millowners. Any attempt to impose or increase an import duty in India was resisted strongly by this lobby because India was one of the most important markets for British textiles. India bought about 30 per cent of British textile export in 1865. On the conflict regarding issue of customs duty, India's financial interests were represented by the government in Calcutta and the interests of British export furthered by the India Office at London. Calcutta wanted to use customs duty as a means to reinforce Indian finances. London denied it that freedom until the First World War. Until then, rates of import duty on textiles were low. Such duties were removed and reimposed from time to time, and were partly offset by excise on competing goods produced by the mills in Bombay.

During the war India's contribution to the war effort was critical for London. After the war, the government of India's point of view on the financial question could not be ignored. Tariffs were a convenient way to raise revenues at a time of strained finances. Partly because of the war, the need for state aid to industrialization in India was beginning to be recognized. Indian business had become a significant voice by then. It made a claim for state aid to industry in the form of protective tariffs. Indian sentiments in favour of industrialization were growing too. And finally, the influence of Lancashire on British policy, or indeed within the imperial economic system, was on the decline. At the same time, Japan began to emerge as a competitor of Britain in Asian markets. These shifts eroded the resistance to raising customs tariffs. There was steady and significant increase in average tariff rates after 1920.

Protection for industry has already been discussed in Chapter 5. Briefly, protection was given very hesitantly and in only a few cases. Tariffs led to significant expansion in those industries that did receive protection. But the experience also illustrates the dangers of using tariffs as an instrument of industrialization. In theory, protection gives an 'infant' industry the chance to expand, utilize economies of scale, and eventually become internationally competitive. In some cases such logic did work in India. Perhaps the most important example is the Tata Steel in the first few decades of its history. In reality, protection was sometimes given to producing units that were rather old and poorly managed, such as many of the cotton mills of Bombay. In any case, the success of protection in improving efficiency could not be tested in near future. For, soon after independence tariffs were made, almost with a vengeance, a major instrument of industrialization. The average rate was raised steeply and universally. This regime remained in force for 40 more years. When it did end, large segments of the Indian industry built in the meantime had become globally uncompetitive.

If the tariff experience is ambiguous, there is much stronger ground to argue that the government's control on the Indian exchange rate hurt India's exports in the interwar period. On the question of exchange rate control, London's concerns took precedence over those of Indian commerce. It has been argued that in the interwar period, the two were clearly in conflict. This episode has already been described in Chapter 7. The scale of the impact of such control is open to debate.

## PUBLIC FINANCE

The government's capacity to make productive investment was constrained by its rather primitive public finances. To understand the nature of this weakness, it is necessary to study some essential details of public finance.

### Structure of Revenue and Expenditure

The structure of revenue and expenditure will be described by using data that combines central and provincial finances. At any time in the nineteenth century, the most important tax was land revenue. In 1858–9, land tax was as high as 50 per cent of total revenues. Next in importance were two commodity taxes of a rather special nature. One was levied on export of opium, and the other on the sale of salt. Government had a monopoly on the production of opium, and a near monopoly on the production of salt. Together, the taxes collected on these two items accounted for 24 per cent of revenues in 1858–9. More modern types of taxes such as the income tax, customs and excise accounted for a small proportion of revenue (about 12 per cent in 1858–9). Two features of this tax structure were against the modern principles of taxation: it was regressive; and it was income-inelastic. A tax on salt was incident upon rich and poor alike, for both consumed the same quantity. On the other hand, the limited reach of the income tax left many prosperous people out of the tax net. Salt tax also meant, taxing a commodity whose demand was relatively income-inelastic. That is, even as the economy expanded, tax revenues from salt would not expand automatically.

Over the next 90 years, and especially after the First World War, this pattern of taxation changed. The importance of land tax decreased steadily to about 20 per cent of revenue in the 1920s. The opium tax became negligible and salt tax was a much smaller source than before. On the other hand, income tax, customs and excise had expanded their combined share to over 50 per cent. There were two major political-economic factors associated with the decline of land tax and increase in the other sources.

First, land tax as a proportion of the value of agricultural production declined from possibly 10 per cent of net output in the middle or early nineteenth century to less than 5 in the 1930s. Sustained campaign by associations of landlords against taxation was one factor behind the fall in the importance of land tax. Another factor was the income-inelastic nature of the tax. During the latter half of the nineteenth century agricultural output grew in value, but land tax did not grow to the same extent. Besides, in permanently settled areas, the tax amount was fixed. Attempts to revoke permanent settlement on financial grounds did not succeed.

Second, financial stringency had forced the government to experiment with customs and income tax right from the mid nineteenth century. In this effort the government could succeed only in the interwar period. The conflict over customs duty has been related in the previous section. Income tax was again an area of considerable debate. The government simply did not have the machinery to implement a tax on self-employed people of all kinds. There were some experiments in the nineteenth century, but no real and permanent income tax emerged from these experiments. The groups that could be more easily targeted and assessed were those closest to the government. These were the landlords, government employees, and owners of modern industry many of whom were Europeans. The landlords stoutly resisted being taxed. The resistance of the other two lobbies is less visible, but can be presumed to have been at work. Over time, these groups expanded, diversified, and their resistance to taxation could not be sustained. Income tax, therefore, increased in importance.

For most of this period tax revenue as proportion of national income remained very small and almost static at about 5–7 per cent. Small as it was, the proportion was falling in the interwar period (see Table 7.9 in Chapter 7). Thus, the shifts in the structure of taxes did not make the government richer. Nor did they enable it to expand relative to the economy. The government continued to

have very limited spending power. It also had to rely steadily on
borrowing.

TABLE 8.1

Composition of Government Revenue and Expenditure,
1858, 1900, and the 1920s

| Per cent of total revenue | 1858–9 | 1920–30 (average annual) |
|---|---|---|
| Customs | 8 | 26 |
| Land revenue | 50 | 20 |
| Salt and opium | 24 | negligible |
| Excise | 4 | 17 |
| Income tax | 0.3 | 10 |

| Per cent of total expenditure | 1900–1 | |
|---|---|---|
| Defence | 22 | 34 |
| Administration | 24 | 11 |
| Debt service | 4 | 9 |
| Public works | 17 | 7 |
| Education | 2 | 6 |
| Health | 2 | 3 |

Sources: 1858–9 and 1900–1 Dharma Kumar, 'The Fiscal System' in *CEHI 2*, Tables 12.4
and 12.8. 1920–30 calculated in Tirthankar Roy, 'The Role of the State in
Initiating Development: A Study of Interwar South and Southeast Asia',
*IESHR*, 33(4), 1996.

To this fundamental constraint of limited revenue was added
heavy expenditure commitment on defence, civil administration and
debt service. The Indian army was large and costly relative to the
government's resources. It was also unproductive from India's point
of view, being used not only for India's own defence but also to fight
Britain's wars almost anywhere in the world. Modern administrative
institutions are a positive and valuable contribution of British rule in
India. But as the proponents of 'drain' rightly argued, the cost of imported administrative personnel was frequently excessive. Debt service was an expense imposed by the poverty of the state itself.

Usually, not more than about 20 per cent of total expenditure went
to investment, or to the creation and repair of national assets. If we
consider only net investment, that is creation of new assets, the percentage was much smaller because depreciation accounted for about
one-third of the gross investment in the prewar period, and about
50–60 per cent of gross investment in the middle of the 1930s. The

percentage of investment in expenditure fell quickly towards the end of the interwar period, as debt service and administrative commitments took increasing priority over investment (Table 8.2).

TABLE 8.2
Gross Public Investment as a Proportion of
Public Expenditure, 1898–1938

*(per cent)*

|  | Investment–expenditure ratio |
| --- | --- |
| 1898–9 to 1913–4 | 23.5 |
| 1919–20 to 1929–30 | 23.4 |
| 1930–1 to 1937–8 | 15.7 |

*Source:* M.J.K. Thavaraj, 'Capital Formation in the Public Sector in India: A Historical Study, 1898–1938', in V.K.R.V. Rao (ed.), *Papers on National Income and Allied Topics*, Allied Publishers, Bombay, 1962.

In the pre-war period, public investment was mainly financed from public savings. Nearly 90 per cent of the average gross investment was thus met out of the government's own surplus of revenue over current expenditure. But in the interwar period, the percentage dropped sharply to about 65 per cent. Net increase in liability to meet public investment rose from an average of 10 per cent of investment in the pre-war period to about 35 per cent in the interwar. The increase in net debt contracted was not a uniform one. Roughly the contribution of public debt to investment can be periodized as follows:

1898–9 to 1906–07 : small scale with annual increases in liability in the negative

1907–8 to 1909–10 : large increase in liability

1910–1 to 1913–4 : small and negative increase

1919–20 to 1931–2 : consistently positive and large increases in liability

1932–3 : large negative increase.

In short, 1907–10 and 1919–31 were the two major periods of rising indebtedness. The later part of the 1930s saw net repayment.

The major sectors to draw capital were irrigation, roads, railways and telegraph. During the period of study, these four sectors continued to attract the major part of investments (Table 8.3). However, increasingly from the interwar period, such investments went into depreciation rather than creation of new assets. Public investment in railways was well-balanced in the long run. But investment in irrigation, roads and power was quite unevenly distributed. There was a correlation between the initial inaccessibility of a region, its size, and the share of the region in public investment. Burma, for both reasons, was a major recipient of funds. Within British India, western and southern India received much more funds than did eastern and northern India. Further, the composition of public investment in northern India was dominated by irrigation, whereas that in western and southern India was more even.

TABLE 8.3
Sectoral Composition of Public Investment, 1860–1946

|  | 1860–1 to 1918–9 | | 1919–20 to 1946–7 | |
| --- | --- | --- | --- | --- |
|  | Rs million | Per cent of total | Rs million | Per cent of total |
| Irrigation | 1227 | 22.6 | 1968 | 18.6 |
| Roads | 1570 | 23.7 | 2237 | 21.2 |
| Power | 0 | 0.0 | 199 | 1.9 |
| Railways | 3818 | 53.7 | 6168 | 58.3 |
| Total of the above | 6615 | 100.0 | 10572 | 100.0 |

Source: M.J.K. Thavaraj, 'Regional Imbalances and Public Investment in India (1860–1947)', Social Scientist, 4, 1971.

TABLE 8.4
Regional Distribution of Public Investment in Irrigation,
Roads and Power, 1860–1946

(per cent of total)

|  | Madras | Bombay–Sind | Punjab | UP | Burma | Bengal | Others | Total |
| --- | --- | --- | --- | --- | --- | --- | --- | --- |
| 1860–1 to 1918–9 | 16.6 | 15.5 | 8.8 | 8.8 | 24.0 | 6.9 | 19.2 | 100.0 |
| 1919–20 to 1946–7 | 16.2 | 21.7 | 11.9 | 1.8 | 21.9 | 5.8 | 20.7 | 100.0 |

Source: Thavaraj, 'Regional Imbalances'.

In the nineteenth century, the main focus of productive investment by the state was irrigation, railways, roads, and the telegraph. There were several factors motivating this infrastructural investment. First, business interests both in India and abroad urged modern systems of transport and communication to be set up in India. The influence of Lancashire textile millowners behind the construction of a railway system in India is a well-known example. Their interest was in cheaper transportation of Indian cotton. Second, Britain being the pioneer manufacturer and user of these new technologies, to some extent their extension in India was a natural outcome. The knowledge and the capital to build railways or the telegraph were more cheaply available to India than many other underdeveloped countries of that time. Third, famines in the nineteenth century exposed the extreme vulnerability of a monsoon-dependent agrarian population to harvest failure and starvation. The means to reduce such vulnerability were irrigation for efficient usage of water, railways to transport food quickly from surplus to deficit regions, and a system of public works where famine-hit people could be employed for wages. Public works, in these diverse ways, became bound to the idea of famine relief. Fourth, the pre-existing infrastructure of India was very backward given the size and complexity of the land. For example, the road system the British inherited was extremely primitive. In part, the British in India were trying to deal with the failure of past Indian regimes to build worthwhile public assets. Fifth, the needs of defence were initially an important consideration behind investing in the telegraph and to an extent the railways.

By the twentieth century, the public works drive had largely spent itself. On the other hand, the demand for welfare expenditure was gaining ground politically. This demand arose partly from the realization that education was a means of social advancement that had been neglected by the colonial rulers. In a way, it was a result of political decentralization after 1919 whereby provincial budgets, which were responsible for education and health, became more exposed to local political pressures. Extremely high levels of illiteracy and mortality in India in about 1920 showed that being a colony of Britain for over half a century had done little to enable India to approach British standards of social development. The rise in the proportion of public spending on education and health in the interwar period (Table 8.1) reflects some attempt to redress this neglect of social infrastructure. The attempt, however, was a very limited one. For, the government's poverty and expenditure commitments worsened progressively.

## The Political and Institutional Context

Public finance during the colonial period was influenced by certain long-term political-economic variables. Two were especially important: the federal structure, and the economy's exposure to risks.

During the regime of the East India Company, the finances of the three major presidencies were more or less autonomous. But there was a tendency to centralize control over state finances. By 1882, the basic structure of financial federalism was well-established. The centre was responsible for certain heads of revenue and certain types of expenditure. The provinces were responsible for some others. A few other taxes were divided up between the centre and the provinces. Customs, salt tax, opium tax, railway income were the main revenues raised by the centre. The provinces had full control over receipts of provincial administrative departments such as law and justice or education. Land revenue and excise were the most important taxes that were divided between the two. Only the centre could borrow, the provinces could not. As for expenditure, basically the centre looked after defence whereas the provinces were in charge of local administration, education, health, etc.

The history of federal finance was one of constant struggle between the centre and the provinces over heads of revenue. The provinces felt that they were given too few sources of income and too many heads of expenditure. Another source of tension was great inequalities among the provinces in per capita tax burden and per capita expenditure. Generally, provinces with Permanent Settlement such as those in eastern India raised less revenue on average and spent less. Provinces such as Bombay or Madras raised more on the average and spent more. Settlement pattern, however, is only one determinant of these inequalities. There were probably other reasons too that now remain obscure.

The Government of India Acts of 1919 and 1935, and the legislative assemblies that were created after the 1919 Act, both restructured federal finance and exposed it to organized pressures from elected representatives of the people. The divided heads of revenue were abolished. Land revenue was given over to the provinces. The centre took the income tax. The central budget now had to be balanced by contributions for the provinces, which added another bone of contention. These changes did little to meet the basic grievance of the provinces. Namely, they were given inflexible sources of revenue, but were responsible for expenditures that had to expand with growth of population and income. These complaints were not unfounded. Therefore, the 1935 Act went a little further in giving a larger share to the provinces. The idea of a five-yearly Finance Commission to review the structure of federal finance, an institution that continues today, was another result of this Act.

TABLE 8.5

Shares of the Centre and the Provinces in Gross
Public Investment, 1920–37

*(per cent)*

| | Centre | Provinces | Total (including municipalities and local governments) |
|---|---|---|---|
| 1920–1 to 1929–3 | 56 | 35 | 100 |
| 1930–1 to 1937–8 | 46 | 39 | 100 |

*Source:* Thavaraj, 'Capital Formation in the Public Sector in India'.

In general, the government scrupulously balanced its budget. That is, it balanced current revenue with current expenditure. It did need to borrow substantial sums in London mainly to finance the construction of the railways and irrigation. Many Indian economists have criticized these borrowings on two grounds. These imposed a heavy debt service obligation. And these borrowings helped the London capital market and deprived India of a chance to stimulate its own capital market by means of government securities. The former charge is doubtful. For the capital receipts after all were spent on creation of valuable assets that yielded income to the government. The latter charge does have some merit.

The balance between revenue and expenditure tended to be upset by famines, wars and depressions. The wars fought by the East India Company and the uprising of 1857 left a large burden of debt. The famines of 1876 and 1896 also added to debt. Usually these were met from current revenues without serious problems. The large increases in military expenditure during the First World War not only forced the government to borrow, but since the London market was no longer easy to borrow from, the government was forced to turn towards Indian sources. During none of these episodes, was the Indian government's creditworthiness in question, abroad or at home. The Great Depression, however, saw a major crisis in this respect. Political unrest and the weak export situation reduced confidence abroad in Indian securities. The government could in theory devalue the rupee and stimulate the economy. But such a step would have increased the value of India's net government remittance abroad. Fearing that India may fail to meet this commitment, authorities in London prevailed on India not to devalue but to cut expenditure instead. The outcome was a massive contraction in government expenditure that intensified the effects of the depression (see also Chapter 7).

The Second World War again faced India with a deficit situation, but this episode was unique in several respects. The government had to spend much larger proportions of the budget on defence, not only on its own behalf but also on behalf of Britain's war efforts on promise of repayment from Britain later. While taxes and borrowings were increased, these were insufficient to bridge the deficit. By now India had a central bank and substantial monetary autonomy. Consequently, money supply increased to finance the deficit as never before. While money supply expanded and the nominal demand for goods expanded, the supply of essential goods including foodgrains was diverted to the war effort. The net effect was, massive inflation, serious erosion of real incomes especially of the poor people who found food scarcer and costlier, and a fall in the burden of private debt. An extreme example of the resultant hardships is the Bengal famine of 1943 in which some half a million people died of starvation. The last days of the war saw government control on supplies of essential commodities. This was the precursor of the public distribution system with which independent India has been so familiar. The end of the war also saw steady liquidation of India's accumulated foreign debt. This was a result of Britain's obligations to India on account of the war. In fact, India entered independence with a very large credit balance in sterling.

## INFRASTRUCTURE AND INSTITUTIONS

The most important legacy of British rule was modern infrastructure and public goods that it created. The railways, the ports, major irrigation systems, the telegraph, sanitation and medical care, the universities, the postal system, the courts of law, were assets India could not believably have acquired in such extent and quality had it not developed close political links with Britain.

The government also played a role in information-gathering systems, industrial development, legislation, and higher education and scientific education. In scale and effect, government investment in these areas was both limited and disjointed. Major recent works in these areas will be cited in the list of readings. But these will not be described in detail in the chapter.

The initial motivation behind productive public expenditure was rarely 'development' or welfare in the modern sense. Irrigation was connected with the dependence on land revenue. Railways and telegraph were connected with military needs and foreign trade. English education in its first years with the demand for English-educated employees in government offices. But it would be wrong to believe that, once built, such assets only served narrow imperial interests. Each of these forms of capital had immense externalities. Once they were set up, they were in the nature of public goods. That is, they were open to anyone who chose to use them. In the long run, the canals helped the farmers more than it did the revenue department. English education influenced social outlook. The telegraph was a boon for small and large Indian business firms. The railways enabled vast number of labourers to migrate in search of better work and mitigated the effect of famines. Nevertheless, the absence of a unified policy imposed unevenness in the way these assets developed. There was lack of synchronization over time, between regions, and between different types of assets.

## Irrigation

### History of Policy

Irrigation was seen as a fundamental duty of the state by nearly all regimes ruling South Asia over long periods of time. The two important examples of this commitment are cited here. When the Company took control of the upper Gangetic plains, extensive network of irrigation channels existed in the western part of the river Jamuna. This network was attributed to Firoz Shah Tughlaq, and selectively restored by the East India Company's engineers from 1821. The second example is the 'grand anicut' on the Cauvery in the south attributed to the Chola rulers. Sir Arthur Cotton, who was the main spirit and the technical brain behind the Company's irrigation projects in south India, revived it. Such universal recognition of large-scale conservation of water arose from the region's dependence on the monsoon rains and the consequent risk of famines. Conserving or redistributing water not only created productive assets for cultivators, it was also a means of famine relief and insurance against starvation. Apart from reducing the chances of harvest failure, irrigation conferred several other critical advantages. It made multiple cropping possible. It freed the farmers from having to use low-yield drought-resistant seeds. And it enabled application of more fertilizers. Some of these aspects of irrigation were recognized early, and major irrigation projects were begun during the East India Company's rule. Excluding some years of financial uncertainty and shifts in policy, irrigation remained a major duty of the state throughout the period of study.

The relative importance of irrigation, however, fell after railways began to compete for limited public funds.

In the nineteenth century, the basic construction consisted of canals cut out of perennial rivers in north India, and anicuts[2] constructed on the major south Indian rivers. In the north, Punjab, Sind and western UP are the examples of the success of canals in spreading access to water over wide areas of formerly water-scarce territories. In the south, canals mainly redistributed monsoon water, and did not necessarily improve water supply in lean seasons. The north Indian canals were concentrated in areas serviceable by the two major Himalayan river systems, Ganga–Jamuna, and the tributaries of the Indus. Some of the great northern projects, as we have seen, were pre-British constructions restored by the East India Company. The Bari Doab Canal, was a new construction first started as a way of employing disbanded Sikh soldiers after Punjab was annexed to British India. Still others, such as the Ganges Canal in western UP or the projects in Sind were new projects started during Crown rule from mainly economic objectives. The most dramatic effect of these canals was the planned 'colonization' of vast areas of wastes and pastures by migrant cultivators. In Punjab these 'canal colonies' came up between 1890 and 1930. In the twentieth century, major projects included the Sarda Canal in western UP, the Sukkur barrage in Sind, and the Mettur Barrage in the south. The twentieth century also saw increasing attention being paid to the promotion of small-scale and private sources of water supply such as wells. The shift from large to small water sources was partly induced by financial stringency, and partly by the perceived dangers of canal irrigation. Attempts also began in this period to harness the hydroelectric potential of river water.

In the regime of the East India Company, canal construction was left to the engineering department of the army. Lord Dalhousie established the Public Works Department (1854) and entrusted canals to this department. For a few years after the mutiny ended and Crown rule began, the department was busy with army and administrative constructions. But a discussion started almost immediately on its long-term goals, and it was widely agreed, by authorities in India and in London, that irrigation was going to remain one of the primary goals. It was at this time that the first statement of an irrigation policy was made in a series of official writings. A broad distinction was

[2] Weirs, that is, wall or fence across a river to control the flow of water.

made between those works that were built for purely administrative or famine relief purposes (later named 'protective' works), and those built to increase agricultural production (later called 'productive' works). The former class was not expected to yield any income, though they might save the government money that would have to be spent on famine relief if a famine occurred. The latter class could be commercially profitable for the government. That irrigation could be remunerative in both these senses, as money saved and money generated, had already been demonstrated by a number of major works. For large projects that were too costly to be financed by the current revenue of the government, and which therefore needed loans to be raised in London, it was essential that the projects yield at least the interest on these loans.

What did this yield consist of? Irrigation can raise the productivity of land, and therefore, income of the cultivators. The water that raised incomes was charged at a certain rate paid out of that income. This tax accrued to the Public Works Department, and was calculated in the rate of return on capital invested in irrigation projects. However, for such projects that had come up much before the Department itself no proper calculation of increased income or rate of return was possible. On the other hand, increased income from a plot of land also increased the rental value of that land. Land revenue was supposed to reflect the rental value. In areas not permanently settled the government could realize this value. In *ryotwari* areas irrigated land was charged higher land revenue. However, no exact calculation was possible of how much the rental value of land actually increased due to irrigation. Nevertheless, from time to time, land revenue on account of irrigation was estimated as the indirect return on irrigation projects.

The government spending money on large projects with doubtful return was never a favoured idea with policy-makers for India in London. In 1878, the Select Committee on East India Public Works stated that large-scale irrigation projects were by and large a failure both commercially and in preventing famines. Almost at the same time, the 1880s Famine Commission gave a more informative and balanced picture of irrigation projects in India. The Commission concluded that irrigation projects were on balance profitable for the government, yielding about 6 per cent on capital, but only after land revenue collected is considered.

This question of what monetary returns the irrigation schemes really generated for the government is shrouded in speculation. The calculated rates of return vary widely between projects and regions. They also vary widely depending on whether or not the revenue generated or interest payments are incorporated into the calculations. A general pattern, however, did exist. Major works in Madras on the Godavary and Cauvery deltas yielded good returns. Works in Sind were also profitable. The overall return on works in north India was positive but not large. Ill-conceived projects in Bengal, Orissa and Deccan yielded negative returns. Some of these projects were first constructed by private companies for rates of return guaranteed by the government, in the model of railway construction. The government later purchased them at unjustifiably high prices. Generally in irrigation policy there was a powerful opinion against private enterprise. It was felt that allowing the private sector in water supply would complicate the question of property rights in water.

Partly at least, the rates of return reflected the types of projects in different region and, in turn, the topography of different regions. The East India Company's works in south India were generally well-paying. But one of the biggest among new projects taken up in north India, the Ganges Canal, was running at a loss in the 1860s. It was found that the main reason behind this difference was the topography of Madras, which allowed the construction of simple low-cost 'anicuts' on river beds to irrigate large areas. The canals in such a system could also be used for navigation during lean seasons. In north India, on the other hand, irrigation over a large area required extensive masonry work and many more bridges. And canal navigation was not a source of revenue as road traffic was already quite developed in the region.

The Economic Effects of Canal Irrigation

The non-monetary returns on irrigation projects, such as famine relief or increased prosperity for cultivators were also mixed. Canal-irrigated area as a percentage of cropped area was not very different between Madras and Punjab in 1900. Yet, Madras suffered far more from famines. The reason was, canals as such could not prevent water scarcity in the dry months if the region suffered from a general shortage of rains. In other words, the natural supply of water and the capacity of canals to prevent famines were correlated. In several parts of the canal-served agrarian countryside, there were dramatic improvements in wealth and income of the people. But the human and economic costs of these extensive canal projects were also large. These costs were incurred due to a persistent engineering defect, namely poor drainage of excess water. As a consequence north India was afflicted by saline deposits (locally called *reh*) in certain parts, and increase in malaria in others. The authorities knew about these costs. But they felt that the overall return justified them.

On the net effects of canal irrigation, there is an interesting difference in points of view between the two authorities on the subject, Elizabeth Whitcombe and Ian Stone. Both have worked on the Ganga–Jamuna Doab, the hub of most controversies. There is not much dispute that canal irrigation turned near-desert waste lands in Sind and Punjab into cultivable land. The benefits for agriculture were indisputable. But then, these were initially water-scarce regions. The Doab, on the other hand, was different. It was a relatively slopeless plain hemmed in by major rivers. It had a high water-table already exploited through well-irrigation. Here, the blessings of a new system of water supply were mixed.

Whitcombe has argued that the environmental effects were on balance adverse for cultivation. In this tract canals tended to spread water and block natural drainage routes. This led to waterlogging. The excess saturation led to a problem of saline deposits, called *reh*, which reduced fertility in large tracts. It also worsened the incidence of malaria. As for cultivation, the canals induced a bias for cash crops which reduced self-sufficiency in food. The canals (compared to the wells) encouraged over-cropping and attracted pastoral groups to cultivate. As a result the quality of livestock declined. Cash requirements to pay for the use of canals, enhanced rentals, changes in composition of crops, contributed to increasing rural inequality. This assessment provides support for the left-nationalist view of colonialism as an essentially negative form of intervention.

While these environmental distortions cannot be disputed, whether or not they outweighed the positive effects of increasing peasant income and wealth can be questioned. In a more detailed study of irrigation in the region, Stone argues that compared to the traditional irrigation technology, the canals had significant direct and indirect advantages. Canals enabled rise in yield per acre, reduced the impact of harvest fluctuations, raised average living standards, and encouraged limited industrialization, especially sugar-refining. Canal water, however, was distributed unevenly among peasants contrary to official expectations. Its actual distribution had much to do with local social and political structures that the colonial state was too weak to change.

## Transportation

Until the mid-nineteenth century, the most common form of long-distance transportation of cargo within the country consisted of pack animals and small sailing vessels on navigable rivers. Large trains of pack animals were driven by the nomadic Banjaras on roads that connected western India with the eastern and northern regions. For short-distance trade and travel, the common means of transportation were palanquins, small river-crafts and bullock carts. The older systems of long-distance trade were highly time and labour intensive. It is not surprising that the railways destroyed them without much resistance. While the railways cheapened long-distance travel, local and short-distance transportation saw rather little government investment in the British period. In this sphere, the cruder means of transport survived until well into the post-independence period.

In 1849, the Government of India entered an agreement with some British railway companies to construct railways in India on a government-guaranteed minimum return of 5 per cent on paid-up capital. Lord Dalhousie was the Viceroy of India at the time. The beginning of a number of major infrastructural commitments—the telegraph, the railways, the Ganges Canal, postal system, universities, and the Public Works Department itself—owed much to his ambition to extend Western technology in India, and to his political ambitions as well. The idea of the guarantee was to ensure investment in a venture that would be normally seen as risky because it consumed so much capital for an uncertain return. The guaranteed profit imposed a fiscal burden on the state. But since many crucial lines in India (nearly all those in south India for example) ran at a loss for many decades after their construction, it is probable that without the guarantee these would not have been built at all. Railway construction began on a large scale in the next decade, and was continued almost exclusively by the private sector until 1870. By 1870, Calcutta, Bombay, Madras and Delhi had become interconnected by the 'broad gauge' system. Thereafter, the fiscal burden became too heavy to bear due to the depreciation of the rupee, and the rise in interest rates on government borrowing abroad to pay for guarantees. Increasingly, therefore, the government itself entered railway construction. The first major 'metre-gauge' lines were a product of direct government investment. Later in the nineteenth century, the government started buying out some of the 'guaranteed companies'. During the 1920s, all railways in India were brought under direct government management.

By the time the Indian railway network was one of the largest in the world, it had also had considerable impact on costs of commerce and travel in the entire region. Table 8.6 shows the rapid pace of railway development in India, and the growing intensity of railway usage.

TABLE 8.6
Selected Railway Statistics, 1860–1940

|  | 1860 | 1880 | 1900 | 1920 | 1940 |
|---|---|---|---|---|---|
| Total route miles | 838 | 8995 | 23627 | 35406 | 41852 |
| Route miles per '000 square miles | 0.53 | 5.69 | 14.94 | 22.39 | 25.96 |
| Route miles per million persons | 3.40 | 35.00 | 82.90 | 115.90 | 107.00 |
| Passengers carried (in million) | n.a. | 48 | 166 | 524 | 604 |
| Goods carried (net million tonnes) | n.a. | n.a. | n.a. | 86 | 129 |
| Employment in railways | 16789 | 154108 | 338041 | 727184 | 1046843 |

Note:   n.a. stands for 'not available'

Source:   M.D. Morris and C.B. Dudley, 'Selected Railway Statistics for the Indian Sub-continent (India, Pakistan and Bangladesh), 1853–1946–7', Artha Vijnana, 17(3), 1975.

The economic effects of the railways can be classified into two types. First, the railways had significant forward and backward linkages with other sectors of the economy. Second, there was great reduction in average transportation costs. In many industrial countries, railway construction stimulated the engineering industry, the financial markets, and even the labour markets by facilitating migration and by employing large number of wage-earners directly. In India, the first of these three effects was present only on a limited scale until the First World War, when nearly all of the inputs required for railway construction was imported. The government had built railway workshops for repair and production of parts. These were capable of high-skilled work. But they were not intensively used for that purpose. Coal mining was probably the most important case of backward linkage of the railways. After the War, a progressive Indianization in input purchase began to occur. The role of the railways as a major source of demand for the basic metal industries was significant in the interwar period. Tata Steel is the most important example. The second of these effects was almost non-existent in India, since the major part of the capital raised to finance the Indian railways came from the London money market. There is no question that in 1850, Indian money markets could not conceivably supply resources for a new venture on such a large scale. But even after the railways had become an established field of private investment, the government did not seriously try to raise capital in India. The third effect on employment and labour mobility was of great importance indeed. At 1947, the Indian railways employed over a million people, whereas rest of the modern industry together employed just about two million. In other words, this sector was the single largest employer in the organized sector, a distinction maintained even today. Railways themselves were a major employer of migrant labour. Railways facilitated, even opened up, the major channels of labour migration into the cities and plantations. The plantation areas tended to be located in formerly inaccessible terrain that the railways now connected with the cities.

The reduction in transportation costs can be measured. Import and export trade in real terms increased enormously as a result of the reduction. Because transportation costs became a smaller proportion of the price, supply of goods now responded to much narrower differences between local and world price than before. Raw cotton and hides and skins quickly rose in importance as traded commodities thanks to this factor. In turn, this trend transformed the economies of cotton producing regions. Railways also facilitated integration of markets. This is evident from declining regional variability in prices of foodgrains. In other words, supply of goods moved faster in response to relative prices. In nationalist writings, the railways were blamed for intensifying the late nineteenth century famines by facilitating easy export of foodgrains. Scholars have, in fact, attributed the remarkable let-up in the incidence of famines after 1900 to easier interregional crop movements that the railways made possible. There is no reason why the railways should create scarcity in one period and sufficiency in another. It is more likely that the adverse role of the railways in the late nineteenth century famines is exaggerated (see also the section 'food security' in Chapter 3).

A systematic history of roads and road transport in India remains to be written. From the little research that is available on the nature of long-distance trade before the British came to India, it is fair to conclude that good and safe roads were an extremely scarce resource in pre-colonial and early-colonial India. The poor conditions of the roads partly reflected limited engineering capability in bridging the numerous rivers. The East India Company restored and constructed some major roads for military purposes. But regular allocation of funds for roads did not begin until the 1830s.

Thereafter as well, roads were given a low priority in government investment. Road length grew at a much slower pace than the railways. In 1931, the length of metalled roads as a ratio of population was as low as 0.4 miles per thousand persons. For a comparison, the ratio was above 1 in much of contemporary developing Asia (1.5 in Ceylon and 2.2 in Malaya). The public works in colonial India were clearly biased in favour of the railways at the cost of roads. There were possibly three reasons for this. First, road construction was said to have been too costly in India given the terrain, the rivers, and the high repair costs due to the monsoons. Secondly, roads brought the government no direct monetary return whereas the railways did.[3] The government for some reason did not seriously explore the possibility of involving private enterprise in constructing a network of tolled roads. Third, the lobbies that pushed the government into investment in modern transportation such as the Lancashire mills clearly wanted railways. That is, they wanted systems that would cheapen long-distance trade. They were not interested in roads that would facilitate local trade and travel the more. The opportunity cost of the railways was a relatively high level of backwardness in local transportation. There was also a cost in terms of increasing inequality in business prospects between places located on the railways and those located at a distance from them.

In northern and eastern India, and sporadically elsewhere, the major navigable rivers were an important means of cargo transportation. River traffic was cheaper than roads, and carried larger volumes per head. But the role of rivers in long-distance trade was more or less confined to the Gangetic plains. The most important traffic here connected Bengal with western and northern India via Mirzapur. Cargo went along the Ganges up to Mirzapur, and then was carried overland partly along the current Bombay–Allahabad railway line down south. This traffic was of great antiquity. It is known to have declined in the nineteenth century in competition with the railways.

India had a long and rich tradition in mercantile marine and ship-building. The advent of the Europeans in Indian Ocean created

[3] Vera Anstey, *The Economic Development of India*, Longmans Green, London, 1949 (third edition), p. 129.

competition for the Indians in coastal shipping. However, it also stimulated the business of some of the ancient ports like Masulipatnam or Cambay. The final blow to Indian traditional enterprise in large-scale shipping came with the displacement of sailing vessels by steam ships in the early-to-middle nineteenth century. The major ports that carried the bulk of the foreign trade in the colonial period were entirely new sites where railways and modern harbour facilities converged. These were Bombay, Madras, Calcutta, Karachi and Rangoon. Each served as an export outlet for the products of a vast hinterland. The two western Indian ports enhanced their trade several folds with the American Civil War (1865) and the opening of the Suez Canal (1869). Thereafter, Calcutta and Bombay also grew to become industrial centres. Modern harbours developed in these ports as their commercial importance increased. The First World War, while upsetting private business through these ports, emphasized their military importance. Bombay, especially, saw a modernization drive in the early interwar period.

## Posts and Telegraph

The foundations for a government postal system were in place before 1858. But it became a widely used utility only in the late nineteenth century. This was led only partly by the opening of post offices in semi-rural areas. Very significantly, it was driven by the demand for the services of the post office. Migration and money orders, for example, were synonymous. One could hardly exist without the other. In safety, cost, and wide reach, nothing comparable to the postal money order existed in pre-British periods for the remittance of individual savings within India.

Already in 1849 the East India Company had decided to construct a telegraph system along with the railways and along the railway lines. The telegraph became an urgent necessity on account of tensions on India's western frontier (the Afghan war) and the eastern frontier (the impending war with Burma). The first line, between Calcutta and Diamond Harbour opened in 1851 and was immediately used to send shipping news from the coasts to Calcutta. The major lines were completed before 1855. The remarkable speed owed to strategic needs and to Lord Dalhousie's personal interest in the scheme.

The telegraph was a private enterprise in England and America and a state enterprise in continental Europe. In India it was state enterprise for military reasons, despite Dalhousie's general aversion to state monopolies. By 1857, the telegraph had proven itself a critical military tool in a number of conflicts, rebellions and wars of annexation that distinguished Dalhousie's reign. No wonder it was seen as a symbol of evil by the mutineers in 1857. With vengeance, they destroyed telegraph establishments wherever they could (and never used it to their advantage). But as they began to retreat, the restored telegraph lines again became powerful tools of combat in the hands of the government troops. With this lesson behind itself, the beginning of Crown rule saw massive expansion of the telegraph system between India and Europe and within the country. From then onward, the economic and private uses of the telegraphs began to overwhelm strategic needs, leading to extremely rapid rise in the utilization of the system (Table 8.7).

Table 8.7
Selected Statistics of the Posts and Telegraph, 1858–1938

|  | 1858 | 1891 | 1921 | 1938–9 |
|---|---|---|---|---|
| Number of letters, newspapers, packets, parcels received (millions) | n.a. | 347 | 1422 | 1241 |
| Inland money orders paid (Rs millions) | n.a. | 164 | 789 | 808 |
| Paid telegraphic messages sent (value in Rs millions) | | | | |
|     Government | 0.20 | 1.45 | 2.97 | 1.63 |
|     Private | 0.18 | 2.70 | 17.50 | 14.40 |
|     Foreign | – | 1.54 | 5.87 | 3.85 |
|     Total | 0.38 | 5.69 | 26.34 | 19.88 |

Notes: The telegraph data on the last column relates to 1936–7. N.a. implies 'not applicable'.
Source: Statistical Abstracts for British India, Calcutta, various years.

## The Social Sector

In a narrow sense, investment in mass education and health has implications for economic growth because education improves the capability and productivity of human beings, and better health facilities directly or indirectly help in bringing down rates of population growth. In a broader sense, education and health define the quality of life, and thus can be seen as measures of economic growth. Mass education and health are in the nature of public goods. That is, once a school or hospital is established, it is available for anyone who may demand its services. Because of this, investment in education and health is likely to remain inadequate if left to the private sector. It demands government investment in free facilities, and legislation opening out access of existing facilities. The British rule introduced both these features in India in the form of government and government-aided schools and health-care. In these institutions, moreover, the contents of education or health care were radically different from what was available from indigenous sources.

Education

Neither the concept of formal instruction nor organizations to impart it were unknown in pre-colonial India. But typically, literacy was confined to the upper castes, almost exclusively to men, and mainly to certain professions. Data collected in the 1830s revealed that instruction was widespread among the men-folk of the priestly, landed and mercantile castes, but practically unknown among the labouring people and amongst women. Majority was instructed at home. A small number in south India was instructed in temples, some in north India were taught in Persian and Arabic schools. The rest were taught in 'schools' that had no independent existence outside the private dwellings where they were held. The rarity of standardized schools and standard curricula reflects the fact that various castes wanted various kinds of education. Instruction was decentralized. Education was seen neither as a public duty nor as a means to improve human capability.

Generally speaking, the nineteenth century witnessed centralization of the educational infrastructure, and replacement of moral–religious with secular and scientific learning. Government control and government investment played a direct role in shaping the new system. The new system provided better preparation for employment in the modern economy or government administration. The whole informal educational structure steadily crumbled over the next 100 years. It decayed because it could offer no marketable degree, had very little symbolic value, had a small base of patronage, and adopted obsolete media of instruction. In parts of Southeast Asia where Buddhist monasteries organized some form of mass education, colonization did not necessarily imply a steady collapse of the old system. For, the monastic schools were well-organized and powerful cultural symbols. The Indian informal education had none of these qualities.

However, the scale of the new system fell short of requirements, which is why the informal system lingered on. Students as a proportion of total population increased from 1.3 per cent in 1891 to 3.7 per cent in 1931, whereas the proportion of persons of school-going age in total population was about 40 per cent in these dates. Only about a fifth of the students who started school reached secondary levels. The government did not have the money to build a mass education system that could accommodate the 100 million children who had attained school-going age in 1931. Private funding was slow to shed the biases that had long confined education to only a few groups and to the men within these groups.

Given that the supply of formal education was scarce, there was bound to be rationing of what was available. Thus, the schools for secular and scientific learning drew their students from the classes that had been receiving some informal education earlier. Those who had little or no access to education earlier continued to have limited access during the British rule. The social prejudices that once discouraged them from any education at all had begun to weaken, but did not disappear. Thus, female literacy levels hardly changed during the colonial period.

Along with inadequate supply, there was also a problem on the demand side. Those classes of people who were formerly literate eagerly used the new schools and colleges. The formerly illiterate classes were either unable or unwilling to enter these institutions. Among communities and regions, some were clearly more open to education than others. Thus, the average literacy rate among the Parsis was 79 per cent in 1931 (73 among Parsi women), whereas the general literacy rate was only 8.3 (2.3 for women). Among the Jains, the literacy rate was 35 per cent (11 among women). In Burma, which was poorer than most Indian provinces, literacy rate was 37 per cent (17 among women). Clearly, communities differed in their perception and in their opportunities as well. The Burmese case illustrates the tenacity of the monastic schools.

Health

Mortality rate was high in the region before British rule. It began to come down significantly after 1920 (see Chapter 9 for a detailed discussion). Government initiative in the form of sanitation, medical care, and famine prevention contributed to this decline. The first two initiatives started in the barracks. The stress on sanitary reforms had a great deal to do with the exceptionally high death rates in the army. It was related with the growing sense that communicable diseases like cholera, small-pox, or plague thrived on poor water supply, contaminated food, poor drainage, poor sewage, and crowded living conditions. Army death rates dramatically dropped in the last quarter of the century with the reforms.

The Indian Medical Service (IMS) had begun as early as 1764. It recruited health professionals by means of a competitive examination to which Indians were admitted after 1853. The IMS was at first meant to only look after the troops, but its duties gradually expanded. Government hospitals expanded rapidly from the third quarter of the nineteenth century. Dispensaries also increased in number. At first, mainly the Europeans and Anglo–Indians used these institutions. Indians rarely came to these places for treatment. These were concentrated in the towns. For the upper castes, they carried the image of being impure places. The upper castes also had access to the more effective forms of traditional medicine. When Indians did begin to come to government hospitals, a large proportion at first was from lower castes. Gradually, however, prejudices against government hospitals began to decline. One factor in this change of attitude was the latter's success in surgery.

From the 1860s (after the Royal Commission on Sanitation submitted a report in 1863), sanitary reforms began to touch the lives of civilian population and local governments. Large municipal corporations built hospitals staffed with European health officers. Municipalities paid more attention to pure water supply and proper sewage. Public health offices became effective in dealing with major outbreaks of communicable diseases, of which three were especially virulent, malaria, plague and smallpox. Great epidemics, such as the plague epidemic that raged in India between 1896 and 1920, saw some early and rather drastic implementation of the new ideas on how to decontaminate affected habitats. Until the middle of the interwar period, these measures made little difference to the aggregate death rates. Thereafter a steady decline in death rates began to occur. The exact causes of the decline cannot be clearly identified. Sanitation and medical care had very limited reach but still, these measures did contribute to the reduced occurrence of major epidemics after 1920. The other factor, probably the more important one, behind the decline in death rates was the low frequency and severity of famines in the twentieth century (see also the discussion on mortality rates in Chapter 9).

## POLICIES OF THE PRINCELY STATES

A comprehensive descriptive history of the economic policies of the states waits to be written. Some works exist on the three largest states,

Hyderabad, Mysore and Travancore. Based on these studies, a few hypotheses can be advanced.

First, the broad composition of public expenditure and revenue in the states conformed with that of British India. The land tax dominated revenue in the nineteenth century. Administration, including police, justice, and palace expenses, took away a large proportion of the expenditure. For example, in Mysore during 1905 and 1910, these heads accounted for over half the public expenditure.

Second, both the structure of revenue and the structure of expenditure were changing in the same direction as British India from the last quarter of the nineteenth century. The importance of the land tax declined and that of commodity taxes and royalties increased. In Mysore, income from excise, forest royalties, state railways, and royalties from the Kolar gold mines increased substantially between 1880 and 1910. Forest income was also crucial in the numerous sub-Himalayan states. In expenditure, infrastructure began to increase its share.

Third, in the nature of infrastructure expenditure, the priorities in the states by and large followed the priorities in British India. Thus, in the late nineteenth century, the main item of expenditure was the railways. Again, in the interwar period many states began to play a more active and diversified role.

Fourth, at this stage the experiences of different states began to diverge. In this divergence, a major role was played by the nature of local politics and by the technocrat- advisers who commanded influence in some of the states. In Mysore, there was great interest and commitment towards industrial development under the initiative of the state. The debates on industrial policy in Mysore anticipated some of the issues that figured in the 1950s discussion on industrial policy for India (this episode in Mysore history was briefly discussed in Chapter 5). Interwar Mysore also saw the implementation of major projects in irrigation. In Travancore and Baroda, the emphasis fell on the social sector, education and health. In all these states, the role of 'outsiders' in policy matters was significant. In Hyderabad, on the other hand, internal ruling classes and business interests had a larger influence on policy. Hyderabad more or less confined itself to industrial development under the leadership of the local landed and trading communities. In this effort, Hyderabad pioneered the concept of state-backed investment banking, which has been used extensively by central and state governments in post-independence India.

It is unlikely that these four broad hypotheses will be upset when the history of the states is written out more fully. But, admittedly, this is a very bare and tentative outline of a complex and little-known subject.

## Conclusion

In many respects colonial India had a more modern form of government than most previous Indian regimes. It had a more diversified revenue base. It spent less on luxuries and more on the genuine duties of the state such as defence, welfare, infrastructure and institutions. Yet, it spent far too little relative to what was needed to make a significant difference for the average Indian. And the little it spent concentrated in areas that promised the government monetary profit.

The immediate reason behind this poor and biased effort was the government's own poverty. It spent little because it earned little. The extent by which colonial India fell short in its capacity to make a difference can be seen in comparison to UK and Japan (Table 8.8). Even compared to most of its generally impoverished neighbours in South and Southeast Asia, British India was a desperately poor government. In 1920–30, the government of the Federated Malay States spent, on average, more than ten times the money spent in British India per head. That of Ceylon spent more than three times, those of the Philippines and the Dutch East Indies more than double, and those of Siam (Thailand) and French Indo–China 40–50 per cent more. None of these was a significantly richer country than British India. Nor were they formally or informally free from colonialism. And yet their governments could do far more for their people. How?

A closer look at public finance in these countries suggests a much larger usage of flexible sources of revenue such as customs, excise and income tax. This hints at two types of constraints the British Indian government suffered from. One arose externally—the limited use of customs was a result of explicit or implicit lobbying by British trade interests. There was, in this sense, an imperial element in the government's fiscal weakness. To a greater or lesser extent, all the Asian countries mentioned above had to face the pressure of European manufacturers to keep trade open and unrestricted. In India, such lobbying succeeded significantly until the 1920s. The other factor behind the poverty of the Indian government arose internally. The limited use of income tax was partly related to the stout resistance of powerful landlords, the most obviously taxable Indians. On top of these constraints was added the large defence commitment.

TABLE 8.8

India in Comparison:
Size of Government and Social Sector in 1920–30

|  | India | UK | Japan |
|---|---|---|---|
| Size of Government:<br>Government revenue as a ratio<br>of National Income (per cent) | 5.2 | 18.8 | 29.2 |
| Size of Government: Government<br>revenue per capita (£) | <1 | 24 | 4–5 |
| Health Indicators: |  |  |  |
| Death Rate (per '000 persons) | 26.0 | 12.2 | 21.3 |
| Infant Mortality (per '000 live births) | 181 | 74 | 153 |
| Growth of School Education:<br>School-going children as ratio<br>of population (per cent) |  |  |  |
| Primary | 2.4 | 12.9 | 27.0 |
| Secondary | 0.5 | 9.3 | 6.6 |
| Secondary enrolment as a ratio of<br>primary (%) | 20.8 | 72.1 | 24.4 |

Sources: *Statistical Abstracts for British India*, Calcutta, various years, and B.R. Mitchell,
   *International Historical Statistics: Africa, Asia and Oceania*, and Mitchell, *International Historical Statistics: Europe 1759–1988*, Macmillan, New York, 1992.

The limited levying of taxes on the wealthy suggests a more general
and well-known hypothesis about the nature of British rule in India.
A tiny minority of Europeans ruled over an immensely large and
diverse territory populated by a vast number who had proved their
potential for violent rebellion at the time of the mutiny. The situation
was not favourable for large and daring reforms that might affect and
anger the local elite. The general approach to taxation, therefore, was
orthodox and risk-averse. In effect, the internal taxation system was
regressive. Public finance, as nearly all other aspects of governance,
carried an implicit bias for preserving hierarchies among Indians.
Imperialism was not alone in paralyzing the government. The local
distribution of power, which the British were not easily persuaded to
upset, mattered just as strongly.

The sense of inertia that colonialism was powerless to change returns in the discussion on population growth, which is the subject of
the next chapter. The inertia can be seen in indices of social development that were correlated with decline in birth rates.

## ANNOTATED READINGS
### Policies and Policy-making

The institutional structure of decision-making has been described in S. Ambirajan, *Classical Political Economy and British Policy in India*, Cambridge, 1978, Ch.1. See also the Table 3, p. 269, for an overview of government intervention.

### Trade and Public Finance

Free trade and protection in colonial India are well-researched themes. See Ambirajan, *Classical Political Economy*, Ch. 2. A substantial recent study is Basudeb Chatterji, *Trade, Tariffs and Empire*, Oxford University Press, New Delhi, 1992. See also some of the earlier and shorter studies, especially, Clive Dewey, 'The End of the Imperialism of Free Trade: The Eclipse of the Lancashire Lobby and the Concession of Fiscal Autonomy to India', in Dewey and A.G. Hopkins (eds), *The Imperial Impact: Studies in the Economic Development of Africa and India*, London, 1978. On the impact of tariffs on Indian industry, see discussion in Ch. 5 and the readings cited therein.

On public finance, Dharma Kumar, 'The Fiscal System', in *CEHI 2*. The essay touches on all aspects of Indian public finance and the debates around it. Those who wish to read more on specific aspects of taxation and expenditure policy, can follow the readings list given in Kumar. See also the sources in Ch. 7, and especially M.J.K. Thavaraj, 'Capital Formation in the Public Sector in India: A Historical Study, 1898–1938', in V.K.R.V. Rao (ed.), *Papers on National Income and Allied Topics*, Allied Publishers, Bombay, 1962.

### Infrastructure and Institutions

On irrigation, Elizabeth Whitcombe, 'Irrigation', in *CEHI 2*; and Ian Stone, *Canal Irrigation in British India*, Cambridge, 1984, Ch. 1 (on the controversy), Ch. 2 (on construction of the canals), and Ch. 8 (on the effects of canals upon standards of living and the regional economy).

On the construction, financing, administration, technology and employment practices in the railways, read Daniel Thorner, *Investment in Empire: British Railway and Steam Shipping Enterprise in India 1825–1849*, University of Pennsylvania Press, Philadelphia, 1950; I.J. Kerr, *Building the Railways of the Raj 1850–1900*, Oxford University Press, Delhi, 1995; Peter Harnetty, *Imperialism and Free Trade: Lancashire and India in the Mid-nineteenth Century*, University of British Columbia Press, Vancouver, 1972, Ch. 4; Ian Derbyshire, 'The Building of India's Railways: The Application of Western Technology in the Colonial periphery 1850–1920', in Roy MacLeod and Deepak Kumar (eds), *Technology and the Raj: Western Technology and Technical Transfers to India, 1700–1947*, Sage Publications, New Delhi, 1995. On the economic effects of the railways, John Hurd, 'Railways', in *CEHI 2*. Several works cited in Ch. 3 also deal with this theme. For a superbly readable and illustrated descriptive history of the railways, read Chs I–V of *Indian Railways: One Hundred Years 1853–1953*, Railway Board, New Delhi, 1953 (written by J.N. Sahni).

On the telegraph, see Saroj Ghose, 'The Introduction and Development of the Electric Telegraph in India', PhD dissertation, Jadavpur University, Calcutta, 1974. This work is not easily accessible. The following essay by Ghose describes the early history of the telegraph in sufficient detail, 'Commercial Needs and Military Necessities: The Telegraph in India', in Roy MacLeod and Deepak Kumar (eds), *Technology and the Raj: Western Technology and Technical Transfers to India, 1700–1947*, Sage Publications, New Delhi, 1995.

On education, see Syed Nurullah and J.P. Naik, *A History of Education in India*, Bombay, 1951, for a detailed descriptive study. On scientific and technical education, a subject not covered in this chapter, see Deepak Kumar, *Science and the Raj*, Oxford University Press, Delhi, 1995, Ch. 4. On the development of health care in colonial India, see David Arnold, *Colonizing the Body–State Medicine and Epidemic Disease in Nineteenth-Century India*, Oxford University Press, Delhi, 1993, Ch. 6; Arun Kumar, *Medicine and the Raj, British Medical Policy in India, 1835–1911*, Sage Publications, New Delhi, 1998. The last thirty years of British rule continue to be inadequately researched. There are, however, works on specific aspects. For example, V.R. Muraleedharan, 'Development of Preventive Health Care in the Madras Presidency: The Case of Malaria during the Interwar Years', in S. Bhattacharya et al (eds), *The South Indian Economy*, Oxford University Press, Delhi, 1991.

## Princely States

As mentioned in the text, only economic policies of the three larger states have been researched. See Bjørn Hettne, *The Political Economy of Indirect Rule: Mysore 1881–1947*, Curzon Press, London and Malmö, 1978, Part III; T.M. Thomas Isaac and P.K. Michael Tharakan, 'An Enquiry into the Historical Roots of Industrial Backwardness of Kerala—A Study of the Travancore Region', Centre for Development Studies, Trivandrum, Working Paper No. 215; Raman Mahadevan,

'Industrial Entrepreneurship in Princely Travancore: 1930–47' and C.V. Subbarao, 'Role of the State in Industrialization: The Case of Hyderabad', in S. Bhattacharya et al (eds), *The South Indian Economy*, Oxford University Press, Delhi, 1991.

# 9

# Population and Labour Force

India's population, long stagnant, began to grow rapidly after 1921. Given the large initial size of population in India, demographic change in this region was a major turning point in world population history with overwhelming consequences for economic growth within India. In theory, population can become either a productive resource or a burden. It can become a resource if the average capability of the people increases at the same time as their number does. It can become a resource if increased supply of labour and consumption potential enable better utilization of other productive resources.[1] In either case, growth in productivity can be expected to occur along with growth in numbers. Population can become a burden if other resources are already scarce, and average capability does not improve. In that case, supply of more labour to work the same stock of resources can simply lead to diminishing returns. A quick look at colonial Indian demographic data suggests that population growth accelerated at a time when agricultural growth decelerated. This coincidence surely intensified poverty in the rural areas. It also leads to an analytical question. Was the simultaneous occurrence just a coincidence? Or was there a causal connection between population growth and economic stagnation?

The present chapter will suggest an answer to this question. However, its main purpose is to present a descriptive outline of demographic history. The chapter is divided into two parts. The first deals

---

[1] This is a view associated with the writings of Ester Boserup. See *The Conditions of Agricultural Growth: The Economics of Agrarian Change under Population Pressure*, Allen and Unwin, London, 1965.

with population growth. The second deals with population characteristics, especially occupational structure.

## POPULATION SIZE AND GROWTH

Population growth is basically influenced by three sets of factors: (a) the economic rationality of having large or small families, (b) the socio-cultural context influencing preferences for large or small families, and (c) health care systems and nutritional status, which determine human ability to control or cope with biological processes. Long-term trends in population reflect changes in all three sets of factors. The different paces at which these factors change have led to long periods of high population growth or low population growth.

'Demographic transition' is a theory about the uneven pace of change in these three factors. The original statement of this theory is as follows.[2] In pre-modern times, death rates tended to be high in all societies because of the risk of diseases and famines. It was economically rational then to sustain high birth rates. Net growth of population was generally small. Sustaining high fertility was achieved via religious doctrine, moral codes, laws, customs, marriage habits and family structures. From the nineteenth century, death rates, first in the western societies, and then in the developing world began to fall. These fell because of changes in health care systems and nutritional improvements. The 'social-cultural props' (doctrines, customs, etc.) sustaining high fertility were no longer needed in the economic sense but they are ingrained beliefs and not prone to change easily. Hence, they did not decay as quickly as improvements in health and nutrition. So, as mortality began to fall, fertility remained stable and the world entered a period of high population growth. Eventually, the economic costs of having large families began to be seen as excessive. In the west, this happened in the course of industrialization, urbanization, and increasing women's participation in the labour force. Mass education made individuals aware of the costs and benefits of large families, and enabled more women to enter labour force. So, the social outlook began to change, fertility declined, and societies entered low population growth regimes.

In many developing countries including India, the first part of the transition has already occurred. A high population growth regime began from the interwar period. But the second phase, the return to

[2] See F.W. Notestein, 'Population: The Long View', in T.W. Schultz (ed.), *Food for the World*, University of Chicago Press, Chicago, 1945.

a low population growth regime, has not yet occurred. The theory states that, sustained high rates of growth in population may persist in modern times as a consequence of slow decay of the social props, due to, say, an absence of mass education.

In later restatements, the element of economic rationality behind the decision to maintain high fertility before or after mortality decline has been stressed, and the role of the social-cultural factors in sustaining high fertility somewhat de-emphasized.[3] But, their role cannot be ignored totally precisely because the preference for large families is almost always expressed in cultural terms. For example, the bias for a male child is strongly prevalent in northern India and weak in southern India. This bias is believed to lead to higher family size. This difference across regions cannot be explained purely in terms of economic differences.

In turn, high rates of growth of population influence the level of public services, availability of common property and natural resources, modes of using these resources, and condition of the labour market. These implications of crowding for economic growth are yet to be studied systematically. In the rest of this section, we shall study mainly the beginning of the demographic transition in India.

## Before 1881

Comprehensive census of population began to be conducted every ten years from 1881. Before that, incomplete counts were conduced for some regions and cities. In fact, such attempts began from the early nineteenth century when officials of the East India Company realized the administrative need for population data. In Britain, the first census had been conducted in 1801.

For the pre-1881 period, and especially for the pre-British period, population has been estimated by using different assumptions. One method, now discredited, is to assume that population grew steadily at a constant rate until 1881, and thus estimate a figure for the late eighteenth century.[4] But the assumption has no factual basis. It is not a plausible one either. There is an implicit belief here that the British rule brought with it political stability and must have led to a growth in population. Political instability and insecurity of property might have been greater in the pre-British period, and wars more frequent.

---

[3] Kingsley Davis and Judith Blake, 'Social Structure and Fertility: An Analytical Framework', *Economic Development and Cultural Change*, 4(2), April 1956.

[4] See the discussion in Leela Visaria and Pravin Visaria, 'Population (1757–1947)', in *CEHI 2*.

These factors can depress population growth. They can do so directly by causing deaths, and indirectly by causing destruction of crops in areas through which armies pass. Yet, with a few exceptions, this was probably a minor source of mortality at any time in India's history. The major source was disease, epidemics, famines, inadequate nutrition and poor hygiene. The British rule until 1881 changed these conditions only very slowly and sometimes for the worse.

In more recent times, a few other estimates have been made based on the incomplete regional data and less questionable assumptions. One such study owes to P.C. Mahalanobis and D. Bhattacharya. Their work created a series for 1801–1871 by means of certain assumptions that adjusted for the underenumeration and undercoverage. The method was to make a list of common 'disturbing factors', that is, episodes that usually killed a large number of people in India, for each major region and each decade. The existing estimates were then adjusted for these episodes to create a time-series, using some informed guesses about how severe these episodes were. The result is shown in Table 9.1.

TABLE 9.1
Population Estimates, 1801–71

|  | Population in millions | Percentage change over the decades |
|---|---|---|
| 1801 | 207 | – |
| 1811 | 215 | + 3.9 |
| 1821 | 205 | – 4.6 |
| 1831 | 216 | + 5.4 |
| 1841 | 212 | – 1.9 |
| 1851 | 232 | + 9.4 |
| 1861 | 244 | + 5.2 |
| 1871 | 256 | + 4.9 |

Source: P.C. Mahalanobis and D. Bhattacharya, 'Growth of Population in India and Pakistan, 1801–1961', *Artha Vijnana*, 18(1), 1976.

The figures in Table 9.1 suggest a low but positive growth rate of population in the nineteenth century. The period was prone to violent fluctuations, the severity of which seems to have declined to some extent after 1841. That fact seems to support in a rather crude way the view that the consolidation of British rule in India improved welfare of the Indians. However, such a reading will be hasty. For the very first census decade, 1871–81, saw a catastrophic famine and near-zero population growth. Further, the incidence of fluctuations was regionally variable. Not all regions in India were equally famine-prone. In a recent estimate of Bengal based on the quantity of salt produced,[5] Sumit Guha shows that the population of Bengal grew without major reverses between 1790 and 1860. Based on inter-district variations within Bengal, he concludes that the extent of growth was positively related to density.[6] This seems a generalizable point.

## 1881–1941

For comparison over long periods of time, population estimates must be adjusted for change in territorial extension over time. Table 9.2 shows census figures after these adjustments. The table adds figures for the post-independence period to make the time-frame long enough. Five major conclusions can be drawn from the table.

(i) Population growth rate was very small (on average about 0.4 per cent) between 1881 and 1921.

(ii) The growth rate sharply increased from the decade 1921–31.

(iii) There were sharp fluctuations within the period 1872–1921. In particular, the 1876–7 famine and the influenza epidemic of 1918–9 caused unusual mortality just before a census count. Thus, both 1872–1881 and 1911–21 censuses show near-zero growth. But the intervening censuses show somewhat higher rates of population growth.

(iv) After independence, population growth accelerated steadily, until 1981 after which a small decline is in evidence.

(v) Acceleration of growth on an expanding base has led to exponentially larger numbers added every 10 years. The last column in Table 9.2 shows this net addition. For some purposes, such as measuring changes in the balance between natural resources and people, this incremental figure, and not the growth rate, is the true measure of the economic impact of population growth.

There were differences across major regions in population growth, the most important determinant of which was the regional impact of famines. Growth was positive and above average in eastern and southern India. Both regions suffered from fewer and milder famines and food scarcities after 1881. The worst south Indian famines in the colonial period occurred in the 1870s. Western India experienced below average growth rate and great fluctuations. The reason, again,

[5] Salt consumption is plausibly believed to be correlated with population size and poorly correlated with incomes.

[6] 'The Population History of South Asia from the 17th to the 20th Centuries: An Exploration', IUSSP Conference on Asian Population History, Taipei, 1996.

was the occurrence of famines, the worst of which occurred in 1896. Northern India also experienced slow growth. Parts of this region, falling outside the Gangetic delta, were more susceptible to scarcity and famines. The Gangetic delta was better off in terms of natural water sources as well as canals dug during and before the British period. This region did not escape famines. But it was less badly affected by them.

In British India as a whole, as well as at the regional level, the age-composition of the population remained remarkably stable throughout the census period. Children, or persons of 0–14 years, formed about 39 per cent of the total population. The elderly, defined as persons of 60 years or above, formed about 4–5 per cent. Persons of working age (15–59 years) formed about 56–7 per cent. One of the main factors influencing age-composition is the fertility rate. And the stability in the former derived mainly from a stability in this rate, as we shall see.

TABLE 9.2
Population of Colonial India and the Indian Union, 1881–1991

| | British India and the states excluding Burma | | Present territory of India | | |
|---|---|---|---|---|---|
| | Total (millions) | Average annual growth rate (per cent) | Total (millions) | Average annual growth rate (per cent) | Number of persons added every 10 years (millions) |
| 1881 | 257 | – | – | – | |
| 1891 | 282 | 0.9 | – | – | |
| 1901 | 285 | 0.1 | 239 | – | |
| 1911 | 303 | 0.6 | 252 | 0.6 | 13 |
| 1921 | 306 | 0.1 | 251 | 0.0 | –1 |
| 1931 | 338 | 1.0 | 279 | 1.1 | 28 |
| 1941 | 389 | 1.4 | 319 | 1.4 | 40 |
| 1951 | – | – | 361 | 1.3 | 42 |
| 1961 | – | – | 439 | 2.2 | 78 |
| 1971 | – | – | 548 | 2.5 | 109 |
| 1981 | – | – | 683 | 2.5 | 135 |
| 1991 | – | – | 846 | 2.4 | 163 |

Source: Leela Visaria and Pravin Visaria, 'Population (1757–1947)', in CEHI 2. The 1891–1911 estimates are based on Kingsley Davis's work. Post-1947 estimates are from Statistical Abstracts of India, Delhi, various years.

Sex-composition was about 1030–70 males per 1000 females. From 1901, there was a steady increase in the male-female ratio. The excess of males was not a universal feature. In north India, the excess of males and deficit of females was stark. In south India, there was an excess of females. Why did the number of males exceed that of females in north India? Three hypotheses have been offered at different times: systematic under-enumeration of females, systematic under-reporting of female births, and greater risks of death for women both at birth and at the time of child-bearing. Of these, the third is the most widely accepted view. The risks arose from social biases against the girl child. They arose more specifically from such practices as female infanticide and neglect of female babies. The sex composition varied significantly by region with varying social attitudes.

## Determinants of Population Growth, 1881–1941

In a statistical sense, there are three main factors determining population growth. These are mortality or death rate, fertility or birth rate, and net migration. Generally speaking, in the transition from low to high population growth rates, the birth rate has been the relatively static factor and the death rate the more dynamic factor. It is a decline in mortality that initiated the change in regime. British India is one example of a class of developing economies that experienced such a decline at various times in the twentieth century. Why mortality declined is one of the central questions of economic demography, a question still not completely answered.

TABLE 9.3
Crude Death and Birth Rates, 1881–1951

|  | Death rate (deaths per 1000 persons) | Birth rate (births per 1000 persons) |
|---|---|---|
| 1881–91 | 40–2 | 47–9 |
| 1891–1901 | 38–50 | 46–51 |
| 1901–11 | 41–4 | 44–8 |
| 1911–21 | 42–50 | 45–9 |
| 1921–31 | 33–8 | 42–8 |
| 1931–41 | 30–2 | 43–5 |
| 1941–51 | 25 | 40–2 |

Notes: The figures for death rate and birth rate show the range of different estimates. See Visaria and Visaria, 'Population', for these estimates.

Mortality: Causes of High Death Rate

Table 9.3 shows the general tendencies in death and birth rates. It is clear why population growth rate was low until 1921 and accelerated thereafter. Birth rates did not change dramatically. Mortality rate, initially very high by world standards, declined steadily and quickly from 1921. Why was mortality rate so high in India before 1921? Why did it decline after 1921? Why did the birth rate not decline at the same time?

The most striking aspect of India's population history is the high mortality rate. Mortality was determined by both long–term and short-term factors. The key long-term factor leading to high mortality was a consequence of India's location on the tropics which implies intense summer heat and heavy dependence on monsoons for survival. Rains are so unevenly distributed by season, that even small delays in arrival could upset the agricultural cycle and push the region close to desert-like conditions by drying up water reserves. The conditions are precarious in areas that receive relatively less rain even under normal conditions and have fewer perennial rivers, such as the Deccan plateau. Thus, the possibility of crop failure, water scarcity and famine is built into the geography of the region, and famines did strike with almost predictable regularity until 1900. In recorded history of famines, some of them were known to destroy millions of lives, sometimes as much as 20–30 per cent of the population of the area affected.

Because famines were primarily environmental in origin, the situation could not have been fundamentally different in the pre-British period. It can be safely assumed that the mortality rate in the eighteenth and early nineteenth centuries was very near the levels of the 1880s. Birth rate could not be biologically much higher than what it was found to be in the 1880s. These two assumptions lead to the inference that population must have grown rather slowly in pre-British India.

The disappearance of famine from about 1900 was an important reason for fall in death rate. The other factors behind mortality were diseases and epidemics, nutrition, sanitation, and social institutions.

Three diseases—cholera, plague and malaria—took heavy toll of life in the late nineteenth and early twentieth centuries. Cholera and plague epidemics were known to have occurred with equal ferocity from much earlier. Cholera was directly related to unsanitary living, polluted water and congestion. For these reasons cholera often started in pilgrim towns, during fairs, or after floods. Famines also were responsible for epidemic outbreaks as sustained and acute food shortage reduced immunity. Malaria outbreaks in the colonial period have been attributed to construction works that created stagnant pools of water, such as the canals in UP. Even without this factor, in regions like the present West Bengal, malaria was prevalent in the nineteenth century. These were not the only diseases that could cause deaths en masse. There were many others, including a few that specially affected children. Some like the influenza epidemic of 1918–9 became fatal only in certain years.

Along with famines and diseases, mortality was also a consequence of prevalent social practices that exposed certain segments of the population to exceptional health risks. Extremely high maternal and infant mortality in British India reflected this as none other.

Infant Mortality: Social Causes of High Deaths

Infant mortality per 1000 live births was above 200 at 1901. It came down to 180 at 1931. This level did not compare too badly with the poorer countries in South America or even Europe, and was somewhat above the rates in British Malaya. But it was still among the world's highest. The causes of infant mortality were not necessarily the same as the causes behind high mortality in general. High infant mortality was a stable feature of Indian society. It did not need famines or epidemics. It derived from the poor health of the mothers. That, in turn, was a result of child marriage, frequency of motherhood, primitive obstetrics, and insanitary conditions during childbirth. Strangely enough, women in the cities were not necessarily better off in this regard. In some cases they were even worse off. An enquiry in Bombay found that women mill workers had fewer children than in the rural areas. But they did have much less rest during and after pregnancy than in the rural areas.[7]

Government hospitals could bring only marginal improvement in the infant mortality rate. One of the basic causes of child mortality as well as the birth of a large number of children with impairments was the early age of women at marriage and commencement of child bearing. India as a whole practised child marriage, but some regions had a much worse record in this respect than others. The age at marriage tended to be the lowest in eastern India (Greater Bengal, eastern UP, but not Assam), and large parts of central India. Age of consent laws existed in British India. But these were universally disregarded until the enactment of the Child Marriage Restraint Act of

[7] *Census of India 1931* Vol 1, Part I, Report, Delhi, 1931, pp. 92–3.

1930. This act made the marriage of women below the age of 14 punishable, but not invalid. The Act was no more than a piece of paper for a long time after it was passed. Marriages were held in public places in open defiance. Different religious communities had different views on it. In western India, marriages could be held a few miles away from the village, inside the territory of a native state where British laws did not apply. Nevertheless, the Act, and the few actual convictions under it, may have had a mild deterrent effect after 1930.

### Mortality: Causes of Decline

Why did mortality decline sharply from the interwar period? In the larger literature relating to the developing world as a whole, there are basically two positions on the origins of mortality decline. The first emphasizes public health measures that led to better treatment of communicable diseases. The four pillars of successful medical intervention in the early twentieth century were malaria eradication, immunization programmes, improved sanitation, and the use of antibiotics. However, critics point out that, none of these measures was universally applied before mortality began to decline. And they do not explain such prior episodes of accelerated population growth such as was experienced by eighteenth century Europe. An alternative view is that, worldwide improvement in nutrition led to increased resistance to diseases. The change owed less to the quantity of food consumed and more to better distribution of food intake. 'Better food distribution in Europe followed in the wake of the Industrial Revolution and reached the developing countries late in the nineteenth century as the Third World came increasingly under the political domination of the West'.[8]

In India, the specific variables that are believed to have played the most significant role in mortality decline illustrate the second view, though the first effect was undoubtedly important after 1920. Three specific factors need to be considered. First, a well-developed government machinery for famine relief came in place. Secondly and more importantly, long-distance private trade in grain expanded. As the railways grew in density and reach, grain could move into scarcity areas much faster than before in response to higher prices of grain. This simple market mechanism that distributed food more evenly across regions and over time gained in efficiency with development

---

[8] Carter L. Marshall, 'Health, Nutrition, and the Root of World Population Growth', *International Journal of Health Services*, 4(4), 1974.

of railways and the telegraph. Thirdly, in some regions a network of irrigation canals contributed to stability in food supplies (see also Chapter 3). Along with these, there had been major breakthroughs in disease prevention and control around the turn of the century.

There is some scope for debate on the interpretation of mortality trends during the British rule. Some estimates suggest that population grew at a significantly positive rate in the period 1801–72. If these are believed, then it might seem that population growth rate actually declined during the period 1872–1921. Such a decline would derive from a rise in mortality during 1872–1921. This was the period when the modernizing benefits of British rule were made available. A rise in mortality at the same time is incompatible with the belief that these modernizing benefits had much impact on mortality. Ira Klein has put forth this argument.[9] Klein followed it with the hypothesis that the spread of major epidemics in the third quarter of the nineteenth century led to the rise in mortality during 1872–1921. The spread was aided by better infrastructure and greater population movement. Increasing immunity to these diseases thereafter led to a fall in mortality after 1921. The argument hinges on the assumption that population growth was higher before 1872, which is questionable and not well established in Klein's study. Further, several major episodes of high mortality in this period derived from famines and famine-induced diseases. It is not proven that famines in pre-census periods were any less severe. Nevertheless, Klein's stress on the outbreak of new diseases and on the role of increasing natural resistance to these diseases, are both noteworthy.

Birth Rate

Why the birth rate was high is a less debated question. But why it remained high even as mortality declined is not easily answerable. A high death rate itself can induce a high birth rate. The smaller the chance of survival of children the more are parents induced to produce more children. This reasoning explains why historically birth rates in India have been high. The Indian fertility rates did not attain the biological maximum but were high by international standards— high enough to maintain population stability in the face of high death rate.

There are various social means of ensuring high birth rate. The

[9] 'Population Growth and Mortality in British India, Part I: The Climacteric of Death', IESHR, 26(4), 1989; and 'Population Growth and Mortality in British India, Part II: The Demographic Revolution', IESHR, 27(1), 1990.

most effective is to get women married early. The age of marriage has thus been low throughout the Indian subcontinent. Early marriage, however, also increased risks of death and impairment of further childbearing capacity due to early pregnancy, and to that extent reduced overall birth rate.

On the other hand, there were several social practices that had a depressing effect on the birth rate. The most important were female infanticide in north India, and prohibition on widow remarriage among the Hindus.

Why did fertility remain high even after mortality began to decline? No clear answer to this question is available yet. The long-term stability of the 'social props' is the most reasonable hypothesis. For a very long time in the past, the social status of women had been largely determined by the biological need to adapt fertility to the great risks of early death. Early marriage usually went with little participation of women in commercial work, low levels of female literacy (practically zero literacy before 1901), a social attitude that did not see women as directly productive workers, and therefore, did not see them as legitimate claimants to property. Mortality rate began to fall in the colonial period but social attitudes did not change so easily. The persistence of these values well into our own times has contributed to the relatively low levels of women's social development and lack of freedom in decision making. Scholarship dealing with more recent data has found a strong negative correlation between levels of women's social development and birth rates.

Migration—International

International migration was never a significant influence on population growth. In 1881–91, for example, net emigration from India was about 700,000, a mere 0.3 per cent of the 1881 population. In the next decade, the percentage was a little higher, but it declined thereafter. Still, migration did increase quite dramatically during the colonial period, especially after 1870. It could be attributed to the growth of British enterprise elsewhere in the world. The steam ship, the railways, and new trade routes played critical facilitating roles.

Organized emigration began in the 1830s when recruiting agents contracted with large parties of potential workers and arranged to send them abroad. During 1830–70, Madras and Calcutta were the main ports of embarkation. Migrants through Calcutta came from eastern India. The destinations were the British colonies in Southeast Asia, Burma, the Pacific and the West Indies. The Madras port sent several hundred thousand Tamils to Ceylon and Burma. The migration to Mauritius, South Africa, and the West Indies took place via Madras and the French ports in south India.

During 1871–1930, every year about two to six hundred thousand persons left India to work abroad. But the majority returned to India after a few years, so that net emigration was rather small. Eighty per cent of the migrants migrated within Asia between 1830–1900, and almost 100 per cent between 1900–37. From the early 1920s, net emigration began to fall quite sharply even as the number of migrants increased for, after 1920, return migration speeded up.

In the nineteenth century, the source areas of migration happened to be specific districts, not evenly spread over a large region. This fact suggests that the source areas shared some common features such as high population density and a high propensity for harvest failure. Further, rural labourers and artisans formed a large part of the migrant population. These classes tended to be especially vulnerable to drought because they had no store of grains. The famine years gave rise to mass scale migration. Also, the concentration of source areas in a few districts suggests the role of limited information—the fact that a known person had migrated with subsequent economic success, encouraged migration. For it promised some support at destination for the new migrant. Returned migrants encouraged persons known to them to leave. Systems of recruitment worked more intensively in areas where it had once succeeded.[10]

Why did migration not flow on a much larger scale? The difficulties of the sea voyage and vast differences in ways of life at the destination discouraged many people. More importantly perhaps, internal migration became a major substitute for international migration for persons who were ready to move. From the 1870s, plantations and public works inside India recruited large numbers from more or less the same districts that had once sent thousands of people abroad.

Migration—Internal

International migration represented a worldwide trend towards increasing labour mobility—a joint outcome of new economic opportunities and revolution in long-distance transportation. Within India, internal migration also increased as a consequence of the same process. Internal migration had no impact on the population growth of India as a whole, but it did have a significant impact on the population growth of certain regions within India. Relevant data on internal

[10] See also the discussion on migration in Chapter 5.

migration is not sufficiently detailed for the pre-1901 period. So the following description relates to the period after 1901.

Persons who declared themselves as 'immigrants' formed about 1.8 per cent of the total population of India at 1901, and 3 per cent in 1931. In absolute terms, there had been an increase of about 5 million persons. The percentages varied between regions. For example, 12–15 per cent of Assam's population consisted of 'immigrants' in 1901–31. It is certain that the all-India percentage of immigrants was much smaller than 1.8 about 20 or 30 years before 1901. For, internal migration in 1901 followed a certain pattern that was propelled by causes of recent origin. The vast majority of migrants moved into specific occupations and areas of opportunities that were a consequence of colonial influence. The examples were, labour in plantations, labour in large-scale industry, services in Burma, and so on. The major movements happened along lines indicated in Table 9.4 and Map 9.1.

TABLE 9.4
Major Channels of Internal Migration, 1901–31

| East India | 1. | Bihar and UP to Assam plantations |
|---|---|---|
| | 2. | Bengal (mainly Mymensingh district) to Assam, peasants migrated in search of land for resettlement |
| | 3. | Bengal to Burma, to work as labour and in the tertiary sector |
| | 4. | UP to Bengal, to work in industry, mines, and the tertiary sector |
| Central India | 5. | UP to central India, to work in mills |
| | 6. | Chhattisgarh to Berar, to work as agricultural and mill labour |
| | 7. | Hyderabad to Berar, mill labour |
| South India | 8. | Madras (Tamil Nadu) to Mysore, labour in mines, and into the tertiary sector |
| | 9. | Madras to Burma, labour and the tertiary sector |
| North and Western India | 10. | Within Punjab, east to west, peasants and pastoralists resettled as peasants in the canal areas |
| | 11. | Rajputana to Punjab, trade |
| | 12. | Rajputana to Bombay, trade |

*Source: Census of India*, Vol. I (Parts 1–2), 1901–31.

The table and the map show at least five broad types of migration: (a) movement out of high population density regions (UP, Bihar, Bengal), (b) circulation of agricultural labourers among neighbouring

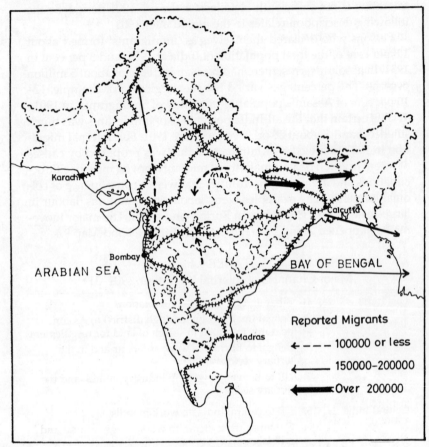

MAP 9.1:  MAJOR CHANNELS OF INTERNAL MIGRATION

regions, (c) traders and professionals seeking out new fields, (d) peasants seeking out cultivable land, and (e) agricultural labourers moving into non-agricultural labour. To these we can add one more type, the movement of artisans from north India and the Deccan and their resettlement in western and eastern India. Being relatively smaller in scale than those shown in the table and the map above, this movement is not adequately captured in census data. It has been studied recently and shown to be quite significant for the history of the textile and the leather industries at least.[11]

What factors determined internal migration? We have seen ('labour', Chapter 5) one explanation suggesting that the 'reserve price' of labour was low in the source regions.[12] This theory of migration in the Indian context has not been seriously questioned. But it needs to be supplemented by others. Many individual migrants owned land back in the villages they came from. Such people do not fit this model. What city work meant for them was perhaps a reduction of risks, the choice of a portfolio of occupations.[13] Even agrarian labourers, the type that fits the 'reserve price' model best, may have had other reasons for migration. Many of the source areas displayed at least two other features apart from very low and insecure wages, surplus labour or excessively high population density such as in eastern UP, and social deprivation of labour. A large number of people who took up jobs in the mills were from the 'untouchable' castes who experienced a distinct improvement in the social climate when they came to Calcutta or Bombay. Their social status was not forgotten but cities for them were certainly much less hierarchical than the villages. Also, cities created wider job opportunities, whereas the village would have offered them nothing but agricultural labour and a degraded lifestyle. When we account for this factor, migration was a change undoubtedly for the better. There is so far no work on internal migration in India that can satisfactorily account for these diverse movements in one framework. The common factors behind all of them seem to be, (a) socially and economically depressed conditions in source areas, (b) new economic opportunities that arose during the colonial period, and (c) easier transportation.

[11] Douglas Haynes and Tirthankar Roy, 'Conceiving Mobility: Migration of Hand-loom Weavers in Pre-colonial and Colonial India', *IESHR*, 33(1), 1999; Tirthankar Roy, *Traditional Industry in the Economy of Colonial India*, Cambridge, 1999, Chapter 6.

[12] Lalita Chakravarty, 'Emergence of an Industrial Labour Force in a Dual Economy—British India, 1880–1920', *IESHR*, 15(3), 1978.

[13] See the discussion in Chapter 5.

## Famines as Demographic Events

Famine was a more important cause of death in colonial and pre-colonial India than old age or diseases. Mortality figures for the three major famines of the nineteenth century were, about 8 million during 1876–8, 2–4 million during 1896–7, and 3–4 million during 1899–1900. Between 1872 and 1881, a 'normal' or long-term average 0.5 per cent annual growth rate in population would have meant an addition of about 10–12 million persons. Almost the entire expected increment was carried away in two years of drought and epidemics in 1876–8. The 1876–8 famine was extremely severe in Bombay–Deccan, and comparatively mild but intense in northern and southern India. Famines of similar scale were probably rare occurrences. But more localized famines of equal ferocity occurred in 1868–9 (Rajputana), 1837–8 (Punjab and Western UP), 1854 (Madras–Deccan), 1865 (Orissa and Madras), and 1873–4 (Bihar). Famines capable of causing mass destruction of lives became rare from 1900, with the exception of Bengal famine in 1943–4. The Bengal famine was an exception in that it was the only famine that was not preceded by a harvest failure. All the others were preceded by a shortage of monsoon rains. Rains continued to fail from time to time in the twentieth century, but famines became rarer.

The first few months of a severe drought saw sharp rise in food prices. The resultant mass starvation led to a decrease in conceptions, followed by increase in deaths. The middle months of the famine saw soaring deaths. These deaths had an association with age and sex. Usually, famines increased male mortality because men tended to leave their villages in search of food and work. Famines also affected children and the elderly severely because they could not withstand sustained malnutrition. Finally, it affected the lower castes because they commanded smaller 'exchange entitlements'.[14] These were the vulnerable groups. The return of the rains did not necessarily

---

[14] Amartya Sen suggests that famines can occur not due to declines in food availability, but because groups of people are deprived of their entitlement to exchange some goods or services for food at the normal price of food. See his *Poverty and Famines: An Essay on Entitlement and Deprivation*, Oxford University Press, Delhi, 1984. With the exception of the Bengal famine of 1943, in all other major famines of colonial India, there occurred a sharp decline in average food supply due to failure of the rains. However, mortality and diseases were almost always distributed unequally between castes and occupations, which suggests that entitlement failure was present even in a weather-induced famine. For example, groups of people could be deprived of claims upon food stocks because of their low caste.

improve the situation. Sustained malnutrition exposed the survivors to parasites, especially cholera, dysentery, diarrhoea and pneumonia. Malaria outbreaks were very common in some regions such as Bengal. Finally, by the end of a famine the population profile changed completely both in numbers and in age and sex distribution. A smaller work-force supported a larger number of dependants per male and a large number of widows. These conditions delayed the return of normalcy to agricultural production. After the shock passed, birth rates usually rose above pre-famine levels, and death rates fell below the latter.[15]

The government's response to famine was to establish relief camps where starving persons could get free or cheap food in exchange for work on public projects. The idea of relief camps took shape slowly. They were relatively new and a still debated institution in 1876, but a well-established one by 1900. Food-for-work programmes set up after 1947 followed this colonial precedence. Relief camps helped mitigate the effect of famines. They were a means by which major railway lines and other public works were constructed in the third quarter of the nineteenth century. But they were far less effective especially in the earlier years in the prevention of mass death. Why was the government slow to act, and why did it act on a restricted scale? The reasons were a combination of budget constraint and ideology. Key personalities in charge of deciding famine relief believed that relief made people lazy and dependent on government subsidies, and that relief tended to interfere with free trade in grains by changing relative prices between regions. It so happened that such hesitation suited the government's intense reluctance to spend its limited income on any kind of public good.[16] The force of both these arguments weakened after the 1876–8 famine. This event was much discussed both in governmental and non-governmental media. It had a singular influence on perceptions about the impact of British rule on the welfare of ordinary Indians.

An interesting question in India's demographic history is why

[15] Tim Dyson, 'On the Demography of South Asian Famines', *Population Studies*, 45(1–2), 1991; Arup Maharatna, *The Demography of Famines: An Indian Historical Perspective*, Oxford University Press, Delhi, 1996, 'Summary and Conclusion'; D. Rajasekhar, 'Famines and Peasant Mobility: Changing Agrarian Structure in Kurnool District of Andhra, 1870–1900', *IESHR*, 28(2), 1991.

[16] David Hall–Matthews, 'The Historical Roots of Famine Relief Paradigms', in Helen O'Neill and John Toye (eds), *A World Without Famine?*, Macmillan, Basingstoke and London, 1998.

famines became rare even as food availability per capita began to decline after 1920. This puzzle can be resolved if we make a distinction between sudden large shortfalls in food intake, and sustained mild decline in food intake. Individuals can adjust more easily with the latter. But the former always leads to violent demographic consequences.[17]

## The Economic Impact of High Population Growth

In classical writings on sustained high rates of population growth, economic impact in the form of 'Malthusian checks' was highlighted. Reduced availability of food per head due to high rate of population growth can make famines and diseases more likely, which would reduce population to the level sustainable by food supply. In the postwar period, the Malthusian impact became an obsolete and unpopular theory, mainly for three reasons. First, even if average food availability declines in a country over time due to population growth, Malthusian checks need not occur because of better world trade and distribution of food now compared to a century ago. Second, populations can adapt quite well to gradual decline in average food intake. Segments of the population, such as children, may get mildly undernourished if food availability per head declines, but may not die as they would during famines. Third, it was found that increasing density of population can sometimes lead to more efficient utilization of resources (see the beginning of this chapter).

Indeed, Malthusian disasters more or less vanished from India after 1900. It is probable that increasing density did lead to increasing efficiency in some contexts. At the same time, from 1921 South Asia entered a regime of exceptionally high and sustained population growth. What economic effects such a regime can have remains an important question. Critique of Malthusianism does not deny the prospect of overpopulation. Food is not the only index to measure overpopulation. If capital or land becomes short in supply relative to labour diminishing returns can follow. This can depress wages and depress the productivity of land.

In Chapter 3 we have seen that productivity of land was stagnant or declining in the early twentieth century. So were agricultural real wages. Both tendencies were probably stronger in eastern India, a region of very high population density already about 1901. Both these

---

[17] Sumit Guha argues that the later rarity of famines derived from the rarity of violent harvest failures, leading to a change in mortality trends, 'Mortality Decline in Early Twentieth Century India: A Preliminary Enquiry', *IESHR*, 28(4), 1991.

tendencies have been present, with exceptions, in post-colonial India as well. Population growth has accelerated from early in the twentieth century. A causal connection between depressed yield and wages, and high population growth is a plausible hypothesis.

Let us see a little more closely how this connection might have worked in the long run. Land-use statistics suggest that the main determinant of economic growth in the nineteenth century was expansion in cultivated area. Expansion in cultivated area occurred by two means, (a) expansion in cultivable area, and (b) conversion into cultivated land of what were hitherto uncultivated wastes. Irrigation made some of these wastes productive land. After 1900, irrigation and land development slowed down. Further expansion in acreage had to be slow. After 1947, the same process restarted. More waste was converted and brought under the plough. In the pre-independence period, the acreage cropped per capita could be roughly maintained by this strategy. In the post-independence period, it began to fall. The direction of change in acreage (net sown area) per capita can be gathered from following data:

|  | Acres per capita |
| --- | --- |
| 1885 (British India excluding Burma, includes current fallow) | 0.69 |
| 1938 (British India excluding Burma, includes current fallow) | 0.67 |
| 1951 (Indian Union) | 0.81 |
| 1996 (Indian Union) | 0.38 |

It is clear from this description that population growth has led to at least two effects, reduction in arable land per capita, and destruction of the commons.

Reduction in land per head means a reduction in the assets of the average peasant household. In turn, this means reduced capacity for investments in land. Land improvement methods that carry economies of scale are not easy to implement in this situation. Further, land expansion is likely to have led to the use of inferior land in the long run. Finally, the destruction of the commons has also affected forests and water-resources. Even as the area under the forest department expanded, it is common knowledge that the quantity and the quality of the forests have universally declined. Reduced access to the commons can, directly or indirectly, restrict productivity of land. It can also make productivity expansion too costly in terms of environmental damage.

Two other impacts of population need to be mentioned. The first relates to labour markets. The availability of a pool of surplus labour can lead to a labour-intensive industrialization based on the growth of small-scale industry. Colonial India saw the beginnings of this process. But such industrialization is not capable of generating rapid growth in wages and productivity. Secondly, one measure of over-population is the balance between people and the government's capacity to supply public goods. The government needs to provide for food security, education, health care, and security of property. The larger the population size, the larger the demand for the above. A crisis can develop if the government's income does not increase at the same rate as population. Such an imbalance was beginning to unfold by the end of colonial rule. It has been acute in the post-independence period.

## LABOUR FORCE AND OCCUPATIONAL STRUCTURE
### Census Data

Census data on employment by occupation is available from 1881. However, the early censuses, especially 1881, 1891 and 1901, involved a number of problems of definition. Scholars who have written on occupational structure have had to reconstruct this data somewhat, and suggest ways of getting around these problems. Two sets of work are especially noteworthy, that by Daniel and Alice Thorner in the 1950s and the early 1960s, and by J. Krishnamurty in the mid-1960s. Based on these works, the main problems with census data on employment can be briefly summarized.

(i) The 1881, 1891–1901, and 1911–31 censuses use different occupational classifications.

(ii) The data on women workers is suspect in almost all the censuses. In particular, the earlier censuses are believed to have inflated the number of women workers. Some members of the working family participated in commercial activity very marginally. The earlier censuses are believed to have treated them as workers.

(iii) There was a category called 'general labour' in the early censuses that was meant to include non-specialized rural labourers. In reality, nearly all such people were agricultural labourers by main occupation, and performed other work when no agricultural work was available. This category of workers, therefore, can be seen as agricultural labourers.

(iv) Many broad sectors in the earlier censuses clubbed manufacturers and traders of industrial goods, and included all of them under industry. This gave inflated shares of industry in 1881–1901. To avoid a misreading, industry and trade data should be seen together and not separately for the early censuses.

(v) The 1931 census used a definition of worker much stricter than its predecessors.

(vi) In 1951, there was a category called 'services otherwise un-classified', which was probably equivalent of agricultural/general labour.

These differences across censuses require some re-adjustment and guidance before they can be studied for trends. Table 9.5 shows what the occupational data looks like after the basic adjustments.

TABLE 9.5
Labour Force and Occupational Structure,
the Indian Union, 1881–1951

|  | 1881 | 1901 | 1911 | 1921 | 1931 | 1951 |
|---|---|---|---|---|---|---|
| Population (millions) | 213.2 | 238.1 | 251.9 | 251.2 | 278.7 | 356.6 |
| Work-force (millions) | 100.8 | 115.7 | 121.0 | 117.7 | 119.4 | 139.5 |
| Participation rate (%) | 47 | 49 | 48 | 47 | 43 | 39 |
| Participation rate for men (%) | 63 | 63 | 62 | 60 | 58 | 54 |
| Participation rate for women (%) | 31 | 33 | 34 | 33 | 27 | 23 |
| Occupational structure (% of work-force): |  |  |  |  |  |  |
| Primary sector[a] | 74 | 75 | 76 | 77 | 76 | 76 |
| Secondary and tertiary sectors | 26 | 25 | 24 | 22 | 22 | 24 |
| Industry and trade[b, c] | 20 | 16 | 16 | 15 | 15 | – |
| Industry[b] | – | – | 10 | 9 | 9 | 10 |
| Trade and transportation | – | – | 7 | 7 | 7 | 7 |
| Other services | – | – | 7 | 6 | 6 | 7 |

[a] Includes animal husbandry, forestry, hunting, fishing, and 'general labour'.

[b] Includes mining, construction.

[c] For all of British India, including Burma.

Sources: Alice Thorner, 'The Secular Trend in the Indian Economy, 1881–1951', Economic Weekly, 14(28–30), special number, July 1962; Daniel Thorner, '"De-industrialization" in India, 1881–1931', in Daniel and Alice Thorner, Land and Labour in India, Asia Publishing House, New York, 1962.

## Occupational Structure

Three major conclusions emerge from studying Table 9.5 These are:

(i) Participation rate fell in the long run. One obvious reason be-hind this trend was changing age-composition in favour of children and adolescents. In the case of women, participation rate was lower than men because even many adult women did not participate in paid work. The number of such adults must have increased during 1921 and 1951, when women's participation fell sharply.

(ii) If we confine ourselves to comparing the primary, secondary and tertiary sectors only, there was no change in occupational structure in the long run.

(iii) Divisions within the secondary and the tertiary sectors can be drawn only broadly. The 1881 data for industry is suspect, and if that is ignored, the same conclusion of stability emerges.

These three points are well-known in the literature on occupational structure. However, four further points have not been sufficiently explored in earlier work: These are,

(iv) Why women's participation rate declined is an open question. In earlier work, there was a tendency to treat the high rates in the earlier censuses as a reporting problem that got corrected for over time. It has been suggested that women who did commercial work only as members of the household production unit, and were marginally involved in such work, tended to be misclassified as 'workers' in the earlier censuses (see also the discussion in Chapter 4 on this point). But it is not so clear that this is a correct view.[18] It is possible that large numbers of adult women in fact left commercial work because the household as a production unit tended to decline along with increasing commercialization and specialization of work.

(v) The presence of a large category 'general labour' in the earlier censuses has also been explained similarly as a reporting problem. This category too, like adult women workers, shrank gradually. Once again, a different explanation can be offered. The 'general labour' category arose because in the late nineteenth century village, there was present a large group of people engaged in diverse work. Such people were village servants, artisans, agricultural labourers at the same time. That such workers tended to disappear over time can again mean increasing commercialization of labour, increasing specialization of tasks, and the creation of a labour market in rural India.

(vi) There were segments of growth and segments of decline within industrial labour. Similar divergent tendencies were present

---

[18] In a more recent essay, Alice Thorner takes the position that women's participation rate may not be purely a reporting problem. See 'Women's Work in Colonial India, 1881–1931', School of Oriental and African Studies, London, 1984. The essay comparing regions and occupations is perhaps the only detailed investigation into this trend now available.

within the broad categories of services as well. The industry picture we have seen in Chapter 4. The services picture has not been fully explored.

(vii) In fact, for the tertiary sector, there is an almost complete lack of detailed research. The only work, and a pioneering one, by Dharma Kumar on South India, suggests that commercialization of the services occurred. It created segments of growth and segments of decline within this sector.[19]

While there was an apparent inertia in occupational structure, the structure of national income changed significantly, as we have seen in Chapter 7. Between 1900–01 to 1904–5 and 1942–3 to 1946–7, agriculture's share declined from 67 to 58 per cent, industry's share increased from 21 to 25 per cent, and services' share increased from 12 to 17 per cent. These shifts resulted from two processes. The first was the rather slow growth rate of real income in agriculture during this period. Second, within industry, and possibly within services as well, there were both organizational and technological changes that led to growth in labour productivity.

Within agricultural employment, the share of agricultural labourers increased and that of cultivators declined. These trends were broken only in 1921 and 1951. These statistics need to be read cautiously, as we have mentioned in Chapter 3. Further, the relative proportions of cultivators and labourers varied somewhat across regions.

If in 1881–51, there was inertia in occupational structure, was there a change in the earlier part of the British rule? Some scholars have argued that the share of manufacturing in total work force was higher at 1800 than by the end of the nineteenth century (see Chapter 4, 'deindustrialization'). The database to test such a hypothesis is weak. Furthermore, as it has been argued in Chapter 4, even if the share of manufacturing in employment had been higher earlier, that does not necessarily mean a larger share of industry in national income. For, many manufacturing workers in the nineteenth century worked only part-time. Their number was probably higher about 1800. The share of such non-specialized workers has been declining in the long run.

## Quality of Labour

A people's ability to exploit new opportunities and create new opportunities must depend on their state of education and health. Without education, manual labour and traditional occupations will tend

---

[19] 'The Forgotten Sector: Services in Madras Presidency in the First Half of the Nineteenth Century', *IESHR*, 24(4), 1987.

to restrict the possibilities of economic growth. Poor measures of health are usually symptoms of incapacity showing poor quality of labour and social-cultural conventions that lead people to work below their capacity. Poor health status is also causally associated with high birth rates and population growth. The record of colonial India in these respects was among the poorest in the world. The state of education has been discussed in Chapter 8. While overall mortality declined several key indices of health improved much more slowly. Infant mortality is a revealing example, discussed earlier in this chapter.

## CONCLUSION

Population history in British India is a story, simultaneously, of both transformation and inertia on an immense scale. Population growth began to accelerate due to decline in mortality rates. The decline reflected new standards of health and sanitation. It was also a result of the disappearance of famines after 1900. This latter development reflected India's newly acquired ability to adapt to its basic climatic condition. This was an outcome of the railways and market development along with public relief. On the other hand, birth rates, infant mortality, sex-ratio adverse to women, changed little. In short, there was rather little change in women's status in society and in the low value they commanded as commercial workers.

This low value of women as paid workers had roots in Indian culture and society. The British rule did not create these conditions. It is possible, however, that commercialization of labour in some cases reinforced that cultural bias. As we have seen in Chapters 4, 5 and in this chapter, commercialization encouraged work participation and occupational mobility for men and simultaneously it seems to have discouraged mobility for women. At any rate the latter greatly lagged behind the former. Better value for men seems to have been associated with a devaluation of women. The long-term stability in occupational structure and the retreat of women from the workforce reflect that devaluation to some extent.

## ANNOTATED READINGS
### Population Size and Growth

Leela Visaria and Pravin Visaria, 'Population (1757–1947)', in *CEHI 2*. P.C. Mahalanobis and D. Bhattacharya, 'Growth of Population in

India and Pakistan, 1801–1961', *Artha Vijnana*, 18(1), 1976. Ira Klein, 'Population Growth and Mortality in British India, Part I: The Climacteric of Death', *IESHR*, 26(4), 1989; and 'Population Growth and Mortality in British India, Part II: The Demographic Revolution', *IESHR*, 27(1), 1990. Sumit Guha, 'Mortality Decline in Early Twentieth Century India: A Preliminary Enquiry', *IESHR*, 28(4), 1991. Arup Maharatna, *The Demography of Famines: An Indian Historical Perspective*, Oxford University Press, Delhi, 1996, 'Summary and Conclusion'. David Hall–Matthews, 'The Historical Roots of Famine Relief Paradigms' in Helen O'Neill and John Toye (eds), *A World Without Famine?* , Macmillan, Basingstoke and London, 1998. Ira Klein, 'When the Rains Failed: Famine, Relief, and Mortality in British India', *IESHR*, 21(2), 1984.

The economic effect of population growth is not a well-researched field. In historians' writings, demography as a possible source of agricultural stagnation has been discussed. But it is not a popular line of enquiry. See Chapter 3 ('resource endowments') for a discussion. For the post-independence period, the following piece is strongly recommended. N. Krishnaji has explored the impact of drastic reduction in land-man ratio in post-independence India on agriculture and rural labour, 'Land and Labour in India: The Demographic Factor', *EPW*, 25(18–19), 1990.

## Occupational Structure

J. Krishnamurty, 'Occupational Structure', *CEHI* 2. Alice Thorner, 'The Secular Trend in the Indian Economy, 1881–1951', *Economic Weekly*, 14(28–30), special number, July 1962; Daniel Thorner, '"Deindustrialization" in India, 1881–1931', in Daniel and Alice Thorner, *Land and Labour in India*, Asia Publishing House, New York, 1962. Alice Thorner, 'Women's Work in Colonial India', School of Oriental and African Studies, London, 1984. Dharma Kumar, 'The Forgotten Sector: Services in Madras Presidency in the First Half of the Nineteenth Century', *IESHR*, 24(4), 1987.

## 10

# Conclusion

### SUMMARY

The broad picture of colonial India described above is a mixed one. India was changing rapidly under the impetus of commercialization, a strong state, modern infrastructure, government intervention in agriculture, and other changes brought on by colonialism. But these changes, both political and economic intensified competition and produced both segments of growth and segments of decline.

In the most popular world-view of India under colonial regime, what we have called the left-nationalist interpretation of Indian economic history, it is suggested that the decline outweighed growth, and that both growth and decline derived mainly from colonial policies. The economic interests served by the British rule led to the exploitation and impoverishment of India. The chapters found no quantitative evidence to prove that decline outweighed growth. Throughout the colonial period Indian real incomes were growing. Nor is there strong enough ground to believe that the dominant source of economic transformation was colonial policy. Direct government intervention was, after all, limited in most sectors other than agriculture. 'Exploitation' cannot be unambiguously defined in this context. In part, new opportunities and competition were a result of India's integration in the world economy, and extension of market exchange and integration of markets within India.

One task historians often face is that of identifying segments in decline and segments of growth, and explaining where they differed. In agriculture, growth tended to occur under a combination of relatively high levels of commercialization and investment. Else-where, growth was small, temporary, or absent. Employment declined in small-scale industry as a result of two processes: compe-tition with large-scale industry, and competition within small-scale industry. Due to this latter process, older and less efficient organiza-tions like the households declined in favour of small factories and wage labour. The outcome was a decline in employment, but rise in labour productivity. Large-scale industry experienced significant growth. So did mines and plantations. In the tertiary sector, organ-ized financial services like modern banks and insurance were grow-ing in employment and output. But there was also significant decline in some traditional services. We do not know yet whether that decline derived from competition with the organized sector, or from changes in the nature of demand.

What at first sight might appear as overall economic stagnation of colonial India is, in fact, a result of aggregating over these contradic-tory experiences. Why colonial India met with stagnation is not a valid question. But why agriculture met with stagnation in the interwar period, and why eastern India stagnated, are valid ones. The question why more rapid economic growth did not occur is a rather speculative one. But it does deserve an answer. Chapter 3 discussed a set of explanations. Colonial policies were important in specific contexts and in a rather indirect way. Also important were resource-endowments, caste and rural power, demography and ecology.

One of the messages of the book is that Indian economic history is an evolving discipline with many researchable questions still unan-swered. The last section gives some examples that arise from the chapters above.

## Research Topics

### Agriculture

There are a number of unexplored questions about agricultural his-tory that deal with risks. High uncertainty is built into monsoon agriculture in the tropics. What was the quantitative dimension of risks of harvest failure or price fluctuations? How far were these risks climatic in source, and how far manmade (for example, related to world market fluctuations)? How did risks influence saving and in-vestment of the agricultural population? What traditional systems of insurance existed and how effective or far-reaching were they? How did these traditional systems change from the nineteenth century? How did market structures adapt to risks?

The rural credit market has been extensively studied. But key issues have remained unresolved. Rural credit has tended to be seen as an expression of power and dominance. More realistically, it was a field where social power, creditworthiness of borrowers, harvest risks, portfolio choice of lenders, demand for working capital, and market structure, interacted to give rise to a variety of terms in diverse contexts. Can this interaction be brought within a conceptual framework or simple descriptive typology?

## Industry

We know little about informal systems of financing small-scale industry, and about that part of the informal money or capital markets which dealt with industry. Modern small-scale industry as a whole raises several questions. Where did its capital and labour come from? How were these firms managed? Did these firms originate from sources closer to small-scale industry, or from those closer to traditional small-scale industry? Surplus labour was an important factor behind long-term survival of labour-intensive industry in South Asia. But as technological choices and consumption patterns change worldwide, labour-intensive industry needs to adapt labour to making new goods or learning new methods. We see signs of these changes in small-scale industry in colonial India. The subject needs further research.

Scarcity of capital, especially long-term capital, was an overwhelming constraint for industry. It led to a variety of financial innovations. It also led to abuses and distortions in the product and capital markets. How did pervasive rationing affect the use of funds? The subject has been dealt with rather indirectly in Indian business history. A more focused study is needed. Large-scale industry used machinery. But it used it in a context of surplus labour, cheap labour, and a culture of hierarchical employment. What did this rather anomalous condition mean in terms of shop-floor practices?

In industrial finance, several basic questions await answers. What were the size, structure and operations of the informal money markets? The largest and the most financially stable banks in India had mainly European clientele. On the other hand, the Indian entrepreneurs tended to deal more heavily with a segment of banking that was not only smaller by average size but also differently managed. Why did this segmentation in the organized money market arise?

Was it due to colonial biases or to information problems? Given that the different segments of banking transacted with different types of client, how did the nature of clients influence financial structure, behaviour and rules?

## The Macroeconomy

Key areas of national income research need statistical work. Examples are, estimates of provincial incomes, income distribution, and consolidated wages and earnings by occupation and region. Given the great significance of gold in Indian macroeconomic history, what influenced choice of assets by saving households is a question that needs to be researched further.

## Population and Labour Force

The census data on occupational structure has been explored. But well-known works on this subject have raised questions and pointed out stylized facts that are yet to be answered. The most important example is the following. Women's participation in non-agricultural work in South Asia fell for nearly a hundred years between 1881 and 1971, and has been rising slowly between 1971 and 1991. Why did it fall? Why has it been rising again? The answers are expected to illustrate the conditions for entry and exit of women in paid work, changes in the nature of jobs where women enter, and in turn, long-term patterns in industrial organization. The most widely known hypothesis on the decline is that it is essentially a reporting problem. This hypothesis is not satisfactory for three reasons. First, it is a speculation. Second, it suggests, unrealistically, that it took the census 90 years to correct an error. And third, it rules out the presence of structural changes leading to the same effect. Work on changes in industrial organization suggests the decline of household production systems, which is one example of structural factors that may produce a decline in women's participation in the work force. There are almost certainly several other such factors.

Little research has been done on changes in tertiary sector employment in India. We do not know the answers to such basic questions as, what kind of occupational shifts have taken place in the long run within the service sector, or what caused employment growth and decline in this sector.

More generally, studies on occupational structure have not gone far beyond the census data. It is necessary to see census data in relation with histories of specific occupations or types of worker.

Demographic behaviour by occupation also needs to be explored. Economic changes that entail (a) increased need for labour, and/or (b) family as the main unit of work, can encourage families to become larger in size. There are many historical examples from the world over. That these conditions existed in colonial or post-colonial Indian agriculture, small-scale industry, and the service sector, cannot be questioned. How binding were they, and what role did they play in raising population growth?

Population history and economic history need a sustained and closer dialogue, given that one of the outstanding facts about the region's economic history is its long-maintained high rate of population growth. How does sustained excess supply of labour influence employment contracts? How does family structure interact with capital ownership in rural India, or how relevant is a Chayanovian model of peasant history? How has population impacted the commons? How did population affect government budgets and fiscal policy in the long run?

The list above is a small subset of research possibilities. One purpose of stating some of these questions (and indeed of the whole book) is to remind students of economic history that much of the actual and potential work on colonial India is engaged, not with making or unmaking images of imperialism, but with unfolding long continuities in institutions and behaviour. In that sense, studying economic development and studying history are not separate occupations.

Appendix A

# Imperialism

Connected with the question of whether or not Britain exploited and impoverished India, is the bigger question about the significance of imperialism. India in the nineteenth century was a colony of Britain, and a part of the British Empire, which in turn was one of several imperial systems. Was there an economic basis for the expansion of empires in the nineteenth century? Was there an economic need for the European industrial nations to rule over countries in Asia and Africa?

In the early-twentieth century, a view developed that the motivation behind imperialism was indeed an economic one. It stemmed from 'underconsumption', which was a tendency of internal consumption to rise more slowly than production. Underconsumption arose from increasing inequality of incomes in the industrial countries. The labouring classes did not experience rise in purchasing power, whereas the capitalist classes saved much of what they earned. This drove the latter to look for markets overseas, and force open these markets with the aid of superior military power. The economic philosophy of imperialism was therefore, free trade and freedom of foreign investment. This view can be called the classical theory of imperialism. It was first stated by J.A. Hobson. In the writings of Lenin, Rosa Luxemburg, and the postwar Marxists, the theme that imperialism was driven by the need to find external markets was restated with minor variations. In the more recent 'world systems' school, the idea that such contacts via trade and investment impoverished the colonies was further explored.

While the empire was at its prime, the majority of British writers believed that it was a beneficial and modernizing influence on the colonies. They argued that modern infrastructure, increased political stability, and security of life and property, came as a result of colonialism. Usually, such writings underplayed or glossed over the negative or disruptive impacts of imperialism.

In the postwar period, the Marxist theories came under a more powerful attack. A critique developed of its mono-causal, Eurocentric, 'mercantilist' view of the origins of imperialism. D.K. Fieldhouse, for example, criticized Marxist theories for asking the wrong question.[1] The question cannot be, were economic transactions with the colonies economically advantageous for the rulers? Of course, they were. But so were transactions with countries that were not colonies. Why, then, was colonialism needed? The correct question would be, did these advantages in some cases require political domination? If garnering these economic advantages for the rulers depended on power, such advantages could be called 'exploitation'. Examples of such advantages would be looting, unfair terms of trade, or 'drain'. During the nineteenth century, such forms of exploitation were either non-existent, or not clearly definable.

Over the 1950s and the 1960s, J. Gallagher and R. Robinson redefined imperial expansion as 'a set of bargains between European agents, sometimes with little backing from the metropolis, and their local allies and opponents, who were primarily concerned to defend or to improve their position inside their own societies'.[2] There was no doubt that a propensity to, or sometimes even a conscious policy of, expansion existed. Nor is there any doubt that economic motives formed a key driving force behind that propensity. But the actual outcome—that is, the empires as they actually came into existence— was less a result of that policy, and more a result of the interaction between these expansionary tendencies and local circumstances overseas. The interaction took no standard form either in politics or in economics. In some recent work, the question of how imperial economic policies were shaped has been reexamined. It has been suggested that the power of industry lobbies to influence political decisions in Britain should not be exaggerated. In Britain, the main political decision-makers were a class that represented landed wealth rather than industry. The work of P.J. Cain and A.G. Hopkins

[1] D.K. Fieldhouse, *The Colonial Empires*, Weidenfield and Nicholson, London, 1965, p. 380.

[2] Anil Seal, 'Preface', in J. Gallagher, *The Decline, Revival and Fall of the British Empire*, Cambridge, 1982, p. viii.

suggests that the main economic interest group that increased its political influence in Britain from the late-nineteenth century was financial rather than industrial. In fact, the government was willing to sacrifice the interests of industry when they clashed with those of the City of London, the financial centre.

Quantitative work also seriously questions the classical theory and some of the key predictions of the modern 'world systems' school. There is now sizeable statistical work comparing the scale of transactions between the colonists and their empires on the one hand, and the rest of the world on the other. In trade, migration, investment, and factor income movements, the links with the rest of the world appear to have been much more extensive than the links within the empire. Economic gains from colonies were neither as large as was imagined nor as crucial to the origins of industrialization. International comparisons also suggest that average incomes in South Asia were already lower than they were in Europe before colonial rule established itself.

The adverse effects of trade, foreign investment, and colonial domination on the colonies themselves were implied in the classical imperialism literature. The early nationalist writers in India dealt more directly with these effects. The key elements in their argument were, de-industrialization, drain, excessive revenue burden, and famines caused by food exports. Arguments that were for them not much more than political tools, were reestablished later by the left–nationalist historiography as correct and valid descriptions. The criticism of the Marxist theories of imperialism applies equally to the left–nationalist paradigm. The left–nationalist argument has been discussed in Chapter 1, and specific elements in it discussed in various other parts of this book.[3]

## READINGS

This topic was introduced in Chapter 1. See Chapter 1 for a list of readings.

---

[3] See 'critique of the left-nationalist paradigm' in Chapter 1, 'de-industrialization' in Chapter 4, the role of revenue policy in Chapter 3, 'drain' in Chapter 7, and interpretation of infrastructure development in Chapter 8.

## Appendix B

# The National Accounting Framework

The essential national account is a series of definitions about how national income is constituted and how it is spent. It is a simple and useful method available for describing the structure of an economy. For colonial India, the basic national accounts needs slight modifications. In this appendix, this modified accounting system is explained first. Next, it is shown how the analytical arguments of Chapter 7 can be simply stated in accounting language.

The national accounts deal with a set of 'flow' variables. That is, these variables are measured over a period of time, for example, income per year or saving per year. Five main definitions constitute the system. These are about (a) how national product is constituted, (b) how income is spent, (c) balance between saving and investment, (d) balance between government income and expenditure, and (d) balance between inflow and outflow in transactions with the rest of the world. By convention, national accounts are developed in such a way that every flow appears twice in the system, once showing where it arises from, and once describing how it is used. Whether this convention has been followed, that is, whether the complete system has explained every variable's origin and destination, is tested simply by adding up the definitional equations, which must add to zero.

## (a) National Product

Goods and services produced in the economy, excluding goods and services used up as raw material in the production of other goods, form the Gross Domestic Product or GDP at market prices. It is made up of 'GDP at factor cost' (Y) plus the various direct and indirect taxes paid to the government (T). GDP is the most important component of the income of a nation. GDP consists of four main types of goods and services. These go to meet consumption (C), investment (I), government demand (G1), and export (X). If the country receives foreign investment, we can write total investment as $(I + N_{in})$, where I stands for investment goods demanded by domestic producers, and $N_{in}$ goods demanded by foreign investors. Finally, consumption, investment, government expenditure or export can not only be met from output of the nation, but also from goods and services imported (M). Combining these definitions we can write:

$$(Y + T) + M = C + (I + N_{in}) + G1 + X \tag{B.1}$$

or

$$Y = C + (I + N_{in}) + (G1 - T) + (X - M) \tag{B.2}$$

The second expression shows government budget and foreign transactions separately.

## (b) National Income

Expenditure must be equal to income. GDP net of taxes is the main component of national income. Apart from that, citizens can also receive income from abroad $(F_{in})$, or have to make payments to foreigners for various services $(F_{out})$. The net factor income from abroad is $(F_{in} - F_{out})$. Added to the GDP net of taxes, the total gives us disposable national income. This income can be either consumed (C), or saved in the form of different financial assets. Four types of financial asset have been historically relevant for India: government securities sold at home (B1), net import of gold and silver $(M_{gold} - X_{gold})$, deposits or securities with the private sector (S), and foreign investment abroad $(N_{out})$. We can write the income-expenditure balance as:

$$C + S + N_{out} + B1 + (M_{gold} - X_{gold}) = Y + (F_{in} - F_{out}) \tag{B.3}$$

## (c) Saving–Investment

Investment by domestic investors must be equal to deposits or securities left with the private sector (S), that is,

$$I = S \qquad (B.4)$$

## (d) Public Finance

Government expenditure must equal government receipts. There were two main types of government expenditure in British India: expenditure in India (G1) and expenditure abroad (G2). The two most important types of government expenditure abroad were pensions paid in sterling to retired employees, and interest on public debt raised in London. The government can finance its expenditure by three means: current revenues (the bulk of which are raised in taxes (T)) borrowings from abroad (B2), and borrowings at home (B1). We can write:

$$G1 + G2 = T + B1 + B2 \qquad (B.5)$$

## (e) External Transactions or Balance of Payments

Receipts in foreign currency must equal payments in foreign currency. There were four main heads of external transactions in British India, (a) net export, (b) net capital movement, (c) net export of gold, and (d) net factor receipts from abroad. The symbol for each one of these elements has already been introduced. We can write the balance of payments as:

$$[X - M] + [(N_{in} - N_{out}) + B2] + [X_{gold} - M_{gold}] + [(F_{in} - F_{out}) - G2] = 0 \quad (B.6)$$

The four items under square brackets are, respectively, commodity trade balance, net capital movement, net gold export, and net receipts on account of services. In British India, the first two items were usually positive, and the second two were usually negative.

These five definitional statements complete the system. Let us write them together.

$$Y = C + (I + N_{in}) + (G1 - T) + (X - M) \qquad (B.2)$$

$$C + S + N_{out} + B1 + (M_{gold} - X_{gold}) = Y + (F_{in} - F_{out}) \qquad (B.3)$$

$$I = S \qquad (B.4)$$

$$G1 + G2 = T + B1 + B2 \qquad (B.5)$$

$$[X - M] + [(N_{in} - N_{out}) + B2] + [X_{gold} - M_{gold}] + [(F_{in} - F_{out}) - G2] = 0 \quad (B.6)$$

It can be checked that this account is 'balanced', that is, if the left-hand and right-hand sides are added up, all items cancel out.

The correspondence between the text in Chapter 7 and the system described here can be shown simply by means of Table B.1.

TABLE B.1
The National Accounts

| National account | Text section in Chapter 7 |
| --- | --- |
| National Product | 'National income' and 'Composition of national income: By type of product' |
| Income–expenditure | as above |
| Saving–investment | 'Saving and investment' |
| Government account | 'Public finance' |
| Balance of payments | 'Balance of payments' |

Most of the arguments about growth and stagnation in Chapter 7 can be simply illustrated using the national accounts system. For example, the Story 1, that colonial policy was responsible for low levels of income and investment, boils down to three short statements. First, given total government receipts, a larger G2 must lead to a lower G1, or government expenditure in India. Second, for a given net receipt of sterling from abroad, a larger G2 implies lower M or lower capacity to import. Third, in the 1920s, overvalued exchange might have depressed export (X) and encouraged import (M), which would mean a smaller Y than that under a flexible exchange rate regime. One of the hypotheses stated under Story 2 is that, other things remaining the same, if $M_{gold}$ becomes larger, two effects can follow. First, savings usable for productive investment (S) can fall. And second, import (M), a large component of which were machinery, can fall. Both are adverse for investment and economic growth.

READINGS

This topic was dealt with in Chapter 7. See the readings list of Chapter 7.

# Index